'. . . reveals how espionage networks are the hidden force behind many events in world history . . . *The Puppet Masters* speaks with . . . gravitas . . . At a time when the accuracy of intelligence has been questioned, Hughes-Wilson is clear as to what and whom it should serve'   John Cooper, *The Times*

'Just the week for an ambitious book on intelligence . . . [Hughes-Wilson] shows that the traditional purpose of intelligence – to win battles – has changed radically because of global terrorism and new technology . . . His claims for intelligence as our most important weapon are convincing'

Peter Lewis, (Critic's choice) *Daily Mail*

'. . . a penetrating analysis of the way that Intelligence chiefs have led – and very often misled – politicians' thinking during war'   Andrew Roberts

'. . . readable, entertaining and deliberately provocative . . . Many of Hughes-Wilson's balder statements are calculated to stimulate debate and get the heart racing, and this objective he undoubtedly succeeds'

Royal United Services Institute Journal

'. . . contains some hilarious tales. If you want a definitive examination of the modern world's intelligence scene, read this. It won't reassure, but it will enlighten'

Scottish Legion News

'. . . an enjoyable read . . . Hughes-Wilson provides a readable history that will appeal to readers of all types'   *Military Intelligence*

'There are sufficient plots . . . contained in the book to keep the average thriller writer in material for the rest of his working lifetime. Once picked up, *The Puppet Masters* is hard to put down. If for no other reason than it exposes the convoluted workings of the political mind, I strongly recommend it'   *Royal Tank Regiment*

'A powerful book . . . there should be a well thumbed copy of this book on every general's and every intelligence officer's bedside table'

Prof M. R. D Foot, *The Spectator*

'First and foremost, *Puppet Masters* is an enjoyable read . . . John Hughes-Wilson provides a readable history of intelligence that will appeal to readers of all types'

Military Books Review USA

Colonel John Hughes-Wilson broadcasts for BBC television and radio, presenting military events and is a fellow of the Royal United Services Institute and an archive fellow of Churchill College, Cambridge. He is the author of *Military Intelligence Blunders* and *Blindfold and Alone* (with Cathryn Corns).

the PUPPET MASTERS

spies, traitors and the real forces behind world events

JOHN HUGHES-WILSON

CASSELL

Cassell Military Paperbacks

Cassell
Wellington House, 125 Strand
London WC2R 0BB

1 3 5 7 9 10 8 6 4 2

Copyright © John Hughes-Wilson 2004

First published in 2004
by Weidenfeld & Nicolson
This Cassell Military Paperbacks edition 2005

The cartoon on p.328 is from the John Murray Archive, and is reproduced by
kind permission of Lady Lancaster. The document on p.358 is reproduced by
courtesy of the NSA Archive, Fort Meade Maryland, and those on p.391 &
464 are reproduced by courtesy of The National Archives, ref Prem 15/1010

British Library Cataloguing-in-Publication Data.
A catalogue record for this book is available
from the British Library.

ISBN 0 304 36710 9

Printed and bound in Great Britain by
Cox & Wyman Ltd., Reading, Berks.

Typography by Gwyn Lewis
Cartography by Technical Art Services

www.orionbooks.co.uk

Contents

Maps and diagrams

Introduction

When as an infantry officer in 1970 I was invited to join the Intelligence Corps, my own surprise at being selected for such a remarkable corps was only matched by that of my friends and colleagues. I promptly looked around for a good comprehensive read on my new career specialisation. I couldn't find one.

There were plenty of technical tomes and histories of the Second World War, accompanied by the usual crop of racy journalistic accounts masquerading as instant history. In vain I sought one single readable history of intelligence and its impact over the years. Now, thirty years on, I have at last found the time to write the background book that I would have liked to have bought and read as a young infantry captain transferring to intelligence all those years ago.

One thing confused me from the start: every time I picked up a book on military history I discovered that it invariably had little or no reference to *intelligence* in the index. This puzzled me greatly (and still does). It is quite astounding just how many historical books by acclaimed authors, and hailed as outstanding works, somehow manage not to contain the word 'intelligence'. It is as if all those great generals fought bloody campaigns without anyone bothering about the enemy.

This is obviously nonsense, and I began to go from bewilderment to irritation. Great campaigns and conflict between nations have never been 'intelligence-free zones', other than in the sense of incompetence by boneheaded generals or politicians – and they are the ones who usually lose. The truth is that intelligence as a general subject has been shamefully ignored and it is a very serious omission.

My own experiences since then in war, peace, Whitehall and with international alliances have reinforced my fledgling suspicion that intelligence is much more important than I realised. Experience has also confirmed another suspicion that dogged me from the start: that there was a lot more going on behind the scenes than was ever released in the press or in books. In many cases someone really *was* pulling the strings behind the scenes – or at least was trying to. Hence the title of this book – *The Puppet Masters*.

I began to realise that modern intelligence is a much misunderstood activity. It is *not* all about secrets and daring deeds. Thanks to the rash of fiction in both films and books many people have come to believe that intelligence is all about spies. It isn't. James Bond and his creator Ian Fleming have much to answer for. Nor, thanks to unwanted – and sometimes unwarranted – publicity, is intelligence just about the SAS or its counterparts in other countries, like the Russian Spetsnaz or America's Delta Force. Despite the distorted popular view that these Special Forces are manned by some bizarre species of supermen of unlimited physical endurance, the truth is that they are merely collectors of intelligence when nothing else can do the job.

The fact is that intelligence is not some gritty testosterone-laden adventure story. It is really a straightforward, often mundane, office *routine* of collection, collation, interpretation and evaluation, followed by dissemination to decision makers with a need to know. As they are the people who tasked the intelligence agencies in the first place, it follows that these intelligence masters ought to ask sensible questions. It equally follows, with an elegant inevitability, that in order to answer the questions posed by these important decision makers, those who report on intelligence should stay honest, objective and impartial at all times if they are to fulfil their duties efficiently.

This need for honesty has never been more important, because the sudden upsurge of interest in intelligence since the start of the twenty-first century has thrust the subject into the world's headlines in a way never before seen. Intelligence has now become regular front page news. This is unprecedented. It poses a serious challenge for intelligence organisations in many Western countries, because intelligence agencies are under pressure as never before. The temptation for career bureaucrats to tell their political masters just what they would like to hear, and not the truth, is strong. Wide is the path and straight is the gate: but it is a dangerous mistake.

For intelligence officers, however senior, to be sucked into the policy makers' world of excitement and crisis, which in my limited experience invariably surrounds great decisions, is a serious error. Moreover, once intelligence officials are is drawn into the magic circle of complicity surrounding contentious *policy* decisions, impartiality goes out of the window. They just end up as their boss's mouthpiece. Worse, a dangerous line has been crossed. Intelligence, if it is to stay honest and objective, cannot do its job impartially if it allows itself to be lured into becoming an advocate of any one particular policy. The taxpayers expect their intelligence services to be impartial, accurate and above all *honest* to alert them to any threat to their well-being. That is after all why the British taxpayer spends over two billion pounds a year on his or her intelligence services. Taxpayers do not hand over their hard earned money for intelligence officers to become cheerleaders for government policy or party politics, any more than they would tolerate their intelligence services being corrupted by any other inducement or foreign bribe.

Paradoxically, as intelligence hits the headlines there are those who downplay its importance, maintaining that only brute force can ever win conflicts. Even if this crude premise were true, then a moment's thought shows that intelligence still remains vitally important. Because if the only thing that counts in war is brute force and combat power alone, then professional soldiers and diplomats know that to back such a primitive theory, three key elements are essential for victory. First, warriors who believe in their cause and who are prepared to risk their lives for what they believe; secondly, a plentiful supply of the weapons, ammunition, logistics and sinews of war to demolish any enemy;

and lastly the knowledge of where that enemy is and exactly what he intends to do, so they can beat the hell out of him. This last point is called intelligence.

Of course, there is another much older, cleverer and subtle advantage that good, accurate, timely intelligence can bestow to anyone wise enough to recognise the real truth. It is much less costly than any victory amid the blood, fire and horror of the battlefield, and it should be the ultimate goal of every professional soldier, diplomat and even politician. It is the ability, in the words of an ancient Chinese sage, 'to subdue your enemies and bend them to your will *without having to resort to force*'. Only intelligence can do that.

This book is dedicated to proving that intelligence – and the men and women who pull its strings behind the scenes – has been trying to do that since the dawn of time.

1

On Intelligence

Spies occasionally manage to conduct successful espionage: your family, friends and work colleagues are on that mission every day...

ANON.

In the beginning there was sex. Or to be more accurate, there was prostitution according to those who maintain that intelligence is 'the second oldest profession'. This is, of course, absolute nonsense.

The need to know is just as deeply embedded in our biological and social make-up as the need to reproduce. 'Real time information' on the world around us, whether we are in a cave or a spaceship, is as essential to our day-to-day survival as any other human function. Indeed, our primary survival reflex actually depends on a keen awareness of the threats around us, as any sparrow hopping around looking for food in a cat-infested garden knows. Intelligence on the threat as the key to survival is, therefore, the *oldest* profession and not the second – if profession it is. Intelligence is part of mankind's basic survival instinct and as old as humanity itself. Perhaps if Adam had had a little more intelligence about what Eve and the Serpent were up to, we may not be in quite the mess we are in today.

There are many different meanings of the word 'intelligence'; but we all admire it and we all recognise the real thing when we see it. Intelligence is *good*.

One of the best examples of intelligence in its many forms was demonstrated by the bored and hung-over members of a British Field Security Section in Germany on New Year's Day 1946. Faced with the prospect of handing the captured Berlin suburb of Magdeburg back to the Soviets, including full lists of all those Germans wanted for questioning as ex-Nazis, the members of Britain's Intelligence Corps lived up to their name. One of its members asked:

> Why are we wasting our time and effort chasing Germans around
> in the freezing cold trying to arrest them? The Germans are a
> disciplined people, used to obeying orders. Why don't we just put
> an official advertisement in the local papers ordering all ex-Nazis
> to report to the Security Officer?

What seemed a good idea over the wine the night before was – unusually – carried through and the advertisements duly appeared. To the astonishment of the duty officer, at 0745 on the appointed day a long queue of Germans were found standing in the snow outside the Field Security Office at the town hall, stamping their feet and complaining of the cold. 'We have come to report, as ordered', their leader said to the startled NCO on the gate. 'Where do we have to register?' Thus truly was the lie given to that cheap old jibe, 'military intelligence is a contradiction in terms.' This was *intelligence,* in all its forms, of a very high order.

From the dawn of time mankind has been snooping on its neighbours. This natural curiosity is not only a common and deeply inherited trait but has often been an evolutionary lifesaver. Even chimpanzees like to know what their neighbouring troop is up to. Most humans and their institutions have their own secrets, things that we do not wish our neighbours to know. Whether from fear, weakness, greed or shame we all have things we wish to conceal. The same is also true of humanity writ large: the nation state.

The fact is that there exist two mutually opposed forces: curiosity versus secretiveness. Inevitably this will lead to natural competition. One party wants to hide something: the other wants to find out what it is. This deeply rooted contest is at the heart of all espionage. The quest for intelligence defines the clash between enemies and sometimes even between friends and allies.

During the last century, intelligence became a public obsession for the first time. Just as the nineteenth century gave us Sherlock Holmes and the detective novel, so the twentieth century spawned the spy thriller. The books of John le Carré and Len Deighton arguably define the truth of our age far more accurately than any of the self-conscious literary deliberations of the Booker Prize committee.

Spy mania started early in Britain. F. N. Maude's *Coming Waterloo* (about a French attack on an unsuspecting Albion) greeted the new century. It was followed rapidly by the pulp fiction of William le Queux and his splendid villain, Gaston la Touche, as improbable a moustache twirler as any of Ian Fleming's later creations. By the time 1914 erupted into violence, the books of Erskine Childers and John Buchan had replaced France by Germany as Britain's enemy of choice, aided and abetted by the yellow press of Harmsworth's *Daily Mail* and a literate, if credulous, public. The age of the secret agent as hero had arrived. The twentieth century was the century of intelligence and spy fever.

As the age of espionage dawned, so governments began to translate public fears into national organisations. While authoritarian Russia had always had its secret police, in Britain men like Vernon Kell and Mansfield Cumming (the founders of MI5 and MI6) and their fledgling agencies merely reflected two emerging trends of the new century: public paranoia and the growth of government. In every country secret police and intelligence organisations proliferated. Two world wars later, George Orwell was to record the drab bureaucratic consequences of this alarming conjunction in *Nineteen Eighty-Four*, perhaps the ultimate secret police novel.

These growing intelligence organisations were not just confined to their homelands. Their secret struggles and shifting alliances often charted and underpinned much of the twentieth century's international relations. In every country intelligence grew to become a major department of government. The more authoritarian the state, the more powerful the secret agencies, and the more bureaucrats it employed to protect the national interest – as well as looking after their own jobs, status, promotions and pensions, all paid for by a frightened or coerced taxpayer. For the intelligence agency professional, and for his masters, economic survival depended as much on maintaining a healthy level of public paranoia about real or imaginary 'threats' as on any actual need to gather intelligence.

Most of these intelligence agencies, in whatever country, set out to collect as much intelligence as possible as the quickest way to meet the demands of their political masters. The collection of intelligence is a relatively straightforward part of the intelligence process; provided enough money, resources, time and technology can be thrown at the problem collecting intelligence is achievable if sometimes expensive. However, as the history of the Cold War proved, it is interpretation, not collection, that presents the real intelligence challenge.

True objectivity is rare. Intelligence assessments, especially in the Soviet Union, were invariably skewed to reflect the prejudices of those in power and the demands of the leadership. The world was seen through the distorting prism of the 'Party line'. The betrayal of the KGB Archive by Vladimir Mitrokhin was confirmation that the real contribution of the KGB inside the Soviet apparatus during most of the past eight decades 'was little more than to sustain the longest lasting one party state of the twentieth century.' There is certainly a grim irony that such a statement should be proved by, quite literally, the *trahison des clercs* of a disaffected KGB diarist.

This problem of misperception was not, however, just confined to the USSR. During the 1980s there was no rush of Western intelligence agencies clamouring for the politicians' ears, eager to explain that the Soviet Union's woeful economic performance inevitably meant the collapse of Communism and guaranteed victory for democratic liberal capitalism. On the contrary, for the time-serving Western intelligence analyst with a wife and children to feed, to have presented such a report would have meant professional suicide. For, just as the detective needs a regular supply of criminals to justify his long-term existence and his pension, so too intelligence agencies need the reassurance of a permanent adversary, as good needs evil, competing in the ideological shadows like Milton's angels and devils and locked in the reassurance of permanent battle. Intelligence needs good solid enemies and a reliable threat, actual or potential.

The end of the Cold War changed all that and for a brief moment encouraged many false hopes. Some commentators talked of the 'end of history' and dreamt of a massive peace dividend. Like Marxism's theories of the State, optimists mused that war would somehow wither away. Sadly, reality soon reasserted its bloodstained grip.

In the words of the haiku: 'When the glaciers melt and retreat, old weeds bloom afresh.' Without the controlling hand of the Cold War superpowers to keep them in check, ancient enmities boiled to the surface in the Balkans, the Middle East, Afghanistan and the collapsing Russian Empire.

Surveying these new world struggles after the fall of the Berlin Wall, a CIA director observed ruefully that although the 'dragon' was slain the world now faced 'a bewildering variety of poisonous snakes'. By the mid 1990s the poisonous snakes of war and conflict were everywhere. Yet again, the armourers thrived. And where the catalysts for conflict lead, and politicians directed, the secret intelligence war inevitably followed. The struggle continues to this day. New threats, new enemies and new wars have forced intelligence firmly back onto the front page of every newspaper. Hitherto invisible puppet masters, manipulating world events behind the scenes, have been dragged, blinking heavily, out of the shadows and into the arc-light glare of publicity.

The truth is that there never was any real prospect that the intelligence industry would wither away. There is just too much money, too many jobs, too many big budgets locked up in the institutions of spying and intelligence for the mere lack of any serious threat to encourage self-denying ordinances from the secret organs of Government. By the mid 1990s on one issue the KGB/SVR, CIA, SIS, GCHQ, NSA, MI5, DGSE, FSB and NRO were all solidly agreed and spoke with one unanimous voice. New threats and new problems would have to be found, and quickly too, to justify the agencies' existence and to prevent the unthinkable – bureaucratic reduction or even extinction.

For a time in the 1990s some of the intelligence agencies' new targets smacked of job-saving desperation rather than any real defence requirements. Britain's Security Service (MI5) may yet live to regret its leap into criminal intelligence to try and become part of some 'British FBI', once its anonymous officers begin to be hauled into court to face, on oath, the probings of clever defence lawyers into the undercover workings of a service now working on 'big crime and drugs'. As one anonymous officer observed: 'it all depends on how you define the threat to the realm ...'.

This post Cold War panic by many of the intelligence agencies for their jobs may have been premature, for it turned out that there really *were* new threats to confront. The horrifying images of fully laden airliners slamming into burning skyscrapers sent shock waves around the world. Global terrorism was here to stay. 'Kill one, frighten ten thousand', said Stalin. Al-Qaida brought this profound truth on terrorism home to a world audience, reinforcing the observation of Stalin's partner in crime, Lenin: 'The purpose of terror is to terrify.' Osama bin Laden and his kamikaze teams of Muslim fanatics rammed the point home publicly and brutally. A frightened world discovered that it needed intelligence as never before. To feel secure, we need good intelligence about the threats to our well-being. Intelligence suddenly began to dominate the headlines.

Politicians quickly capitalised on this post Cold War mood of public insecurity. As every advertiser knows, in order to sell insurance, first you have to create a climate of fear or insecurity – intelligence agencies were being encouraged to tell the public just how truly dangerous the situation was. Sadly, some ambitious government servants need little encouragement to exaggerate the threat and are only too willing to compromise their impartiality in the hope of a bigger departmental budget and promotion by the men with political power. After all, currying favour to satisfy the powerful is nothing new.

Intelligence will therefore continue to stay firmly in the limelight and remain a critical tool of national defence. Nuclear proliferation and non-state terrorism using unconventional weapons have provided us with a threat that will be hard – if not impossible – to eradicate. Islamic fundamentalist terrorism's anti-Western 'empire of the mind' will not just go away. New threats and new intelligence targets beckon as grim as any Cold War stand-off.

This issue of new targets for intelligence is not just confined to global terrorists, international drug dealers, WMD proliferation and money launderers, however. Barely hidden from the public, a bitter new intelligence war broke out in the last decade of the twentieth century that may signpost one of the new roles of the national intelligence agencies. In the global market place, commercial intelligence is increasingly seen as the new tool to guarantee national advantage and justify lavish intelligence staffs and budgets. Some indicators already exist of this trend. One of the more obvious examples was the French Secret Service's blatant shift of priorities to steal American trade secrets and the subsequent tit-for-tat of diplomatic expulsions in the 1990s. They are not alone: Tokyo's unusual variant of the Public/Private Finance Initiative (whereby major Japanese corporations finance and run secret national commercial intelligence operations on behalf of the government) and the more traditional efforts of Beijing to acquire the West's defence secrets by good old-fashioned spying are other current examples of the emerging global commercial war.

Perhaps the clearest indicator of these new priorities was President Clinton's boast that by deploying national intelligence assets to support Boeing-McDonnell's bid to supply airliners to Saudi Arabia he had scotched French hopes of selling the Airbus to the Saudis and thus 'saved US industry ten billion dollars'. Against this background, the WTO may turn out to be just another cockpit of commercial rivalry, spying on trade rivals, and a symbol of the new demands for commercial intelligence to make money.

This is not, however, intelligence as we, le Queux or even Ian Fleming's James Bond knew it. Defending the realm or 'Save the Free World from Tyranny!' will always remain more potent calls to arms than, 'to ensure that US business can maximise its competitiveness in the context of the global economy in order to attain an appropriate level of national corporate profit.' Such a dreary newspeak 'intelligence mission statement' smacks more of greed and old-fashioned protectionism than any moral crusade. Intelligence and its consort, treachery, may have many motives, some of them even honoured by a higher cause, but the theft of others' commercial secrets for personal greed or the share price will always remain an improbable candidate for genuine heroism.

Other changes to the well-worn patterns of intelligence emerged in the early years of the new century. Intelligence became more politicised in the West. Although in the US there had always been savage turf wars between the intelligence agencies over political priorities, these had traditionally been associated with internal problems and budgets rather than questions of national policy.

Britain's 'Rolls Royce' system of a Joint Intelligence Committee (JIC), on the other hand, was supposedly designed to remove intelligence from the hurly-burly of the political process, delete doubtful reports and report objectively to ministers. In 2003, however, in the aftermath of the second Iraq War it became clear that even the sanctity and impartiality of the JIC process had been subverted by the insidious demands of the politicians in power.

In a blatant bid to justify the decision to go to war by ensuring that that the 'right' intelligence was published by the JIC, the British Prime Minister directed that the National Intelligence Assessment was to be 'sexed up' to meet his policy demands. In a shameful episode worthy of Stalin's infamous dictum to his intelligence chief Gorlikov: 'Correct intelligence reports are only those with which I agree ...', the JIC meekly allowed the Prime Minister's personal hatchet man to redraft intelligence assessments to conform with his master's policy needs and become blatant government propaganda for a war with Iraq.

Despite carefully managed 'independent enquiries' by hand-picked Whitehall trusties, which (unsurprisingly) declared the Blair government to have been blameless, it slowly emerged that the Prime Minister had *lied* to parliament over Saddam Hussein's Weapons of Mass destruction. Whether Blair was a fool or a knave remained unproven, despite calls for the impeachment of a sitting British Prime Minister. Whatever the politics of the matter, the British intelligence community's reputation for strict political impartiality had been seriously compromised.

Intelligence had become *very* politicised. Intelligence was changing and was allowing itself to be bullied into producing the intelligence its masters wanted to hear in a bid to retain its influence around the table of political power. Intelligence, for the first time in Britain, had become just another spokesman for the state and government policy. It was a development worthy of the KGB in its heyday.

Sadly, as we begin the twenty-first century, there are no indications that the power and influence of any of the various 'KGBs' – or their pale shadows in the West – are in any way really diminished. William le Queux would have been proud of his foresight over the rise of intelligence a century ago, but horrified at the outcome. His bright new twentieth century of progress and imperial glory turned out to be a sordid and bloody century of spies, a new information-rich world of which he could never have dreamt, but one in which intelligence was at the very heart of affairs.

Ominously, our new century shapes up to be even more dependent upon intelligence, in all its forms. As the future unfolds the indications are that we will be relying on intelligence as never before, and on the skills of the men and women in our intelligence agencies who struggle to protect and warn us of the coming threats to our daily lives.

We can only hope that they have the moral courage to tell the truth as they see it without fear or favour, because intelligence matters. It always has, right from the beginning.

2

In the Beginning

It is essential to know the character of your enemy and of their principal officers ...

FLAVIUS VEGETIUS

From the earliest recorded times, we have proof of intelligence collection. The Sumerians, who invented writing, also give us the first evidence that intelligence was an essential element in their military prowess. Similarly, the Egyptians appear to have gone to the trouble of codifying their intelligence needs long before the birth of Christ and the dawn of the modern era. From about 3000 BC there still exists one of the earliest recorded intelligence reports to the Pharaoh from a scout group on Egypt's southern border: 'We have found the track of 32 men and 3 donkeys.' Today we can still see occasional flashes of these early methods of intelligence collection in, for example, the Jivaro Indians of Ecuador whose rule was always to count the number of huts in an enemy village before attacking it for plunder and women. That way they could work out the likely number of warriors they might be confronting.

Most books on intelligence tend to look to the Bible as the first evidence of military intelligence and in particular, its reference to Moses' famous spying expedition into present-day Israel. On the run from Egypt and trapped in the inhospitable burning wastes of the Sinai desert, the wandering Hebrew tribes needed somewhere to settle, and somewhere with abundant water, fertile soil and green trees for preference. The Hebrew tribes knew exactly where to turn for assistance in their hour of need, for, as the Psalmist advises: 'I will lift up mine eyes unto the hills; From whence cometh my help.' The Israelites duly lifted up their eyes unto the hills, and especially to those in the north: Canaan. As the Old Testament says:

> And the Lord spoke unto Moses, saying, 'Send thou men that they may search the land of Canaan ...'. ... And Moses sent them to spy out the land of Canaan and said unto them, 'And see the land, what it is; and the people that dwell therein, whether they be strong or weak, few or many. And what the land is that they dwell in, whether in tents or in strongholds ...'

In modern parlance, Moses had issued his critical intelligence requirements.

The fact is that the Bible is full of such tales of military prowess, battles, deception and, above all, intelligence gathering. This is hardly surprising, as many modern scholars believe that the Hebrews' chosen god, 'Jehovah', was the god of war from their original pantheon. Later Moses' successor, Joshua, sends two spies to report on the walled city of Jericho and its defences, about 1200 BC. According to the Bible story, the two spies are hidden by a friendly prostitute called Rahab – the first, but by no means the last, evidence of close collaboration between the first and second 'oldest professions'. Betrayed by an informer, the Hebrew agents flee the city with Rahab's help, for which service her house and life are spared when the well-briefed Jewish army later storms and sacks Jericho. It is a classic example of intelligence in action.

Another accessible Old Testament example is the story of Delilah, the earliest recorded example of a honey trap, or in KGB parlance a 'swallow'. The Philistines – who get a really bad press from their Hebrew rivals – decide that Delilah is the ideal tool with which to entrap the Israelites' strongman, Samson. She succeeds brilliantly at her covert mission, luring the drunken and infatuated Jewish champion into her boudoir. Thus ensnared, and presumably in some fit of post-coital intimacy, Samson blurts out the secret of his strength (his hair) before, like so many men before and since, falling into the deep sleep of the 'just after'. His fatal doziness costs the Jewish champion his eyesight and his liberty. Shorn of his strength by a gentle barber and blinded by not so gentle Philistines, Samson languishes in captivity before finally pulling down the columns – and the roof – of his prison on the heads of his tormentors once his hair has grown back. It is a cautionary tale of the power of women and the weakness of men confronted with a suitably seductive and available honey trap.

There is more permanent evidence of ancient intelligence in action other than Jewish biblical legends of sexual entrapment. Set in stone on the wall of the great temple at Karnak in Egypt is the graphic story of Tutmoses III's triumphant campaign against the Syrian uprising of 1488 BC. According to the hieroglyphs, the warrior pharaoh's speedy reaction to the rebellion was made possible by his secret agents in Megiddo. These undercover spies noted Khadesh's growing army in the north and promptly rode south to warn the Egyptian outpost fort at Tjuru (near present day Port Said) of the gathering storm, months before the rebels were ready to move against their new young pharaoh.

The ancient Greeks also bequeath to us an interesting tale of unusual secret communications, worthy of a James Bond novel. When Histiaeus, the ruler of Miletus, was sent to the court of King Darius of Persia the Persians took him, quite rightly, for a possible spy looking for any weakness in the Persian Empire. Not wishing to offend a past ally, now a potential adversary, they offered Histiaeus hospitality at the royal capital, Sousa. Once there he was effectively placed under house arrest and all communications back home blocked. Languishing in his golden cage, Histiaeus thought that he had identified the weak spot in the Persians' grip on their sprawling empire; but how to tell his fellow Greeks? And how to evade the Persians' total block on messengers or letters?

Histiaeus's solution was simple but brilliant. He allegedly cut the hair off a servant's head, tattooed the crucial message onto the shorn scalp, then let the hair grow back. The servant was then dispatched home. Despite an intimate and comprehensive search by his Persian guards, he carried no message and Darius's men let him pass, little knowing that on his head were the crucial words: 'Histiaeus bids thee to incite the Ionians to rise up and revolt against Darius'. (Quite why the servant messenger was not asked to remember this simple message is unclear; perhaps as a way of avoiding him blurting it out if he were captured and interrogated.)

The ruse worked. The servant returned home bearing the vital intelligence on, if not in, his head. Legend has it that Histiaeus's son-in-law Aristagoras had quarrelled with his Persian overlords and was sitting contemplating total ruin or something even worse – the Persian Empire was notoriously ruthless with its Greek vassals – when the travel-stained servant was brought in bearing his secret message, plus the bizarre request, 'Thy father-in-law Histiaeus bids thee to shave my head …'. The Greeks took note and Aristagoras duly incited Darius's Ionian vassals to rise against their unpopular overlord. If nothing else, the legend stresses the need for very clear and very brief secret communications. There is, after all, only so much space on the human scalp.

We have plentiful other evidence of the importance of intelligence in antiquity. Mithridates, the youthful king of Pontus, is alleged to have spent no less than seven years of his adolescent exile wandering Asia Minor collecting intelligence in the bazaars and markets dressed as a camel boy or a merchant, before finally taking up his crown at the age of 21. Then, at the head of a small but tactically competent army in 88 BC, he launched a devastating assault on Asia Minor. His commanders seemed to know every pass, every road in advance. More dangerously, they knew the identities of the disaffected, the traitors and the would-be turncoats who would rally to their side everywhere they went. City after city yielded to his arms. Within a few short years, Mithridates ruled Asia Minor; a resounding victory based almost entirely on good intelligence.

Mithridates' great enemy was Rome. As her power grew in the Eastern Mediterranean Roman emissaries and traders were viewed with increasing suspicion by their reluctant hosts. When Mithridates finally did go to war against Rome, one of his first acts was to order all Romans in his territories to be slaughtered forthwith as potential spies and traitors.

One of the problems of intelligence in Roman times was a deeply held cultural belief that spies and intrigue were somehow an affront to 'old Republican values'. This cherished view of some golden age of heroic virtue is best summed up in the poet Macaulay's words:

> For Romans in Rome's quarrel
> Spared neither land nor gold,
> Nor son nor wife, nor limb nor life,
> In the brave days of old.
>
> Then none was for a party;
> Then all were for the state;
> Then the great man helped the poor,
> And the poor man loved the great ...

The Romans of the first century AD were no more immune to this kind of sentimental nonsense about the past than we are ourselves today. Romans prided themselves on winning their battles by superior organisation, moral uprightness and strength of arms – or at least they claimed to. Sneaky and underhand tactics were beneath contempt for such a virtuously Republican, upright and moral race.

That at least was the theory. Close examination, however, reveals that the Romans ran as sophisticated, dirty and underhand a secret service as any other great power. The difficulty is that the Romans' security seems to have been very tight. Secret operations two thousand years ago seem to have remained commendably secret. Hard facts about intelligence do however emerge from the mists of the past during Rome's lengthy period of pre-eminence. It is also easy to forget that 'Rome' lasted for nigh on eight hundred years. The real question confronting any account of Ancient Rome is, 'which Ancient Rome'?

It appears that Rome used spies from the start. According to Livy, as early as 300 BC Consul Q. Fabius Maximus had sent his brother undercover, disguised as an Etruscan farm worker to infiltrate and spy out Umbrian areas behind the enemy lines. By the time Hannibal and his elephants had burst into Italy following their surprise march from Spain a century later, Rome found itself on the receiving end of a very sophisticated intelligence effort. Hannibal used spies and agents widely to keep himself informed about Carthage's arch-enemy, even infiltrating his spies deep into Rome itself. Well might Cato thunder angrily from his seat in the Senate at the close of every speech, 'Carthage must be destroyed!' On the evidence, at least some of his distinguished audience were probably paid agents of Carthage.

By the time Scipio 'Africanus' took over the Roman effort against Hannibal in 210 BC he had learned that old-fashioned Republican values of honour and stoicism were of little value other than in helping to swallow the sour cup of defeat. And Rome had suffered too many defeats at the hands of Hannibal's all-conquering and well-informed Africans.

Scipio controlled his own intelligence effort from the start, once even ordering centurions to disguise themselves as slaves to accompany a peace delegation into the enemy camp. As mere slaves they could wander around unchecked, while secretly reconnoitring the enemy positions, strengths and numbers. It was a clever choice of cover. For a proud Roman senior non-commissioned officer to stoop to pretend to be a member of the despised underclass was a remarkable thing.

Even more remarkable was Scipio's order when one of Hannibal's Numidians recognised one of the undercover soldiers, Lucius Statorius, as a centurion in the legions. Scipio denied the claim and ordered the accused 'slave' to be publicly flogged as a demonstration of his servile status. Gritting his teeth, the unfortunate Statorius endured his painful ordeal, doubtless consoling himself by reflecting on the moral value of the Republican virtues of fortitude and stoicism demanded in the service of Rome. His cover held. The dubious Numidians were convinced. No self-respecting Roman centurion would ever tolerate or endure such a public humiliation. We can only hope that a grateful Scipio duly rewarded the unfortunate NCO once his back had healed.

By the time of Julius Caesar in the first century BC we can clearly see the first recognisably modern system of intelligence in action, although Roman intelligence organisations of the day were privately run, usually by the rich: senators, merchants and politicians. For example, Crassus, Caesar's senior partner and moneylender, obviously possessed an intelligence organisation second to none. After crushing Spartacus's slave revolt in southern Italy in 71 BC, Crassus set up an intelligence network covering the whole of the then Empire and designed to warn him of every development, whether a threat to Rome or, more importantly for the richest man in Rome, any shift in the market forces that governed the Empire's far-flung trade. Crassus understood the need for good intelligence as well as any modern Wall Street banker.

Crassus had used informers from the start. He had made his fortune by running the Roman fire brigade and made sure that it was closely linked to his contacts in every city block. These paid agents had orders to tip him off immediately a fire started in the packed and incendiary streets of Rome. Once his private fire gangs arrived, they offered to put the fire out: but only if the owner would agree to sell the burning building on the spot at a knock down price. The minute that the distraught owner agreed to this hasty negotiation, Crassus's men promptly put out the fire. Suddenly Crassus owned yet another prime building. It was even rumoured that his men actually started some of the more lucrative fires. The ruthless application of these novel house insurance policies swiftly made Crassus rich beyond belief and the owner of large parts of Rome, both real estate and, because money draws new friends, many of its influential citizens too.

On this financial empire Crassus could turn his attention to politics. With his spies in every city and a reward for accurate reporting, Crassus's private intelligence network was both comprehensive and timely. It is easy for us today, living in an age of global television and instant information, to overlook the vital importance of speedy reporting from far afield. Crassus's network of spies was a vital tool in making him not just the richest man in Rome but also the richest man in the Empire. With the right agents, informers and placemen, he could influence every political development and outwit and out-manoeuvre his envious rivals, eventually becoming co-consul with Pompey in 55 BC.

Despite having founded his fame and fortune on a superlative network of spies, Crassus's greed eventually overcame his caution. In an ill-judged bid to seize the gold and lands of Parthia for himself, the greedy Roman was trapped deep inside Persia and cut down at the head of his legions. Crassus's exact death is unknown. One legend, however, has him executed by having molten gold poured down his throat as a contemptuous gesture of his avarice. His legacy lived on, however, in his extraordinary intelligence network, which passed to Julius Caesar.

Caesar developed the first real 'national' intelligence system for Rome. As a successful soldier he realised the importance of timely, accurate information about his enemies and the need for fast secure communications to keep his own plans secret. His *Gallic Wars* contain numerous references to intelligence collection, the most well known perhaps being the reconnaissance of Britain by his agent the Tribune Gaius Volusenus in 54 BC just before Caesar's landing in Kent. However, the organisation remained essentially Caesar's, not Rome's. Intelligence, even national intelligence, was still a private venture, run by a successful warlord.

With Caesar's own murder in 44 BC, the network passed on to Octavius, 'Caesar Augustus'. As the final beneficiary of the bloody civil war, Augustus was taking no chances. He rapidly drew all the existing military and diplomatic intelligence into his own hands and established an Empire-wide network of communications, the *Cursus Publicus* that was to become the core of Rome's Imperial secret service.

The upshot was that Imperial Rome could now build on Crassus's and Caesar's private foundation to establish what was a recognisable police and intelligence service designed to give early warning of any threats to the Imperial throne and of corruption and unrest in the Empire. Trajan and his successors further refined the Roman secret service with a network of spies and informers to cover the civilised world in support of their central needs for Imperial security and commerce, and to back up the legions guarding the long frontiers. These undercover secret agents were backed up by official intelligence officers: the *Speculatores,* drawn from the intelligence officers of the legions and, from the Imperial military procurement system, the *Frumentarii,* whose ostensible role was to obtain grain for the army at the best prices.

The *Frumentarii* were aided by their more sinister counterparts the *Peregrini,* who were based in a special barracks on the Caelian Hill. As their name implies the *Peregrini* acted as a 'go-anywhere' secret military police and enforcement unit for the Emperor's orders anywhere in the Empire. By the early second century AD this organisation was firmly under the command of a *princeps* reporting direct to the Emperor and his chamberlain with specially appointed *sub princeps* and centurions commanding the secret police units.

The Rome-based *Frumentarii* in particular quickly acquired the happy reputation common to all such organisations. These agents of Rome's secret police were heartily detested by their fellow citizens. Their role as a kind of early Gestapo in the great cities started from the first century AD, with Christians one of their special quarries. Any political movement that advocated both the equality of slave and free, plus the existence of some heavenly kingdom clearly posed a serious challenge to the Roman social order and as such was considered deeply subversive to domestic security.

The *Frumentarii* were tasked to hunt down these dangerous revolutionaries. Like most secret police and security services, however, the *Frumentarii* seem to have lacked imagination. One early Christian, Dionysius, evaded them by the devious expedient of hiding *in his own house.* This particularly cunning ploy confused the increasingly frustrated secret policemen as they scoured Rome for four days, fruitlessly searching for such a tricky and dangerous dissident. Dionysius was eventually smuggled to safety by the Christian underground, thus proving the truth that a repressive regime will as often as not inspire an equally determined and resourceful Resistance movement to respond with its own intelligence networks and spies.

By the end of the second century AD, two centuries after Caesar, Imperial Rome was effectively running a sophisticated and remarkably modern secret service with two clear tasks: overseas intelligence and internal security. Although these networks still tended to be personal organisations reporting directly to the emperors, Rome, as in so many other matters, had developed the first recognisable intelligence bureaucracy, and one that foreshadowed modern governmental institutions. For not only was Rome *big* government: it was also *intrusive* government. By the third century Rome's network of secret agents and their greedy hangers on had become such a source of unpopularity and discontent throughout the Empire that Diocletian disbanded the *Frumentarii*.

This high-minded gesture was, however, like so many such reorganisations of intelligence agencies throughout history, merely cosmetic. Diocletian simply replaced his military secret police with a new *civilian* secret police, the 'general agents' (*agentes in rebus*). These agents in 'things general' reported to the Emperor's own head of the intelligence service in the Imperial Palace. Old habits died hard. Rome may have had an intelligence service: but it remained privatised and inward looking to the end, and not especially efficient. Most Roman emperors fell to the assassins' deadly stroke, and not in their beds. In the words of the distinguished historian of Imperial Rome's grubbier past, Professor Rose Mary Sheldon, 'Ironically, for all their reputation as empire builders, the Romans were never as good as watching their enemies as they were at watching each other ...'.

With the collapse of the Western Empire and the fall of Rome itself in AD 476, the surviving Eastern Empire remained to carry on the genius that was Rome. Byzantium's administrative institutions, dynastic complications and fortunes for the next thousand years depended to a large extent on the competence or otherwise of Constantinople's spy network; and the evidence is that Byzantium's secret intelligence service was very busy indeed.

For example, under the Empress Theodora (AD 530) the intelligence service flourished and emerged from the shadows as a major element in the rule of the Eastern emperors. It was good and timely intelligence as much as Theodora's refusal to flee the city that helped Justinian put down the great Nika insurrection of AD 532. The plotters were condemned to death and a frightened Emperor's conviction that only good intelligence and ample gold had saved his throne and his life was powerfully reinforced.

The political complexities of empire in the east have given us the adjective 'Byzantine' and Constantinople's detailed intrigues need not concern us today. What does emerge from Byzantium's long struggles, however, are two clear and long-lasting intelligence themes: the need to preserve the secret of 'Greek Fire' and the requirement to report on the constant threat from Islam and the heirs of the Prophet. The latter was to absorb a great deal of Constantinople's effort and can only have been done by a comprehensive and reliable system of informants, agents and spies in the Muslim camp over many centuries. Across the years details are understandably sparse, but it is fair to conjecture that their most likely sources would have been the major trading routes and flow of commerce that flourished in the Near East at the time as it still does today. Intelligence would undoubtedly have followed the great caravan routes as Byzantium followed Baghdad's every move – and vice versa.

Baghdad, in its turn, showed equal zeal in keeping an eye on its own internal preoccupations. From the historical record we know that the Abbasid Caliph, Haroun-al-Rasheid (AD 786–89) of the 'Arabian Nights', was prone to disguising himself and wandering the streets and souks of Baghdad to collect his own intelligence on what the people really thought about their ruler: 'Uneasy lies the head that wears the crown.' Secret police and internal security intelligence on the views of the faithful has remained a feature of Islam over the centuries, and still remains a priority for Islamic leaders today, as the citizens of Cairo, Damascus, Baghdad and Tehran know only too well.

Byzantium's other great intelligence preoccupation highlights intelligence's mirror image: security. For nearly four hundred years, Constantinople's principal counter-espionage problem was to prevent the secret formula of their ultimate terror weapon, Greek Fire, from falling into the hands of their Islamic foes.

Greek Fire appears to have been a viscous liquid mixture of naphtha, liquid bitumen, turpentine resin from pine trees, sulphur and quick-lime. It could be dropped on to men or ships in clay pots, flung from catapults and, suitably diluted, even be projected from siphons or tubes like a flame thrower. It burnt with a tenacious, all consuming flame and only sand, urine or vinegar could extinguish it swiftly; water merely helped the fire to spread. Some reports even claim it burnt on water. Greek Fire produced a spectacular explosion, like petrol, when ignited in a confined space and gave off thick black smoke. A small pot of Greek Fire hurled like a hand grenade into a cluster of Moorish warriors would ignite their flowing cotton surcoats and stick tenaciously to armour and skin, turning men into flailing human torches, burning in their own fat. It was an effective and terrifying 'secret weapon'.

Not surprisingly, the Islamic armies of the Caliphate were anxious to discover the secrets of Byzantium's terror weapon. For several hundred years, its formula became a Moorish intelligence priority. Equally, for the hard-pressed defenders of Christendom's Eastern Empire, the preservation of this great secret became their counter-intelligence priority. Astonishingly, and despite the systematic torture of thousands of captives over the years, and the lure of treachery and gold, the Byzantines appear to have kept their jealously guarded secret safe until about 1100, by which time the Saracens could turn their own instrument of torment against Byzantium's ambiguous allies and fellow Christians, the Crusaders of Western Europe. Of Greek Fire's potency we have no doubt; the flower of Christian knighthood reacted with awe and horror to this terror weapon as it flew through the air, 'like a winged long-tailed dragon, the thickness of a barrel, with the report of thunder and the velocity of lightning …'. The search for intelligence on what were, for their time, considered 'weapons of mass destruction' is by no means just a modern concern.

Islam's internal divisions and its preoccupation with dissenting voices started early. Policing the faithful required good intelligence if Islam's rulers were to sleep easy. Backsliders and heretics, wherever they might be, were to be sought out and punished. By the high Middle Ages, one particular fanatical Muslim sect was meting out its own brand of justice, terrorising both Muslim and Christian rulers alike: the Assassins, sword bearers of the Ismailite sect of Islam.

The Assassins took their name from hashish. Not because, contrary to most ill-informed opinion, the followers of Hassan ben Sabbah (the Old Man of the Mountain) were regular users of the drug (*hashishin* means hashish eaters) but because, in the opinion of the moderate Muslim world of the time, anyone who behaved quite as wildly as the Assassins must have been drugged up to the eyeballs. Marco Polo, that intrepid recorder of things oriental for his Venetian readership, recounted the first real Western account, and the one that has since defined our view of the Assassins' murderous exploits:

> At his mountain stronghold at Alamut (in the Persian mountains north-west of Teheran) ... the old man kept a number of young men from 12 to 20, each with a taste to be a warrior, and told them stories of Paradise, as had the Prophet before him .... When the old man wanted a lord killed, he would say to a youth, 'Go thou and slay so-and-so and if you return my angels will carry you straight to Paradise. Even if ye die, my angels will convey you thence, to the realm beyond Earthly joys ...'.

While Hassan stayed safe in the 'secret garden' of his mountain fastness, his fanatical young killers secretly set out to cut down 'impious princes' and the 'enemies of God', Muslim and Christian alike. The Assassins favoured bold, daylight suicide missions to proclaim their cause, preferring to strike down a crusading count in front of his congregation at mass or an Islamic ruler in front of his shocked courtiers. 'Armed propaganda' as an instrument of Islamic terrorism is nothing new.

Hassan's stealthy retainers were the first modern international terrorists. Their exploits struck genuine terror into the rulers of the Middle East for over two hundred years and kept many a notable looking over his shoulder, fearful of the sudden knife thrust, or poison in the feast. Although the Assassins did, like their Japanese counterparts the Ninja, take money for their deeds, for them at first this was the exception. The

Assassins preferred to warn their victims of their misdeeds temporal and spiritual well in advance and then suggest that a more moral life would be healthier, in return for a payment as 'an offering to God'. Should the warning fail, then and only then, would the lethal blow be struck, and as publicly as possible.

Such a sect relied almost entirely on good intelligence and inside knowledge to focus its murderous activities. By the twelfth century the Old Man of the Mountain's secret service allegedly had a spy, informer or paid agent 'in every Lord's tent'. Against this far-flung network, attempts to stamp the Assassins out proved fruitless. Their excellent intelligence service forewarned them of impending attacks and allowed them to interdict any threat well in advance, sometimes by unusual and subtle methods. When, for example, Sindjar, Sultan of the Seljuks, decided to move against the Ismailite order in the twelfth century, the Assassins' leader ordered his agents to ask the Sultan to desist – or else. Sultan Sindjar ignored the approach and the Assassins resorted to direct action – but direct action far more potent than mere murder. One morning, the well-guarded Sultan awoke to find an Assassin's dagger thrust into the floorboards alongside his bed. As the shocked potentate was coming to terms with the implications of this rude awakening, a slave entered carrying a message. It read:

> Were I not well inclined toward Sultan Sindjar, the hand that planted
> my knife in the floor would have plunged it into the Sultan's bosom.
> Let him know that I, from my mountain far off, guide the hands of
> those who surround him. Peace be with you ...

Faced with this unnerving 'double whammy' Sultan Sindjar needed little convincing of the Assassins' reach or their penetration of his household. From that moment on, the Assassins flourished, spreading their net across Asia Minor and, after Hassan's death in 1124, the al-Qaida of its day had added extortion to their piety. By the middle of the thirteenth century the sect had degenerated into little more than a group of professional anti-Shi'a murderers and extortionists, living off blackmail and protection money like Mafia bandits.

Their undoing was not to be at the hands of Moor or Christian. In 1256 the Mongol Horde fell onto Northern Persia. Rukneddin, by then leader of the Assassins, found that he was powerless to kill the Mongol leaders, or even penetrate their ranks. Like many an intelligence officer before and since, he discovered that his intelligence operation was powerless against another ethnic group. Worse, he fell into their hands and, desperate to save his skin, offered to surrender the Assassins' impenetrable mountain fortress at Alamut in exchange for his life. The Great Khan agreed to the trade and then contemptuously ordered the Assassin leader and all his followers slain in true Mongol style.

In the final analysis even the much-feared Assassins were no match for Genghis Khan's own superlative intelligence service which penetrated far beyond the borders of south-western Asia, reaching deep into the capitals of Europe itself.

The Western idea that the Mongols, or Tartars, were some kind of vast travelling army of gypsy nomads wandering aimlessly about the Steppe in search of grazing, like some North American Indian tribe is an over-simplification. The Mongols were a well-organised and well-led force, capable of extraordinary military feats and controlled by a central authority that brooked no opposition. Fresh from his victories in the East, by the late 1230s the Great Khan's army was on the march west, looking to new conquests.

By 1241, when the Mongol Horde's leading general was poised to launch his assault on Eastern Europe from the Donetz Basin, the Mongols had established a stable military and civil organisation and set up an elaborate system of intelligence gathering to discover the strengths and weaknesses of their enemies. It was an organisation that was incomparably better than anything that the Europeans had devised or could even envisage. It was a very modern intelligence organisation and exploited European divisions, with agents deep inside Europe. The Venetians, anxious as ever to gain a commercial advantage over their rivals the Genoese, willingly collaborated with the Mongols to act as their paid undercover European intelligence service. In return they received secret trade concessions in the East and indemnity from ruin should the Mongol wolf ever arrive at Venice's door, which in 1240 looked a real possibility.

One Ye Lui Chutsai appears to have been the principal intelligence coordinator of the Mongol Empire at the time. For over a decade his agents had penetrated virtually every European court and major city and revealed not only the Europeans' capabilities and intentions but also their fears. For the Khan's intelligence service, Europe was an open book. Even the knowledge that the Pope was delaying a call for a Holy War against the Mongol Horde to defend Christendom (because he hoped to convert the Mongols to Christianity!) was the result of astute Mongol information planting, deception and disinformation. Subutai and Chutsai, the two great Mongol generals, appear to have been running a remarkably integrated – and modern – intelligence operation, building up a detailed intelligence picture of their next conquest and running advance spoiling operations against potential adversaries in Europe as the Horde's seemingly inexorable assault rode westwards.

In the spring of 1241, the Mongols struck, swiftly overrunning Poland and Hungary. Although outnumbered, they struck at the Silesian army at Leignitz on 9 April and, well forearmed, surprised Wenceslas of Bohemia the next day, before falling on the coalition army of King Bela and his Hungarian, German, French and Croat knights from the flank and rear. These well-timed and devastating blows were not just luck. They could only have been possible with good intelligence and a thorough knowledge of the Mongols' enemies' locations, strengths and plans.

The Venetian Fra Carprini was sent as an envoy to the Mongols. From his chronicle and other accounts we can piece together the basics of the Mongols' intelligence system. First, sometimes years ahead, came the 'merchant spies', always travelling in pairs and reporting back, diligently hunting for every scrap of basic intelligence on the potential victim: topography, climate, roads, bridges, cities, the political and demographic make-up of the region and the loyalty of its tribes. Inevitably, military forces, weapons and fighting ability figured large on the Mongols' collection plans. It is reasonable to conjecture that such low-key but all pervasive penetration of the enemy was reported back to the Mongols' 'front commanders' (and ultimately to the Great Khan himself) by means of commercial codes used by merchants travelling along the great caravan routes of Asia.

Such information was diligently and independently checked at Mongol headquarters against the testimony of any captives or informers to double-check its accuracy and veracity; an early example of 'critical analysis' and 'source evaluation'.

Behind the secret merchant-spies came the great *schwerpunkts* of the invading Mongol Horde itself, reporting back by a 'pony express' service called the *Yam*. If the secret of modern warfare is to 'get inside an enemy's information loop' and be able to react quicker with fresh intelligence, then Genghis Khan and his Mongols could probably give lessons today. The Khan's immense realm was connected winter and summer by a network of 10,000 horse staging posts and 300,000 'fast horses'. Like its pale imitator The Pony Express, the couriers galloped for 20–25 miles, then changed horses until they had accomplished their 'six stages' – an astonishing 150 miles a day. By this means, Carprini's claims that the Great Khan could receive intelligence from 1,500 miles away in ten days now appears wholly credible. The Mongol secret service not only was thorough, painstaking and accurate, it was also quick.

The columns themselves included a group of 'interpreters, mandarins and informers' who advanced behind a cloud of skirmishers and scouts thrown out to front and flank, usually about two days ahead, thus not only ensuring good and up-to-date contact intelligence on the foe, but also guarding against surprise attack.

We have several other classic indications of the seriousness with which the Mongols regarded their intelligence service. Genghis Khan's code of law, the *Yass*, was a complex synthesis of tribal laws and customs. Of the twenty-two articles that we know of, two in particular reinforce the Khan's preoccupation with intelligence:

> ... send out spies and bring in captured informers who must be
> questioned and made to give information that we can check off
> against the spies' reports ...

and, as a second order prescribes:

> Spies and false witnesses are to be condemned to death ...

For the Mongols, intelligence was a priority – by law.

The popular Western view of the Mongols is, certainly as far as intelligence is concerned, very wide of the mark. The Great Khan and his heirs organised and ran an efficient secret service, a reliable system of military intelligence and an objective assessment and evaluation staff, all linked together by rapid and secure communications, at a time when the majority of Europeans could barely communicate with their nearest big town.

It was a formidable achievement and one that would have won the approval of the Khan's Oriental ancestors. For it was during the ancient civilisations of the Orient that the first ideas on intelligence and the concepts behind warfare were written down as theories, principles and even, to use the modern jargon, 'standard operating procedures'. In Ancient China and India successful generals were setting down their thoughts on intelligence long before Machiavelli's musings.

The first known 'codifier' of intelligence in the ancient world appears to have been Sun-T'zu, about the time that Ancient Greece was emerging from the historical shadows. Proof of Sun-T'zu's durability as a pundit on intelligence and conflict can be found in the numerous modern books about his writings on warfare and how best to wage it. Ironically most of them are to be found on the bookshelves and web sites of business organisations and companies advocating new methods for commercial intelligence and profit. The market place is invariably the first to spot advantage and good counsel. And Sun-T'zu's reflections on his chosen profession have undoubtedly stood the test of time.

Sun-T'zu was a diligent and serious soldier who lived and fought around the Yellow River province of Wu around 500 BC, well before

Rome's greatness. Like many a professional soldier before and since, Sun-T'zu realised that there was far more to war than just battles. Sometime towards the end of his career he wrote a classic textbook called *The Art of War* (*Ping Fa*). If proof of his military experience, professionalism and common sense was needed it is in his emphasis on intelligence.

Not for Sun-T'zu the arrogance of many a Western staff college trained peacetime general or Defence Ministry bureaucrat who ignores intelligence on exercises and in peacetime 'because it just ruins the whole exercise' or is 'too expensive', only to bewail the malign fate that gives him no intelligence once war strikes. Realising only too well that any half decent and well-led enemy will rarely have the good grace or courtesy to conform to his own highly polished wishes and plans (and indeed, may even have some tiresome ideas of their own), Sun-T'zu thought deeply about intelligence, and made it a priority for soldiers and statesmen alike.

He classified his collection agents into five main groups:

1 Local inhabitants

2 Government officials in the enemy camp who would betray their government in order to stay in their jobs

3 Enemy spies who could be 'turned' and doubled to play back disinformation

4 Expendable agents who could be sacrificed to feed false information to the enemy

5 Spies who could be relied on to penetrate the enemy, survive and report accurately from inside the enemy camp

For this latter group of 'peerless spies', he wrote:

As living spies we must recruit men who are intelligent but appear to be stupid; men who seem to be dull but have strong hearts; men who are physically fit, vigorous, tough and brave; and men who can live the simple life and survive, enduring cold, hunger, dirt and humiliation ...

These observations could come straight out of any modern textbook as the basic criteria for selecting intelligence operators and Special Forces' soldiers. Perhaps, more clearly than anyone, Sun-T'zu realised that the relatively small amounts spent on garnering intelligence in peacetime were in fact investments: insurance policies against having to spend far more if – or once – war broke out. To Sun-T'zu, good intelligence in peacetime was as much a part of national defence as an army on the march in war: and a damned sight cheaper too.

His philosophy is best illustrated by his clear understanding of intelligence, or 'foreknowledge':

Now the reason that the enlightened Prince and wise general conquer their enemy is foreknowledge. What is called foreknowledge cannot be divined from spirits, Gods, comparison with past events nor from calculations. It must be obtained from men who know the enemy's true situation ...

Sun-T'zu's judgements were by no means isolated examples of the wisdom of the Orient. A century later in India the great warrior ruler Kautilya was setting out very similar concepts of collecting intelligence as the best way to secure the state and to disrupt an enemy. Kautilya, often called the Indian Machiavelli, had uncompromising views on how to be a successful commander and the vital importance of good intelligence. In the fourth century BC he set them down in his *Arthashastra* or testament.

For all their antiquity, his and Sun-T'zu's thoughts and observations have stood the test of time. They and the Great Khan remain as proof that, from the mists of time, intelligence is crucial not just to survival, but to battlefield success and political power.

From the very beginning, intelligence has been the hidden hand of victory.

3

Church and State

Nam et ipsa scientia potestas est ...
(Knowledge itself is power)

FRANCIS BACON

The Mongols' intelligence service may have been a superlative instrument, or 'force multiplier' for war. Catholic Europe, however, possessed an equally effective, if not better, intelligence organisation, albeit one geared for essentially internal intelligence: the Church.

It is almost impossible for us nowadays to grasp the sheer power of the Church in medieval Europe. Its reach was all pervasive and it had agents in every city, town, village and hamlet. Wherever there was a priest, there was an intelligence agent of Rome. There is nothing sinister in this. It was just that the Catholic Church had an enormous number of dedicated members, a well-trained hierarchy of bureaucrats and a secure international network of communications back to the centre on which to draw. For over eight hundred years, Rome monitored, checked, steered and often dictated European policy based on its control of information.

In fact, the Catholic Church's net was so wide and so all pervasive that it is as hard now as it was then to distinguish or to disentangle its 'intelligence systems' from its normal day to day activities. The Church was so all powerful, so all encompassing of peoples' lives in the Middle Ages that its intelligence collection and reporting function is often simply overlooked or taken for granted, just as it was in its heyday from about AD 700 to 1500. Of course, the Church reported everything to Rome. That was what it was for. That was its job.

The Catholic Church's intelligence service rested on four principal pillars: the power of the confessional; a monopoly of literacy and learning; good communications; and the Inquisition. A cynic might add for good measure, that the fear of hell and the control it exercised over men's minds helped as well. Medieval man might have striven for heaven, but the fear of eternal damnation and the burning pit was a far more potent bridle. For medieval men and women hell was very real. As the founder of the Salvation Army said, centuries later, 'Nothing moves the People ... like the fear of Hell Fire flashed before their eyes.'

The terrors of hell and the power of the priests enforced obedience and, more importantly, through the all-important confessional, timely intelligence of man's temporal intentions was gained for the benefit of Holy Mother Church. The sacrament of confession and penance rested on the simple theory that sin – except for the most mortal crimes of all – could be purged and cleared by confessing all to God's ordained priest. He, drawing on the somewhat dubious authority of Matthew's Gospel was endowed (ostensibly through the apostolic succession) with the power of none other than Christ himself to forgive sins. Such a hot line to the divine was a useful tool for both collecting information and for social control. The confessional heard everything and forgave much. This marvellous intelligence apparatus pervaded the Church from top to bottom. To hold back was to risk damnation and so, either through faith or sheer superstition, for hundreds of years, millions of people from peasants to princes poured out their innermost secrets to Catholic priests across Europe. The confessional was quite simply a fabulous information gathering system.

Of course, it was meant to be secret. Priests were supposed to carry the secrets of the confessional to their grave, and many honest clerics clearly did. The system, however, had an in-built flaw: the priests themselves had to confess. Thus, in this way, the *mens rea*, or guilty knowledge, would be passed up the Church's hierarchy like a pyramid sales force, until it reached Rome itself, the *fons et origo* of Christ's true faith. It was not meant to happen, but it would be naive or disingenuous to pretend that it did not. Moreover, it flies in the face of all our experience of human nature and the way hierarchical organisations operate, from government ministries to international corporations, to pretend that confessors did not warn their bosses of impending trouble or some juicy titbit. Knowledge has always meant power and the control of populations.

Occasionally the clouds of secrecy part and a shaft of hard fact illuminates confessional practice with its cold light. For example, we know that in about 1550, the Archbishop of Milan gave clear orders to his clergy that they were to reveal the names of any heretics or suspected enemies of the Church obtained through confession in order to collect intelligence on Rome's protestant foes. Of one thing we can be sure: this may be an isolated breach of the Church's normally solid security over the use of the confessional for intelligence purposes, but it would fly in the face of reason or our intelligence to suppose that it was the *only* example.

To back up this unrivalled intelligence collection system, the Church effectively controlled the dissemination of information through its almost total monopoly of literacy. The clerics (hence *clerks*) were all priests, monks, friars or at the very least lay brothers. Even the lay assistants swore absolute allegiance to their local abbot or prior. For every national, regional and local government, the Church and its servants provided the only efficient and literate civil service. A veritable army of monks and clerks across Europe daily transcribed letters, copied books, annotated tally sticks and accounts ledgers, and carried on the day to day work of administration. Few princes and even fewer commoners could read or letter. At higher levels, chancellors, cardinals and archbishops whispered daily into princes' ears or chaired key committee meetings on behalf of their masters. Emperors, kings and courts could only function thanks to the Church's ability to read and write for all Christendom. Even the medieval guilds relied on the support and blessing of the Church to record their commerce.

To say that the medieval Church's tentacles were like an octopus is a crude and inadequate understatement, let alone a cliché. The Church *ran* Europe; it provided the complete nervous system for the whole body politic. And all roads led to the Holy Father, the Pope. Woe betides a king, however mighty, who gainsaid God's vicar on earth in Rome. For example, when King Robert of France defied the Pope in 998 and married his blood cousin, he was promptly excommunicated and abandoned by all his courtiers, terrified of the contagion of hell and damnation. Even his two loyal squires who stayed on treated him like a leper by throwing all his uneaten food on the fire, 'for fear of contamination'. The papacy's weapon of excommunication was a powerful temporal tool. Henry II of England, who ruled an empire from the Pyrenees to Hadrian's Wall, was flogged through the streets of Canterbury on the orders of Pope Alexander III for his alleged complicity in the murder of that turbulent Archbishop Thomas à Becket. Popes, and the Church they governed, were well informed, essential to society but above all, *powerful*: and their power of excommunication was in its day as terrifying and effective as any modern weapon of mass destruction.

With such a powerful and all pervasive bureaucracy spread Europe-wide, controlling virtually all civil service administration, plus a privileged secret collection system to hoover up every scrap of intelligence, the Church needed good communications. A constant stream of petitions, updates, situation reports and analysis of information trotted across the muddy tracks of Europe to flow from abbey to chapter house, from cathedral to council chamber, then on to Rome, while a steady stream of papal pronouncements, instructions and warnings filtered back by the same route. Such relatively good communications served to reinforce papal control; but Rome wanted more. Popes wanted obedience from those far away. So from 1059 every bishop had to swear primary allegiance to the Pope and papal visitors or legates were appointed to regularly go out to inspect and supervise their charges. The tithe, or church tax, was making Rome richer than ever before, and the Pope's army of priests, bishops and primates were dispatched to act as the eyes and ears of Rome's empire from Scotland to Spain, and from Portugal to Poland's eastern marches. By the start of the thirteenth century, the Church's total grip on the administration of Europe, from people's wills to international treaties, rested solidly on arguably the best civil and intelligence service the world had ever seen, running what was effectively a European superstate.

It was not enough. In 1138, Innocent III had decided that the papacy was the supreme authority on earth, stating, 'The Lord left to Peter the government not only of the Church but of the whole world.' Although Innocent was shrewd enough not to challenge the powerful secular lords who reigned over his temporal empire, he nonetheless was drawing a clear line in the sand to protect the Church's authority, rights and possessions. Any committed position, strongly held, needs to be defended or it is worthless. Innocent's successor as Pope, Gregory IX, decided that Mother Church needed to collect intelligence on any threats to Rome's supremacy and a mechanism to deal with them. In 1231, he authorised the Holy Inquisition, the final instrument in the Church's orchestra of control.

The Church had always been threatened with internal opposition, heresy, schism and by those reluctant to yield to Rome's claim to divine omniscience. The Humiliati in Italy, with their tiresome insistence on 'Holy Poverty', the Waldenses (who rejected the Church's monopoly of godliness and preached an apostolic proto-communism) in France and even the Franciscans in Italy, all felt the lash of papal disapproval for their temerity in daring to contest Rome's all governing power. (In the case of the Franciscans they were lucky not to share the same fate as the Humiliati and Waldenses, who were ruthlessly suppressed and went to the stake for their pains.)

The problem was that as the Church had grown all powerful so, inevitably, had it become a target for criticism for its failings and envy of its wealth and power. In the twelfth century, dissent and resistance movements to the established Church spread across Europe like a rash. By 1190 one bishop was writing that 'the cities are full of false prophets.' From the Balkans to Spain, a storm of opposition arose. From every side, the bishops and their palaces were assailed, often physically so, but more often by new cults or sects. All believed that they knew better than Rome.

Of these sects, the Albigenses or Cathars were the most prominent and, from Rome's point of view, by far the most dangerous. It had originally begun in the Balkans, mainly in Bulgaria (hence the modern corruption of 'bugger', a reflection of the Bulgari Cathars alleged sexual practices). The Cathars, who based themselves around Albi in south-western France, believed in a simple life, aspired to live as the Gospels claimed that Christ had done, sharing their possessions in community, and strove to live without sexual congress. Those that achieved this remarkable unearthly goal and self-denying pinnacle of faith were revered as *perfecti*. Above all though, the Albigensians rejected the Church, relying only on their own *perfecti* priesthood to administer their rites and deliver the true message of God.

Worse, they denounced the Catholic Church as corrupt and venal, and Rome itself as the 'Great Whore of Babylon'. The Pope was, to them, the Antichrist on earth, bloated with money and power and greed. By the 1190s, the Albigensian heresy was spreading across the Languedoc and Toulouse of south-west France, Catholic churches were being sacked and pillaged, clergy evicted and tithes ignored. Even excommunication didn't work; many of the region's nobles had cheerfully embraced the Cathars' view of religion and rejected Rome's rule. Although, given their high-minded rejection of the procreative act, the Cathars should theoretically have died out in three generations, in the short term the Church faced a mortal threat to its power. A strategy of waiting for three generations of sexual abstinence to do its worst flew in the face of human nature and might prove too long for Rome to wait.

By 1198 Innocent III could stay his hand no longer. The threat to both Church and State was far too great. In 1209 he issued a follow-up to his original letter damning the Cathars, and called on the head of the Cistercian order 'to make inquisition throughout France' to snuff out the Albigensian heresy. To ram the point home, the Pope excommunicated all the nobility who supported the Cathars and offered their lands as a fat bribe to any who would rid him of these false and turbulent priests and their pernicious doctrine. Under this cloak of religious zeal, the greedy knighthood of northern France fell on the Languedoc like a bunch of marauding pirates and, in an orgy of bloodshed and looting, stamped out all traces of the brushfire of heresy while enriching themselves and the kingdom of France in the process. To Pope Innocent III and his successors, heresies such as the Cathars were far worse than any external enemies. They were not only a threat to the power of Rome but were traitors to God himself, and would have to be investigated and extirpated as quickly and as publicly as possible in future. To deal with such threats intelligence was needed. Only a proper secret intelligence system or 'great inquisition' could keep check on the next likely threat to the Holy Father's empire.

The Inquisition drew its moral legitimacy and legal authority from a scriptural basis in the Bible, especially Deuteronomy 13: 1–9:

> If there arise among you a prophet or dreamer ... saying, 'Let us
> go after other Gods' ... neither conceal him, but thou shalt surely
> kill him.

The gentle teachings of Christ himself were even quoted as the basis of the Inquisition's most feared practice, burning at the stake:

> If anyone abide not in me he shall be cast forth as a branch and
> wither: and they shall gather him up, cast him into the fire, and
> he burneth. (John 15: 6)

Killing off dissenters before they could do too much damage was standard practice in the ancient world. For the Jews, the Greeks and the Romans, any failure to worship the State gods or proclaim false gods was a capital crime, punishable by death. Roman magistrates were legally obliged to summon any suspect charged with this crime – which was codified along with treason – and make an *inquisito* into the affair. By the early thirteenth century Classical law, 'capital crime' and the need to stamp out opposition to the authority of Rome led to the formation of the Inquisition by Pope Gregory IX in 1231. The Church's hounds were to be unleashed to hunt down heresy.

The first task of the Inquisition was to collect intelligence on the faithless. For this, the Church was well equipped with its new armies of friars (the so-called 'mendicant' orders) being available to spread out and gather information. Chief among these were the Dominicans, whose punning nickname *Domini Canes* (Hounds of the Lord) best sums up their task. They were astonishingly successful. Both as gatherers of intelligence who could be guided to their mission ('controlled sources') and as agents of papal intimidation, spreading fear and a desire to collaborate wheresoever they roamed, the black 'Army of Priests' of the Holy Inquisition were a powerful tool in the papacy's armoury of information gathering and control. By the year 1250 the secret service of the Church was no longer playing a passive collection role. Its 'hounds' were actively engaged sniffing out valuable intelligence on behalf of Mother Church. The cleansing faggots of holy fire would then purify Christendom and hold the line against false dogmas.

The most notorious and most successful achievements of the Inquisition were in Spain. Despite the clash of cultures between Moor and Christian, Jewish and Latin, Spain was, certainly until the early 1200s, a relatively mixed and tolerant society. The *Reconquista* altered all that. By the mid 1300s, the *convivicencia* (living in harmony, coexistence) of Spanish life was beginning to unravel and 'ghettoisation' increased. Tensions rose between Christians and Jews, and hostility flared. The Jewish ghettos, or Aljamas, were burned.

To save their own and their families' lives, many Spanish Jews reluctantly converted to Christianity in a desperate bid to appease the Christian authorities. These *conversos* were allegedly Christian, but for many it was merely a cosmetic change, an external fig-leaf to keep the aggressive and fanatical Spanish Christians at bay. Behind closed doors many *conversos* remained staunchly, if secretly, unconverted. To the old and faithful Jewish community, however, these *conversos* were little more than traitors, not only prepared to save their skins in return for the ability to carry on their trade or profession but potential informers, denouncing their former co-religionists. Tensions rose as a beleaguered Jewish community, now desperately split, fought to survive in an increasingly hostile Spain. The choice before most of them by the 1490s was simple: convert to Christianity, risk exile from their homeland or worse.

In 1492, Ferdinand and Isabella finally grasped the nettle of expulsion. In their Edict of 31 July 1492, the Christian rulers of Aragon and Castile offered the Jews of Spain a stark choice: either convert to Christianity or be expelled from Spain. The full Inquisition had been established in Spain twelve years before the decision was taken to expel the Jews. It was already active in both collecting intelligence and prosecuting false *conversos*, many of whom fled. The Decree of 1492 merely accelerated and ratified this process. From 1492, the Inquisition swung into action with a clear mission to uncover any false conversions and any heresies against papal dogma.

The Inquisition's intelligence process was worthy of the preparatory backup to any modern interrogation. Spies, agents and informers built up a comprehensive 'database' on likely suspects long before the Inquisition proper arrived in town. The Holy Inquisition's advance guard of friars would arrive and preach a list of heresies. They would then offer an Edict of Grace. This was a formidable inducement to denounce others. If the faithful came forward within a month (the so-called 'period of grace') and confessed all, then their sins would be pardoned – for a price. (This was usually used to defray the Inquisition's costs.) They would then be reconciled to the Church without further penalty. To a backsliding or half-hearted *converso* this offered an invaluable insurance policy against his own arrest and confiscation of property. Even stronger insurance against the Church's savage laws could be obtained if he or she provided information on any other likely suspects who were not 'good Christians'. The Inquisition's intelligence officers were only too happy to collect all snippets of information: however unworthy they might seem to be.

Hardly surprisingly, a blizzard of self-seeking denunciations and confessions assailed the Inquisition when it rolled into town. This had two effects: first, it confirmed their worst fears that Catholic Spain really was riddled with widespread heresy; secondly, it encouraged a further climate of denunciation. The Inquisition's determination to strike hard and root out the merest sniff of heresy was unmistakable. For self-protection many *conversos* denounced enemy and friend alike, the more the better. Those Jews who still remained angrily denounced their own kind as 'false Christians', whom they felt were just pretending to have been converted and were now busy betraying their old friends to save their own skins. The torrent of accusation, counter-accusation and denial often overwhelmed the clerical abilities of the visiting Inquisitors; an early case of the sheer 'noise' masking any real intelligence – if intelligence it was.

To control this flood of potentially valuable information, the Inquisition built up a network of informers across Spain that makes even the bloodstained excesses of Stalin's and Hitler's secret police seem relatively mild. The Inquisition's outward sign was their guard force, the Militia Christi, whose black cloaks and white crosses became synonymous with fear and terror. But the uniformed guards of the Inquisition were not the only men willing to take Torquemada's gold in exchange for the guarantee of immunity, freedom from civil lawsuits and total relief from taxes conferred by being a supporter of the papal secret police. Across Spain, 'men of all professions, dignities and callings' became spies and informers for the Inquisition. The Inquisition's police state was a chilling portent of the excesses of twentieth-century secret police, and sometimes more efficient. The Inquisition's secret intelligence service terrorised all Spain and far beyond, even burning captured English seamen as Protestant heretics. In the opinion of many, the Inquisition was 'the most wonderful police system that the world had ever seen.'

We know something of the Inquisition's secret intelligence collection methods from an unparalleled source, the 'Inquisition of Canariote' acquired by a British peer, the Marquis of Bute, in 1890. From these records, the Inquisition's diligent collection, collation and use of intelligence is laid bare. For example:

> Deposition of Diego de Mondragon, 17 May 1499: 'Gonzalo de Burgos is an heretic, with a Hebrew book hidden in his house …'

Deposition of Pedro de Bibliosa, 18 May 1499: 'Juan Bernal said to Juan Marquez, "Welcome, Jew." The latter replied, "You honour me calling me a Jew", to which the said Bernal replied, "Then son of a harlot, you must then be a Jew!"'

Deposition of Marcia de Alcazar, 14 June 1499: 'She had heard that Juan Crespo's slave has said that his mistress cooks two dishes of stew, but only puts pork in her husband's ...'

Deposition of Gonzalo de Sugera, 10 November 1505: 'Luis Alvares (a convert) is in fact the secret Rabbi (of Tenerife) and his house is the Synagogue. One Friday he saw the wife of Juan de Crespo entering the said house ...'

Deposition of Diego de San' Matinez, 27 November 1505: ' ... many converts have been seen clandestinely entering the house of Luis Alvares, where it is commonly believed Jewish ceremonies are held ... Luis de Niebla's house is known as "the little Synagogue" ...'

That the Inquisition's reach was long and it did more than just file these snippets of unevaluated gossip is borne out by the case of Alvaro Gonzales, a Jewish cantor who fled Portugal after pretending to convert to Catholicism in 1496. Hunted by the Inquisition, he fled to Gibraltar and then on to the Azores where he was discovered and arrested. In 1504 he escaped his jailors and was smuggled to safety in La Palma in the Canaries. According to the records of the Inquisition, he subsequently lived as an orthodox Jew, preparing his food by the Law and observing the Sabbath, Jewish feast and festivals. He refused to allow his slaves to be baptised and did not hesitate to speak out against Christianity. When one of his 'old Christian' neighbours taunted him for being a Jew, he replied, 'Better to be a good Jew than a bad Christian ...'.

In 1524, the combination of informers and the Inquisition's intelligence system finally caught up with their 70-year-old wandering Jew. After interrogation, a secret trial and lengthy imprisonment, Alvaro Gonzales was found guilty of heresy and handed over to the civil power.

No defence testimony was heard at his trial. To testify before the Inquisition in a heretic's defence was to invite a death sentence on the witness and ruin on his family. Even lawyers were forbidden to stand in defence by Torquemada's grim decree that all lawyers were to 'abandon their defence duties the instant they believed their client was guilty.'

In sixteenth-century Spain, Canon Law was the civil law and the civil power knew exactly what to do with backsliding heretics uncovered by the Inquisition's all seeing spies. Even monarchs and princes feared its power and rarely challenged its findings. On 24 February 1526, Alvaro Gonzales was led out at the La Palma *auto da fé* and burned alive at the stake. The Holy Inquisition had claimed another soul for God. The Church's secret intelligence police had done their job well.

The Catholic model of intelligence based on the medieval Church and the Inquisition was to survive for centuries: indeed it survives in diluted form to this day. The Vatican's intelligence gathering apparatus is still rightly respected for both its organisation and its reach. At the time of the Counter Reformation it served to remind foes and backsliders alike of the might of Mother Church and her readiness to strike at the enemies of God.

Elsewhere in Europe, where men's minds were already questioning and rejecting the power of Rome, a grim calculation was being made. If papal terror and Holy Inquisition were being used to enforce the Church's stranglehold over individuals, perhaps one day they might even be used to try and enforce the Pope's control over any prince or state bold enough to break away from the authority of Rome.

A new kind of struggle was looming. Information on the threat was needed.

4

Money, Money, Money

Nervos belli pecuniam infinatam
(Endless money forms the sinews of war)

CICERO

It used to be a favourite trick of staff college entrance examinations, particularly in the Oceanic World, to pose the question: 'Does the Flag follow Trade, or Trade follow the Flag?' to staff college candidates. From Portugal to Pensacola, this riddle was presumably designed to tease out deep thoughts from the aspiring general staff officer on the nature and roots of conflict.

The joke among the examiners was that *both answers could be right*. Either proposition could be defended. Presumably the hope was that some wrinkle-browed infantry officer, fresh from the delights of supervising trench digging all night while hungry, wet, tired and cold could be prevailed upon to come up with some new and profound academic insight, thus selecting himself for future military greatness. That rarely happened. Of one thing, however, the academic staff college advisers could be sure: virtually every intelligence officer taking the exam paper would reply, 'Not necessarily, but wherever there is commerce or trade, there will intelligence also be …'.

If we accept 'enlightened self-interest' as being the motivator for much of human behaviour, then where there is money, there is intelligence. Commerce flourishes and survives nourished on a blood supply rich in the oxygen of trade: information. The culture of economic intelligence is of such antiquity that we can only apply our own common sense and experience to fill in any gaps in the primary sources. Of course, the Babylonians traded information along the great caravan routes of the east. Of course the price of silver in Ancient Athens, and the price of Egyptian corn in Ancient Rome were of such all-consuming importance as to be almost unworthy of special comment. The Roman Army even had its own special commercial intelligence officers called *Frumentarii*, dedicated originally to supplying grain by finding out the best price. They were taken for granted. As we draw nearer to our own era, however, we begin to see echoes of something recognisably modern and something that looks surprisingly familiar in the records of trade: market intelligence.

Nowhere is this modernity more obvious than in the annals of Venice. *La Serenissima* survived – and thrived – on a mercantile society deeply rooted in international trade. And, for Venice, just as for New York, the City of London and Hong Kong today, international trade meant money; and money demands good information and intelligence. From 1250 onwards, Venice set up probably the finest intelligence system in the world, for its day. No matter that it was primarily commercial; Venice's prosperity and national security were indivisible from her market intelligence. The markets in their turn needed every scrap of political and military intelligence in order to operate for the greatest benefit of the ruling oligarchy and citizens of Venice. By 1300, Venice was built on other men's gold and the best intelligence money could buy. Insider trading is nothing new.

The key to Venice's economic success and power was her geographic position, situated at the tip of a secure sea and nestling among a natural fortification of lagoons. Inland lay mountains and bad roads. Venice was hard to get at. More important than her secure base, however, was her location at the vital trade crossroads of West and East. From Venice the sea lanes led straight into the heartlands of the Ottoman Empire, Byzantium and, past them, on to Africa, Asia, and Cathay. To the north were the lands of the German emperors, the Hanseatic League and Britain. To the west lay Spain and France, the powers of the age. All had to pass Venice's door on their way to northern Italy, Florence, Genoa and, crucially, Constantinople or Rome. Along these flourishing international highways, Venice sent her bankers, merchants, ambassadors and spies.

By far the two most important links for Venice were Rome and the Ottoman Empire of the Turks. Of these two, monopoly access to the Ottoman Empire was, economically, Venice's trump card. In their turn, the Ottomans needed Venice. Despite their lack of ambassadors in Europe the Turks ran their own sophisticated spy rings wherever possible. The Sultans Murad II and Mohammed II ran intelligence networks deep into the Balkans, their own 'Near West', and kept careful watch on the supporters of Hungary, Romania and Bulgaria throughout the fourteenth and fifteenth centuries. But the reason why the Turks rarely concerned themselves with ambassadors and intelligence collection in Europe is often overlooked. They didn't need to. Venice spied for them. Venice not only collected intelligence – like the good mercantile trader she was – in return for favours from the Turks, she sold intelligence, too. It is no surprise then that Venice was often referred to by her contemporaries as 'an untrustworthy whore'.

Once Venice had conquered Cyprus and brought Constantinople under control she effectively became the hub for all trade – and information – with the East. Venetian merchants' unique access to the trade routes with the Ottomans and the Mongols of Asia meant a continual flow of information as well as goods. In its turn this monopoly of intelligence conferred enormous power. By 1310 Venice controlled the all important – and hugely profitable – European spice trade, the exchange rates for gold and silver, and was also effectively bank-rolling not just the wool trade from England and Flanders but also the silk routes from China. These alliances and links between Venice, Constantinople, the Ottoman Turks, the Mongol Khans, China and India ensured Venice's economic power and influence far from Europe.

To further ensure her economic power, politically Venice ran a 'very tight ship'. The oligarchy which ran Venice's affairs, the Council of Ten, were elected solely by the principal mercantile families and exercised their authority ruthlessly to control the commercial and political interests of the city-state. In a later phrase, 'the business of Venice was business'. Nothing was allowed to interfere with the teeming shipyards, glass making or busy trading warehouses by the sea front. Dissent was monitored closely by internal spies and denunciation. If necessary, malcontents, traitors and critics' mouths were quietly stopped by secret trials and discreet strangling with a silken cord. From 1310 onwards the Council of Ten reigned unchallenged and supreme, and brooked no interference from within or without. Even papal excesses were suppressed. When the Inquisition did eventually creep into Venice in 1248 it did so on sufferance. The Venetian Council through its *Savii del'Eresia* always remained the final arbiter of guilt and not the Pope's henchmen, whose activities were always carefully monitored. Many a medieval monarch envied the Venetian rulers' control and power.

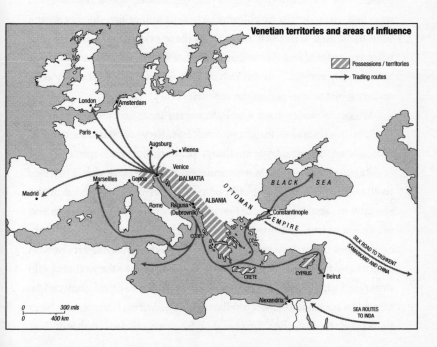

There was never any question about Venetian political aims or policy goals. The prime task of Venice's rulers was always to ensure that both Venice's commercial monopolies were never compromised and that trade flowed freely. To do this, the oligarchs built up and ran a secret intelligence service that was the envy of the rest of Europe. Exactly how the Venetians controlled and operated their intelligence system remains only partially revealed across the centuries. The close-mouthed Council was, quite rightly, intensely secretive about their intelligence organisation. The names of *esploratores*, or spies, are hardly ever recorded in the public documents of the day. Nor are the identities of the *persona degne di fide*, the 'trusted agents' or informers. We know Venice had them and used them to back up its powerful network of ambassadors and representatives distributed throughout the courts of Europe and the Levant. As a matter of policy ships' captains and 'travellers to far lands' were routinely debriefed on returning to Venice by the Doge (Venice's supreme councillor) himself, with by law a witness and a scribe present. We also know that the menacingly named *signori di notte* could be relied on to detain troublesome citizens and police the city with a firm hand after dark. But apart from these occasional glimpses into what was undoubtedly a well-organised, well-run national intelligence and security service, it is difficult to unravel all the details of Venice's secretive operations across the centuries.

We do, however, have a unique mirror image of Venetian intelligence methods and an insight into just how they worked. The detailed intelligence records of one small city-state still survive.

Ragusa (Dubrovnik) was an independent city-state only 250 miles to the south on the other side of the Adriatic. It prospered in the shadow of Venice during *la Serenissima*'s century of greatness and modelled many of its institutions on its large and dangerous neighbour, albeit on a much smaller scale. Like Venice, Ragusa survived on its wits and for its security relied on, uniquely, one of the first properly organised intelligence services in history. If three institutions can be argued to have had the best intelligence – the British Empire, the Swiss Banks and the Catholic Church – then Ragusa's original contribution is also worthy of those remarkable organisations. Like Pisa, Genoa and its role model and big brother, Venice, Ragusa lived on trade and intelligence. It so closely mirrored and imitated Venice that it was often described as 'Venice's monkey', perched on the shoulder of its big brother.

Ragusa's security policy relied on a unique doctrine based on intelligence alone. From 1301, the Ragusan governing council formally decreed that:

> ... for the fortification and security of the City ... to choose good and competent men to explore where they consider best, both inside and outside the Republic, all information and inform the Prince as necessary for the good and prosperity of the state.

Ragusa's first three 'gatherers of news and information' are identified as Miha Procula, Per Prodangelli and Marin Drizich. One of the prime targets of this first intelligence service was Venice itself: powerful, close by and greedy as a pike with a minnow within reach. By 1348, we see the Ragusan senate ordering the council to assign 'five men of knowledge and wisdom to enquire and check on intelligence from Italy and Serbia' and the Dubrovnik archive contains numerous 'collection requirements' sent out to agents in the field as part of the Ragusan intelligence and security service's normal work. Ragusa's main agents were, like Venice's, consuls or ambassadors sent far afield with specific orders to report everything they saw or heard. Between 1250 and 1590 the number of deployed intelligence service agents abroad on the city payroll rose from three to over forty, all reporting back to Ragusa's senate. So in 1558 Ragusa could warn Philip II of Spain that 'our agents in Belgrade report that the Grand Turk is preparing to attack Hungary next spring', (while at the same time cannily identifying for themselves that the price of animal skins and pelts would go up soon, as there was an acute shortage in the Balkans). Intelligence was the Ragusans' key to survival.

Like Venice, Ragusa had to keep a close eye on the Ottomans, and often behaved as a vassal state. We know that her ambassadors to

Constantinople (Istanbul) rotated every two years and had written orders instructing them:

> If something happens you consider important, we order you to
> inform us and not to spare horse couriers, for we shall pay them.
> Be cautious in sending them ...

Ambassadors were also given 12,000 gold ducats with clear instructions as to exactly whom should (or should not) be bribed at the sultan's court. The Grand Vizier was always a prime target – and not just for Ragusa, but also for Spain, Venice, England, France and the Emperor. With such a wide range of bribes available, it is no wonder that grand viziers became rich. Ragusa also picked up a valuable Venetian saying, as part of their written ambassadorial instructions: 'Polite to all, sincere to none.'

Ragusa's intelligence collection priorities, however, went much wider than mere conventional spying and diplomatic reporting. Like Venice, as early as the sixteenth century, the Ragusan senate realised the value of the primitive first news-sheets then beginning to circulate. Within the next hundred years Ragusa was formally buying, and using as an 'open source' of intelligence, the *Gazetto di Toscan*, the *Gazette de Leyde* from the Netherlands and inevitably, Venice's own very first news-sheet, the *Notizie de Mondo*. Like some latter day Special Branch, Ragusa subscribed to and supported her adversaries' newspapers.

In addition to collecting and collating intelligence, Ragusa clearly used its intelligence wisely in its own interests. For example, when Venice seized the island of Lastovorno (Lagosta), uncomfortably close to Ragusa's vital sea lanes, the little Adriatic city-state Ragusa promptly provided their ambassador to the Sultan of the Ottomans with a comprehensive brief, setting out the adverse consequences for the balance of power for all concerned. The surprise of Venice's ambassador (at a meeting designed to ingratiate himself with the great man) can only be guessed at when the Sultan began the meeting by brutally informing the startled diplomat in public: 'If you don't ask your government to withdraw from Lastovorno immediately, I will have your head ...'. Such undiplomatic directness had its effect. Venice pulled out of Lastovorno, and both the Sultan and Ragusa had scored points.

Ragusa like Venice also regularly traded intelligence to its neighbours, so much so that sometimes it rivalled Venice as the hub of Europe's intelligence machinations, known in every court and chancellery. In every case the intelligence was aimed, as the original charter of 1301 made clear, at providing for and maintaining the security of the tiny city-state. Thus:

> To Louis, King of Austria, May 1373
> We are sworn servants of your Majesty and bound ... to inform you of everything we learn that the Venetians are doing against your lands ...

> From Sultan Bajazit II, April 1495
> Thanks the Senate of Ragusa for the intelligence that his brother Dzem has died at Rome and requests more information ...

> From Sultan Suleiman [undated]
> I order that you shall not interrupt the flow of your information ...

> To the Sultan, 11 November 1570 (Before Lepanto)
> Twelve Papal Galleys have united with 49 of the King of Spain and passed Corfu to join up with the Venetian fleet ... 185 large galleys ...

However, like the careful insurance brokers they also were, Ragusa actually had ships fighting for *both* sides at Lepanto.

Ragusa's extraordinary use of intelligence as both a survival strategy and to ensure economic prosperity continued until well into the nineteenth century. As late as 1806, Talleyrand – an arch intriguer himself and a man who could recognise duplicity of a high order when he spotted it – wrote:

> Too weak to defend itself, Ragusa always looked for foreign protectors. Its system consisted of bending to the will of the strong and sliding through great political events without somehow being involved in them ...

Venice, on the other hand, Ragusa's permanent threat across the lagoon, had no wish to 'slide through' events. She wanted not only to be involved, but to shape them. Using the state's unique access to commercial intelligence, in the early 1300s the Council of Ten allowed the city to speculate in what was to become the biggest banking crash in history. Unlike Ragusa, Venice was playing for the very highest stakes, politically and commercially. Venice was bidding to become Europe's first commercial superpower. Venice's power play was to bring much of Europe to its knees and shape the next two hundred years. At its heart, Venice's policy rested on two key factors: commercial greed and an unrivalled machine for gathering economic intelligence. Intelligence played a major part in the coup.

The story started late in the 1200s as Venice's trade – and intelligence – tentacles gradually sucked much of Europe's commodities into her net. In an age before national sovereignty, let alone control of economies or money supply, Venice's unique centrally directed and powerful system of oligarchal despotism could dictate and control policy in a way impossible for mere monarchs elsewhere in Europe. By the year 1300 Venice was in a position to manipulate the currency market across Europe.

Merchants from all over Europe could raise guaranteed bills of credit to buy goods with the great banking houses of Lombardy and Florence. Increasingly, these would be underwritten and paid out in new Venetian gold. In an unusual twist of economic theory, 'good' money was buying up 'bad'. Silver flowed from all over Europe into Venice. In return Venice was laying out gold to the rest of Europe. As a result, by 1330 Venice was effectively controlling the European international money market.

The secret was simple. Through her trading monopoly to the East, Venice was able to buy large amounts of gold *at a very low price*. The rest of Europe was only too happy to exchange their second-rate silver for Venice's first-rate gold. Venice made a profit on both ends of the deal: she bought gold cheap from the East and exchanged it at 34 per cent profit for European silver. Venice's bulging warehouses enabled her by 1330–40 to control the price of silver *and* gold in the European market. To add insult to injury, Venice then sold the European silver on to her Mongol friends in the East at a good mark-up (so much so that by the mid 1300s the Mongol Empire's basic portable unit of high currency was the Venetian silver bar, or *sommi*). As the demand for silver in the East increased, the Venetians could even boost the selling price of silver out to Asia, despite the record quantities flowing into Venice's warehouses. The result was that Venice was becoming the mint for all Europe, not just the great trading port and slave market between East and West.

Venice was now not only the centre for gold and bullion trading but effectively, because of her hidden assets, the banking capital too. Between 1290 and 1330, she ensnared the surrounding bankers of Genoa, Pisa and Florence into a web of financial derivatives and trades that were designed to ruin her rivals and establish her pre-eminence. All Europe's bankers turned to Venice and her bulging coffers. Even the famed Fugger family of bankers from Augsberg based themselves in Venice's *Fondacio de Tedeschi* (Warehouse of the Germans) and worked from the Rialto, where cashless bank drafts, transfers and credit lines were available all over Europe – at a price.

And what a price! The Florentine 'bills of exchange', which were theoretically backed directly by the gold and silver stored in the Bardi and Peruzzi banking houses, and which were traded as speculative commodities, could show a profit of 40 per cent a year, sometimes yielding 1,640 per cent! These 'derived trades' were further stimulated by the bankers' knowledge that the big Italian banks literally owned and could fall back on the national revenues from several European capitals to back their trades. For example, England's Kings Edward II and III had mortgaged their complete revenue income to the Italian banks in exchange for huge loans up front.

In return, the bankers collected their taxes, took over the state monopolies and sold wool and hides on their own account, usually at vast profit to themselves. By 1325–30, the big Italian banks had effectively 'privatised' the royal incomes of England, France, Castille and Naples for their own benefit. To make matters worse, they controlled the national money supply too. By 1340, Florence reset the value of their Italian gold florins well above the level of comparable English coin; 15 per cent higher, thus devaluing the English currency and making Edward III pay 15 per cent more for every international transaction, to his cost and the banks' benefits. Uncontrolled primitive capitalism, human greed and slow communications led the banks to extend themselves for profit and to make forward bets on money they didn't have.

By 1330, Venice's intelligence agents knew exactly who was overextended financially and who was vulnerable. The oligarchy of Venetian ruler merchants was now ready to strike and make a killing. Sitting now on the biggest pile of gold and silver in the world, Venice rigged the market and deliberately began to drop the price of gold by flooding the market with her own precious metal coins. Gold which was once fifteen times the price of silver now began to slide until it was only nine times the value. Everywhere, except Venice, kings, people and banks found it difficult to cope with the sudden drop in the real value of their land, their assets and their commodities – all of which were, thanks to Venice, now priced in cheap, devalued gold. They could not pay in silver: most of Europe's silver was now sitting in Venice's coffers or far away in Asia. Banks began to fail. Demands by bankers to the royal debtors of Europe to pay more were contemptuously dismissed, as one by one the captive kings defaulted on their debts and refused to pay a penny more. Suddenly the big Italian banks were in trouble.

Uniquely vulnerable and exposed to these huge single clients, in 1342 the two Vatican banks collapsed. In 1345, the bubble burst as Florence's greatest banks went under when the Houses of Bardi and Peruzzi defaulted on their payments. Just as the Black Death struck, reducing the Europe population by 25–40 per cent, so did the international monetary system collapse. It was a social and economic disaster.

Across Europe trade slumped, prices rose, and labour was scarce. The only state to benefit had been Venice, whose government had helped to rig the whole thing in the first place and whose network of commercial intelligence agents had kept the Council of Ten well informed at all times. Venice's great rival Florence was ruined for a decade or more; Venice now stood supreme, Mistress of the Mediterranean, with an ambassador at every court in Europe and an unrivalled network of commercial intelligence agents in every counting house and trading centre. For Venice the flag didn't follow trade – trade had been the flag, and her bulging coffers proved the point.

There are few schools as efficient at teaching as the school of financial disaster. Across Europe the survivors of the Great Plague and the great financial crash of the 1340s and 1350s determined that they wouldn't be caught twice. Two things stood out clearly from the Great Crash. To succeed, kings needed to control their own currencies; secondly, a system of market intelligence was vital for economic survival. By 1400, every international merchant in Europe was running – and paying for – a network of market intelligence agents based on the Venetian model and looking uncannily like today's financial press.

Inevitably, Venice led the way. Information was her life-blood. By 1500 dozens of apprentices, trained in Gutenberg's revolutionary new technique of printing, had been brought into the city, lured by rich rewards and the Venetian council's realisation that with printing went control of information. As the sixteenth century dawned Venice printed as many books and papers as the whole of the rest of Europe combined and encouraged the import of 'every printed matter'.

This interest in new technology did not, however, curb Venice's more traditional methods. On the contrary economic intelligence became, if anything, more important. It certainly became more open and systematic. Thus we find Venetian agents openly collecting market intelligence at the great European trade fairs from the mid 1400s onwards.

The correspondence of the period reflects this constant need for economic intelligence. As the letters flowed between the great commercial centres, surprisingly modern information is listed: 'spot prices' – for gold and silver, wool, timber and grain – feature just as regularly as in today's *Financial Times*. Venice's agents in Antwerp, van Bombergen and van der Molen, for example, had clear briefs not only to buy and sell items for their Venetian masters (they were on commission) but were also tasked to report formally on key items of market – and other

– intelligence. Sometimes van Bombergen (1532) was briefed to visit trade fairs solely for the purpose of collecting information. His successor, van der Molen, bureaucratised the system even further. From his Antwerp trading house, Venice's key agent in the Low Countries in the 1540s sent back regular written reports on commercial intelligence as instructed by his masters. His office was set up in the form that would be easily recognisable to us today, with the usual day books, accounts and ledgers. Traders from all over Europe flocked to these trading houses to buy, sell and exchange information. A daily market intelligence report was dispatched back to Venice to keep the merchant's masters up to date; and by the early 1540s to London, for the traders around St Paul's were by then in constant touch with the Low Countries.

By 1540 a recognisable commercial intelligence system based on the flow of trade and the markets of Europe was firmly established, centred on Antwerp. These new intelligence networks were to prove the economic springboard for the European mercantilist expansion of the next 500 years, especially in Holland, Switzerland and England. Nowadays New York, Tokyo and London all rely heavily on computers and electronic information: but the banking and market intelligence systems established by their forebears 500 years ago remain broadly unchanged. The market intelligence network established in the 1400s and 1500s still remains in place.

Such an intelligence system was far too valuable to be left to mere merchants in the troubled 16th century. As the political upheaval of the Reformation exploded through Europe the fledgling spy masters and intelligence collectors of the various courts and governments began to realise that in this extraordinary network of money, market and commercial intelligence there was an intelligence system that would work for them too. Venice's legacy was to be much more than a domestic security police and a protective network of commercial spies abroad.

For England in particular, Venice's intelligence system was to provide a model for the defence of the realm.

5

States and Churches

Intelligence is never too dear ...

SIR FRANCIS WALSINGHAM

On 8 February 1587, Mary Queen of Scots was led into the great hall of Fotheringay Castle to face execution. The first hesitant stroke of the axe struck deep in her shoulder without cutting off her head. Appalled onlookers heard the mortally wounded woman choke out, 'sweet Jesus ...' before the second stroke hit home, tumbling her head into the basket as a final jet of arterial blood spurted from the gaping neck. The shocked but still alive brain kept her lips moving until final extinction occurred fifteen minutes later.

Mary Queen of Scots was dead at last, executed for plotting high treason against Queen Elizabeth of England. She was the victim not just of her own political naivety but also of a cunning and well-planned intelligence 'sting' operation by the English secret intelligence service, working on behalf of a Protestant state and its newly independent Church.

Despite the best efforts of the Catholic Church, by 1520 Rome could no longer contain the torrent of criticism and dissent hurled against it. The dam finally burst on 15 March 1517, when Pope Leo X promulgated a Bull of Indulgences to fund the building costs of St Peter's in Rome. Spurred on by the blatant sales of 'pardons for cash' being peddled by a salesman Dominican friar called Tetzel, an obscure professor of philosophy at Wittenberg University called Martin Luther finally snapped at this flagrant abuse of power and piety. For years Luther had been calling for Church reform. The door-to-door selling of papal indulgence for money was the last straw. There are few so angry as the disillusioned. The good Catholic Luther nailed his 95 Theses to the door of the Castle Church in Wittenberg on 31 October 1517, disputing the sales of 'pardons for pardon' by quack salesmen and money raisers. From motives of piety and good Catholicism, the Reformation had begun.

When seeds fall on fertile and well-watered ground, they flourish. The German remains of the Holy Roman Empire harboured deep anti-clerical resentments and were ripe for revolution. Freedom from Rome was a heady lure. An explosion of support for Luther's challenge rocked first Germany, then, as the echoes of the blast reverberated further afield, all Europe too. Land hungry magnates and princes allied themselves to the cause of the 'Protestants', cheerfully joined by an army of peasants all bent on freeing themselves from the greedy yoke of Rome's taxes and tithes. Some extremists called Anabaptists even tried a primitive form of communism. The new Protestant princes suppressed such unwarranted excesses by the lower classes with a practised ease. Even rebellion needs to be carefully managed. And rebellion against the Pope it undoubtedly was. From Brussels to Berlin and from Basle to Bordeaux, the Church of Rome stood assailed on every side. The wars of religion had begun: State against State and Church against Church. Previously, under the Inquisition, a man's – or a woman's – religious beliefs could land them in deep trouble. Now they led to wars, massacres and genocide.

Both sides of the great religious divide armed themselves for the battle. Whenever Christian soldiers, of whatever stamp, march on as to war they will need intelligence. By 1545, Europe was drifting into a new kind of war and every ruler from the Pope to the most minor German princeling needed information for the emerging struggle. Information on who was planning what; information on which side was winning; and information on who to side with in the great battles ahead.

This new emphasis on intelligence meant that secret organisations and intelligence services flourished across Europe. In England as early as 1525 an underground heretical organisation of 'Christian Brothers' was active in London selling Luther's adherents Protestant tracts and then Tyndale's English version of the Bible. The Lord Chancellor, Cardinal Wolsey, hired his own secret agents to hunt down this threat to Rome's monopoly of divine guidance and spiritual instruction. Undercover operators were dispatched to stamp out the fires of heresy both abroad and in England. Tyndale himself was finally tracked down, betrayed and burned alive for his pains near Brussels in 1536. Back home, Wolsey and his secretary Thomas Cromwell merely imprisoned those undercover Protestants arrested by his undercover agents. Catholic England was still prepared to hold the line against the contagion of German Protestantism. Wolsey's planned reforms for the English Church were for reform through gentle evolution, not some savage rupture with Rome.

His master's inability to pass on a Y chromosome changed all that. The tale of King Henry's divorce from his first wife because she had 'failed' to bear him a son and heir is too well known to need repetition. One of the gravest consequences was that staunchly Catholic England (whose coins still proudly bear the Pope's award of *Fidei Defensor* – Defender of the Faith to Henry VIII) suddenly became part of the great breakaway from Rome. At a stroke, Catholic France and more dangerously the superpower of the age, Catholic Spain, were religious adversaries. Cold war or hot, England was now at odds with the great European powers as well as the Pope.

By the time the Protestant Queen Elizabeth inherited the throne of England in 1558, twenty years of growing alienation from Catholic Europe was threatening the whole security of her new realm. Elizabeth's turbulent childhood had taught her that she lived in dangerous times. Her sister Queen Mary had actually married King Philip of Spain and returned the country to Catholicism. To ram the point home, she had ordered the burning of 283 Protestants during her short reign. Elizabeth, however, was a Protestant by both conviction and nationalism.

Thus, while the new queen was all for not making 'windows in men's minds' she quickly realised that by turning England back towards the Protestant cause she had made both herself and her country a target for every papal fanatic bent on furthering the cause of Rome's Counter-Reformation. Only diplomacy and intrigue could save her throne. Like many a ruler before and since, Elizabeth turned to her secret service and to the enigmatic figure of Francis Walsingham.

Walsingham was a dedicated Protestant who in his early twenties had been forced to flee abroad during the reign of Queen Mary. While on the run in exile Walsingham had learned French and Italian plus the arts of intrigue and secret service as practised by the Europeans, especially in Venice. In particular, the Venetians' skilful and ruthless use of secret diplomacy and secret intelligence for politics, trade and international influence had made a deep impression on the young Englishman. Living and surviving abroad, always on the edge of ideological conspiracy and political assassination, was a good training for Britain's first great intelligence officer. Once the new queen's reign made it safe to return to London, his good contacts inside the French court, his Venetian-style tradecraft and above all, his quiet, discreet efficiency made him a natural choice as the principal agent runner for William Cecil (later Lord Burghley), Elizabeth's principal secretary of state.

Walsingham was successful from the start. A vicious undeclared and undercover war was raging between the English secret service and the Jesuits, a fanatical new order of Catholic 'Soldiers of Christ', swearing direct allegiance to the Pope as the spearhead of Rome's Counter-Reformation. The Jesuits had been founded by Ignatius Loyola in the 1530s and were busy training a new breed of young zealots in their Continental seminaries, who seemed (according to contemporary visitors) to be imbued with a single aim – to die as blood martyrs in the service of Christ and the Pope. In their fanatical pursuit of martyrdom and hatred for their opponents these religion-crazed Catholic youths appear to have been little different from their modern counterparts, the Islamic suicide bombers, and just as dangerous. Religious terrorism, in whatever cause, is nothing new.

For England and for Walsingham, the interests of Church and State were now one as he helped to uncover a series of plots and secret operations driven by Catholic Europe and designed to remove England's new Protestant queen.

In 1559, Sir Nicholas Throgmorton was appointed ambassador to the French court. Traditionally ambassadors were the primary source of all foreign reporting. A natural and diligent intelligence collector, he promptly began to report on French capabilities and intentions. By the standards of the day, the intelligence appears to have been a model of good reporting; clear, accurate and timely. Unfortunately, Throgmorton's excessive diligence gave him away and blew his cover as a mere diplomat. A suspicious Queen Catherine de Medici ordered travel restrictions to be imposed on the ambassador's access, and thus his value as an intelligence agent was severely restricted.

One of Throgmorton's aides was the young lawyer, Francis Walsingham. As Throgmorton's stand-in for intelligence reporting from Paris his stature swiftly grew. By the mid 1560s, he was reporting directly to Cecil and appears to have been running agents to watch out for any plots against the English crown. Wisely, he did not side with any of the factions at court, merely concentrating on the task in hand with a discretion and single-mindedness unusual for its day. Between 1568 and 1570, Walsingham, by now an MP, was back in England and engaged in domestic counter-espionage and subversion, sniffing out anti-Protestant plots festering around the Catholic ambassadors to the court of St James'.

Having proved himself a trusty servant, new postings beckoned. Cecil and the queen clearly trusted him, because in 1570 he was appointed ambassador to Paris. There he promptly began to set up intelligence networks all over the Low Countries, France, Italy and even Spain itself while at the same time negotiating a possible dynastic marriage with France. As ambassador Walsingham played his hand long and with considerable skill, understanding only too well that the queen's policy aim was, above all, to stall and play for time. He also appears to have been clear that his role was not – as with so many other

Renaissance civil servants – to feather his own nest with foreign gold, but above all else to keep the crown of England secure on his sovereign's head. When Elizabeth's meagre secret vote ran out, Walsingham actually paid his agents out of his own pocket. He had good reason.

While ambassador in Paris he and his friend Philip Sydney witnessed the appalling bloodbath of the Saint Bartholomew's Day massacre on 24 August 1572, when every Protestant (or 'Huguenot') in Paris, on the orders of King Charles IX, was attacked as the church bells tolled for mass. The resulting slaughter made the gutters of the city literally run red with Protestant blood as, in a frenzy of killing, the Paris mob ran riot. Protestant Europe branded the massacre as pure barbarism. For a dedicated Protestant onlooker such as Walsingham the Paris massacre of the Huguenots must have served two purposes. First, it served as an awful warning of what the result might be for himself and his fellow Protestants should the Catholic faction ever come back to power in England. Secondly, the experience must have steeled his resolve to ensure that such a thing must never be allowed to come to pass. His own life and many others would be on the line.

By 1573 he was back in London again as principal secretary, now privy councillor and effectively head of the secret service. His orders specifically tasked him, 'to have care to the intelligence abroad'. Walsingham performed his duties to the letter. Although Dr Conyers Read, Walsingham's distinguished biographer, claims that too much emphasis has been placed on the intelligence aspects of Walsingham's career and that his diplomatic and civil service work was of greater consequence, it is not too much to say that Sir Francis Walsingham invented – and ran – the first English secret service. Like the Venetians who seem to have been his role model and major influence, he made no distinction between 'military' and 'diplomatic' intelligence, scorning such artificial demarcation lines in the interests of what today is regarded as an 'all source analysis' of the totality of the threat to England's survival. By 1577 he was knighted and responsible for coordinating all intelligence collection and operations on behalf of his sovereign and her realm.

Walsingham assessed – correctly – that the ultimate threat to England came from Catholic Spain, rich from the stolen silver of the Americas and the most powerful European country of the age. Madrid therefore became his critical intelligence priority. Like many great intelligence officers his successes were numerous and mostly unsung; but it can be no coincidence that England avoided the perils of open war with Spain for so long.

It had not been easy. Throughout the last forty years of the 1500s the problem came to the boil. The flashpoint was Holland. By 1566, the serious-minded and deeply religious Dutch were openly holding Protestant prayer meetings in the large towns and calling for religious freedom – and much else besides – from their Catholic rulers, the Habsburg kings of Spain. In 1567 Philip II of Spain moved 10,000 regular Spanish infantry into the Low Countries to cow his rebellious northern subjects. It was to no avail. By 1568 open rebellion broke out in the coastal provinces of Holland and Zeeland.

For Protestant England the Dutch Protestants' rebellion posed difficult questions. Ten thousand well-armed Spanish regulars, the best troops of their day, just across the North Sea were a potential threat not just to the Protestant cause but to England too. 'The Great Bog of Europe' may have been one Englishman's view of the Low Countries but over the next ten years they were beginning to represent England's vital strategic interests on the continent. If the Dutch went under then it might well be England next. Spain was the superpower of the age. In increasing numbers English 'volunteers' began to drift across the North Sea to help the cause of their Dutch brethren. By 1578, with the Dutch Protestants trapped behind the flooded landscape and the Duke of Parma's avenging Catholic 'Army of the Low Countries' now closing in for the kill, Elizabeth had no choice but to send in her own troops to save the increasingly beleaguered Protestant rebels. An open clash with Spain was inevitable. Walsingham's greatest challenge had begun. He was more than equal to the challenge.

Walsingham's reputation as an outstanding spymaster rests principally on three coups: running the double agent Sir Edward Stafford; his comprehensive uncovering and thwarting of Philip of Spain's plan for a seaborne invasion of England – the Spanish Armada; and the Babington plot which tricked the Queen of Scots to the block.

The Edward Stafford case is one that reveals Walsingham's skill, patience and craft as an agent runner. Based on his own experience, Walsingham regarded all English ambassadors as potentially venal, corrupt and at risk from bribery from foreign agents. In 1583 Sir Edward Stafford was appointed ambassador to Paris in place of Sir Edward Cobham.

It was a poor handover. Stafford lacked any background in diplomacy and was soon in trouble, short of money and floundering at the sophisticated French court. Sensing a vulnerability that could lead to recruitment, the secret talent spotters and compromisers of the day moved in to snare the unwary diplomat. By 1585, de Mendoza, the Spanish ambassador in Paris, triumphantly informed Madrid in a secret letter that he could bribe the English ambassador into showing him 'secret despatches from London', adding, 'this ambassador is much pressed for money'. A delighted Madrid promptly authorised a bribe of 2,000 golden crowns.

It worked. Stafford took the Spanish gold. Madrid had recruited an English ambassador, no less, as their secret agent with direct access into English government foreign policy. It was a triumph for Spain and the Catholic cause.

Unfortunately, neither the Spanish nor Stafford had reckoned with Walsingham. The English spymaster already knew all about the ambassador's treachery. In his turn, Walsingham had been intercepting and reading the Spaniard's mail between Paris and Madrid. As backup he even had his own agent in place inside Stafford's embassy, a trusted informant called Rogers. Acting as security officer to the 'embassy', from the start Rogers had reported the whole breach of security back to Walsingham in London. Moreover, he had also identified Stafford as being in contact with Catholic agents of Mary Queen of Scots and was convinced that the ambassador was in fact a trusted courier and go-between for Catholic plotters in England and France.

By Elizabethan standards, this was the deepest treachery. Stafford could easily have ended his days in the Tower, laying his neck on a wooden block one cold morning while the executioner raised his axe. A recall or a quiet assassination beckoned. Walsingham did neither. Like the canny agent runner he was Walsingham realised that he now had a priceless opportunity to scam Madrid, using Stafford's treachery as a conduit. He could exploit the Spaniards' and Stafford's ignorance of the fact that *he knew* by pumping his own disinformation down the pipe to his unsuspecting victims. It was a deception and double-cross operation worthy of any age, as the unsuspecting Stafford discreetly let the Spanish see London's secret 'instructions' – in fact misinformation and chicken-feed dictated by Walsingham. By 1586, Stafford's value as an 'unconscious' double agent in place was further reinforced when he became aware of Spanish plans of an impending invasion of England a good two years before the Armada sailed.

Walsingham's patience and subtlety were vindicated. His long game of deception and double bluff, using Ambassador Stafford as an unwitting – if treacherous – pawn, was of far more value to England's cause than yet another ceremonial beheading of a minor figure on Tower Green. It was a classic example of taking the long view in agent running and exploiting the knowledge of others' treachery to the benefit of the betrayed. When Sir Edward Stafford did finally retire to his estate in 1587, he seems to have been blissfully unaware that his treachery was known and had been used against his foreign paymasters. He had in fact been an extremely useful ambassador, although perhaps not quite in the conventional sense of diplomacy.

For Walsingham and his queen, Stafford's confirmation of the Armada represented the biggest crisis thus far. England was now finally faced with a mortal threat and needed a policy and a plan to disrupt any attempt at an invasion. In the spring of 1587, Secretary Walsingham put down his detailed thoughts on the problem, leaving us with the first professional intelligence system and operational plan to survive. His remarkable 'Plot for Intelligence out of Spain' still rests in the

National Archives. In it we can trace the workings of Walsingham's mind as he sketched out his three main intelligence initiatives to delay and thwart Spain's plans.

In the document he first spells out the requirements of his collection plan. Secondly, he proposes to deploy a network of agents across Europe as trusted sources to collect as much information as they could to meet his collection priorities. Last, he plans to launch a series of special secret operations to disrupt and slow down the Spanish plans for their great Armada. From the sources available we know that his agent network looked at least like the diagram below.

We know a little about Walsingham's secret agents, how they were recruited and how his system worked, from the life of the playwright Christopher Marlowe.

Marlowe was a member of the tight little circle from Kent, which was to dominate much of Elizabeth's reign behind the scenes. He was

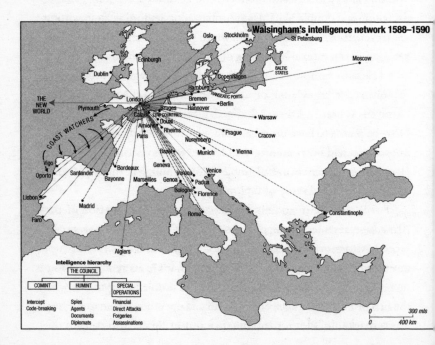

a protégé of Sir Roger Manwood, First Knight of the Exchequer, and a judge on the Queen's Bench. Manwood's propensity for accepting bribes was legendary, even by Elizabethan standards. However, he was also closely linked with the Walsingham family by office and marriage. It was almost inevitable that one of his favoured scholars from the King's School in Canterbury would drift into the world of intelligence and intrigue once Marlowe had gone up to Corpus Christi College Cambridge in 1580 as a bright young 17-year-old. Sometime while up at Cambridge Marlowe was recruited by Walsingham for his secret service.

In 1581 Father Robert Parsons, a dedicated Jesuit undercover agent, reported to Rome that 'seven very fit youths' had been dispatched from Cambridge to Rheims. One of these was the Cambridge scholar from Corpus Christi. Marlowe had become allegedly a potential convert to, and sympathiser with, the Catholic cause: or so thought the Duc de Guise, his sponsor. But in reality young Kit Marlowe was one of Walsingham's undercover men, sent to the Rheims Seminary to smell out plots against Elizabeth and to identify Catholic agents under training. According to Tom Nash, Marlowe was 'a Machiavellian' and 'cloaked bad accions with Common Wealth pretences ...'. His job of identifying enemy agents done, Marlowe fled back to England.

Marlowe's subsequent reappearance in London in 1587 and his career as a successful playwright took up the next six years. But his mysterious death points to some hidden hand at work. On 30 May 1593, Christopher Marlowe was in the house of a Mrs Bull at Deptford with three known government spies, all agents and members of the now dead Walsingham's intelligence web: Ingram Frizer, Nicholas Skeres and Robert Poley.

The local coroner, William Danby, recorded Marlowe's death. It was claimed that there was an argument over paying for the meal and a drunken Marlowe is alleged to have grabbed Frizer's dagger and lashed out. Frizer then turned the dagger in Marlowe's hand and 'gave the said Christopher then and there a mortal wound over the right eye of the depth of two inches ...'. Marlowe fell dead, his brain pierced. Frizer was arrested, tried and acquitted after pleading self-defence. Poley, a known agent of Walsingham and a close colleague of Thomas Phelippes, Walsingham's secret codebreaker and forger, disappears back into the shadows. But we know he was on the Crown's payroll at the time, paid for by Elizabeth's Vice Chamberlain Sir Thomas Heneage, who appears to have taken over many of the spymaster's tasks on behalf of Walsingham's successor, the Earl of Essex. Poley's next appointment was in the Walsingham family's own household – a strange coincidence.

We will never know, across the years, what really happened that evening in the Deptford house. What we do know is that Marlowe's great friend and protector Sir Roger Manwood of Sandwich in Kent had just died. We also know that on 18 May 1593 the Privy Council issued a warrant for Marlowe's arrest. Two days later he had been hauled before the Star Chamber, a special court of privy councillors charged with the correction of slanders, heresies, libels and riots. Marlowe was apparently accused of 'atheistic practices and denying the divinity of Jesus Christ' and ordered to 'give daily attendance upon their Lordships until he be licensed to the contrary.' Twelve days later Kit Marlowe was dead.

From the evidence, it seems that before his mysterious death he had either briefed the Privy Council or been interrogated by them on some unknown matter in conditions of great secrecy. The sources talk of backsliding or even going back to the Catholic camp. No ordinary person, even in Tudor England, would have been 'done away with' on the orders of the highest council in the land merely on some point of dubious theology, however. 'Dubious theology' was the talk of every college and alehouse in the land. The story has all the appearances of a smokescreen, spin and disinformation over something much more serious. All three of his companions that night were known government undercover agents and one at least was a notorious cut-throat. Frizier's wounds were adjudged superficial and Marlowe's 'mortal wound' seems too small to have resulted in an 'instantaneous death'. The tale as told to the court is strange to say the least. Putting all the pieces together, Marlowe's death looks suspiciously like a cleverly executed 'wet job' – the killing of a dangerous and garrulous double agent who knows far too much and must be silenced at all costs. If nothing else it highlights the reality – and the risks – run by Walsingham's undercover agents. Human intelligence has changed little since then, because human nature remains unchanged. Spying has always been dangerous work.

Walsingham's further intelligence initiative to interdict Spanish intentions was perhaps the most cunning of all. Using his agents in northern Italy he got the Spanish government's invoices and Bills for Loans 'contested', or queried, when they were presented for payment to the banks at Genoa (who were lending the capital to bankroll the Spanish project to invade England). Contested bills had to be rechecked for errors, reauthenticated and re-presented. In an age before computers that could take months. Delay followed delay and by autumn 1587, Walsingham could confirm that the Armada was delayed for at least another year as his secret hand choked off the vital supply of Italian gold Spain needed to fund their 'enterprise of England'.

When finally the Armada did sail in the summer of 1588, two years late, they were observed from the start. Walsingham had deployed a screen of small fishing boats off the Spanish ports and a network of harbour watchers to act as 'contact intelligence'. Their brief was to report back to Lord Howard of Effingham, Admiral of the English fleet, the exact size, composition, course and speed of the approaching threat the minute it appeared. Surprise was lost from the moment the great expedition sailed.

With an intelligence professional like Walsingham up against them the Spaniards never really stood a chance. Harassed by the English fleet up-Channel, attacked at night by fireships off Gravelines, unable to embark Parma's invasion force, the Armada split up and ran into the North Sea. Desperately short of water and leaking like sieves in the ferocious Atlantic gales as they rounded the North Cape, many of the stricken galleons were forced to put into the west coast harbours of Scotland and Ireland or simply ran ashore to their shipwreck and doom. But even at this long range Walsingham's long arm extracted a final price on the queen's enemies.

On 23 September 1588, the 800-ton Ragusan battleship *San Juan di Sicilia* limped into Tobermory Bay in the west of Scotland, her rigging in tatters, taking in water and chronically short of drinking water. Her captain struck a deal with the local Clan Chieftain, Lachlan MacLean of Duart. In return for sweet water and supplies he would 'loan out' fifty of his well-armed Spanish soldiers to assist the Highland chieftain in the usual Highland clan local squabble over cattle rustling. The exhausted crew relaxed. Safe ashore among the hospitable Highlanders they could gather strength, dry out and prepare for the long journey back to Spain and then Ragusa. Unfortunately for the crew of the *San Juan di Sicilia* other eyes were watching.

Five hundred miles to the south, Walsingham had learned of this unusual visitor to Scotland. Over the next two months arrangements were made to revictual the ship. Obliging factors and ships' chandlers were only too willing to help prepare the galleon for her long journey back to Spain and then Ragusa. Everything would take a little time but, with the plentiful gold ducats available on board, anything was possible – at a price. One agent in particular, a Mr Smollett of Dumbarton was especially helpful. So helpful in fact that he was allowed on board to make the final arrangements.

On 5 November, Mr Smollett came aboard one last time. On the forecastle the deck crew were spreading damp gunpowder to dry out in the open air. With pleasantries and good wishes Mr Smollett concluded his business below then went ashore. Shortly afterwards the *San Juan di Sicilia* blew up in a catastrophic black powder explosion, killing all on board and showering timbers and wreckage all over Tobermory Bay. Mr Smollett, merchant from Dumbarton, was in fact one of Walsingham's trusted agents. He had dropped a piece of smouldering lint near the drying powder before leaving the battleship. The destruction was complete. With a puppet master of Walsingham's calibre pulling the strings, England's arm was long and his vengeance sure.

Storm and shipwreck finally completed what the Royal Navy and Walsingham had already begun. Of the 130 ships and 15,000 men who set out, only 35 ships and 6,000 exhausted survivors finally limped home to Spain in September after their 3,000 mile voyage. Spain was ruined at sea for a decade. It was Walsingham's greatest triumph of military intelligence and defending the realm.

But Walsingham's quiet genius was not just confined to straightforward intelligence on military matters. The Babington plot, which was to lead the Queen of Scots to her cold block in Fotheringay great hall one February morning, was a triumph of the darker arts of intelligence: black operations, false flag recruitment and codebreaking.

The doomed Queen of Scots had endured a turbulent career. Married young to the Dauphin of France, after his untimely death she had returned to her native land to take her rightful place on the throne of Scotland. Mary of Guise behaved like a true French dowager queen, spending her own fortune to try and bring art, civilisation and culture to the grim rock of Edinburgh and its festering slums below. For her, even as a Catholic, legitimate power was more important than religious differences and she tried to please her newly Protestant people and their dangerous Lords.

She should have saved her time and her money. Scotland of the 1500s was a primitive and backward country. The Scots nobles of her day were like a bunch of Sicilian Mafia chieftains, 'men of honour' fighting and feuding between themselves for the honour of their families and the power to rule the land. Mary was an outsider. She was also weak. They moved in for the kill: literally. The nobles had a blood feud with Lord Darnley. They settled in the only way they knew how. Following the murder of her new Scottish husband as a result of this vendetta by his fellow nobles, Mary – probably in desperation – married the most powerful chief of the clans to ensure her security. Even this marriage to Bothwell for her own protection proved a disaster. He was promptly exiled by his peers and the dour Scottish nobles now closed in to imprison their own rightful queen. Men of honour they might claim to be, but to the grim and bloodthirsty Calvinists of Edinburgh might was right, and a mere woman, and a flighty French Catholic one at that, full of her intrigues and scheming, was no true Sovereign Lord for Scotland. By 1568, she had escaped her stern Scottish jailors and fled to England and safety, throwing herself on the mercy of her fellow queen south of the border.

For Elizabeth, however, this unwelcome royal guest represented nothing but trouble. Not only was the wretched woman suspected of having ordered Lord Darnley's murder, but English Catholics were also duty bound to acknowledge Mary as the rightful heir to the English throne, since Queen Elizabeth was the daughter of Anne Boleyn, Henry VIII's *second* wife. The Church of Rome had never accepted Henry's 'divorce' from Catherine of Aragon. To Rome, Henry VIII had never been legally married to Anne Boleyn.

Elizabeth of England was therefore, in Catholic eyes, the bastard daughter of a non-marriage. She was legally illegitimate and thus her claim to the English throne was equally as illegitimate. Mary of Scotland, on the other hand, was a true granddaughter of Henry VIII's eldest sister, Mary Tudor, and so had clear dynastic precedence over the 'usurper' Elizabeth, *whether Elizabeth was Catholic or not.*

For Protestant England, Mary Stuart was political dynamite. From the start she had become involved in the intrigue and plots against the Crown. In 1571 a Florentine banker called Ridolfi was uncovered acting as the go-between for a conspiracy involving Pope Pius V, King Philip of Spain and the Catholic Duke of Norfolk to put Mary on the English throne. The plan was for a Spanish invasion followed by an uprising of England's oppressed Catholics: Mary's role was to be married off to the duke once Elizabeth had been dispatched. Cecil's secret service soon uncovered the plot and pounced on a courier at Dover carrying letters incriminating the plotters. Norfolk was tried for high treason and went to the block on Tower Hill on 2 June 1572. Although Mary denied all knowledge of the plot – and Elizabeth believed her – her advisers were now more than ever convinced that Mary Queen of Scots posed a deadly threat to the security of Protestant England.

Walsingham's luck – if luck it indeed was – eventually began to snare the Scottish queen. In 1582 a 'stranger in a graye cloake' was stopped by an English patrol on the Northumbrian Fells near the Scottish border. The man, who could well have been a Jesuit agent, bribed his way clear and escaped. But the contents of his saddlebags revealed a breviary and a mirror. When the finds were examined at Alnwick Castle by Sir John Forster, Elizabeth's warden of the Northern Marches, a coded message was revealed tucked behind the mirror. On reaching London, Walsingham's codebreakers soon cracked the code. It was nothing less than Mary Queen of Scots' secret pipeline to her sympathisers in France. Wisely, like the great intelligence officer he was, Walsingham did nothing. He watched and waited. Sooner or later Mary would incriminate herself.

Parliament and council fears were reinforced in 1583 when Walsingham's agents arrested Francis Throckmorton, a Catholic agent. Under torture he revealed that yet another plot was coming to fruition, again with the aim of placing Mary on the English throne. Throckmorton and his accomplices were executed and Bernadino de Mendoza, the Spanish ambassador, was declared *persona non grata* and given his marching orders from London. But by now it was clear to an increasingly worried English political Establishment that as long as the Queen of Scots lived, she offered hope to the Catholic cause and a legitimate contender for Elizabeth's throne. She would always be a focus for treason, the more so as, despite Elizabeth's Fabian tactics and ruses to stall her overseas enemies, the threat of open war with Catholic Spain was growing.

As a result, by 1586 the dangerous Scottish queen had virtually become a prisoner under close house arrest, with all her mail in or out being intercepted and unable to move from her house. Pleas to Elizabeth to 'get rid of' Mary fell on deaf ears. Whether through compassion, squeamishness or the realisation that if she ordered one queen executed, then she might be setting an unfortunate precedent for her own demise, Elizabeth stayed her hand. The queen was adamant. She would not order Mary's death. Cecil, Walsingham and the rest of the Privy Council would have to look elsewhere if they were to rid themselves of their royal cuckoo in the nest.

A solution was at hand, however. A disaffected young Catholic called Anthony Babington, resentful of the Protestant police state that had declared his Catholic mass an act of treason, planned to rescue Mary from her rural prison. By 1587 Catholics like Babington had good cause to be resentful of the Protestant establishment's draconian anti-Catholic laws. Catholic priests were ordered to quit England on pain of death. For saying the Mass a Priest could go to jail for life. Catholics harbouring priests were hanged and Jesuit priests executed on sight. No known Catholic could travel further than five miles from their house.

Everywhere good Catholics lived in fear, with denunciation and betrayal by the lowliest scullery maid from the village a constant threat to their worship, lives and families. Everywhere the Catholic flame burned low and resentment smouldered among the faithful. In circumstances like these, the Queen of Scots' escape would be a coup for all Catholics and give her supporters an important new asset in their bid to oust the Protestant usurper. They could then offer the crown to a legitimate, Catholic heir of Henry VIII and restore the true faith. If the plot succeeded then Elizabeth's life was in mortal danger.

Sadly for Mary, Babington's plot had been penetrated from the start. Walsingham not only knew all about it; he was actually *running* it. Worse for the Catholic cause, he was yet again playing it long, hoping to ensnare the Queen of Scots in his own web and this time get her to incriminate herself in the conspiracy. If Walsingham and his boss Cecil could get the Queen of Scots to commit a clear and unequivocal act of treason against Elizabeth, Mary would be doomed. Could Walsingham's secret service trick Mary into committing an act of mortal folly?

In 1585 a young Catholic called Gilbert Gifford, who had trained as a Jesuit before abandoning his faith, wrote to Walsingham offering his services. Part of Walsingham's genius was his willingness to employ rogues and villains as his agents. Provided he could control them, he was prepared to use whatever human material was to hand: turncoat, crook or thief, cheat, liar or forger. Walsingham's knowledge of human motivations and weaknesses must have been profound. Like many an intelligence officer and policeman before and since he knew only too well that the key to success lay in talking to the enemy, however distasteful. Detectives have to deal and consort with criminals every day if they are to do their job; in their turn, intelligence officers and spymasters have to rely on turncoats and traitors. In matters of secret intelligence, high moral causes and lawyers' posturings should only rarely be allowed to obstruct the need for success.

Walsingham interviewed Gifford – a convicted crook and renegade who had written to him from prison – and offered the young man a job as agent provocateur for the most dangerous job he had for a renegade Catholic: to trap the Queen of Scots. Freedom was Gifford's bait; but Mary was Walsingham's catch. Gifford was briefed to act as a trusted courier from Mary's Derbyshire prison and pass coded messages, smuggled out disguised in beer bungs.

The plan worked. At last Mary was in touch again, so she thought, with sympathetic Catholics 'on the outside'. Hope must have flooded into her heart at the thought of rescue from her grim jailors and the prospect of freedom. It lowered her barriers of caution as Walsingham then moved to the next phase of his 'sting' operation.

On 6 July 1586, Gifford suddenly arrived on the doorstep of the chief conspirator himself, Anthony Babington, and gave him a coded letter from Mary. Well briefed by Walsingham, Gifford explained that he was working for the French Embassy and that Mary had heard of Babington from her supporters in France. Could he help?

Babington could. He dictated and enciphered a reply, effectively sealing his own death warrant. He wrote:

Myself and ten gentlemen and a hundred of our followers will undertake the delivery of your royal person from the hands of your enemies. For the despatch of the usurper, from the obedience of whom we are, by excommunication, made free, there be six noble gentlemen, all private friends, who for the zeal they bear to the Catholic cause and your Majesty's service will undertake that tragical execution ...

Gifford duly gave the letter to Walsingham to copy before sealing the original in its bung and smuggling it back to Mary at Chartley Hall. The trap was baited.

Mary was delighted and on 17 July 1586 replied, making the fatal mistake of endorsing the plan. She promised rewards to those concerned if the plot succeeded. She would have been less delighted if she had been aware that every ciphered letter was being cracked and decoded by Walsingham's tame cipher expert Thomas Phelippes, who could speak and read six languages, 'write any man's hand', and was an expert on cryptography. Mary and Babington's supposedly secret cipher was a crude substitution system, easily unbuttoned using simple frequency analysis. When Phelippes passed the damning decrypt back to Walsingham, he marked the copy with the sign of the gallows. The message was clear. The Queen of Scots had condemned herself by her own hand. She had, in writing, encouraged Englishmen to kill their own queen. It was a fatal mistake. The trap was sprung.

Not quite. Like a good intelligence officer he was, Walsingham wanted more. With the patience of a spider in its web he waited to bag Babington and any other conspirators red-handed, preferably while they were making their move. It was very nearly his undoing. For on 5 August 1587, to everyone's astonishment, Anthony Babington himself walked into Walsingham's outer office and requested an official passport for France.

Recognising the most wanted man in England, Walsingham's stunned assistant John Scudamore played for time and suggested they repair to a nearby tavern while the paperwork was sorted out. This they did, but Babington smelt a rat when a written message was delivered to Scudamore telling him that soldiers were on their way. Telling Scudamore that he was going to use the privy, Babington casually ambled out the back leaving his hat and cloak on the table. Once outside he was over the back wall and away just as armed guards burst in to arrest him.

His escape did not really matter. The whole plot had been hopelessly compromised. Walsingham's trap had worked to perfection. His plan had been nothing less than to remove the Queen of Scots as a threat to England once and for all. With Mary dead there would be no focus for any plots, no figurehead to lay claim to the English throne. It was he who had instructed Phelippes the forger to copy Mary's handwriting and cipher, asking Babington for the names of the would-be assassins. Duped by the forgery, Babington had obliged, sealing his own fate. In her turn, Mary's reply on 17 July had effectively egged him on to commit the highest of high treason. Her encouragement to the plotters had spelled her own doom. Walsingham's trickery from the middle of the spider's web had lured them in and incriminated them all.

Once Babington had run there was no more reason for England's secret service to delay. For ten days the plotters went on the run, before finally all being captured by 15 August.

Mary's hour had come a week earlier. On 11 August, a week after Babington had fled, Mary was given permission to ride in the grounds of Chartley Hall. A group of horsemen appeared in the distance coming nearer and riding hard. We can only speculate on her thoughts. Was this the group of Catholic gentlemen intent on rescuing her? But this time Mary's luck had run out for good. The horsemen were Royal Guards from the Lord Chancellor and Walsingham in London, sent to arrest her. Within the week, Walsingham's secret service had rounded up the whole plot. For the conspirators there could be only one end.

The final fate of Babington and his co-conspirators was that of any traitor in that dark age. They and six other members of the plot were flogged until they bled, then dragged on hurdles through the filthy streets, hanged by the neck until nearly strangled and then 'drawn'. First, their genitals (privites) were sliced off. We can only guess at the agony and horror as a skilful executioner then sliced open each wretched man's belly in turn, before slowly drawing out coils of intestines to burn on a brazier in front of their eyes. Merciful release from this howling wilderness of pain only came with a final decapitation. The terror of the wretched prisoners, seeing their friends butchered alive and awaiting their own fate, is beyond our imagination. Finally, the bodies were quartered like hogs' carcasses and the heads ceremonially displayed on pikes at the city gates. 'Thus perish all traitors!' was the ritual cry of the executioner to the shocked crowd. Death for High Treason in Tudor England was a grim and grisly warning to any other would-be traitor. It was meant to be.

The Queen of Scots was tried in her turn under the 1584 Act of Association, which said that 'anyone involved in criminal conspiracy against the Queen's majesty' was a traitor and their lives forfeit. Mary was found guilty – which she undoubtedly was – and finally bent her neck to her own execution block on that cold February morning in 1587. Mary Stuart was a victim of her own naivety, born of desperation, but also of a cunning intelligence entrapment operation devised and its string pulled by Sir Francis Walsingham, Elizabeth Tudor's spymaster and probably one of the greatest Britons of his time. He is certainly one of the most unsung.

Sir Francis Walsingham died in 1590, almost bankrupt. He had funded many of his intelligence and secret service operations from his own pocket and nearly ruined himself and his family in the service of 'Gloriana' and the Protestant cause. When he received the news of Walsingham's death, King Philip II of Spain wrote in the margin of the report: 'Good news from England ...'.

His queen may not have fully recognised Walsingham's worth as an intelligence officer *sans pareil*, but in the ultimate accolade, his enemies certainly did.

6

Making the Mould

To outwit a rival use all artifice, all means are permitted against your enemies.

ATTRIBUTED TO JEAN DU PLESSIS, DUC DE RICHELIEU

By the time of Queen Elizabeth's death and the accession of Mary Queen of Scots' son, James Stuart, to the English throne in 1603, the old European balance of power had splintered apart. The big bang of the Reformation had reinforced the individual nationalisms of Europe's states. The papacy's historic position had been reduced to just another piece on the chessboard of European politics and sometimes a mere pawn of the new nationalism at that.

In this fevered climate, intrigue seethed. To the normal combustion chamber of international dynastic rivalries and economic competition had been added the catalyst of religious war. Wherever there is intrigue and war, intelligence is needed. The information requirements of each of Europe's rulers expanded as never before. Every nation had developed its own commercial intelligence network in the preceding 150 years. By the start of the Thirty Years' War, the great war of religion, in 1618 competing intelligence networks were establishing themselves across the European continent.

Two key rivalries defined the conflict by 1630: a north-south split between the Protestants of the north and the Catholics of the south. Running across the grain of this great struggle was an old-fashioned, and much more familiar, competition for European supremacy between the growing power of a united France and the increasingly over-extended might of imperial Spain.

The arch-intriguer and spymaster who inherited Walsingham's crown as Europe's controlling intelligence officer was French and a church-man. Armand Jean du Plessis, Cardinal Duc de Richelieu, was from 1624 to 1642 the controller of France's destiny. If Louis XII and Henri IV had made France whole, then it was Richelieu who orchestrated the deeds of Louis XIII and built the foundations of Louis XIV, 'The Sun King's', great-ness. A man of the Church he may have been, but Richelieu never allowed mere faith in some distant deity stand in the way of his duty to France. In an age before policemen, post offices, the Inland Revenue or even good roads, Richelieu controlled sixteen million French souls with an iron grip through his unrivalled network of spies and informers. And not just France. To his domestic security service, the cardinal added the tentacles of an international secret intelligence service designed to keep Paris informed, warn of likely threats from abroad and execute secret operations to destabilise any opposition. From London to Vienna, Stock-holm to Madrid, Richelieu's tentacles reached.

Richelieu controlled his own security service personally, alert to the first whiff of conspiracy, ever ready to unmask treason and prepared to strike down the king's enemies with a ruthlessness that was feared by friend and enemy alike. But Richelieu delegated much of the intel-ligence work to his director of secret service, another churchman, Père Joseph du Tremblay. This clever, subtle and painstaking priest has bequeathed to us a title that reflected not just his Capucin friar's habit but his true role: *l'éminence grise*. François Joseph le Clerc du Tremblay was a religious fanatic. As a boy he had undergone some kind of con-version experience. Thereafter he committed himself to a life of prayer and closer union with God, passionately embracing his mystical experience of personal divine revelation. On this path of absolute conviction, shared by committed Marxists and Sufi mystics alike, du Tremblay genuinely appears to have believed that he had been given some unique insight into God's revealed purpose.

Deeply religious he may have been: deeply Christian he most certainly was not. Despite – or perhaps because of – his deep detestation of women and sex ('uncloistered females are as wild beasts and horrific mysteries' in Huxley's vivid phrase), like many a friar before him he was irresistibly drawn to these forbidden objects of desire, even using a closed order of Calvary nuns as 'praying machines' to pray at his bidding for his latest cause. The nuns (who may have been as equally misguided as himself) thus prayed for such deeply uplifting and spiritual causes as the 'deaths of Huguenots' and even 'that the King should apply his whole mind to the prosecution of the present war ...'.

We should not be surprised that so many of God's revealed solutions to du Tremblay tallied so closely with the interests of France. Like many others who attempt to walk the mystic's path, du Tremblay was in reality a deeply neurotic and dangerous individual with the moral values of a fanatical religious terrorist. Even in the middle of a war he would pray for hours and go into a meditative trance then come out and reveal God's answer to the waiting court. Such Rasputin-like piety was deeply impressive, if a little unnerving to normal mortals like the king. Within the court of Louis XIII l'Éminence Grise was feared and detested. But for the unscrupulous Richelieu this charismatic religious fanatic and deeply flawed man was the perfect tool for his purpose. Between them, du Tremblay and Richelieu would rule France in the king's name and bend soldiers and princes across Europe to their sacred cause: *la France*!

Across Europe Richelieu and du Tremblay assembled a network of spies and informers. The cardinal reputedly favoured Englishmen overseas as his undercover agents, allegedly finding them unprejudiced, trustworthy and reliable. Given his problems with Frenchmen at the time we should not find this too surprising. He was, after all, a child of the religious wars between the French crown and its over-mighty nobles. From the start he set out to ensure that the great magnates not only would never, but *could* never again challenge the supremacy of the kings of France. Early in his career he suffered a stinging rebuff that taught him a hard lesson about life at the French court. It undoubtedly steeled his resolve and shaped his path of intrigue and duplicity for the years ahead. Within just a year of becoming secretary for foreign affairs to the young King Louis XIII he was out of office, deposed from his influential post by a skilful intrigue orchestrated by enemies at court determined to lessen the Queen Mother's hold over her youthful charge. As a member of the queen's party, Richelieu lost his post.

The experience seems to have given Richelieu the very lesson he needed to survive – and to prosper – in the viper's nest that was the French court of the early seventeenth century. In future, in secret matters of intrigue where others had led, du Plessis would follow and learn. Following an intrigue of his own he was back in power by 1621, this time as a cardinal. From then on, this highly intelligent, driven and subtle man never looked back.

At the heart of de Richelieu's intelligence network was the *cabinet noir*. Originally intended as a codebreaking office, its influence grew until it effectively became the secret chamber of the French executive arm of government. Richelieu ruled France – in the king's name, naturally – with an iron hand. His drive to consolidate and extend French power appears to have been exceeded only by his drive to ensure that 'France' herself was not betrayed, or worse, its weak king disgraced. Thus internal enemies were hounded down and suppressed with a vigour normally reserved for external foes. Plots to seize the throne by nobles like Orleans and Cinq Mars were laid bare by the cardinal's secret army of spies and regional agents (*intendants*) and the Huguenots brought to heal. Abroad France might hazard its fortune; but at home subversion or rebellion was to be crushed without mercy. The cardinal's policies and he himself were hated and feared throughout France, but especially by the old nobility who saw him as a tyrant and dictator pulling strings to use King Louis's power for his own ends.

At times Richelieu's rule must have seemed harsh indeed. But a contemporary comparison may have softened even the lash of the cardinal's harsh rule. For example, his *lettres de cachet*, which consigned suspected traitors or noble plotters to Paris's grim version of the Tower, the *Bastille* – or some grimmer fate – were but a pale reflection of a far more savage regime, that of Ivan IV ('the Terrible') of Russia. Richelieu and many educated Frenchmen must have been well aware that compared with Ivan's secret police, his own 'tyranny' in France could be represented as merely that of a strict parent dealing with some unruly children.

For Ivan's rule was far worse than the cardinal's. A generation before, the first 'Czar of all the Russias' had confronted the same problems of unifying his own powerful nobles that Louis and Richelieu now shared. His solution was particularly Russian, and one that was to cast a shadow that shapes Russia to this day. In 1565, Ivan founded an organisation called the Oprichniki to ensure that he was informed of all potential treason in his extended Muscovite kingdom and to whip his nobles and boyars into line. The Oprichniki's members seem to have been the very models for J. R. R. Tolkien's *Nazgul* in his *Lord of the Rings* trilogy. The Czar's new enforcement agents wore black uniforms, cloaks and armour, rode coal-black horses and carried a flag showing a mastiff's head and a broom to symbolise their role – to sniff out dissent and treachery and then to sweep it away with a ferocity designed to impress and cow any thoughts of rebellion. The Oprichniki soon justified their dreadful reputation. In 1570 they moved into the city of Novgorod looking for traitors. When they left the city, just over a month later, the majority of Novgorod's citizens were either dead, exiled to Kazan in the east, or in prison. Women and children had been violated, the menfolk butchered. Word of the Oprichniki's dreadful atrocities went out through Ivan's kingdom like a bush fire and spread wider still, losing nothing in the telling.

The tales of the Oprichniki's tortures and executions of women and children shocked all Europe. Even the Czar himself began to question his minions' excesses. By now probably half-mad, Ivan turned to an unlikely quarter for intelligence and support for what he felt was his embattled regime – Queen Elizabeth of England. He even attempted unsuccessfully to bribe the queen's tame astrologer (and undercover intelligence officer) John Dee to the service of Muscovy. 'With such a man at my side, I would need no further intelligence', he is reported as saying, as part of an attempt to open up Russia to the West. Sadly Dee wasn't playing. Elizabeth and Cecil were, however, the real beneficiaries of Ivan's clumsy approach, both from the imports from England's new trade embassies to Russia and the Baltics and the intelligence which accompanied them. By 1585, Walsingham was even running his own English agents out of Russia as well as the Baltic and Hanseatic ports.

Ivan's Russian Oprichniki made Torquemada's Inquisition appear to be a model of restraint. Their job done, the Oprichniki was forcibly disbanded two years later, but the tradition of state repression and conspiracy that they founded left an indelible impression on Russian minds for the future and on Europe as a whole. Compared to the Oprichniki's crude and unsophisticated practices, Richelieu's Gallic subtleties stand out as the sophisticated alternative for its day. Given central control, good domestic security and above all, stability at home, the cardinal could turn his mind to the great game of European power politics.

Once he became the king's first minister in 1624 Richelieu's three key policies crystallised and came together. All needed the very best intelligence. It is a measure of his success that he succeeded in all three. For domestic security, first he had to control the Protestants (Huguenots) and stop them becoming a state within a state, which in the France of the early 1600s seemed a very real possibility. Second, he had to crush the power of France's feudal lords, many of whom had never really accepted the Bourbon supremacy of Paris. Finally, abroad he had at best to control and if possible weaken the power of Habsburg Spain and Austria. All three tasks were essential, Richelieu reasoned, for the good of France. Above all else, national unity and the interests of France were his only criteria. For the cardinal, even the Church was merely a political tool for the implementation of his central policies and the consolidation of central power in Paris. France was Richelieu's true God.

The Cardinal's spy networks were in action right from the start. In a startling reversal of fortune Richelieu's intelligence agents had so penetrated the Duke of Buckingham's expedition to aid the Huguenots of La Rochelle in 1627 that he knew every detail of that sorry English foray long before it had even left port on its disastrous mission. In stark contrast, Buckingham's less than encouraging policy for intelligence on departure must have come as little comfort to his ramshackle fleet and its rag-bag army of pensioned-off Marines: 'The courage of the soldiers and sailors must make up for our want of intelligence!' Buckingham had obviously never heard of Sun-T'zu, but he should at least have known of Walsingham. England's great spymaster must have been turning in his grave. Such idiocies as Buckingham's should be emblazoned on every statesman and general's wall. (They were to be heard again 250 years later from a cynical British intelligence officer watching the Falklands Task Force set sail in April 1982.)

Richelieu's great international challenge was not, however, in dealing with an enfeebled and incompetent Protestant England. The Habsburg power of Spain and its friends to both East and West could, if they ever combined, at the very worst crush his newly united France, and at the very best, stunt its growth. Imperial Spain and Austria were the Cardinal's real enemies and therefore his intelligence targets. Though he may have never read him, Richelieu was clearly a firm believer in Sun-T'zu's maxim, 'What enables enlightened rulers to conquer the enemy at every move, is intelligence'.

Forearmed by his agents with the knowledge of every move from Madrid and, above all, hard intelligence out of Vienna, the seat of Habsburg imperial power, Richelieu, the Catholic cardinal, set out on as ambitious and duplicitous secret operation as any in the murky history of espionage and double-dealing. His plan was nothing less than to bring the *Protestant* princes of the North in against Austria's Catholic armies. For Henry IV, 'Paris may have been worth a Mass...'; for Richelieu, France was worth a Protestant Eucharist, if it came to the push and helped the French cause. What mattered was France, not religious labels.

The series of religious wars known to history as the Thirty Years' War had broken out in 1618 and pitted the Protestant North against the imperial Catholic South. The longer these great religious wars ravaged Germany and the east reasoned Richelieu, then the less chance there would be that the Habsburg Imperial forces could ever turn on France. Moreover, any enfeebled Spanish-Austrian coalition would leave France supreme in Europe. Although Richelieu and his chief agent, du

Tremblay, were both devout Catholics, for very clear *raison d'état* they set out to secretly encourage the Protestant armies of Gustavus Adolphus, king of Sweden, to attack Catholic Austria and the Habsburg Emperor Ferdinand II. It was a scheme of breathtaking duplicity. It could even have been denounced as heretical. This secret treaty with the Lion of the North was only the beginning, however. Richelieu's intrigue went much further.

The Imperial force's greatest asset was the Emperor's commanding general, a brilliant Czech Protestant general known to history as Wallenstein. Albrecht von Waldstein's was no ordinary career. Born a Bohemian noble, and raised by the Jesuits, he had married an heiress who obligingly died, leaving him her fortune. This he multiplied by buying up confiscated estates and then managing them as they should have been managed. As they prospered, so did he. By 1619 Wallenstein was able to lend even the Emperor vast sums: for example, half a million gold ducats in 1623 alone. By 1625, Wallenstein was effectively financing Ferdinand. He asked for no security. To the magnate who owned a quarter of Bohemia, he could well afford an emperor's word to be his bond.

By 1626, at Ferdinand's request, Wallenstein had recruited and armed 50,000 men and brought them into the battle line alongside the armies of the Catholic League under a grateful Tilly. This victorious Catholic army now surged north, laying waste on the route to Lower Saxony, Hannover, Holstein and even Denmark itself.

By 1627 Wallenstein's armies controlled most of northern Germany and were close to the borders of France. To balance his 140,000 experienced troops the Catholic League of Tilly and Maximilian of Bavaria could only muster a mere 30,000. Wallenstein's wealth, his power and his successes in battle now seemed to pose a threat: not just a threat to France but to the established order and the European balance of power. When Ferdinand arbitrarily removed the Elector of Mecklenburg and gave his electorate to Wallenstein alarm bells rang throughout the motley community of minor German princelings. If Mecklenburg could be deposed by the Emperor, who next? Even German princes had rights; particularly against ambitious foreigners from the South with a large army to give weight to their orders. Jealousy and whispering against this overmighty Caesar intensified. Bavaria warned Ferdinand that she might not ratify the Emperor's son as imperial successor should Wallenstein stay on as commander of the Imperial forces, exacting tribute and enriching himself by force of arms.

Ferdinand stayed his hand: he had one last task for this brilliant and powerful man. In 1629 as part of a Jesuit inspired campaign of enforcing the Counter-Reformation, Ferdinand issued the 'Edict of Restitution', ordering all lands lost in the Reformation to be returned to their owners – which meant mainly to the Church. Wallenstein's horde swept through Germany enforcing the edict, restoring the Catholic faith and evicting Protestants everywhere. Towns and cities fell to the host. Only Magdeburg resisted where places as far apart as Augsburg and Dortmund fell one after another to the avenging Catholic armies of Wallenstein. His great task for the Emperor completed, Wallenstein was promptly dismissed.

With their charismatic and successful general gone, the mercenary troops of the Imperial Army began to desert. It seemed only a leader like Wallenstein had held their professional ranks together. Well warned by Richelieu, Gustavus Adolphus of Sweden, the leader of the Protestants, offered these hungry veterans of a dozen victories good food, a warm campfire and regular pay in his own well-ordered ranks. Thousands of ostensibly Catholic mercenaries defected, to re-enlist in the Swedish king's army of the Protestant North, allowing him to further consolidate his hold on the northern ports.

It was a breathtaking coup and a piece of double-dealing only possible through timely, accurate intelligence. Richelieu had achieved a masterstroke; he had weakened the Imperial forces of the Habsburgs, immeasurably strengthened the Protestant counterweight to the Emperor's power, got rid of the Habsburg's Empire's outstanding general and reinforced Gustavus's Protestant army. And all while pretending still to be a staunch Catholic, an ally and a friend of the Emperor. Many thought that they had benefited from the switches and betrayals of the early 1630s; in reality there was only one clear winner and that was Richelieu's France.

Within two years Wallenstein was back. Tilly was dead. Everywhere the Imperial armies were in retreat. Gustavus Adolphus of Sweden had resurged into Germany carrying the Protestant cause on his pikes and muskets as far south as the gates of Munich. Only Wallenstein it seemed could stem the Northern tide. A stricken Bavaria begged for his recall to stop Gustavus Adolphus's avenging Protestants. The Emperor reappointed his mighty subject to command of the Imperial forces. Once more Wallenstein set out to bring Gustavus and his all-conquering Swedes to battle.

They met at Lützen near Leipzig on 16 November 1632. By nightfall the battle was over. Wallenstein's men were driven from the field. But this time it was the victors who were grieving and the vanquished rejoicing. Gustavus Adolphus, the Lion of the North, was dead, cut down by Imperial cuirassiers in the swirl of battle. Men whispered that he had been murdered by a conspiracy directed by Richelieu and du Tremblay. It mattered not. Wallenstein was again supreme in *Mitteleuropa*. His reputation and his power were at their zenith. Like some free-booting Mongol of old he now stood at the head of the most powerful private army in Europe. Wallenstein was now independent, rich and well armed enough to do whatever he chose.

Richelieu now planned a secret intelligence and diplomatic operation to remove this dangerous hero. The cardinal's intelligence service had long since alerted him to the fact that Germany's Catholic princes and electors were jealous of Wallenstein, both for his military success and for his close links with the Emperor. His power and wealth had already made him a target of much envy and intrigue by his rivals and fellow generals. Now fate – and good intelligence – alerted Richelieu to a useful weapon of intrigue.

Pressing internal issues such as who was to be selected as the next king of Bohemia stood large at the time and threatened to split the Catholic camp. The Habsburg Empire was divided on the choice. The German electors' votes mattered to the Emperor, struggling with party faction and internal politics in his imperial capital. Du Tremblay was dispatched to Vienna to further muddy the waters. His orders from the cardinal were to advise Ferdinand and to sow division in the Catholic ranks. 'It would be well to oblige the Electors in this trifling matter', encouraged Richelieu's agent, pressing the cause of the anti-Wallenstein faction. It was as much a matter of faith, he urged, as of politics.

To a man in debt to the tune of 2,000,000 gold ducats to his most powerful subject and moreover, a subject with a large army at his back, these were persuasive arguments. Fearful of losing the political support of the Electors, his German princes, and especially of his Spanish and Italian senior officers, the Emperor banished Wallenstein to his Bohemian estates. The great leader took himself off with dignity and a positive army of servants.

This time Wallenstein's retirement was permanent. Shortly afterwards the Emperor declared his overmighty subject an outlaw, and on 25 January 1634 Wallenstein was murdered by renegade Scottish and Irish officers in the pay of his jealous Catholic rivals. France's secret triumph was complete. In Liddell Hart's words, 'It is difficult to overestimate the influence this tremendous weakening of the Imperial Army exercised on the fortunes of the war ...'.

Of course, the secret of Richelieu's double-dealing could not be kept for ever. When the full duplicity of du Tremblay's 'counsel' was finally revealed to him, Ferdinand's rage was terrible: 'This worthless friar has disarmed me with a rosary and put six Elector's hats into his narrow cowl!' But it was too late. The Protestant armies of the north German plains were now too well established to be thrown back into the sea. With his best general gone and his armies weakened the Emperor had to accept the inevitability of a long war or negotiate a peace. All over Europe men said that the hand of Richelieu lay behind it. Only France had really benefited from the long chain of events that left Gustavus Adolphus dead, Wallenstein murdered and the Habsburg Empire prostrate and weak.

The Habsburgs took their revenge, although not on Richelieu. It was du Tremblay, his *éminence grise* who paid the price of his master's double-dealings. When that 'worthless Capucin' was proposed as a cardinal, Pope Urban VIII, wary of Habsburg wrath and Spanish power, refused the honour.

Richelieu's skills were not confined to agent running and skilful secret intelligence operations, however. His *cabinet noir* relied heavily on intercepting others' codes and ciphers and usually deciphering them. At the siege of the Huguenot fortress of Realmont in 1628 the Royal Army captured a Huguenot courier trying to run the blockade and get a message for help through the siege lines. Richelieu was present as he was at so many internal battles. He had heard of a local man called Antoine Rossignol who was reputed to be able to break any code and invited him to unbutton the Huguenot's message. The obliging Rossignol duly did so, revealing that the Fortress's spirited defence and plentiful expenditure of shot was a bluff. The defenders were in fact nearly out of supplies, ammunition and food.

Richelieu's great ability as a politician was to use others and information to his own best advantage. His response was simply to send the secret message back into Realmont under a flag of truce, with a copy of its decoded version attached and an invitation to the garrison to give up their pointless struggle. Realising that the game was up and their weakness known, Realmont tamely surrendered to the king's forces. Richelieu's bloodless coup reveals his skill as a master of not just collecting intelligence but in *using* intelligence wisely.

Richelieu's blueprint for intelligence survived his death in 1642. Although Mazarin, his successor, never confronted the great challenges of Richelieu's ministry, he could nonetheless rely on a peerless network of agents both at home and abroad that would be the political and military intelligence model for France and Europe's intelligence services for the next century and a half.

By 1650, the spotlight turned back to England. The 'great rebellion' of the 1640s had torn the kingdom apart. The Puritan Protestant faction in Parliament had pulled down the House of Stuart's edifice of royal despotism and, to make sure that their victory was permanent, had cut their king's head off. The Anglo-Catholic rump of the Royalists fled abroad to plot their return. The countryside may not have been despoiled but to the protagonists the English revolution was every bit as bloody and full of intrigue as any of the Continental wars of religion.

The English dictator, Oliver Cromwell, was a stern no-nonsense soldier. From his enlistment as an amateur leader of an East Anglian cavalry regiment in 1642 to his assumption of supreme military and political power in 1650 he had acquired the virtues and the vices of the professional military commander. Clear thinking, focused and determined, this stern unbending authoritarian brooked no interference with his mission, which appears to have been nothing less than to establish a Puritan heaven on earth. His gloomy Christmas- and dancing-free regime may have sat uneasily with the newly 'liberated' English but his Lord's men and his major generals undoubtedly ran an *efficient* despotism. And efficiency needs good intelligence. With the disciplined single-mindedness of the soldier, Cromwell and his chief agent, John Thurloe, set up a new English secret service devoted, as Walsingham's and Richelieu's were before them, to two clear tasks: the unmasking of subversion and treason at home and the identification of threats from abroad, mainly from the exiled Royalists. Protector Cromwell may have been a God-fearing man, but he never forgot that divine guidance can usually be enhanced by a good dose of earthly intelligence on one's enemies and especially on those who dare to disagree with the Lord's work.

Secretary Thurloe ran the Commonwealth's secret service. The years of England's republic may have been few, but Thurloe and his master put an untarnishable lustre on them, at least in military terms. Cromwell's regime was simply the most efficient and for its size, the most powerful, of the age.

For a tiny nation in the aftermath of schism and a debilitating civil war, the Lord Protector's achievements are prodigious. Algerian pirates who had happily been raiding the south-west coast of England to seize ships and slaves were driven back to their Mediterranean lairs. The Scots and Dutch were humbled and controlled. Would-be Royalist assassins and regicides were exposed and neutralised to the admiration of Mazarin in France, and not a mouse squeaked among the Royalists in exile without Thurloe – and therefore Cromwell – becoming aware of it. Some of his subjects even believed that, 'my Lord protector had supernatural powers.' Good intelligence was the secret of Cromwell's survival and that of his government. Compared with Elizabeth's parsimonious regime Oliver Cromwell did not stint his 'Postmaster General'. According to Pepys's diaries, the secret service vote under the Lord Protector was no less than £70,000, an unimaginable sum to Elizabeth's spymaster. His predecessor George Downing had been a successful 'scoutmaster' to Parliament's 'New Model Army' but the hazards of Whitehall and Westminster in peacetime demanded different skills to basic cavalry reconnaissance, military bravery and contact military intelligence, however bravely and hard won.

Thurloe was first and foremost an interceptor of others' communications, as his title Postmaster General reveals. As a result of both his communications intelligence and his army of spies throughout Europe ('subtil and sly fellows …') Thurloe enabled his master to 'carry the secrets of all the Princes of Europe at his girdle' in Pepys's vivid phrase. But crucial to his reputation in an age which relied on the written word was his 'secret office' or chamber, where the letters of half of Europe were intercepted, decoded or ended up. His fellow professionals gloomily noted his success: 'There is no government on earth that divulges affairs less than England, or is more punctually informed of those of others', Ambassador Sagedo of Venice warned his government back home. Richelieu's successor Cardinal Mazarin, no slouch at intelligence himself, conceded that no sooner had the French cabinet met behind closed doors in Paris than Secretary Thurloe and the English were informed 'within a few days'. The key element was not just 'collecting' intelligence, however; Thurloe's genius lay in his interpreting intelligence. To do this he needed skilled codebreakers.

Codes and ciphers have been used since time immemorial, by the practitioners of Venus as much as by those of Mars. Purists point out (correctly) that a code is different to a cipher. A code can be anything from symbols and dots, to modern strings of computer nulls and ones, (e.g. '…'0011001001 etc.). A cipher, on the other hand, is the substitution of one letter for another. Traditionally secret writing (e.g. invisible ink) and simple substitution codes were the staple of the ancients. Julius

Caesar is credited with the schoolboy system of using one letter of the alphabet to represent another according to some prearranged agreement; the so-called substitution code.

Byzantium and Islamic mathematicians soon improved on such unsophisticated practices. By the 1400s the Florentines and, inevitably, those arch-intriguers the Venetians were seeking new and more secure methods of 'secret writing' to protect their secrets. By 1500 even the use of double alphabets to muddle the frequency of letters had been superseded by a new toy, the 'cipher disc'.

Invented by a Florentine called Alberti, the cipher disc was simply two flat copper discs, one outside the other like a wheel rim and its tyre. Each had an alphabet inscribed on its rim. The letter on the outer ring could be aligned to coincide with any letter on the inner ring. However, by changing the setting of the discs in relation to each other, say, every ten letters, the message could only be deciphered by someone who had access to – or had cracked – the secret list of settings.

Alberti's disc was followed, in about 1580, by 'Vigenère's Square'. Vigenère, whose *Treatise on Ciphers* was printed in 1586, proudly dubbed his invention, *'le chiffre undéchiffrable'* and indeed for nearly three centuries, until the advent of Babbage's primitive computer in the 1840s, the Vigenère Square remained the standard for high security ciphers. Despite Vigenère's boast, it never truly was unbreakable.

To crack into these increasingly sophisticated ciphers Thurloe's 'black chamber' relied on the skills of two master codebreakers, a brilliant mathematician called John Wallis and Cromwell's own brother-in-law, Bishop John Wilkins. Between them, these two remarkable men effectively kept both the Royalist plotters and England's foreign foes permanently neutralised. As fast as a plan was hatched, it was uncovered. Thurloe's cryptanalysts ensured that Oliver Cromwell could read most of his enemies' secret intentions like an open book. It was a remarkable achievement.

Only one group alone eluded Cromwell and Thurloe's reach. Despite many near misses and countless penetrations by the Commonwealth's agents, the Sealed Knot, a secret Royalist group dedicated to King Charles II, somehow just managed to elude the Puritan's all-seeing eye and long arm. There were close shaves aplenty; but Charles Stuart somehow always managed to evade his would-be captors. Cromwell's agents had every reason to hunt down his old adversary's son and heir to the English crown. In 1654, from exile, the 'King over the Water' had offered £5,000 (a huge sum) and a knighthood to any 'stout man bold enough to slay a certain base mechanic fellow called Oliver Cromwell.' For Thurloe and his master, it was a real grudge match and the stakes could not have been higher.

Cromwell's undercover intelligence men redoubled their efforts to unmask traitors and plots against the Commonwealth, uncovering a host of half-baked ideas to smuggle explosives and ammunition into England disguised as soap or wine, as well as plots to poison the Lord Protector. This extraordinary underground battle between the Sealed Knot and Thurloe intensified as the 1650s wore on. The Commonwealth finally managed to get a spy, Richard Willys, inside the Knot, but it was too late. At the last it was Thurloe's number two, Samuel Morland, who would eventually betray the Commonwealth to Charles Stuart. Even Cromwell himself became personally involved in the 'great game'. One gentleman of unknown sympathies was given a passport to travel to Germany. On his return he was invited to an audience with the Lord Protector, Oliver Cromwell himself, no less.

Had he, enquired Cromwell, kept his promise not to meet Charles Stuart during the visit to Cologne? The traveller swore he had. Cromwell continued his remarkable personal interrogation. 'Who, then, snuffed out the candles when you met Charles Stuart?' The flustered traveller denied any such meeting. Cromwell pressed him further: 'So you deny carrying any letter for the said Charles Stuart?'

The man swore his innocence. He knew of no such letter. Cromwell said nothing, but took the man's hat and slit open the lining. Concealed inside was a letter from Charles Stuart to his supporters in England. Contemptuously, the Lord Protector tossed the incriminating package onto the table and ordered the unfortunate Royalist thrown into the Tower to await his fate as a traitor and a spy.

When the Royalists in Cologne discovered that they had been betrayed, Charles's security men searched all the baggage and every room of his entourage in exile. In the belongings of a trusted Royalist aide, a gentleman called Manning (in reality one of Thurloe's best and most trusted agents), they discovered secret ciphers, codes and letters. Confronted with this evidence, Manning confessed all. He was an under-cover agent for Cromwell and excused his treachery by pleading financial necessity for he had received the princely sum of £1,200 for his work.

Manning's only hope was for a spy-for-spy exchange, with him being swapped for one or more of the Royalist agents in prison in England, rather like the famous exchanges at 'Check Point Charlie' during the Cold War in Berlin. Thurloe rejected such a plan out of hand. Manning was expendable. But for the unfortunate prisoner a ray of hope gleamed still. The Elector Prince of Cologne flatly refused to condone any killing on German soil by his troublesome English guests, however elevated. Charles's hard-nosed Royalists were undeterred. The wretched Manning was marched out through the woods and over the border into Julich to pay the ultimate price of the undercover operator caught by those he has betrayed. 'Two gentlemen of the court' shot him down as a spy. Like any good intelligence officer, however, Thurloe had many more undercover agents to fall back on. Reliance on one single source has always been a dangerous practice.

By the time of Charles Stuart's restoration as king in 1660, Richelieu in France and Thurloe in England had effectively made the mould for a national intelligence system. Both countries used basically the same model. At its heart was a single controlling brain and a few trusted lieutenants, each responsible for one or more of four key intelligence operations:

1 Domestic security, plots and subversion

2 Interception and the deciphering of potential enemies' communications

3 Human intelligence, spies and agents to collect foreign intelligence

4 A special operations capability to reach out and execute 'deniable operations' and to spread disinformation

It was – and is – a surprisingly modern construct and was to set the organisation and pattern of intelligence until the coming of the industrial revolution.

In England, the Restoration confirmed the importance of intelligence in national policy if only by the furious public debate which broke out over such weighty matters as the secret intelligence vote in Parliament and who was to be in control of such a dangerous organisation. There, England and France split. The canny Charles, whose whole life had been based on intrigue, treachery and mistrust, ran his own private intelligence service, preferring to 'divide and rule' the component parts of Thurloe's intelligence organisation rather than to trust his fate to the loyalty of yet another Puritan busybody. Slowly, England's State intelligence system withered and contracted.

Louis of France on the other hand, had a firm and certain grip on his own realm thanks to the legacy of Richelieu and Mazarin. The underage Sun King had succeeded to the throne in 1643, and from 1655 onwards was ruling France and her affairs with an increasingly sure hand. It needed to be; for from 1667 onwards Louis embarked on a series of wars against most of the powers of Europe. In these new wars of nationalism, intelligence flourished as never before.

Louis was passionately interested in intelligence and took enormous pains to be fully informed on everything, as St Simon tells us: 'He had spies and reporters everywhere and of all descriptions.' Many of them sent their secret letters direct to the king by 'secret channels of his own devising.' The aim was clear: Louis was going to keep as tight a grip on everything in his kingdom as he could. This burning need to know allowed his lieutenants of police to assume a dangerous authority. Richelieu's personal network of intrigue was now backed by the heavy hand of absolute power. Like Thurloe, Louis relied heavily on communications interception. St Simon's account cannot be bettered:

But the cruellest of the king's methods of obtaining information was the opening of private letters. Years passed before the practice was generally suspected; and even afterwards many ignorant and foolish people continued to feed him .... He read extracts of those containing any matter which the Postmasters or their minister decided he should see ... A single word of abuse or disparagement of the king or of the Government ... was enough to finish a man's career without further enquiry ...

With sources like this at his fingertips and the power to strike at unsuspecting traitors Louis XIV's power was complete – in France. Abroad, Louis's power was helped immeasurably by two key factors in France's dealings with England. Charles II had spent much of his early life in France and was therefore heavily indebted to the French king, in every way: survival, financial, emotional. He liked France and he liked the French. Secondly, Charles was a noted libertine and ladies' man. To put it bluntly, Charles was only too easily compromised. In modern parlance, he was 'a sucker for a honey trap.'

Louis, whose ambition was to neutralise turbulent Protestant England, and keep her that way, had a splendid instrument for controlling his fellow sovereign and his potentially powerful little country across the Channel. She was fresh-faced, dark and sexy. Her name was Louise de Kéroualle (sometimes Queroualle), and her mission from Louis was nothing less than to ensure King Charles II of England would faithfully carry out Louis of France's wishes by bedding him for France.

Of the fact that it was an intelligence entrapment special operation we can be in no doubt. Her instructions from Louis were 'to see what may grow out of this situation'; Ambassador Colbert wrote back from London to Louvois, the Minister of War, 'We hope that she will so behave that the attachment [i.e., to Charles] will be so durable as to exclude all others ...'.

France could hardly have selected a better choice of agent of influence. Louise, with her soft, dark good looks, swept Charles off his feet. Indeed, she appears to have nearly overplayed her hand. Realising, like many a woman before and since, that physical unavailability merely encourages desire, she played hard to get. A worried Colbert cautioned her about playing her game too long: 'Do not repulse temptations too strongly' urged the nervous ambassador, knowing Charles's limited attention span and notorious flightiness. He need not have worried. A besotted Charles was hooked by such a luscious bait.

After an increasingly frantic wooing Louise finally allowed herself to be persuaded by her royal suitor, even allegedly going through a form of mock marriage before surrendering her virtue to his eager demands. It is said that Colbert, Arlington and Lady Sunderland were present as presumably astonished – or amused – witnesses when she yielded gracefully to the 'the dribbling dart of love' while Charles promptly bedded her there and then in public.

Soon she was created Duchess of Portsmouth. Charles could not think of a world without the sensual Louise at his side. For such a worldly woman, the rest of her mission must have been simple. Now came the French sting. It was a secret proposition from Louis. In return for three million gold francs a year, would Charles sell his kingdom's neutrality and declare war on the Dutch? English control of the Channel ports on Walcharen and the Scheldt were thrown in for good measure.

For an embittered Charles, whose requests for money from a parsimonious Parliament were constantly being rebuffed, the offer was like manna from heaven. It freed him from the yoke of tiresome and sanctimonious Puritans and accountants. No matter that he had effectively sold out his staunchly Protestant country to a Catholic overlord. With good French gold in his pocket and the compliant, sexy Louise as *maîtresse en titre* by his side, the Merry Monarch could get back to the pleasures of his Restoration.

Rarely can a single secret agent of influence have scored such an intelligence coup. However, Louise de Kéroualle probably achieved one other triumph. Although it is hard to prove definitely, there is enough circumstantial evidence to believe that Louise may have induced Charles to finally commit himself to becoming a secret Roman Catholic. For

Protestant England, such a revelation would have been explosive. The Treaty of Dover and its full ramifications were too dangerous to be allowed the light of public scrutiny. As rumours began to spread of secret treaties, Popish plots and treachery in high places an anonymous notice appeared on the door of Charles's bedchamber:

> Within this place, a bed's appointed
> For a bitch from France and God's anointed.

The ever volatile London mob voiced its disapproval, hissing at Louise's coach as it clattered through the streets and screaming, 'French whore!' One day, mistaking Nell Gwyn's coach for her French rival's, they booed it and forced it to stop, whereupon the brazen ex-orange seller leaned out and called to them:

> Nay, nay, good people. You are mistaken! I am the King's *Protestant* whore! I am the English one!

The London mob cheered her to the echo.

The mob would have rushed to arms if they had known the final stinging affront of Louis's extraordinary deal with Charles II. If the English Protestants were ever to try and expel Charles, then under the Treaty, Louis's Catholic legions would land in England and protect his person and his throne. And establish French control over England, of course …

In such a climate, Charles's intelligence inheritance withered. There was little need to read French diplomatic traffic and Charles's enemies were in Parliament and the English court, not abroad. By the time of Charles II's death in 1685, real intelligence matters occupied but a small part of English life.

Intelligence flourishes when nourished by the fertile soil of intrigue, however. The Merry Monarch had left no legitimate heir. His brother James had succeeded, and James was a staunch Roman Catholic with all the stiff-backed Stuart hauteur of his father, whose neck had felt the axe only thirty-five years earlier. Yet another religious confrontation loomed as rebellion broke out first in the West Country and then in

London itself. Yet again, civil war loomed. Men had to choose. Finally the unpopular James II, England's last Catholic king, abdicated in 1688 and fled abroad, carrying with him the last hopes of the House of Stuart. In a clear indication of who exactly was in charge, Parliament invited the Dutch Prince of Orange, leader of the Protestant cause, and his English wife Mary to become England's next joint monarchs.

With a new Continental court, and a new Stuart 'King over the Water', once again intrigues flourished as the men, and women, of power jockeyed for position. The struggle between the Catholic Stuarts at St Germain and the Protestant ascendancy in Westminster would absorb much intelligence effort in the years to come as the Dutch and English tried to contain Louis XIV's France at the zenith of its power. William and Mary's dour Dutch courtiers needed intelligence from abroad as never before in order to re-establish the balance of power in Europe. The age of the spy and the intelligence agent had arrived with a vengeance.

But as the eighteenth century dawned it brought with it another intelligence development, and one that would one day have far-reaching consequences. For in the gloomy winter fastnesses of Russia, Peter the Great, that tireless reformer and advocate of novelty, established in 1697 a new organisation, the Special Office of the Czar.

This Special Office was to be controlled by a specially selected, diligent, but above all, trustworthy bureaucrat called Makaroff, reporting exclusively to the Czar. In future, by order of the central authority in Moscow, all questionable political activities, disloyal officers, treasonable crimes against the State or even denunciations from members of the public would be centrally investigated and punished accordingly.

Of course, there had been similar groups like this before. Ancient Sparta had had its own undercover organisation to control the Helots and to stamp out any signs of incipient rebellion; the *Vehmgericht* of medieval Germany and (inevitably) Venice's Council of Ten had policed their citizens with a ruthless eye for dissent. But there had never been anything planned to be quite so efficient or so all-powerful as Peter the Great's Special Office.

Russia had invented the secret police.

7

The Age of Battles

No war can be conducted without early
and good intelligence, and that such
advices cannot be had other than at very
great expense

JOHN CHURCHILL, 1ST DUKE OF MARLBOROUGH

With the arrival of William III on the English throne in 1689, the political landscape of Europe altered dramatically. William was Dutch, he was Protestant and he had been at war with France for years. No greater contrast in either personality or policy could there be to the relaxed Francophile reign of his predecessor Charles Stuart. William's United Provinces of the Netherlands had been fighting Louis XIV since 1672, and England's new Dutch king could have been forgiven for thinking that this new addition to his tithes was going to be a welcome reinforcement to the Dutch struggle.

He was rapidly disabused. England's tiny and ineffective army had one foot, not for the first or the last time, stuck firmly in the Irish bog. At first, rather than England coming to the Netherlands' aid, it was William and his generals who were to spend their time and effort saving the English from being driven out of Ireland.

William's eventual defeat of the Stuarts' Franco-Irish forces at the Boyne in 1690 transformed both his war and Europe's strategic landscape. At last he could devote his energies, and those of his new kingdom, to his life's work: evicting the French from the Low Countries and consolidating Dutch Protestant rule. For the last decade of the 1600s, William of Orange grimly plugged away at Louis's dominant France in a protracted and largely unsuccessful struggle. However, 'even unsuccessful warfare', in Correlli Barnett's perceptive analysis, 'can exhaust an opponent, provided it is pursued for years.'

Even for the glories of Louis XIV's France, twenty-five years of ceaseless campaigning had proved too costly. By the time the new century was dawning it was clear that France was not only expansionist and greedy, she was also over-extended and tired. After half a century of glory, Louis's all conquering armies looked vulnerable. At Ryswick in 1697, his ministers had signed a peace treaty with the stubborn Netherlanders. The question was, how long could it last? The European agenda for the eighteenth century was thereafter to be defined by one simple grand strategy: control French ambitions. To accomplish this, her opponents had to know French intentions. And for that they needed intelligence.

William III may have been an unimaginative and unsuccessful plodder of a general. His skills as an administrator and organiser, however, were of the highest calibre for his day. Where Charles II had been slapdash and untroubled by such routine matters as papers of state and an efficient bureaucracy, William's tidy Dutch mind wanted things to be 'correct'. As he had to spend at least six months of every year out of his new kingdom, he delegated his powers to capable and trustworthy ministers. Intelligence matters were clearly and 'tidily' handled by William Blathwayte. Blathwayte's brief as secretary of state was unequivocal and was to define Britain's overseas intelligence effort for the next half-century: keep an eye on the Stuarts in exile, and look out for French plans.

At first it was the 'King over the Water' who absorbed most of William's intelligence efforts. Between them the deposed King James and his son Charles Stuart had raised conspiracy to a fine art. Across the years it is difficult for us to envisage just how threatening were the Jacobites at this time. Rather like the expectant disciples awaiting the imminent second coming of Christ, the 1690s and early 1700s were times of high tension, expectancy and nervous strain for English politics. With the might of Louis XIV at his back, who knew when the 'Old Pretender' might suddenly reappear unannounced on England's shore, bringing more political upheaval and even another civil war? And where then should men's loyalties lie? It was an age of trimming, compromises and a time when the prudent took out political insurance by keeping a foot in both camps.

Fortunately for William and Mary, James's court in exile had been thoroughly compromised and penetrated by Blathwayte's agents. That the threat was real there can be no doubt. On one occasion James actually dispatched the Royalist Duke of Berwick to England to front up a plot to assassinate King William. Led by Sir George Barclay twenty highly trained undercover soldiers, the SAS of their day, were infiltrated one by one into London from France and prepared to strike as the king went riding on Turnham Green on 15 February 1696. It was the biggest plot since the Gunpowder Treason of 1605 and about as successful. Somewhere along the line the plot had been penetrated and betrayed. King William did not ride that day, warned of the attempt. The plotters waited in vain for their target. When no one turned up they fled or were arrested. Another Stuart plot that could have changed the course of history had been defeated, not by force of arms but by good, timely, accurate intelligence.

The man charged with countering these Stuart intrigues on the Continent was a writer, one Matthew Prior, who had been England's ambassador at The Hague. He seems to have been a remarkably perceptive and professional intelligence officer. From his correspondence we know his views on his undercover spies, as like the true professional he was, Prior 'handed over' a list of agents to his successor listing their virtues and their weaknesses.

One in particular appears to have been ideal, and a natural choice for intelligence work, being described by Secretary Prior 'as cunning a fellow and a true debauchee'. Such a description would make him a perfect choice in any age for his sleazy trade.

By the time of William's death and Queen Anne's succession in 1702, war with France was looming yet again. French claims to the Spanish throne scared the smaller fry of Europe, who were terrified – rightly – of the consequences and power of any Franco-Spanish super-power axis ruled from Paris. French moves to seize the vital frontier fortresses facing present-day Belgium finally precipitated the conflict. By 1703, Europe was yet again at war. Louis XIV's ambition and grand designs were to set a pattern of battles and warfare on the Continent that would last for the rest of the eighteenth century.

For the English – soon to be the British following the Act of Union with Scotland signed in 1707 – the intelligence tasks of spying on the French as well as the exiled Stuarts in St Germain were not unduly onerous and appear to have fallen into a well-defined pattern. The tightly controlled collection of bored aristocrats assembling at Versailles every season leaked like a sieve, while the gossipy Stuarts were an open book, with the Channel Packet boat scarcely able to handle the volume of two-way traffic between the rival courts. Contraband, spies, gossip and travellers regularly criss-crossed between London, Paris, The Hague and Rome, plus the hired agents of a dozen German princelings. Warnings of new insurrections being planned were the essential currency of intelligence as politicians trimmed their sails to catch every passing breeze or rumour of rebellion. For London it was a busy, fevered time for those in power – and in the money – and for the impoverished Stuarts abroad a desperate scramble to survive.

In this kind of atmosphere where intrigues flourished in every coffee house, information could be bought and sold like any other commodity. A cynical Thurloe had said, a generation earlier (when writing to his 'head of station' in Rome, about suborning a new agent onto the books), 'These people cannot be gained but for money, but for money they will do anything.' Eventually Thurloe authorised a large payment in gold and wearily advised that only a 'Cardinal, Monsignor or a good secretary' was really worth recruiting. Such an unsentimental view of men's motives proved only too true for his successors as well.

But not all the intelligence traffic and treachery was one way, as the case of the spy William Gregg proves. Gregg was a native of Montrose in Scotland and educated at the grammar school before graduating from the university at Aberdeen. Like many an educated Scotsman since, the best sight he could see was the high road leading to London, there to try his luck south of the border and 'seek for advancement of state' at Westminster. Soon he was appointed secretary to the ambassador to Sweden. Sadly, like many another junior embassy member he fell into a 'number of irregularities', of which 'debauching a Swedish lady' cannot have endeared him to his ambassador. He was dismissed the service and sent home on the first boat.

First Minister Harley, ever alert to exploiting human weakness, promptly engaged the educated and broke young Scot as a copy clerk in his confidential office. Today, in an age of photocopiers, faxes and word processors, it is easy to forget just how labour intensive 'wordsmithing' used to be. A great man – or a politician – would stride up and down the office, dictating as he went. A scribe or clerk would desperately try and catch the sense of these mighty thoughts and set them down on paper to be literally hand copied by a circle of copy clerks peering at the prime copy pinned to a board. What obtained at the highest level of State applied equally to the meanest lawyer's office. Every letter or document had to be copied out by hand unless it was printed.

The dangers of such a system were twofold. First, the possibility of human error in copying was ever present, but secondly, it was inherently a very insecure method of conducting classified business. Where confidential letters and secret treaties have to be hand copied by clerks, leaks are almost inevitable. (Even today, the written word still presents a security risk. Britain's intelligence services admit to losing up to two hundred laptop computers a year) Gregg's new job at the heart of Britain's political intrigues gave him access to all the clandestine foreign policy twists and turns of Harley's increasingly beleaguered administration. For an impoverished and ambitious young Scotsman, the temptation to make money by access to State secrets was just too much.

It was Harley's policy to leave his confidential postal packages unsealed until the last minute before dispatch. Gregg took the opportunity to slip a note of his own into a letter addressed to one of Harley's Royalist contacts on the Continent. In it he offered to work as a spy for the Stuart court in exile at St Germain. To demonstrate his access to secrets and value as a spy he quoted from a secret letter from Queen Anne to her allies, urging an invasion of Spain.

This was a mistake. Unfortunately for Gregg, Harley's onward bound 'classified correspondence' was routinely screened by Dutch security officers at the Duke of Marlborough's headquarters looking out for this sort of material. William Gregg had not only condemned himself as a traitor by his own hand; he had actually signed his own inserted letter just to be sure.

In normal circumstances Harley would probably have jumped at the chance to exploit this situation by using Gregg as an unconscious double agent. There was much advantage to be gained by allowing this duplicitous clerk to send material to Britain's enemies and to pump 'chicken-feed' and disinformation into the Stuarts' camp via the would-be traitor. Unfortunately Gregg's treachery was publicly revealed as part of a wider scandal involving another two of Harley's undercover French couriers, named Baras and Valiere. It turned out that these two regular travellers between Dover and Boulogne had been taking more information back to France than they had been passing on to London. The two spies were in fact *French* double agents and had been having a field day passing details of British convoys and shipping movements to the privateers and corsairs of Dunkirk and Calais. Depredations among British merchant ships in the Channel had been particularly severe and Harley's political opponents sensed their chance. Gregg, Baras and Valiere were all arrested. A committee of the House of Lords ruled that Gregg was a traitor but had been caught before he could do any real harm. The two Frenchmen on the other hand, proudly confessed to the damage they had caused, claiming that they had acted as true soldiers of France. In Bishop Burnett's words, 'These men, as they were Papists, so they behaved themselves insolently boasting much of their power and credit.'

It transpired that suspicion had fallen upon the two French agents before, but Harley had always protected them, claiming that they were his own double agents. Now with their guilt openly admitted, there was nothing he could do with his network. The smuggler-couriers game was blown: it was he, Harley, who had been fooled by the French and not the other way round. Harley was personally exposed as a dupe of French trickery, his government was compromised and there was very little he could do about it. However, if a scapegoat could be found he might escape some of the censure now being heaped upon his head. William Gregg of Montrose was the perfect choice for a legal sacrifice. The wretched Scot was convicted under the ancient Treason Act of Edward III. Immediately after the Scots clerk's trial both Houses of Parliament petitioned the queen for his execution as a spy for 'Treason against the Realm'.

On 28 April 1708, William Gregg was hanged as a spy at Tyburn. On the scaffold, he handed a signed confession to the Sheriff of Middlesex acknowledging the justice of his sentence and begging the queen's forgiveness. He professed that he 'died an unworthy member of the Protestant faith', but that 'the want of money to supply his extravagances' had tempted him to commit the fatal crime that cost him his life.

Gregg's dismal fate as an unsuccessful mercenary spy offering to betray his country for money seems not only familiar but also rather modern. There have been many William Greggs since, in many lands. After the burning resentment of revenge and 'getting even', money still remains the most attractive lure for would-be traitors.

Not all spies of the period were as unlucky as Gregg or motivated by greed. The creator of Robinson Crusoe, no less, admitted that he had worked for Queen Anne's government 'in several honourable tho' secret services'. Daniel Defoe was being too modest by far. While the Duke of Marlborough wrestled with his sovereign's enemies on the battlefield, in Europe Defoe had been living almost as dangerously as an undercover government agent ever since Monmouth's rebellion in the reign of James II. He had seen three of his school friends hanged for their part in that affair, so Defoe could genuinely claim to have been 'well schooled in intrigue'. A prison sentence for parodying the Tory notables of the day and a spell in the stocks seems to have convinced the young writer that the way to success lay in following the Vicar of Bray's cautious counsel, 'That whatsoe'er King may reign' he intended to stay close to the men of power. (In this he seems to have been anticipating the Kremlin's later adage for political survival in a Communist dictatorship: 'sniff out, suck up, *survive*'.)

By the year of Blenheim, 1704, Defoe is to be found wandering the Highlands as 'Alexander Goldsmith' and reporting to the council in London on his findings about the Scots' political attitudes. His success and his pithy and trenchant insights into the politics of the day for his master in London, Harley, earned him a ringside seat at the negotiations for the Act of Union in 1707. Indeed, from 1709 onwards Defoe was not just a collector of intelligence but also an agent of influence trusted by the Whig administration in London to advise on, and if necessary to influence, policy. That he thought deeply about intelligence is clear; as early as 1704 he had drafted a paper for his paymasters in London advocating a 'Scheme for General Intelligence'. He also understood the other face of the intelligence coin as well, adding to his proposal: 'For as intelligence is most useful to us, so keeping our enemies from intelligence among us is as valuable a hand.' Like the true professional he obviously was, Defoe understood that intelligence, counter-espionage and security are an essential *troïka* for success.

His career flourished. As one of the leading writers and pamphleteers of his day, his undercover value to the administration as a sympathetic journalist and agent of public influence was immense. He could write freely and produce pamphlets to order; politically supportive, seditious or even straightforward honest ones. He was the perfect 'spin doctor', aided enormously by the fact that his prestige as a writer was high and his work much sought after. With such a reputation he worked undercover for the government and could thus insinuate himself into the opposition's camp and write for them without his true role or loyalties ever being known. By 1716 he was actually editing the principal *Jacobite* news-sheet, but in such a way 'as to keep the Jacobites amused' and to deflect them from resorting to more direct methods. Such a subtle and devious policy speaks volumes for the sophistication of intelligence 'special operations' and black propaganda in the early 1700s. It also shows that the demand for intelligence both at home and abroad remained as high as ever in the hothouse political atmosphere of the early eighteenth century.

And not just for political intelligence, either. From the moment the Anglo-Dutch armies took the field in 1702 to contain the final ambitions of the aging Louis XIV there was a clear need for high-grade military intelligence as well. France was the power of the age. Behind her barrier of fortresses facing the Spanish Netherlands and manned by her well-trained and well-equipped army of 90,000 men, France could threaten the very existence of the Protestant United Provinces of the Low Countries and their British allies.

The man charged with defending the Netherlands and defeating the French armies was John Churchill, known to history as the Duke of Marlborough. He had fought as a colonel of infantry under Turenne, the architect of many of France's greatest victories, rebelled against James II, been jailed by King William and now depended for his position on the favour of Queen Anne through his wife, the queen's 'best friend' at court.

Marlborough has come down to us, rightly, as a 'great captain' and one of the greatest soldiers of his age and arguably of many others. He combined the logistical skill of a Wellington and strategic judgement of Napoleon with Frederick the Great's tigerish aggression on the battlefield. What he appears to have had to an unusual degree, in addition to these martial attributes, was the patience and diplomatic skills of an Eisenhower as a supreme allied commander. Such a superb general and a successful war leader could never have achieved his victories without a clear understanding of the need for intelligence. Marlborough was, in every sense, a 'man of intelligence' and says so clearly in his own writings, quoting that no battle was ever won 'without early and good intelligence'.

One of the severest criticisms that can be levelled against many a general or politician is that he tries to be his own intelligence officer. This implies that the individual in question knows more about the enemy's capabilities and intentions, history, language and culture than his professional advisers. Such an approach carries with it connotations of arrogance and stupidity. While the commander must always have the final right of *decision*, he should never pretend to himself – or to others – that he has the monopoly of wisdom, let alone knowledge of the foe. For example, Stalin insisted on being his own intelligence officer before Barbarossa in 1941, insisting (despite all evidence to the contrary) that he knew more about what Hitler was up to than his own professional intelligence staff, who were awash with ample evidence of Nazi perfidy. The USSR paid a heavy price for Stalin's conceit and his frightened intelligence officers' cowardice. Stalin was merely one in a long line of such leaders.

There is, however, one honourable exception to this rule; when the commander genuinely *does* know more about the enemy than any of his intelligence advisers. Thus it was for John Churchill. His experience of war, the Stuarts, his Dutch allies and his French foes was immeasurably better than those of his subordinates. He had in his career had dealings with every single possible source, both friend and enemy alike. No one had more experience of the problems of his day; no one understood them better; and no one could manage them with greater efficiency than Marlborough himself.

He had to do everything himself. In an age before general staffs, corps and divisions, command was direct and personal. Bribery and corruption were the norm in the public service then just as they are today in many developing nations. To be in office in the early eighteenth century was not only to have power, but an unrivalled opportunity to enrich oneself both from the exercise of authority and from the public purse. In a deeply corrupt age Marlborough inherited a military system where:

> The whole system of military finance ... was one vast entanglement of fraud. Not only did the officers defraud the soldiers, but they defrauded the government also, while the government in its turn defrauded both officers and soldiers ...

Under William of Orange's strict Calvinistic eye such cavalier practices decreased but the British Army still remained an essentially 'privatised' organisation, and was to remain so until the Cardwell reforms of the 1870s.

This then was the unpromising and corrupt raw material from which Marlborough hewed his military triumphs. At a time when administration and logistics were well nigh impossible, Marlborough makes it all look easy. 'Administration was perhaps the most important single ingredient of Marlborough's genius', was Correlli Barnett's judgement in *Britain and her Army* and it was this attention to logistics and intelligence that distances Marlborough from most of his contemporaries.

His victories have a regular pattern and all rely on four essential ingredients: troops prepared to fight like lions, sound logistics, lots of money and good intelligence. Of these, none was so potentially riddled with peculation and backhanders, even by the corrupt underhand administrative practices of the day, as the provision of intelligence. We have already seen the dangers of treachery and money from William Gregg's sorry tale. Money is the lifeblood of intelligence, which like any other commodity, can be bought if the price is right. Marlborough had to buy much of his own intelligence and it did not come easily or cheap. He paid for his spies and agents by creaming off $2^{1}/_{2}$ per cent of all the monies delivered to him from London and his allies alike and then invested the money in his battle-winning secret and 'ace-in-the-hole': intelligence.

Marlborough ran a formidable intelligence apparatus. A network of spies and agents reported back to London from Versailles and St Germain. We know that Marlborough received a steady flow of good intelligence on French dispositions, capabilities and intentions from his political masters in London, particularly Godolphin. However, in addition to this flow of 'national command authority' information, in his independent post as Supreme Allied Commander in the Netherlands, Marlborough ran his own parallel network of high-level agents against those very same targets, charged with strategic reporting. In the Marlborough Archive there are over four hundred letters from an unnamed spy working directly to Marlborough himself from the very highest positions within the French court. He never failed to give this flow of intelligence the highest priority even if it meant buying it. As *Stadtholder* of the Dutch armies he could use both their and Hannover's funds for this vital task. If ever funds went short, he could always turn to his friend Godolphin, to keep the golden 'cavalry of St George' flowing. At the operational intelligence level, merchants and visitors reported on the capabilities and deployments of the French as they travelled around the camps and garrisons in north-east France. And once on the battlefield, Marlborough's experienced eye and superb cavalry kept his foes under the searchlight of his *coup d'oeil* at the tactical level. He might well have collected, collated, evaluated and interpreted all his own information; with his knowledge and skill there was none better. He was, without doubt, a master of intelligence.

He was not completely alone in his task – Quartermaster General Cadogan was his principal assistant as both administrator and secret intelligence officer. More junior officers such as Cardonnel, his aide with special responsibility for intelligence, also helped and were tasked with specific intelligence collection missions. For example there is a rare surviving example of a communication between Cardonnel and a Herr Robotham of Celle, paying the latter for his (undisclosed) services of an intelligence nature. Most of the time, however, Marlborough played his cards close to his chest and acted as his own intelligence officer. All reports went back to John Churchill personally and as a result he could almost always outwit his opponents.

His victories reflect this. Blenheim, his masterpiece, followed an astonishing 250-mile surprise march from Flanders to the Danube to join forces with the Imperial General Eugene. A cynical view might be that Marlborough devoted as much effort to deceiving his suspicious and cautious Dutch allies (who were not keen on expensive pitched battles and would have been horrified if asked to support one so far away from the Netherland's threatened borders) as he did to deceiving the French. France, Bavaria – and all Europe – were astounded by Marlborough's coup and the subsequent destruction of Louis XIV's army, its first real defeat since Rocroi had crowned French supremacy in 1643, over half a century earlier. The crucial advantage lay with intelligence. Marlborough always knew exactly where the French Army was. In Winston Churchill's vivid words:

> He knew exactly where Tallard was baking his bread, where he was camped and when he would march. He heard of the King's orders to Louvois (the Minister of War) as soon as the Marshal received them.

All this Marlborough got from what was effectively his own secret service. His opponent, Marshal Tallard, only discovered Marlborough's army's presence when it was too late and almost upon him. All Europe was stunned by Marlborough's triumph at Blenheim. It was Britain's greatest battlefield victory since Agincourt in 1415.

With his close friend and comrade in arms, Eugene of Savoy,

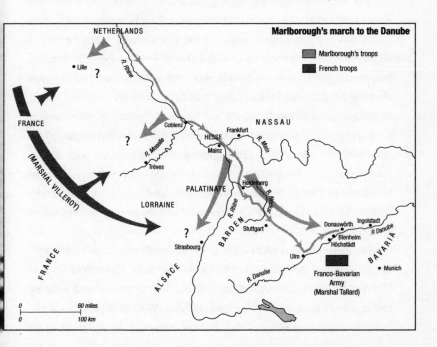

Marlborough subsequently visited humiliation after humiliation on Louis XIV's head. Ramillies, Oudenarde, Malplaquet, the lines of *Ne Plus Ultra* and innumerable sieges brought the France of the Sun King to its knees. Constant war was too much even for the architect of *la Gloire*. It was certainly too much for France.

By 1712 war-weariness in France, a new government in England and the Treaty of Utrecht meant that Marlborough's services were no longer needed. He was dismissed. His political opponents at court had long sought his ruin and his acid-tongued nag of a wife did all she could to assist their project, too stupid or too selfish to see the harm her ill-tempered screeching at the Queen of England was doing to her husband's career. By 1712 Queen Anne was only too pleased to see the back of her erstwhile friend with her bossy, shrewish nagging. Monarchs are only human and can be cruellest in their power to exclude. Sarah was ignominiously dismissed from the Royal Household. With her removal Marlborough went too.

The Marlboroughs' fall from grace left 'Corporal John' to face the final humiliation; a parliamentary enquiry into his alleged misappropriation of Treasury funds voted for the war. Coming from a group of eighteenth-century politicians such a charge seems especially rich; but Marlborough faced down his accusers like a stag at bay, pointing out that the $2\frac{1}{2}$ per cent he had taken had been agreed by all concerned, including Britain's foreign allies, and had been mainly spent on paying for intelligence. It was to no avail. The committee divided on party lines and Marlborough, technically disgraced, took himself off with dignity into private life, becoming a voluntary exile in Germany where he was fêted as a hero. But both his victories and his use of intelligence were to have profound effects. Where he had led so successfully, others would follow.

For example, one of Marlborough's officers was John Dalrymple, second Earl of Stair. He had been on the duke's personal staff in Flanders, working directly to Cadogan and dealing mainly with sensitive intelligence matters. In 1709 he was sent to Warsaw as part of a diplomatic mission to Augustus II of Poland. Although he fell from grace along with his mentor in 1712, by 1715 he was back, this time dispatched to Paris by Britain's new king, George I, Elector of Hannover, invited over from the German state to be Anne's Protestant successor. There would be no Catholic Stuart on England's throne while Parliament had its way.

Stair's role in Paris defines Britain's intelligence priorities at the time. Under cover of his diplomatic duties, he was tasked to run a network of spies and agents to penetrate the plottings of the Jacobite court in exile. With an explosive uprising by the Highland clans in 1715, Britain's new Hannoverian government (on the death of Queen Anne, Parliament had recruited yet another minor European monarch to act as Britain's new Protestant king) needed to be sure that the Stuarts would not try one last throw. Yet again, civil and political intelligence and court intrigue were top of the intelligence agenda in the competition for the British throne.

As the European intelligence struggle became almost endemic and part of the fabric of secret diplomacy, so did the organisations and individuals concerned adapt and evolve to face their new challenges. Perhaps the clearest example of the institutionalisation of intelligence in the 1700s was the growth of properly established *cabinet noirs* or communications intelligence offices by all the big powers. In Simon Singh's phrase, 'cryptanalysis was becoming industrialised'. Intelligence was simply too important to be left to chance by the middle of the eighteenth century in all the capitals of Europe. Walsingham, Richelieu and Thurloe would all have approved.

In Britain, the Postmaster's office recruited a team of permanent professional letter openers, transcribers and copy clerks, and resealers to supplement the cryptanalysts and codebreakers; Paris, Berlin and Madrid all did the same. Perhaps the most efficient was Vienna's Secret Office of the Chancellery, which raised the interception of communications to almost production line standards. The post came in at 0700, en route to foreign embassies and those on a watch list. A hundred letters a day were opened, copied, resealed and sent on their way. Translators and cryptanalysts worked separately in little booths, to break down any enciphered messages and warn the chancellor or the palace of any vital new intelligence or breaking news. To help pay for the operation, Vienna even offered to sell good information on to interested customers. The French Embassy was one keen customer.

Very often these eighteenth-century mail-cracking enterprises were run as 'family businesses'. For example, Britain's 'secret department' of the Post Office was staffed by members of two families, the Willes and the Bodes, the latter having started out as chief clerks to the secret service of Hannover before being summoned to London.

To supplement this regular supply of communications intelligence European governments relied as much as ever on human intelligence and their stables of spies and secret agents. Of these, perhaps the most enigmatic and certainly most bizarre is the Chevalier d'Éon. Clearly he must have been one of the most gifted female impersonators who ever lived. D'Éon exercises a fascination not just for his exploits as an intelligence officer but also for the unusual way in which he carried out his duties. He had a small, lithe, agile body. It concealed a mind just as agile and a will of steel. An accomplished fencer, he had been elected *Grand Prévôt* of the *Salle des Armes* of his native Tonerre at an unusually early age. To a fit body was allied a mind more than fit for undercover intelligence work.

D'Éon had trained as a lawyer, taking his doctorate in both canon and civil law while still well under age for university. He was noted for his prodigious memory; he rode, he fenced, he was academically brilliant and inevitably sought a post in Louis XV's government, even submitting a 'Treatise on the Weaknesses of Louis XIV's Financial System' to demonstrate his practical attainments. For such a talent, a glittering career at Versailles and public service at the centre of events beckoned. Events however dictated a different path.

By 1755, King George of England was concerned that his precious Hannover was at risk from the preying vultures of Paris and Berlin. England's army was small and far away. But half a million golden sovereigns were a powerful lure to the Russian court. Britain's booming new mercantile economy could well afford such an inducement for aid.

In their turn the Czarina's ministers were only too happy to accept such a massive bribe. In return for such a large number of 'the Cavalry of St George', 30,000 Russian peasants would be recruited and armed for Hannover's service in any emergency. France's original efforts to get this deal frustrated not only came to naught; they came to grief with Chancellor Bestucheff throwing the Chevalier de Valcroissant into a Russian fortress for daring to attempt to influence the Czarina directly. Diplomatic relations between Paris and St Petersburg were sundered. In desperation Louis XV's council decided to try a different tack to disrupt the alliance with London and re-establish good diplomatic relations.

D'Éon was dispatched to St Petersburg, as the niece of a Chevalier Douglass, travelling 'for his health'. Douglass's attractive 'niece', Lia, was, in fact, d'Éon in drag, bent on getting a clandestine audience with the Czarina and handing over a secret letter from France plus a private code to reply, concealed in a book of Monstesquieu's *L'Esprit des Lois*. This extraordinary deception was made possible because d'Éon's mother had, for reasons best known to herself, dressed and raised him as a girl since the age of four. Only on reaching manhood had he reverted to masculine ways and clothes. But with his light voice, good skin and small body, d'Éon was well practised in the world of women and could easily carry off his disguise as a shy, young female. Shy 'she' may have been, but this 'small and slight girl, with her pink and white complexion and pleasing gentle expression' attracted unwelcome masculine attention everywhere she went. On arrival at St Petersburg, she was a sensation at court. The Czar's official painter went into raptures, begging to paint this 'slight beauty, Mlle de Beaumont'.

History does not relate quite how Mlle Lia dealt with such masculine attentions, but a meeting was contrived between 'Mlle Lia' and a charmed Minister Woronzoff, Chancellor Bestucheff's rival for the Czarina's ear. Woronzoff presented this delightful flower of 'French maidenhood' to his mistress, where d'Éon became a favourite overnight, even becoming a maid of honour to the aged Empress. A glum British ambassador wrote back to London shortly afterwards, 'I regret to inform you that it is impossible to induce her Majesty to sign the Treaty which we so earnestly desire ...'. By 1757, full diplomatic relations between Russia and France were re-established and Hannover had become yet again a hostage and potential prey to French or Prussian territorial ambitions.

Having performed so brilliantly on his secret undercover mission, d'Éon was recalled to Paris. The Czarina was devastated. She had long since discovered d'Éon's secret but it had merely strengthened her attachment to him. She begged him to stay, even offering him Russian rank and title. D'Éon smoothly declined and returned laden with Russian gifts and French gratitude for his diplomatic coup.

From then on, d'Éon appears to have combined a career as the perfumed bewigged 'Lia de Beaumont' for the secret missions of French diplomacy, with occasional forays into the more testosterone-laden and martial atmosphere of the battlefield as a French officer of Dragoons. He was even commended for his bravery under fire in bringing an ammunition resupply forward and saving a dangerous situation. His efforts were well rewarded. At the age of 35 he was raised to the order of the Cross of Saint Louis, conferring noble rank and the title of chevalier.

It was an extraordinary double life. In Paris as a Foreign Ministry assistant to Nivernais, he managed to 'borrow' and copy out Britain's diplomatic instructions from Lord Bute to Bedford, the British minister in Paris, while a gullible and thirsty British courier was sampling Nivernais's superlative Chablis in the very next room. A furious Lord Bedford later stormed out of his fruitless and compromised negotiations, convinced that there was a traitor back in London.

D'Éon's influence and power grew and was ultimately to be the cause of his downfall. As ambassador in London he had established a regular personal correspondence with the king, much to the suspicion of Madame Pompadour and her faction at court. Hell may truly have no fury like a woman scorned, but the jealousy of a king's mistress can often make for an equally uncomfortable female colleague. Pompadour was worried that d'Éon's access to the king and the amounts of money he was getting would endanger her own position. She decided to clip the wings of such a turbulent potential rival. After a little string pulling at Versailles, a nobleman of superior rank and family to the chevalier was dispatched to London to take over as Minister Plenipotentiary to Britain. For d'Éon, as ambassador *en poste,* this was a public demotion and a serious snub. In vain he pleaded with Paris. Paris and Versailles ignored him. In vain did he point out his greater grasp of diplomacy and the London scene. It was to no avail. Paris ordered him home. Finally, in desperation, the chevalier threatened to reveal incriminating royal correspondence if not treated well.

Paris promptly changed gear. D'Éon's threat was no idle one. Louis XV had been secretly planning an invasion of England. His undercover agents had visited d'Éon in London and done clandestine reconnaissances along the south coast. D'Éon, like the prudent intelligence officer he was, had taken precautions against the possiblity of bureaucratic intrigues at 'head office'. He had kept copies of all the incriminating correspondence. If the English ever found out the true extent of French planning for a surprise attack on the Island then it could easily lead to a major war. The chevalier should come home, begged Paris, preferably bearing his explosive packets of letters. All would be well, only come back to France.

D'Éon was by now too canny and tired of court intrigues to trust either to the gratitude of princes or, even less likely, the magnanimity of his enemies. In a stunning volte-face, the late French ambassador sought asylum in England. A delighted London took him to their hearts as France tried everything they knew to bribe, lure or trick their errant spy back into the fold. The campaign was fruitless. For every attempt at blackmail or an informer up the chimney, d'Éon released more and more damaging French diplomatic correspondence, culminating in 1764 in a book revealing many, but not quite all, of France's diplomatic secrets.

Eventually, in desperation, France dispatched Caron de Beaumarchais, creator of the *Barber of Seville* and the *Marriage of Figaro*, and an undercover agent of the French government, to lure or bribe d'Éon back on peaceful terms. Beaumarchais eventually ran Mlle de Beaumont to earth in a London tavern dressed as a woman, but 'smoking, drinking and swearing like a German trooper' Beaumarchais nonetheless took to this strange apparition and eventually managed to negotiate a deal that would satisfy all parties. In 1777 d'Éon returned to France to meet his new king, Louis XVI. However, when France joined in the American colonies' rebellion against George III a year later, he was arrested and flung into prison, despite his offer to rejoin the colours.

For the rest of his life, d'Éon returned to London where he lived on his reputation and faded from active service, although still dressing as a woman when the fancy took him. Horace Walpole wrote that 'her [*sic*] hands and arms seem not to have participated of the change of sexes but seem fitter to carry a [sedan] chair than a fan ...'. After the French Revolution, d'Éon lost his pension and faded into genteel poverty, still dressing as a woman, but living with the widow of a British admiral. Wags took bets on his true sex. On his death, in 1810, the post mortem revealed him unmistakeable as a man. It was an ignominious end to a remarkable undercover career – in every sense.

D'Éon's fellow secret agent, Caron de Beaumarchais had enjoyed an equally chequered career. Publicly outlawed in front of the French Parliament, he nonetheless enjoyed the acclaim of the mob as the popular scoundrel who had exposed the corruption and bankruptcy of pre-revolutionary France. De Sartines, the *Ancien Régime*'s chief of police, often used this undercover 'outlaw' for his secret missions, even sending Beaumarchais to deal with a notorious blackmailer and fellow 'outlaw' Morande, who was threatening to publish his recollections of a certain amorous young lady. As the young lady in question was none other than Madame du Barry, the king's mistress, much was at stake. Beaumarchais's orders from an anxious chief of police were to bribe the black-mailer and buy him off 'in the good name of France'. Beaumarchais was a good choice for such a Richelieuesque mission. After certain discussions the would-be publisher gladly ceded all his legal rights, even allowing his memory to be wiped clean in exchange for 32,000 gold Louis. Suddenly Morande recalled that he 'might have been in error' and now clearly remembered that the king's mistress was a lady of irreproachable character ...

Beaumarchais's meeting with d'Éon in London is notable for one other key event. During his stay in London, d'Éon had become very friendly with the notorious Hellfire Club, which celebrated its orgies under the lively chairmanship of Sir Francis Dashwood. The club included such members as John Wilkes, the radical libertarian Member of Parliament, as well as other senior political figures. One of them was the representative of the American Colonies in London, Arthur Lee. Lee found Beaumarchais (who was travelling as M. Norac) good company and the two men became firm friends. It was a friendship that was to have historic consequences. For when the American colonists rebelled against London in 1776, it was Beaumarchais who promptly came to the aid of the insurgents, offering clandestine French arms shipments to his old friend Arthur Lee through a specially created 'export' company at Bordeaux, called *Hortalez et Cie* on behalf of the French government.

Such spying exploits as d'Éon's and Beaumarchais's were not, however, confined just to steely-eyed swordsmen and crude bribes, even by secret agents dressed as women. In 1782 the English press reported the extraordinary story of a female agent who had been introduced to the Prime Minister at Downing Street and found favour with the king. Lord North was much taken with this lady of quality and as the British intelligence spies at Versailles were 'too notorious' or were 'so idle that they had completely failed to report on necessary matters', 'Mrs A' was dispatched to Brussels suitably kitted out with an entourage befitting an American aristocrat, even a daughter of the recent Revolution.

After a decent interval the lady moved on to Paris, where she professed herself charmed and settled down to enjoy the season. Benjamin Franklin himself welcomed his 'fellow countrywoman' to his house. Pretending that she spoke no French she was warmly encouraged by her French hosts, becoming a firm favourite at court and a regular guest at Marie Antoinette's *soirées*. With access like this, Mrs A rapidly became aware of many of the inner secrets of French politics as she 'struggled to learn' even the most basic French and her hosts talked openly in front of their charming but stupid 'American' friend. A torrent of intelligence poured out and was diligently transcribed and reported back to London via couriers out of Ostend. The British had an undercover agent at the heart of the French court listening to all its secrets.

Eventually the artless Mrs A overplayed her hand. The French authorities became suspicious and a team was sent to bring her in for questioning. Another British agent, this time a 'legal' resident posing as a merchant, warned her that the police were waiting at her house. Knowing only too well the fate that awaited a convicted spy, Mrs A did a bunk and fled in disguise to Ostend leaving her whole household and valuables behind. But she had succeeded brilliantly in her undercover mission. For she had not merely hoovered up the gossip of the court: she had also, according to the reports, passed on the secret departure of the French fleet to the West Indies and warned of an attack on Gibraltar as well as 'some American intelligence of great importance'. Mrs A was handsomely rewarded for her undercover intelligence work, receiving a pension of £300 a year from the king – a small fortune in those days – and retiring to her native Cornwall. Her identity remains obscure: but she had served her country as well as any man and had not had to cross-dress like d'Éon either.

Her use of an American identity was highly significant. The link between the New World and the Old symbolised the changing face of European politics. For, as the 1700s drew to their close, huge shifts were beginning to creak the long-established tectonic plates of European politics apart and new battlefields were beckoning. The kings and princes of the Continent had been ceaselessly at war with one another for over a century. France had been broken economically by Louis XIV's dreams of glory and finally ruined by the Seven Years' War mid century. Every-where new and radical ideas were stirring. The Age of Enlightenment was challenging old values and existing institutions. Britain was begin-ning the long and explosive economic expansion that would make her 'the workshop of the world', with all the social and political conse-quences to follow. The search for intelligence between all nations was now a ceaseless and full-time pursuit occupying a major place in both political activity and national budgets alike. From the limited battles of the century of limited wars, the undercover intelligence war between states was now developing into not just an institutionalised struggle but was threatening to become part of the open warfare between the nations of Europe. Everywhere statesmen were reflecting on intelligence; its importance and how best to carry it out.

This 'thinking about intelligence' was not just confined to politicians and ministers. Men like the elder Pitt and William Eden sought intelligence through open 'diplomatic warfare' as did their counterparts such as de Sartines in Paris. In Berlin, capital of Prussia ('the Army with a State attached'), however, Frederick the Great decided, in his soldier-like way, to set out the subtleties of intelligence work in a form easily understood by his generals. He set out not just national political objectives, but also a set of 'standard operating procedures' for the Prussian military. It was – almost – a modern intelligence collection plan. It is certainly the first recorded set of real intelligence requirements in war.

To describe Frederick as an 'erratic genius' is unfair both to geniuses in general and Frederick in particular. What he undoubtedly was, however, was a twisted growth. Like some strangely pruned plant, his personality had been malformed as it developed, resulting in a man drawn equally to the arts, to philosophy and to the brutalities of war.

This bewildering mix of contradictions was ever the warrior son of a warrior king. The old man, *der Alte Fritz*, had schooled him like a recruit, beaten him, then thrashed him as only a Prussian drill sergeant could. Such brutalities merely steeled the boy's hatred. To his son's free-thinking ideas, Frederick I could only respond with impotent frustration and the fury of a martinet constantly outsmarted and humiliated by his more clever son. His retribution was both decisive and cruel. The younger Frederick's attachment to good-looking and charming *Hauptman* von Katte and their insane plan to flee Prussia to breathe the freer air of liberal England was the last straw and provided the old man with his revenge. The heir to Prussia's crown was thrown into the military fortress of Kuestrin, and his companion court-martialled by a 'court of honour'. The old man's grim satisfaction at the execution of the dashing young captain can only have been matched by the limitless hatred the spectacle must have engendered in his son, forced to witness the beheading of his closest friend. The young Frederick never forgave him.

Only on his deathbed did the old monster repent. 'What a soldier I bequeath to you', he is alleged to have muttered to his generals as he lay dying. It was a fitting epitaph, for *der junge Friedrich* – Frederick the Great – is remembered as that most dangerous of creatures: a thinking soldier.

His life was spent on campaign and as the years wore on, observers are entitled to ask the question, why? True, Prussia was a frontier state and her open borders were an open invitation to the powers that surrounded her. But compromise might have been found: however, diplomacy was not Frederick or Prussia's way. Even when his army was surrounded and destroyed (only 3,000 men escaped out of a Prussian Army of 50,000) by the combined Austrians and Russians at Kunersdorf in 1759 Frederick fought on. He raised a new army and continued to fight them all until his enemies either died, gave up in despair or retired, exhausted. To the end of his days, this restless warmonger led Prussia's army into the field, year after year, emptying his treasury and slaughtering his soldiers. Yet Frederick's Prussian exploits were to cast a long, dark shadow on Europe's turbulent story for the next two centuries. This ceaseless – and largely successful – life of conflict led him to reflect on the art of war, and during his long career he drew up a list of 'Military Instructions to his Generals'.

Frederick's encapsulated wisdom demonstrates clearly that this remarkable man of war understood intelligence very clearly indeed. Of the twenty-eight articles no less than five are directly tailored to intelligence and one, Article 24, discusses security, specifically warning of bad operational security as a direct consequence of treachery.

Article 5 of Frederick's Instructions lays out his intelligence collection priorities, 'for the knowledge of a country', listing all the 'basic intelligence' needed by an attacker, such as topography, rivers, bridges and the civil population. Article 12 talks of 'spies, deserters and double agents' and urges generous payment to spies, 'even to the degree of extravagance'. Frederick concludes this article with: 'the man who risks his neck to do your service deserves to be well rewarded', which seems sound advice. Article 13 looks at the way that 'an enemy's intentions are to be discovered.' Frederick, unlike many a national leader, understood only too clearly the difference between capabilities and intentions. Just because a nation possesses a weapon doesn't mean they have to use it. Moreover, he concluded this article with the dry observation, worthy of a true student of Voltaire, that 'an intelligent enemy is likely to attempt that enterprise most likely to give you the greatest annoyance ...'. Article 14 looks at the advantages of fighting on friendly territory, 'where every man acts as your spy' and vice versa. Frederick had codified national political and military intelligence requirements.

The 'Age of Battles' had brought intelligence a long way. It was now recognised as an integral arm of the rivalry and combat between states, and nations were now openly organised and equipped to fight their wars not just with armies and navies, but with intelligence and its associated operations as well. As the eighteenth century drew to its close, however, it took with it something that would be sorely missed in the years ahead – limited warfare. A century and a half later, after the first Great War, Guglielmo Ferrero put his finger on what Europe had lost since the days of Frederick the Great and Marlborough:

> Restricted warfare was one of the three loftiest achievements of the Eighteenth century. It belongs to that class of hothouse plants that can only thrive in an aristocratic and qualitative civilisation. We are no longer capable of it. It was one of the fine things that we lost in the French Revolution ...

In the years to come the 'rights of man' and the revolutionary ideas of freedom and liberty stirring across Europe, would soon unleash destructive fires which to this day have still not burned themselves out. The spark fell first in the New World.

8

Land of the Free?

The necessity of procuring good
intelligence is apparent and need not be
further urged ... For upon secrecy, success
depends in most Enterprizes of this kind
& for want of it they are generally
defeated, however well planned ...

GEORGE WASHINGTON

The generally accepted view of the United States of America, in the
words of one well known anthology of espionage, is that: '... they are
protected by one of the youngest of the major intelligence services and
that prior to Pearl Harbor they had no intelligence service at all.' Nothing
could be further from the truth. The fact is that the United States of
America was actually founded on the bedrock of a flourishing and highly
sophisticated intelligence service and one run by one of the greatest
intriguers and spymasters of his age: George Washington.

America's first president has come down to us as a stern, forbidding
and deeply moral creature. Traditional American history portrays him
as almost an Old Testament, God-like man, a giant of moral rectitude
and straight dealing. This is a serious misrepresentation of a cunning
and unscrupulous intelligence officer, as devious and duplicitous as any

in Anglo-Saxon history. George Washington was in fact a spymaster of the first rank, with all the moral equivocation which that implies. Walsingham, Richelieu and Thurloe would have instantly recognised him as a worthy adversary, and a fellow spymaster capable of any immoral trickery in pursuit of his aims.

Intelligence work was deeply embedded in early American history from the start. The first clashes with the native 'Indian' tribes meant that the European settlers were always anxious about the threat from the interior of their mysterious new continent. From the very beginning they took pains to establish links with the tribes to ensure good relations and to garner intelligence to warn of Indian raids. For some of the Native Americans could be as bloodthirsty and as cruel as any other similar primitive stone-age group. Not for nothing did the settlers, unfettered by political correctness and only too alert to the cruel realities of the frontier, call them 'bloodthirsty savages'. They often were. Modern American writers may, unforgivably, rewrite colonial reports (some of them by Washington himself) to coyly talk of 'scouting' parties of 'tribesmen'. Such timid circumlocutions and downright dishonesties have no place in the more robust and accurate originals, which speak openly of 'scalping parties' and 'savages'. Dr Thomas Bowdler is still alive and well, this time spouting his Orwellian Newspeak from obscure provincial American universities.

The European rivalry between France and Britain exacerbated the tensions between the colonists from each nation along the eastern seaboard of North America. Both sides employed native Indians as scouts and trackers to boost their intelligence efforts. A slow-burning guerrilla war sputtered on along the frontier with both sides complaining bitterly of the not infrequent excesses of the other's local helpers. The truth was that both British and French colonists tacitly accepted – and indeed sometimes encouraged – the Indians' ability to inspire terror among their enemies by their custom of scalping their victims. Irregular wars are often the most brutal.

By 1757, things were going disastrously for the British. Despite the million or so colonists spread around in New England, the deep disunities inherent among such sturdy independent souls prevented any real cooperation between the colonies and left them as easy individual prey to the depredations of the French and their native allies. In 1757, Montcalm, the governor of French Acadia (Quebec), pushed deep into the Hudson Valley to besiege one of the Anglo-Americans' defensive strong points, Fort William Henry. After an honourable surrender to the French, Montcalm allowed his Indian allies full rein. The British garrison was butchered in an excess of native savagery. The colonists blamed London; the British generals blamed the cowardice of the local colonial-American forces drawn from the settlers' ranks, who one officer described as 'a gathering of scum of the worst people in every country'.

Into this maelstrom of distrust, bitterness and defeat strode the enigmatic figure of James Wolfe. A career soldier since he was 14, Wolfe had commanded the 20th, or Lancashire, Fusiliers and had already seen action at Culloden and Dettingen. By 32 he was a major general, charged by Prime Minister Pitt with evicting the French from North America. It was a tall order, even for a dedicated professional soldier such as Wolfe who had offended many of his peers and superiors with his outspoken views and sharp tongue. Senior members of the Horse Guards complained to the king that Wolfe was barking mad. 'Mad, is he?' George II is alleged to have replied, 'Well, I wish to heavens he'd bite some of my other generals, then!'

The key to France's North American empire was the great fortress town and citadel of Quebec on the St Lawrence River. Seize the French fortress, and the whole strategic balance in America tipped over. Instead of bottling up the British colonists in the eastern colonies and blocking their expansion west, without Quebec's command of the St Lawrence approach to the sea, the French would be cut off in their turn, trapped in Canada and unable to receive stores and supplies from France. The French Canadian colonies must eventually wither and die. It was a master strategy. The only problem was capturing Quebec, a virtually impregnable French garrison brooding over the steep rocks of the Heights of Abraham.

History credits Wolfe with being a military genius for his victory at Quebec. Like so many 'military geniuses', it transpires that the key to Wolfe's success really lay in his possession of timely, accurate and highly secret intelligence about the enemy. On the 12–13 September 1759, the Royal Navy on patrol in the St Lawrence had picked up two men in a canoe heading downstream. They turned out to be a Captain Stevens of Rogers' Rangers, a colonial auxiliary and reconnaissance unit, and a Captain Stobo of the Virginia Militia. The two men had escaped from the French in Quebec and were able to draw up a remarkably clear and accurate report of the approaches to the French fortress for Wolfe. Not only were the French dispositions and defences laid bare, but the two recce officers also identified the topography, paths and approaches in great detail. In particular, they identified the exact locations of the French defences and their arcs of fire. Most important of all, Captain Stobo's detailed paper on Quebec allowed Wolfe not only to see all the cards in Montcalm's hands, but also a clear route through which he could surprise and outflank the French commander by zigzagging up a narrow path leading up the cliffs from the river.

On the night of 16 October 1759 Wolfe seized his moment. Leading his bewildered brigade commanders – who knew nothing of Wolfe's secret intelligence – and their trusting redcoats in single file up the steep cliffs behind the French lines, he deployed his men before the startled French could react. In three shattering, disciplined volleys he blew away Montcalm's infantry as they tried to line up to repel the invaders. In his moment of victory Wolfe fell, mortally wounded. Captain Stobo's superbly clear and accurate intelligence report had done the job for him, however. The Heights of Abraham, and thus Quebec, were British. From now on, French power in North America would shrivel and atrophy. By 1760, Montreal had fallen and Canada was British. The way to the West was open.

Washington missed both Quebec and much of the Indian fighting. He had retired from the Crown Service the year before, having seen active service in the French and Indian wars, where he had been a great exponent of native 'scouts'. He left the army disappointed not to have received a regular King's commission in His Majesty's Land Forces. It was a psychological scar that would have serious consequences for the British. Because Washington really had soldiered. As a 24-year-old lieutenant colonel he had accompanied General Braddock's fatal expedition towards Fort Duquesne in 1755 and witnessed the debacle of the British regulars being cut to pieces in the wilderness by a combined French and Indian close-quarter ambush in the forest. Out of 1,373 British and Virginian troops only 453 escaped unscathed. Washington fled the scene of the disaster with four bullet holes in his clothing.

These intelligence disasters left an indelible impression on Washington's developing military mind. He apprehended only too clearly the need to fight unencumbered by heavy equipment and above all the need to avoid surprise. From then on, Washington would always put intelligence and knowledge of the enemy at the top of his military priorities.

From 1759 to the outbreak of the American Revolution Washington, now retired from active duty, managed his estate at Mt Vernon in Virginia. As tension grew between the distant politicians in London and the independently minded colonists, Washington, like many another Virginian gentleman planter, felt himself exploited and hampered by London's restrictions on his way of life. For him, as for so many other colonists, economic freedom was top of his list. Great swathes of virgin territory had become British land following the French defeat in North America. A massive commercial opportunity was there for the taking. Greed and property fever seized the colonial middle classes. In vain London tried to regulate and control the acquisition of these valuable Crown assets. The colonists – including Washington – illegally bought up great swathes of virgin forest and cheap land at knockdown prices in the expectation of vast profits.

This growing sense of alienation from a distant and uncomprehending parent characterised the unravelling of the thirteen colonies' ties with Britain. To resentment over the Stamp Acts – an honest attempt to make the colonies pay for their own costs – was added ever more irksome restrictions of the colonists' freedom to do just as they pleased. Radical voices were raised against the general authority of far distant legislators in London who dared to dictate American lives in their New World. English goods were boycotted, English taxes flouted. Deliberate agitators like Samuel Adams of Boston fomented even more discontent. A network of anti-British committees was formed by a mixture of malcontents, patriots, libertarians and merchants. The troublemakers went looking for trouble and the British authorities were too stiff-necked to bend or compromise. It only needed a spark.

In 1773, the British Parliament passed an act allowing the nighbankrupt East India Company to have the exclusive right to ship tea direct to the colonies. These tea shipments were to be exempt from any colonial states' import taxes and the East India Company was to have the sole right to sell tea only through their own licensed agents. It gave the East India Company an effective monopoly in North America. In the process it could have ruined many American merchants and tea traders. On 16 December 1773 infuriated merchants and agitators disguised as 'Indians' threw tea chests into Boston Harbor. The thirteen colonies, frustrated by London's scornful rejection of their solemn petition requesting repeal and redress of their grievances, prepared to break away. By 1774, an independent Congress had been formed and a Declaration of Rights published. London arrogantly rejected it all and cracked down hard, increasing its North American garrison, imposing martial law and threatening dire penalties for any rebels against the Crown. On 18 April 1775, a column of British troops moved in to a hamlet called Lexington to seize an illegal cache of arms. An unknown colonial militiaman fired a single shot. The army responded with a volley. Another English civil war had begun.

The British badly mishandled the whole affair from the start. A clumsy attempt to crush the rebellion on Breed's Hill outside Boston by a show of Redcoat force backfired badly when it took the British regulars three attempts and 40 per cent casualties to storm the rebels' trenches and bayonet a determined handful of rebel farmers and breakaway patriots. From 'Bunker Hill', as the battle of Breed's Hill has become known, the fight was going to be to the finish. The Congress at Philadelphia raised a colonists' army to defend the colonial rebel states.

George Washington was appointed as commander-in-chief of this patriot force, the Continental Army of the United States, and both sides settled down for a fight.

Washington's orders from his idealistic political masters in the Congress at Philadelphia were very simple but very hard to accomplish. He was well aware of the difficulties of the task confronting him. Washington realised from the start that he could not hope to defeat the regular British Army in open battle. His first priority was to keep his cadre of would-be soldiers together. Like the experienced soldier he was, he realised from the start that the 'vital ground' of the rebellion was not some geographic strong point like Philadelphia or New York, but the rebel army itself. This was the real centre of gravity for the rebellion. Only they could provide the core of any successful Continental Army in the future.

The truth was that once their army had gone the colonists' rebellion was doomed, however much the politicians and lawyers in the Congress prated on about freedom, liberty, the Rights of Man and their own political goals. All that would be left then would be an irregular guerrilla rebellion: and, from his experiences on the frontier, Washington knew only too well that such a policy would only lead to excesses and render victory very uncertain indeed. He also appears to have grasped that if the Congress's goal of the United Colonies being recognised as an equal, independent sovereign republic by the existing international order was to be achieved, then they would have to fight like an independent sovereign power, and not like a series of provincial uprisings. George Washington may not have been a great battlefield general, but he was undoubtedly a clear-thinking strategist in the Clausewitzian mould and a military leader with few illusions.

Whatever else he did, Washington knew that above all to keep the Continental Army in being he had to avoid a decisive full-scale battle with the British. As a result, Washington's war was characterised, certainly for the first three years, by the need to keep his feeble army intact, to evade pitched battles and to wear the British down by pin-prick raids on unsuspecting enemy outposts. In this unambitious but tightly controlled strategy George Washington emerges as a remarkably successful general, realising from the very beginning that he must dodge any enemy blows. To do this he needed to know exactly where his enemy was and exactly what his enemy was up to.

With this as a core strategy, from the very start, America's first commander-in-chief and later its first president put the acquisition of intelligence at the top of his agenda. On 2 July 1775, the day before he took full command of his new rag-bag army, Washington began to build his network of spies. He knew that only good intelligence would give him the vital advantage he needed to form a real army and then to outwit and wear down and defeat the British colonial power. Despite claims that American intelligence was only really born after 1941, the birth of the United States itself was in fact midwifed by a top class intelligence service, masterminded by a devious, calculating and ruthless ex-British colonel from Virginia called George Washington.

Washington always relied on good intelligence. In this, he was helped by the nature of the civil war in the colonies. Only a minority of colonials, a third at the most, were really sympathetic to the rebels' cause; however, these sympathisers were widely dispersed. In Mao Tse Tung's well-worn phrase, this was the sea in which the patriots' spies could swim undetected. Washington quickly established networks of agents working behind British lines. He ran them himself, writing early in 1777: 'Even minutiae should have a place in our collection', and, 'everything ... depends upon obtaining intelligence'. Washington was under no illusions that he was a great general who would win victory in this war on the battlefield. Intelligence was the key: 'The greatest benefits are to be derived from persons who live on the other side.'

Washington's 'chains' of stay-behind agents soon bore fruit. As early as September 1775, Nathaneal [sic] Greene, the brigadier commanding Rhode Island's troops, brought his commander-in-chief a puzzling message handed by a lady to a Newport baker called Wenwood. Breaking open the sealed packet, Wenwood discovered that it contained an enciphered letter to a 'Major Cane, in His Majesty's Service'. He promptly delivered it to the rebels' headquarters, where Washington ordered the woman brought in for questioning. Frightened by the imposing figure of the commander-in-chief, the woman broke down, admitting that she was the mistress of Washington's colleague and army surgeon general, Benjamin Church. Once deciphered, the letter proved deeply incriminating. Church was revealed as a traitor, passing vital political intelligence on the rebels' Congress direct to the British commander, General Gage.

An enraged Washington handed Church over to Congress to be tried and hanged as a spy. Luckily for Church, in their haste to draft high-minded political declarations of independence reflecting the inalienable Rights of Man the fledgling Congress had omitted a number of practical legalities. Church escaped the hangman on a legal technicality: in drawing up the Continental Army's Articles of War, the Congress had embarrassingly failed to make any provision for the penalties for treason or espionage. Church had committed no crime in the new Congress's laws. Although British law was clear on the penalty for treason, the new Congress's was not. Their only legal punishment was exile. To Washington's fury, Church escaped the noose and was banished.

To add to this early catalogue of misfortune, in the summer of 1776 Washington became aware of threats to his life from an undercover British operation. A forger in jail tried to bargain for his freedom by revealing a secret plot to kill the rebels' commander-in-chief. The plan called for an assassination attempt from within the ranks of Washington's personal security detail. The whole guard force was swiftly arrested and a Sergeant Thomas Hickey was tried, convicted and hanged before the shocked army as an example of the dire penalties awaiting anyone foolish enough to spy for the British. From the very beginning, Washington ruled with a rod of iron, ruthlessly not prepared to countenance any backsliding, dissent or treason. Deep down he knew that if the colonists lost, he would be one of the first to swing on a British gallows.

His concerns about security were aggravated by the sheer amateurism of many of the early US agents' efforts. Barely two months after

Hickey mounted the scaffold in New York's Bowery district, a massive British amphibious fleet landed over 30,000 British and German troops on Staten Island. Washington's army was effectively trapped, outnumbered and in the dark. In desperation he pleaded with his subordinates for more intelligence: 'Leave no stone unturned, nor stick at expense, as I was never more uneasy than on account of my want of knowledge', he wrote. A half-baked scheme was hatched to put in an undercover agent to spy on the British dispositions and intentions. A young officer of a Ranger battalion called Nathan Hale volunteered for this dangerous mission behind British lines.

Disguised as a schoolmaster looking for work, and clutching his Yale University Diploma as cover, Hale pushed deep into New York collecting information. British sentries were nervous and watchful following Washington's order to burn houses in New York. On 21 September the young 'teacher' was stopped and arrested for suspicious behaviour. He was searched and incriminating documents were found. Questioned by General Howe himself, Hale gave his name, rank and regiment and admitted to being an enemy officer working under cover. For such an admission there could only be one penalty then, as in many other ages. Next morning the young man was summarily found guilty of espionage and hanged from an apple tree near what is now 3rd Avenue and 65th Street. The British provost marshal denied the condemned man a bible and ripped up the young man's farewell note to his family and friends. Hale's last defiant words were said to be a garbled quotation from Addison's Cato: 'What a pity it is that we can die but once to serve our country.'

Paradoxically Hale's useless but brave sacrifice did considerable good for the rebel colonists' cause. Although Hale's mission had been a total failure, revolutions of all kinds require martyrs and the blood of sacrifice proved a potent fertiliser to 'water the tree of liberty'. Hale became a posthumous hero and, with Paul Revere, is remembered as a patriot hero of the colonists' revolution. But Washington, the consummate professional, knew that less enthusiasm and more caution were required for undercover intelligence work. Young volunteer

lieutenants risking their necks doing amateur extemporised reconnaissances behind enemy lines would not do. They could not be relied
upon. What was required for intelligence was professionalism.

Washington selected a classmate of Nathan Hale to head up
America's first secret intelligence service. Major Benjamin Tallmadge
of the 2nd Colonial Light Dragoons was invited to put together a
network of patriot undercover agents to spy on the British. With his
shadowy colleague Robert Townsend, Tallmadge swiftly organised a
spy ring based on New York. The 'ring' worked on the chain principle,
rather than cells. The individual agents, often 'in service' to British headquarters and officers' messes, saw and reported back their information,
usually by 'dead letter-boxes'. This involved secreting messages in pre-
agreed hiding places for later collection by the next link in the chain,
who would then be responsible for couriering the information back to
Washington. Tallmadge's New York network was called the Culper
Ring because of the pseudonyms adopted by its principal agents,
Abraham Woodhull, who signed himself, 'Samuel Culper', and
Townsend, his controller, who replied as 'Sam'l Culper, Jr'.

The Culper Ring was spectacularly effective from the start. Right
under the very noses of the British New York garrison, Townsend and
Woodhull ran a swift and accurate intelligence service across the river to
Long Island and the rebels. Townsend openly traded with the British
and their numerous American supporters, or 'Tories'. On occasion he
even drank with the British chief intelligence officer, John André. Both
Townsend and Washington's other undercover man in New York fre-
quented the coffee houses of the city, pumping the English customers
and their friends for information. This was carried back to Woodhull
by a keen young man about town called Roe. Roe was 'horse mad' and
frequently rode out to see his friends – especially a quiet, bookish recluse
at Oyster Bay called Abraham Woodhull. Protected by this 'cut out'
from the undercover sources of intelligence, Woodhull got his maid to
hang out her washing in a pre-arranged pattern: a black petticoat meant
to the American watchers on the far shore that a secret message was
ready. Caleb Brewster, a local boat maker, then conveyed them under

cover of darkness to an expectant Tallmadge, anxiously waiting on the Connecticut shore for the latest intelligence from deep within the British lines in New York City.

Woodhull is a classic example of the adage that only the really fearful can be really brave because they are the most scared. He was a quiet and nervous man, much given to introspection and absolutely terrified of discovery. He knew that if they caught him, the British would hang him out of hand. Despite his fear, like many another brave undercover operative working alone, and ever conscious of the heavy footfall on the stair, Woodhull did his case officer proud. Eventually this timid, frightened hypochondriac was so successful that Washington urged his move into the very heart of enemy territory in New York City, to mingle with the British garrison and their sympathetic American supporters. Reluctantly Woodhull obeyed, though he lived in a positive ferment of terror day in and day out, writing on one occasion, 'I am perfectly acquainted with a whole year's anxiety, which no-one can scarcely have any idea but those that experience it.'

Woodhull's anxieties were well founded, because as the flow of intelligence increased, so did the risk to the Culper network and the value of its product. By now Washington's intelligence networks were uncovering the secrets of the whole British operation in the northern colonies and reporting them back regularly in invisible ink, disguised as letters between friends and tradesmen. The British were no fools and put considerable effort into trying to uncover the traitors in their midst. It was a dangerous game.

As well as managing his networks, or chains, of agents, Washington also ran a stable of 'independents', one-off spies known only to himself. A punctilious public servant, he recorded all the details of these secret agents in a ledger. This read like any other classified financial account, giving details of all the secret payments made to further the colonial rebels' cause and (in code) the details of the recipients. As early as July 1775, he opened his secret account book, paying just over $300 to an agent to go to Boston under cover, 'for the purpose of conveying intelligence of the enemy's movements and designs'.

One of Washington's earliest independent agents was a loutish lump of a man called John Honeyman, a slaughterman of Delaware. Honeyman's job as a stockman was to herd cattle to provide meat on the hoof for General Gage's Anglo-German army. As a Scot who had served with Wolfe at Quebec he was well acquainted with the ways of the army and could pass freely doing his job. On the first winter of the war, he had allowed himself to be 'captured' by the Americans after reconnoitring the British lines across the Delaware at Trenton. His gleeful captors brought their prisoner straight to Washington and claimed a reward for capturing a 'wanted British spy'. Miraculously Honeyman 'escaped' back to the British lines, there to complain to the British commander of his ill treatment by the rebels. He 'confirmed' that the American forces were under strength, riddled with desertion, disease and famine and posed no threat to General Rhall and his Hessian mercenaries, quartered for Christmas at Trenton across the Delaware River.

The papers of General James Grant who fought in the American War of Independence were uncovered in 2003 at Ballindalloch Castle in Scotland. They reveal that Grant 'relayed good information' warning Rhall that he would be attacked across the Delaware on Christmas night by Washington's men. Sadly for the British, Rhall ignored these distracting intelligence reports and relaxed his guard. 'It is some comfort to me that I gave them previous notice', wrote Grant. 'It was rather better intelligence than I could have expected ... No man in America knows the channel through which it came except the Genl. who I let into the secret before this accursed affair happened.' Rhall's disbelief was a fatal mistake. Honeyman the American spy had done his job well.

When, on Christmas night, Washington crossed the Delaware to put his rag-bag army ashore at Trenton and burst upon the unsuspecting German garrison, most of who were sleeping off their Christmas party hangovers, it was a massacre. The tactical victory at Trenton was a strategic coup because it kept Washington's rebel army together at the very moment that it was on the brink of voting with its feet. Washington knew that the Revolution was, quite literally, 'about to go home for Christmas'. But the politically crucial Trenton coup was only possible through cleverly managed intelligence. A week later Washington followed up his advantage by striking again at an inferior force at Princeton, employing similar raiding tactics with his units. His aim was never to confront the superior regular Royal Army in open battle, only to pick it off in small battles and to keep the revolutionary flame alight among his own troops. Thanks to good intelligence and clever misinformation he succeeded brilliantly. Intelligence and George Washington saved the American Revolution.

The truth was that Washington's initial belief that he should never try to defeat the British in a traditional battle had proved correct. His strategy all along was of delay, what later writers were to call the 'war of the flea', and is more reminiscent of insurgency than the traditional eighteenth-century warfare of battles and head to head confrontation. To make sure a policy worked he needed good intelligence at all times to tell him where the enemy was; and to further confuse he needed to dupe the enemy by misinforming him of his own army's intentions.

Washington may not have been a great captain on the battlefield, but he certainly knew how to wage war by other means: he was a master of disinformation. Again and again he fed false information into the British camp, often by the most subtle and carefully worked-out intelligence operations. As early as 1777 he deliberately allowed over-inflated troop lists to fall into the hands of known British spies to mislead the enemy about the strength of the Rebel forces. Before Valley Forge, Washington had even drawn up deliberately fake correspondence in his own handwriting, knowing that General Howe, the British commander would recognise it as authentic once it was passed on. To add to the deception, Washington's mystified brigadiers were ordered to prepare grossly inflated lists of units at their disposal and to forward them for collection to one of his staff officers.

What the puzzled brigadiers did not know was that Washington's staff officer was sharing his winter billet with a known British spy. The staff officer contrived to be 'called away', thus allowing the British agent to copy the false troop lists. Two days later, General Howe was gleefully examining the stolen 'evidence' showing Washington's army to be three times its real size. Convinced that the rebels were too strong, Howe called off a planned attack on their stronghold, thereby effectively saving the American Revolution at a critical point. So convinced was Howe by his 'secret source' that when an escaped British prisoner told him the real rebel order of battle figures, he refused to believe him and sat tight. Truly, this was a misinformation coup of the highest order.

Washington used misinformation both as an offensive weapon to lure the enemy into doing the wrong thing and secondly, as a defensive weapon to disguise his own weakness. His use of false planted 'intelligence' to protect the French landings at Newport in 1780 is a classic example of using intelligence and misinformation as a weapon to force the enemy into doing the wrong thing.

Any amphibious force is at its most vulnerable at the moment of landing, half afloat and half ashore. The Culper network warned Washington that Clinton's Anglo-German army intended to pounce on the French expeditionary forces as they landed and drive them back into the sea. Washington was unable to prevent the British from moving and too weak to confront them in battle. Instead, in a coup which Sun-T'zu and Walsingham would have applauded, he arranged for a copy of a 'top secret' plan to fall into British hands showing that the Continental Army was going to move to attack New York. Clinton's principal base in the colonies was too important to leave unprotected. The British commander immediately stopped the planned march to attack the French landing site and instead prepared to defend his HQ against the expected rebel onslaught. It never materialised. Yet again, by using a combination of good intelligence and misinformation, Washington had bent his enemy to do his will, not the other way round. It was a classic example of 'warfare by other means' and it was as effective as any victory on the battlefield – and a lot cheaper in terms of lives and treasure.

It is often claimed that Washington's principal contribution to the US patriots' cause was to keep the Continental Army in existence until it became a real force. While basically true, this remains an oversimplification, because Washington had realised from the beginning that wars are not fought by armies and navies alone, but also by other means. Undercover operations can be as important as any bloody battle. His mastery of these intelligence-driven special operations was very modern, both in his concepts and in their execution.

Like many a competent intelligence officer, Washington also appears to have been very alert to security, the handmaiden of intelligence: for if the enemy's plans can be known to you, then just how many of your plans have been penetrated by the enemy? Keep your secrets secure. It is always wise to assume that your enemy is at least as clever and as dangerous as yourself. Civil war, by its very nature, breeds double-dealing, and Washington, quite rightly as events were to prove, was always alive to the dangers of treachery from within the American camp.

He had good reason to be. The rebels' cause was by no means popular among the mass of American colonists and both sides were riddled with informers and turncoats, anxious to ensure they backed the winning side. It is pure moonshine to pretend that the American Revolution was universally acclaimed by the majority of colonial Americans. Treachery and betrayal were always at the heart of the 'patriots' campaign. Although once the British were defeated and went home popular history books inevitably portrayed almost every colonial as a hero and a patriot, the reality in civil wars and resistance movements is invariably different. The old Communist barb about the French Resistance best sums it up:

> In 1941, only the criminals and lunatics were in the Resistance; in 1942 only criminals, lunatics and communists were in the Resistance; by 1943, only criminals, lunatics, communists and British spies were in the Resistance; but, after the Allies landed in Normandy in 1944 it turned out that *everyone* had been in the Resistance! So how come we never met them in those earlier years ...?

Thus it was in North America in 1780. And as the war hung in the balance, even the most senior colonial leaders began to have their doubts and looked to betray their 'sacred cause of liberty'.

The most senior of these was General Benedict Arnold. Arnold had led the unsuccessful expedition against Canada in 1776 and fought with distinction at Saratoga. Personally brave, he was a popular leader and a good commander. In fact, he was the classic example of that most dangerous of potential security risks: a clever, ambitious man with a serious grudge against his superiors and short of money. He was obviously a good soldier. Washington himself described him thus: 'Surely a more active, a more spirited and more sensible officer fills no Department of the Army'.

Arnold's growing resentment sprang from a number of causes. Like many of the North American colonists he harboured serious doubts about a total split with Britain. (As sometimes did Washington, too. In his ledgers he consistently refers to pounds sterling as 'lawful money'!) Arnold was also under investigation by the Congress for financial irregularities; and his latest posting as commander of the strong point at West Point overlooking the Hudson River was, if not a demotion, then a job well below such an experienced commander's ambitions. His marriage to a pretty young socialite half his age, who was sympathetic to the king's cause, may have spurred him further to treason. Whatever the reason, sometime in the spring of 1779, General Benedict Arnold, American war hero, opened clandestine communications with the British to negotiate changing sides. It was a dangerous game.

Potential traitors and turncoats who have not made their final choice tend to approach each other like porcupines making love – very carefully. Using Sir Henry Clinton's staff intelligence officer, Major John André, as a go-between, Arnold began to correspond with the British commander-in-chief using a code. Arnold referred to himself as Mr Monk – presumably after General George Monk who delivered Cromwell's Parliamentary army to Charles II – and André called himself Mr Anderson.

By September 1780, the deal was struck. Arnold would surrender the key fort at West Point to the British. This would allow the British fleet to sail up the Hudson and control New York. In return, Clinton promised Arnold a King's commission as a general officer in the British Army, plus £20,000 in gold; equivalent to over a million pounds today.

It was an extremely good exchange. West Point housed nearly all the gunpowder of the American army plus a massive depot of arms and ammunition shipped by the ever obliging French through their front company, *Roderick Hortalez et Cie* of Bordeaux, to the rebels. And with New York firmly in British hands, the Hudson River would be open as a highway for the Royal Navy clear to the Canadian border, splitting the United Colonies apart. Strategically this would have been a disaster for the rebels' cause. With the Hudson River controlled by the British the rebellious colonies would be cut in two. The isolated northern colonies could then be picked off one by one by invasion from British Canada in the North as well as the Redcoat Army around New York. Not for nothing did Washington himself call West Point and its barrier chain across the river 'the key to America'.

The final arrangements for this coup were made in conditions of great secrecy behind closed doors in Clinton's headquarters. The Culper spy ring was aware that something was up, but could not discover what. Sarah Townsend, the agent Townsend's young sister, actually saw a letter addressed to 'John Anderson' pushed into a British colonel's pocket and heard him discussing 'the importance of West Point' with André; but what did it all mean? Who was the mysterious John Anderson? And why were the two British officers talking about West Point so secretively? Concerned, Sarah passed a message to her brother, alerting him to the fact that something was afoot involving West Point and urging him to pass on her sealed message. In his turn, Robert Townsend forwarded the message about the mysterious Mr Anderson up the Culper network back to Benjamin Tallmadge, Washington's intelligence officer on the Delaware side of the river.

What happened next was to change history. For, just a week before, Tallmadge had been handed a note from General Benedict Arnold, warning him that a good friend of his, a Mr Anderson, was coming to see him at West Point, but, as he was unfamiliar with the countryside could Major Tallmadge please furnish him with a guide and an escort of a few cavalrymen? Smelling a rat, Tallmadge tore open the sealed letter from Townsend. Suddenly the whole plot was laid bare. Tallmadge immediately began a man-hunt to discover the whereabouts of any stranger on his side of the river calling himself Mr Anderson.

Meanwhile, in a clump of fir-trees not far away André was deep in conversation with Arnold. Their final negotiations to surrender West Point complete, André tried to return to the sloop HMS *Vulture*, which had brought him across to the American side in the dark. But dawn was breaking, and as the warship dropped down river, the British officer was stranded behind American lines. The two conspirators holed up in a nearby farmhouse to plan André's getaway. General Arnold wrote out a safe conduct pass for Mr Anderson and André, in flagrant disobedience of General Clinton's orders, changed out of his uniform into civilian clothes, stuffing the incriminating papers about West Point's defences and arms supplies into his boots. He would then ride out south by daylight, using Arnold's pass to cross the lines. The two men parted.

At about 9 a.m. on 23 September, André was stopped by an advanced picket who were guarding the American outpost lines. The three-man detail refused to accept the safe conduct from General Arnold. In vain André tried to bribe them. Their suspicions now firmly aroused, the picket searched their prisoner, found his boots stuffed with papers and then marched André straight to the nearest officer at North Castle. The officer in question, John Jameson, later reported to Tallmadge that he had picked up a John Anderson carrying some plans of West Point and had packed him off, under guard, to General Washington's headquarters. 'Odd thing', added Jameson. 'He had a safe conduct pass from General Arnold at West Point.' Jameson had already dispatched a courier to Benedict Arnold to check Anderson's story.

The truth finally dawned on Tallmadge. He convinced Jameson to get Anderson back as soon as possible. It was too late to stop the dispatch rider to Arnold, however. The traitor was having breakfast with two of Washington's staff officers when the courier arrived, telling him that

Jameson had captured a Mr Anderson with plans of West Point in his possession. Arnold stood up, 'looked embarrassed', as one of the officers later recalled, excused himself and went to his wife's bedroom, telling her that they must leave – now. Even as they whispered, an aide knocked on the door, calling: 'General Washington will soon be arriving, General'. There was not a moment to lose. Within minutes the Arnolds had fled, leaving all behind. As George Washington arrived at the house of West Point's commanding officer, the Arnolds were being rowed out to HMS *Vulture*, which was still patiently waiting for André.

Arnold had made good his escape, but André was now firmly in American hands. He eventually admitted that he was a British officer, and was tried and convicted as a spy, mainly because he had been captured in civilian clothes. Washington offered to exchange him for Benedict Arnold, but the British rejected such a one-sided trade, although they petitioned for André's life. Washington and his senior officers were adamant, however; and probably in a reprisal for Nathan Hale's execution and as a reaction to the shock of their colleague's extraordinary treachery, Captain, acting Major, John André of the 54th Foot was hanged before a large and sympathetic crowd at Tappam. No public hangman could be found prepared to do such an unpopular deed, and eventually an unknown man, his face blackened to avoid recognition, 'turned him off' in the graphic phrase of the time, leaving André's body dangling on a rope. Americans – the hard-nosed Washington and his judge advocate general apart – regarded André not as a real spy but as the unlucky scapegoat of the genuine traitor, Benedict Arnold. As the *New London Gazette* put it at the time, 'Perhaps no person on like occasion ever suffered the ignominious death that was more regretted by officers and soldiers of every rank in our army.'

André had been unlucky; but he had been stupid, too. Stripped of its myth and legendary heroics, the André story is a classic example of the intelligence staff officer attempting to dabble in the dangerous world of the undercover intelligence operator, and as usual, getting it badly wrong. André paid the penalty and was, forty years later, buried in Westminster Abbey as an honoured hero: a curious ending to his failed mission. But the fact remains for the professional intelligence officer, André stands as a classic monument of just how not to do it. Washington, the consummate intelligence professional, would not have tolerated such sloppiness and amateur dramatics for a second.

This is not to say that the André case was seen at the time as a triumph of colonial intelligence. On the contrary, the André affair sent shock waves rippling through Washington's whole undercover network. For example, his chief agent, the resourceful Robert Townsend, fled New York shortly after the arrest of André. If Benedict Arnold was a traitor to the breakaway colonialists' cause, then who else might have been betrayed? In a personal letter not three weeks after André's execution, 'Sam'l Culper, Jr' wrote to his boss: 'When I conclude to open another route [i.e. of communication] you shall be informed of it. I do not choose that the person you mention, or any other of his character, should call upon me …'.

Clearly the whole American spy apparatus was in a panic and the impact of Arnold's defection – a traitor 'hackneyed in villainy' in Washington's words – had damaged the confidence of the whole New York spy ring, certainly in the short term. Washington, however, knew better than just to rely on intelligence to frustrate his foes. The 'master of misinformation' had other devious methods with which to confuse and bamboozle the enemy.

By the August of 1781, Cornwallis, the British commander in the southern colonies, had hunkered down in all-round defence at Yorktown. In a deception operation worthy of the Allies' complicated plans to mislead the Germans before D-Day in 1944, Washington masterminded a complex series of intelligence deception operations designed to give the impression that his men were concentrating for an attack against New York in the north. In fact, Washington was pushing his army south as fast as they could march to cut off the British forces at Yorktown while the French fleet under de Grasse pinched off the British sea routes in Chesapeake Bay.

Mesmerised by reports of field bakeries being set up in New Jersey, new roads being built leading to New York, and invasion boats being laid up at Staten Island, Clinton braced himself for what looked like an attack on his main base at New York. Cornwallis at Yorktown must fend for himself until the danger to the centre of British operations in the north had been neutralised. In Chesapeake Bay the French admiral out-manoeuvred and nearly trapped Admiral Graves's ship's unimaginative line of battle. The British fleet headed for the open sea and safety, abandoning Cornwallis, now surrounded and cut off by land and by sea, to his fate at Yorktown.

Washington and Rocambeau, the French commander, reached Yorktown on the very day that the Royal Navy sailed into the Atlantic to abandon their army ashore. Cornwallis was trapped. Clinton realised he had been duped, and tried to save the British garrison, but it was too late. On 20 October 1781, Cornwallis surrendered his army. The colonial rebels had won their first major victory, thanks not just to the French fleet, but also to skilful campaign of misinformation and deception which had trapped the British commander like a rabbit in the head-lights. George Washington may have been a second-rate battlefield general, but as a commander-in-chief, determined to win by any means, he has few equals and ranks high among the clever spymasters of any age.

Washington's intrigues to shape the battlefield at home were not the only contribution made by intelligence operations in the colonists' struggle to free themselves from British rule. The Continental Congress knew from the start that they needed allies. France, still smarting from her humiliations at British hands in the Seven Years' War was only too willing to oblige. Any opportunity to heap equal humiliation on British heads was of great appeal to the French government, especially the Comte de Vergennes, the foreign minister, despite warnings of the cost to France from King Louis's finance minister.

Hotter heads prevailed, however. Clandestine French arms ship-ments and aid were merely the forerunners of French political recog-nition and were to lead to direct French military intervention in the war. To orchestrate this kind of support, the colonists required a mission in France and diplomatic friends at the French court in Versailles. In this they were well served by the enigmatic figure of Benjamin Franklin and his friends.

Franklin was a clever choice as 'Ambassador to France' after 1776. He was a genuine polymath: scientist, man of letters, scholar and inventor. He spoke French 'after a fashion'. He was heavily implicated in the Secret Committee of Correspondence of pre-Revolution days, whose task was to secure foreign guns, ammunition, diplomatic support and supplies for the colonies by whatever means, right from the very first stirrings of the American rebellion. From his elegant house in Passy, Franklin orchestrated the thirteen colonies' diplomatic offensive in Europe.

Like Washington, Franklin's undercover war in Paris faced an uphill struggle. He was under no illusions that the European powers were motivated by any great love for life, liberty, pursuit of happiness or American 'freedoms'. He knew only too well that France and the other Europeans were primarily driven by a desire to undermine British power and influence. French trade benefited from the rebels' cause too; as early as 1775 Beaumarchais's *Hortalez et Cie* and French companies were pumping over $5 million dollars worth of arms and warlike equipment into North America to the benefit of France's tottering economy. The chief commercial attaché in France for the colonists' cause was another agent of the Secret Committee at Philadelphia called Silas Deane. Deane's principal task was to encourage France to join in the war on the colonists' side under cover of his trading activities, and to glean as much support for the rebels' cause as possible. To carry out his task, Deane immersed himself not just in commerce and trade, but also in the secret world of intelligence, undercover dealings and black operations.

The diplomatic circuit around Paris at the time of the American Revolution was a hotbed of intrigue even by the fevered standards of wartime diplomacy. The British were only too aware of the Americans' efforts to woo the French to their cause and resisted them by every means possible. The principal British undercover agent in Paris was a New Hampshire man called Paul Wentworth, who, while posing as a loyal American patriot managed to infiltrate Deane's embassy and place a British spy in its very heart. While Washington had penetrated the British in North America, William Eden, the British Minister responsible for the British secret service had turned the tables in Europe with a vengeance. From his smart Parisian house, Wentworth recruited a network of British agents, earning the accolade of 'one of the cleverest men in England' from Vergennes, the French Foreign Minister, and opening up the Passy mission's secrets to British Intelligence.

Among his team, Wentworth recruited a Dr Edward Bancroft to spy directly on both Deane and Franklin. Bancroft was a known sympathiser to the rebel colonists' cause. Franklin knew him and liked him, regarding him as an 'intelligent, sensible man' perhaps influenced by the fact that Bancroft had invested in one of Franklin's money-making schemes before the Revolution. Whatever the reason, before long, Dr Bancroft was a confidante of both Franklin and Deane at Passy, privy to all the confidential gossip and, as secretary to the American Mission, to all the policy secrets of the rebel colonists' mission in Europe. Deane, knowing that Dr Bancroft commuted regularly between Paris and London, eventually tasked his loyal American friend to act as his undercover agent and to collect intelligence 'on the British' when he was in London. Bancroft readily agreed to be an American spy. Deane and Franklin were delighted with their choice.

They would have been less enraptured if they had known that the loyal Dr Bancroft was in fact also in the pay of the British secret service and a willing agent of its chief, William Eden, in London. Bancroft's case officer in Paris was none other than Paul Wentworth. For the next year Bancroft travelled happily between London and Paris, keeping the British informed of every diplomatic twist and turn the Americans were planning. In return, he brought back 'chicken-feed' supplied by Eden from London and as a sideline, speculated heavily on his inside information. London had effectively turned the Passy residence inside out. Bancroft was their man – not Franklin's.

Not everyone was impressed by Bancroft's efforts. King George III openly ignored Bancroft's intelligence, convinced that the traitor was only feathering his own nest and only spying to make his fortune from insider dealing. Much more dangerously for Bancroft, Arthur Lee, one of Deane and Franklin's American circle, openly accused him of being a British spy and a traitor. As Lee, however, was wont to denounce everyone (except himself) as such at regular intervals, he was not believed and packed off to Prussia on a fool's errand to get him out of the way. Lee's accusations, however, very nearly 'spooked' Bancroft, who swiftly acquired a second passport, should he ever need to flee in a hurry. But suspicion did begin to grow in the American mission; just where did Dr Bancroft's loyalties really lie? For one man, however, there could be no question. Through thick and thin, Benjamin Franklin defended his secretary and remained adamant that Dr Bancroft was a loyal, patriotic American. Despite the allegations he trusted Bancroft implicitly.

Unravelling this knotted tangle of spies, loyalties and double agents across the years is not easy. But the more one looks at the story, the more Benjamin Franklin's own personal loyalties come under the spotlight. He was at the heart of the whole London–Paris–Philadelphia web, and his double-dealings point clearly to one conclusion: that Benjamin Franklin, American Patriot, Hero of the Revolution and Champion of Liberty, was in fact a British agent and spy throughout. The evidence is compelling. He turns out to have had a code number (No. 72) as a paid-up agent of William Eden, head of the British secret service in London. He dealt openly with the British secret service's head of station in Paris. He allowed suspected spies to see his correspondence; he tolerated men accused of treachery in his own entourage; and he himself was insecure and indiscreet. It is a damning indictment.

There may, however, be another explanation for Benjamin Franklin's apparently inept and clumsy handling of his undercover mission. If one judges his performance by its *outcome* and not by its day-to-day activities it is clear that his was spectacularly successful. The intelligence analyst's perennial question to cut through the lies and deceptions of their trade is invariably a useful guide: *cui bono?* Who benefits?

On the evidence it is clear that it was the breakaway colonies that benefited most from Franklin's diplomatic skill. In particular, his brilliant finessing of the French government's alliance with the Congress in 1778 to finally side with the Americans was a diplomatic ace in the hole. By opening 'clandestine' talks with Bancroft and London, Franklin had finally forced the French to make their minds up once and for all. They had to come to a decision, if only to forestall the possibility of a separate peace treaty between the British and their errant offspring, who looked to be losing their struggle for independence in 1778. Such a reconciliation would have left France dangerously exposed and isolated, yet again at war with Britain but this time without a friend in sight. Vergennes and Beaumarchais urged French intervention to prevent such a foreign policy debacle and King Louis agreed. Franklin's apparent wavering and his hints at 'secret talks with the British' had in fact clinched the very deal he wanted and achieved exactly what he had been sent to do: get European support for the colonists' cause. On this evidence, Franklin emerges as a complex character who succeeded in his task: to get European support for the breakaway American colonies.

The old man's string pulling, however, was to rebound on him. Eventually even his French allies saw through their duplicitous ally. Vergennes's reaction in 1782 to the discovery that Franklin really was signing a secret peace treaty with the British behind France's back was scathing:

> I am at a loss, Sir, to explain your conduct ... you have concluded your preliminary negotiations without any communication with us, although your own instructions from Congress direct that nothing shall be done without the participation of the [French] King.

Franklin was unrepentant, replying:

> Nothing has been agreed contrary to the interests of France ... the English flatter themselves that they have already divided us. I hope that this little misunderstanding will therefore be kept a secret and that they will find themselves mistaken.

An embittered Vergennes was soon to reap the fruits of the double-dealing and betrayal by France's faithless friend. The final treaty ending the American Revolutionary war was extraordinarily generous and left the door open for trade and enrichment by both the ex-combatants: not so for France, who found herself impoverished, isolated and seething with internal discontent.

Despite his duplicity, Franklin remained a hero to the ordinary French man in the street. His unsophisticated New World nobility played well to an audience hungry for change and for liberty. He saw through the final peace treaties before setting out on his final journey back to Philadelphia to return home to the universal acclamation of his countrymen as one of the Founding Fathers of the United States. Not all who came into contact with the pain-wracked old man were convinced: to many he remained a slippery, devious character.

There is another explanation, however, less palatable to those who would deify Franklin as a 'god-like hero of the Revolution' or to castigate him as a British spy. It is an explanation instantly recognisable to any experienced intelligence officer wearied of running undercover agents, with all their changes of mind, duplicities, foibles and tricks. Benjamin Franklin was really just a cunning old man who kept a foot in both camps for as long as it took him to see which side was winning and see just how he himself could best benefit. It may not be a particularly edifying epitaph for one of the Founding Fathers, but it does reveal *Bonhomme Richard* as a fitting colleague for the United States of America's other master of cunning, double-dealing and agent running: George Washington.

From the very beginning of its rebellion and its gradual transformation into a new and independent state, the USA ran a very impressive intelligence operation indeed. If proof were ever needed of such a statement, one only has to look at the first Federal budgets. George Washington devoted no less than 12 per cent of his national income to 'Intelligence'. This clear political statement of just how he really waged war reveals more strongly than any other where his true war-fighting priorities lay. In this Washington reveals himself to be an outstanding commander and a true disciple of both Sun-T'zu and Clausewitz: neither of whom he had ever read.

The judgement of history must be that as a master of intelligence and its combination with a coherent and successful war-fighting, political and military strategy, America's first president has few equals.

The victory of Washington and his fellow rebels was a triumph for liberty and a ringing declaration of freedom and the rights of man, worthy of Voltaire, Rousseau and the great French advocates of enlightened progress. French aid to the breakaway Americans went much deeper than mere political tracts, however. The colonists' victory had in the final analysis been made possible mainly by power projection across the oceans and by sea power – French sea power. The irony was that France, while busy supporting insurrection and liberty abroad at such ruinous cost to herself, was still suppressing liberty at home. The genie of freedom from oppression, uncorked so far away, was not going to be tamely rebottled.

Its next visitation would be on France herself, with horrendous consequences.

9

The Age of Revolution

All the business of war, and indeed the
business of life, is to endeavour
to find out what you don't know from
what you do ...

ARTHUR WELLESLEY, 1ST DUKE OF WELLINGTON

The breakaway colonists' victory over George III's government was formalised by the 1783 Treaty of Paris. The enigmatic, if not downright ambiguous, figure of Benjamin Franklin oversaw not just a new country as he signed the treaty, but a new era, too. For the desire to break away from a repressive authority was not to be limited to the faraway British settlers' quarrel with London. The colonies' example, tied in with the great intellectual ferment of the Age of Reason, had raised expectations that would inevitably challenge – if not unravel – the whole social fabric of Europe. The Enlightenment was as potent a catalyst of change as the Renaissance and Reformation had been two centuries before. Everywhere the desire for change was stirring and would not be denied.

This desire for change was not just confined to the developing nations of Europe. In Russia, Catherine the Great's careful reforms were moving even that backward country forward; if not in step with Europe, at least only one or two paces behind. Catherine's intelligence service had, however, always been of the highest quality for its day. Considering the way she came to power, suspicion and paranoia would not only seem to be justified but essential for the survival of the Czarina of all the Russians. What had happened to her wretched and inadequate husband could conceivably one day happen to her. She took steps to ensure that it would not.

Among her many other reforms, Catherine reorganised Russia's intelligence service, under its cover name of the Secret Expedition. When Catherine died in bed in 1796, her son Paul took over control of the office of the Secret Expedition. In the process, the new Czar learned some unpleasant truths about himself from deciphered British diplomatic traffic being intercepted and read in Russia's efficient Black Chamber. The British ambassador wrote, 'The Czar is literally not in his senses ... since he came to the throne his disorder has increased.' A furious Czar expelled Ambassador Whitworth from St Petersburg.

Czar Paul did, however, try to improve on his mother's domestic intelligence service. Taking the old Venetian custom of denunciation as a model, he ordered a post box to be placed outside the Winter Palace into which anyone, regardless of rank, nationality or motivation could place 'items of intelligence' – anonymously. The 'Yellow Box' rapidly became an important source of domestic security intelligence for the Czar; it also, inevitably, fuelled the flames of his paranoia. With such a system of unevaluated information flocking in from a random mixture of self-selecting uncontrolled sources, common sense, judgement and peace of mind fly out of the window. An increasingly mad and frightened Czar became the hunted victim of his own fears and what the Yellow Box revealed. For domestic security a more rational and better managed intelligence system is required.

France supplied it. By 1790, the cultural genius and civilised aspirations of the Enlightenment and the French Philosophers had led to a much more efficient secret police than anything that Russia could devise, and a reign of terror that would set the pattern for all future revolutions. The French Revolution did not break the mould for national intelligence; it made the mould for population control and government by terror. It was not exactly the happy state of enlightenment that Voltaire, Rousseau and Diderot had envisaged. France's Revolution proved that Rousseau had been right: men were indeed savages – but not noble ones.

France's nightmare grew partly because of the American colonists' revolt against government from London. Unable to resist the lure of striking back at England for their defeats in the Seven Years' War, the French had thrown in their lot with the thirteen colonies from the start. The American victory at Saratoga was treated like a French victory, 'with dancing in the streets'. Undercover support and illegal arms shipments grew into a full-scale alliance with the colonial rebels and advocates of liberty. In vain, Finance Minister Baron Turgot urged caution. His protestations were overruled. Led by Beaumarchais and Foreign Minister Turgennes, France flung her arms and treasure whole-heartedly into the war. By 1784, Louis of France could be proud of the triumph of French arms. De Grasse's victory at Chesapeake Bay had not only humiliated the Royal Navy, it had arguably sealed the fate of Britain's Anglo-German army ashore and the hopes of the British in North America as well. Britain's final shamefaced defeat and withdrawal in 1783 marked a high point in France's self-regard.

Pride often goes before a fall. Victory had come at a heavy price for Bourbon France. French victories in North America and Suffren's triumphs off India were undermined by commercial losses elsewhere and ill-judged attempts at reform at home. The costs of the war were ruinous to an already depleted treasury. The French may have been jubilant in the late 1780s, but France herself was in serious trouble. Economic disaster could – just – have been avoided. Absolute rulers, however, are reluctant to change the habits of several lifetimes. The policies of Louis XVI and his advisers merely finished off a process which Louis XIV had begun a hundred years before. Now France was heading for some kind of showdown with economic and political reality.

France's explosive revolution in 1789 changed world history. Not only did this triumph of the Enlightenment and its ideals of *liberté*, *égalité* and *fraternité* (none of which lasted very long) as a replacement for the forces of privilege change France; the Revolution changed almost everything else as well. It is not an exaggeration to say that the Revolution changed the political context and the social contract between states as well as between governed and governments for ever. It began the modern era of politicising almost everything. It was the source of all Communist, Fascist and Socialist conceptions of the State and the governed. It was truly revolutionary.

The arm of revolutionary change was long and extended rapidly to intelligence. Although the revolution failed almost completely in its aims – the guillotine, the Terror and Bonaparte swiftly replaced the era of brotherly love as the Revolution devoured its children and a Bourbon king was back on the throne twenty-six years later – it spawned the idea of domestic control of a population on a hitherto unseen scale. Of course, there had been secret police of a sort before. The Spartans had kept informers busy spying on the Helots; the Inquisition had been efficient wherever its gaze fell and its Black Friars travelled; and Peter the Great's secret police of the Oprichniki had become a permanent feature of Russian life. But none of these sinister instruments of oppression matched what the glorious 'dawn of liberty' was to visit upon the unsuspecting French. Robespierre's and St Just's Jacobin radicals soon began to tear up the moderate reforms of the first revolutionaries. In their place came an internal war on 'enemies of the revolution' and 'traitors' as the Revolution's enthusiastic leaders embarked upon a Reign of Terror against the people of France themselves.

Nothing it seems is more galling to a political leader than to discover that the people are just not worthy of the sacrifices he has made for them. First, the Royalists, then the Moderates (such as the Girondists) were marched to their rendezvous with 'Madame Guillotine' and its lugubrious mechanic, Sanson, in the Place de la Concorde. Then, in 1793 with the terror at its height (1,375 victims were guillotined in one six-week period) the guardians of the Revolution finally turned on themselves. It was a time of genuine and widespread fear as the *Comités de Surveillance* (Committees of Public Safety) – a title ironically borrowed from the much more moderate and restrained American revolutionaries of a decade before – sprang up.

Their role was primarily to spy on the local citizens, to supplement the politically active Republican Clubs and to act as local guardians of revolutionary purity for the all-powerful *Representantes en Mission*, Revolutionary leaders sent out from Paris to enforce France's brave new world by whatever means were necessary. In the cities the *comités* were manned by working men of radical views, the militant urban terrorists of the *sans culottes*. In rural France, however, the *Comités de Surveillance* were mainly staffed by the bourgeoisie, anxious not to allow the fruits of their hard work to be torn from them by working-class political hotheads, or even worse, a return of the landed classes demanding their property back. For the canny French middle class the Revolution – properly managed – could be a rich source of enlightened self-interest, guaranteeing not only survival but also a chance for rich pickings. The *comités* were extremely powerful. They could arrest suspects, denounce traitors and backsliders, and even allocate food resources in the area. *In extremis* they could even confiscate property, always a mouth-watering prospect for the greedy, looking for the opportunity to settle old scores with troublesome neighbours.

The *Comités de Surveillance* were not only influential but all pervasive. For example, in the area of Rhône et Loire there were no less than ninety-two *comités* in the Rhône Department alone. With the local rulers the *commissaires* and the threat of imprisonment – or worse – to back them up, the *Comités de Surveillance* controlled French lives as the Revolution bit deep into French life and society in the last decade of the eighteenth century and reform turned into repression. It became 'a crime to be *suspected* of a crime in this glorious Revolution of ours'. Fear stalked the land.

This swift and unexpected emergence of a modern totalitarian police state from the enlightened ideals of the Revolution took nearly everyone by surprise. The law of unintended consequences set loose in France actually established a model for one-party dictatorships that has survived to this day. Russia, China, Iran and Cambodia have all since demonstrated the revolutionary power of the well-organised ideologue and the power of totalitarianism. One thing, however, became clear very quickly to the radical revolutionaries in Paris: in order to police such an oppressive, controlling regime, they needed intelligence on the French people on a hitherto undreamed of scale.

'Cometh the hour, cometh the man.' Just at the moment that the Revolution faltered and its hand reached for the responsibility of total oppression ('Nobody can rule guiltlessly' acknowledged the bloodthirsty St Just), an individual appeared whose skills would make totalitarian government work on a scale undreamed of by the 'oppressors' of King Louis and his aristocratic *Ancien Régime*. The enigmatic figure of Joseph Fouché came on to the scene: Out of the smoke-filled clouds and blood of the National Convention, the Terror and regicide itself, Fouché demonstrated the three key attributes that would make him for twenty-five years as indispensable – and as unsackable – to French governments as J. Edgar Hoover was later to prove to a succession of nervous US presidents, and a puppet master of legend.

The three attributes Fouché demonstrated to his peers were ruth-lessness, bureaucratic efficiency and, like Hoover, the threat of black-mail over any potential enemies. In marked contrast to his predecessor as chief of police, the oafish Heron (who had convinced Robespierre by a stream of denunciations that 'class enemies' beset the regime of the Commune on every side, and who prowled the streets armed to the teeth with blunderbuss and axe accompanied by a truculent escort of armed bully boys), Fouché was a man of the west, born at Nantes of a working-class family. Under the old regime, his lowly birth restricted his progress but not his education. Only the Church offered a man like Fouché scope for advancement in the old days and for ten years he was a lay brother of the Oratorian order, moving from abbey to abbey to teach mathematics, classics and physics to the brothers. The Revolution catapulted him to Paris as an elected member of the Assembly. Here the roots of his future career were laid down in a welter of revolutionary and republican fervour. Fouché, taking his cue from Robespierre, voted for the king's death and became as radical as the wildest of the Commune's hothead extremists. France's future spymaster was a 'coming man' among his fellow revolutionary fanatics.

This zeal for the cause caught the revolutionary leaders' eyes. They quickly dispatched him as a politically trustworthy governor to the provinces. Here the ex-lay brother unleashed a fierce and sustained attack on Christianity itself, unfrocking priests, seizing Church land on behalf of the State, insisting that clergy marry and even banning religious services at funerals. Who can guess what deep slights and long-harboured resentments against his former ecclesiastical employers conspired to bring this outburst of malevolence and violence? Whatever the trigger, Fouché was marked as a revolutionary zealot among zealots and a ruthless administrator of revolutionary ideals. Private property, the clergy and enemies of the revolution were all dispatched with brutal efficiency. He boasted that he had 'dechristianised' France. As the Terror reached its height, he even turned the cannon of the garrison of Lyon on to its rebellious citizens in his own version of 'a whiff of grapeshot', and guillotined the survivors, earning him the nickname *le mitrailleur de Lyon*. To the rapturous acclaim of his revolutionary masters he reported back to Paris, 'Terror, salutary terror is now the order of the day.'

Ever aware – as all good revolutionaries who wish to survive should be – of the shifting sands of radical politics, however, by 1793 Fouché managed to distance himself from Robespierre's homicidal suspicion as the Commune and Committee of Public Safety consumed itself in a final orgy of executions. On the death of the 'sea-green incorruptible' he was appointed by the ruling Committee of Five Hundred to the Ministry of Police. They felt that his revolutionary credentials were impeccable, and he was a man who could be trusted to keep the Revolution safe from its enemies, inside and out: but mainly inside. From then on, France's chief intelligence officer never looked back.

As quickly as the young Fouché had trimmed his sails from religion to revolution, so did the new minister of police, chameleon-like, reinvent himself into a sober, politically astute administrator and bureaucrat. Fouché the revolutionary firebrand was no more. Sensing general weariness with the excesses of the Revolution, France's new chief intelligence officer settled down to become a conciliatory figure, a socialiser, but, above all, a collector of intelligence on everyone.

His network was formidable. He amalgamated the revolutionary network of informers and *gauleiters* with the old Bourbon regional *intendant* system. The police were reorganised, spies run at home and abroad, and all reports funnelled back to his desk. Spotting Napoleon's ambitious designs and potential through his contacts (and a well placed undercover agent within Bonaparte's own household), he ensured that if or when the First Consul ever came to power he, Joseph Fouché, would be at hand with his hard won secret lists of traitors, enemy agents, black marketeers and damaging personal files on enemy and friend alike. Like many a politician newly arrived in power before and since, Napoleon was entranced at the secret information on his political rivals now available to him from his diligent superspy. Thanks to Fouché he now knew who were betraying their country, betraying their wives, the exchequer and the courts. Knowledge is power and Fouché's files and dossiers were detailed and deeply incriminating; just what a new dictator needed. Napoleon may well have wondered exactly what damaging intelligence Fouché had collected on *him* and his family but prudently went out of his way to ensure that his spymaster was well bribed for his loyalty. He stuffed the omniscient Fouché's mouth with gold, making him, by 1802, 'the second richest man in France'.

Fouche's system of national intelligence was revolutionary and all encompassing. To the existing State intelligence structure of a secret chamber of decoders for intercepting diplomatic letters, spies abroad and informers at home he added the whole revolutionary apparatus of spies, informers and denunciation. The old idea of *intendants* was expanded, with a *prefect* responsible to Paris in every one of the ninety-odd new Napoleonic *departements*. Within every *arrondissement* or sub-district, *sub-prefects* reinforced the flow of intelligence, and single spies and informers informed on *them*. For the first time ever a country had a complete bureaucracy of internal intelligence agents reporting efficiently on the population's every move back to a central capital. It was a considerable achievement.

Fouché's *dirigistique* grip on France was reinforced by the legacy of the Revolution and the Terror. For over four years a culture of denunciation, class envy and informing on your neighbours had sown the seeds of a domestic intelligence and security network without parallel. Fouché reinforced and institutionalised this domestic surveillance system and made it a tool of governmental control, which many would argue, survives in France to this day. In addition to this internal intelligence apparatus, Fouché inherited – and expanded – France's external network of diplomatic and commercial spies. The result was a formidable intelligence machine. Not for nothing did Fouché claim that in France, 'three men cannot meet and talk indiscreetly about public affairs without the Minister of Police being informed about it next day.'

Considering his revolutionary zeal (or perhaps because of it) Fouché's instructions to the *prefects* on their professional conduct have an ironic ring: 'If we were to add a single [oppressive power of arrest and detention] we would be ... agents of tyranny ...', and, 'Never forget how dangerous it is to make arrests on mere suspicion alone.' Coming from the 'Butcher of Lyon' this was a bit rich. But Fouché had clearly moved on to reinvent himself as the indispensable bureaucrat concerned only with the public good at whatever cost. As a secret police chief he was exactly what the true inheritor of the Revolution needed. So did his new boss, Napoleon Bonaparte.

Bonaparte took an early interest in intelligence. He realised only too well how much successful leaders needed local knowledge, as his ruthless orders about 'volunteering' local guides to assist him in finding his way on campaign make clear:

> One orders the major to seize some peasant to be put at one's disposal, arrest his wife as a hostage and dress up a soldier as the man's farm hand ... Such a system always succeeds ...

Like so many military geniuses, Napoleon's victories often turn out on examination to be based more on accurate and timely intelligence than inspiration or genius. However, as these intelligence sources were invariably meant to be secret, history frequently fails to record them and it always serves great generals and public leaders to let the mass believe in their own particular skills or genius. Confronted with a mirror behind one's opponent at cards, anyone can appear to be a poker-playing phenomenon. Men like Napoleon, with one eye on their carefully guarded reputations and the verdict of history, are notoriously loath to admit that the reason they won was actually because they knew their adversaries' intentions all along. Great reputations, let alone 'genius' might even be diluted or worse, exposed as hollow. Napoleon Bonaparte was no exception to this iron rule of ego. Behind the scenes, it was good intelligence that fed his carefully nurtured reputation for military brilliance. The hidden hand of intelligence was as much the guiding light behind Napoleon's 'star of destiny' as any stroke of genius on the battlefield.

Evidence, as with any other enterprise relying on secret sources, is hard to come by. Sometimes the lack of good, clear intelligence reveals that the genius's dependence on it is normal circumstance. Napoleon had an early lesson in the need for vital intelligence at one of his most famous victories, Marengo in Northern Italy in 1800. Marengo was a near disaster.

Napoleon's Italian campaign is often cited – usually by supporters of the reputation of the 'man of destiny', encouraged by the divine revelation of his genius contained in Napoleon's own writings – as a stunning example of military brilliance. Closer examination, however, reveals that the 'great military genius' had a little help from his friends. Napoleon actually bribed the Austrian commander, Argenteau, in the 1799 campaign. Paying your opponent to throw 'the game' is as old as time and Argenteau's subsequent defeat should not surprise us. The 100,000 gold francs paid out by Landrieux, Napoleon's military *Chef de Bureau des Affairs Secretes* was a highly worthwhile investment both for France and for Napoleon's reputation. By the 1800 campaign, Napoleon was running a high-grade spy with access to all his Austrian adversary's plans. The French Army's stunning passage of forty cannon through the St Bernard Pass and Napoleon's subsequent pounce on the great fortified city of Milan turn out to be a direct consequence of an Italian spy in the enemy headquarters. In return for 1,000 gold francs a month, Napoleon's agent revealed that the Austrian Army was defending the Piedmont passes well to the west and concentrating around Turin, not Milan.

It was this unnamed spy who was to let Napoleon down at Marengo; for, like so many spies who work for money, he had had a better offer. He became a double agent. The Austrian Field Marshal von Zach agreed to pay more than the French 'to spy on the French'. It was double pay day. Faced with this agreeable situation, Napoleon's spy rode back to Napoleon's camp to pass on the useful intelligence that von Zach's army was going to pull out to the north. Armed with this (entirely spurious) intelligence, Napoleon decided to strike, and on 14 June 1800, lunged on what he thought was an isolated Austrian rearguard near Marengo.

The military genius had made a bad mistake. He had in fact blundered into the main Austrian army, who turned on the French and began to surround them. In the ensuing battle Napoleon's troops were badly mauled and on the brink of a serious defeat when, purely by chance, Desaix's division, which had been on a fool's errand searching for one of the spy's non-existent Austrian forces from Genoa, blundered into the fight from the side. In response to Napoleon's desperate appeals he was able to come to his rescue. A combination of double agents and bad intelligence had very nearly destroyed Napoleon's reputation before it had really begun. Desaix – who paid with his life at Marengo – had saved it. Napoleon would have been less than human if he had ignored such a sharp lesson about the need for good intelligence at all times in the future. From then on, even if his writings may not reflect Napoleon's obsession with intelligence, Napoleon's actions certainly support the fact the France's dictator took intelligence very seriously indeed both on the battlefield and at home.

The Napoleonic battlefield system relied not only on the famed scouting skills of the French light cavalry, but also at the strategic and operational levels on a network of undercover intelligence agents and spies in the enemy camp. Napoleon relied heavily on Berthier, his chief of staff, to coordinate this system for him and make it work through his staff. He, in turn, depended on Jean-Marie Savary, Napoleon's chief of military intelligence, for much of the Imperial period. Savary had realised from his early experiences with Desaix in Italy that spies were literally worth their weight in gold. By 1800 he was deeply involved in agent running, special operations and political intrigue passed on to Napoleon's headquarters in the field. With Fouché in Paris and Savary at GHQ Napoleon was in fact running an effective political-military intelligence apparatus the like of which had never before been seen.

Fouché had his own agenda, however. Keenly aware that Napoleon's seizure of power and dictatorial rule was not universally popular, he appears to have set out from the first to 'take out insurance' for the day when Napoleon fell from grace. The enemies of Revolutionary and Napoleonic France were both within and without France itself. Fouché was well plugged into both. Like his revolutionary colleague, Talleyrand, Fouché intended to survive, come what may. For the moment however, his loyalties lay with Napoleon, and with bringing the malcontents of post-revolutionary France firmly under control. Two days before Christmas 1800 Fouché and Napoleon got their chance.

As the First Consul was driving to the opera a bomb concealed in a cart blew up in the Rue Nicaise. Houses were destroyed and thirteen people killed. Car bombs are not a new phenomenon; nor is terrorism. Napoleon was unharmed. Within hours, Fouché's army of underground informants had fingered the most likely suspects: Royalist sympathisers and their agents in Paris. The secret police rapidly moved in to arrest the suspects and round up the rest of the plotters. But Napoleon and Fouché used the menace of 'terrorism' to push emergency prevention of terrorism decrees through the Senate and Council strengthening the government's powers to arrest and detain suspected terrorists. Within days, Napoleon had his 'emergency powers'. They were to stay in place for as long as he retained power. Thanks to a ham-fisted Royalist plot, France now was a true police state.

Napoleon's fear of Fouché's power probably balanced Fouché's own fear of his leader's arbitrary authority. As with so many secret police-dictator relationships, both men needed the other. Balzac claimed that

Fouché: 'inspired in Bonaparte something akin to terror.' The tension between the two men grew until in 1802, Napoleon actually sacked his Minister of Police who by then was Duc d'Otrante and a millionaire. Fouché's opposition to the 'rechristianisation' of France through the Concordat with Rome probably contributed to the split. Fouché, the ex-lay brother, was still violently opposed to the Catholic Church. Napoleon could not do without his secret policeman for long, however. Dictators rarely can. Within two years, Fouché was back. Napoleon's autocratic style of governmental control needed him.

Napoleon – rightly – always feared the assassin's bullet. Royalist conspiracies were never far from his throne, even after he styled himself emperor and took the crown from a nervous Pope's hands to place it on his own head to ensure the continuity of his dynasty. That unwitting symbolism said it all: France's Revolution had come full circle. From the absolutism of Louis XVI, the 'sovereign people' were now firmly under the thumb of an even more absolute ruler, and one with a far more efficient secret police as well. Such an irony would not have been lost on Voltaire.

Napoleon had been a relatively junior officer at the time of the Revolution and had thus escaped the taint of regicide. In 1804, however, Bourbon blood was to stain Bonaparte's hands too as he launched a highly secret special operation to seize Louis XVIII's cousin, the Duke of Enghien, in what was an illegal *coup de main*, breaking international law. Fouché's external intelligence service discovered yet another Royalist plot to kill Napoleon and depose him. In what seems to have been a fit of exasperation, Napoleon decided to teach the Royalists a lesson, once and for all, and make an example. A snatch squad of elite French troopers invaded Baden undercover of darkness and kidnapped the Duke of Enghien. He was on neutral territory and had committed no crime. Although the evidence suggests that Enghien had little if any knowledge of any plot to kill Napoleon he was court-martialled as a French citizen and shot on Napoleon's orders by a firing squad in the dry moat of the citadel at Vincennes. His only crime was to have been living on a royal pension paid for by the English. The shock waves of this dramatic intervention outraged Europe and did much to reinforce Bonaparte's image as a ruthless and untrustworthy autocrat. Enghien had been no more than an innocent bystander to Napoleon's desire for vendetta and Baden's sovereignty had been violated. Baden would not be the last European state to feel the self-willed anger of the Emperor of the French. *L'affaire Enghien* proved to be a propaganda gift to France's enemies. The 'Old Europe' of the monarchies could portray the French Emperor as a criminal, a tyrant and a Corsican bandit on the loose. Above all it demonstrated just what a dangerous neighbour Napoleon could be.

Fouché's return to power strengthened his position. After the Enghien affair he settled down to keep his master happy. From 1804 on, every day, except Sunday, Fouché sent an intelligence summary to the Emperor. In it he summarised events on a wide range of subjects:

Crime statistics

Intercepted letters

Enemy agents detained

Agents' reports

Interrogation reports

Rebellions against National Guards, police or *gendarmarie*

Stock Market and economic trends

Currency speculation

Public opinion

Army morale and desertions

Political trends, domestic and foreign

Agitators' reports

Prison population

Reports on suspects under surveillance

Royalist plots

Arrest lists

This list of police, security and intelligence reports is by no means exhaustive. It therefore comes as no surprise that under the secret police-man Fouché, more Frenchmen were arrested without charge and flung into jail than ever were dispatched to the Bastille under the notorious *lettres de cachet* of the *Ancien Régime*. Such a reputation and such power naturally bred enemies. Fouché, however, seems positively to have relished his opponents' plots and enmity and revelled in their naivety or incompetence. De Bourrienne's memoirs contain one particular example, which shows France's intelligence chief actually toying with his political enemies as a cat plays with a mouse.

One day the bumbling, anxious-to-please Paris chief of police Junot placed a list onto Napoleon's desk, including an informer's report that de Bourrienne himself had been seen 'mouthing off' in a Paris café the previous night and advocating a return to the monarchy. Napoleon questioned Junot, who swore that it was true; Napoleon then questioned de Bourrienne who denied it hotly, adding that he, de Bourrienne, had already told Junot that the whole story was a pack of lies invented by someone to discredit him. Moreover, people could swear that he had not been near any Paris café; he had been with friends at Malmaison all evening: and he would damn' well prove it too. An infuriated Napoleon kicked Junot out of his office, shouting 'Imbecile!'

When de Bourrienne related the story to Fouché, according to his memoirs, Fouché smiled and admitted that he himself had planted the story onto one of Junot's agents. He had done it just to see if the policeman was stupid enough to report something as gospel without checking. He added that 'he often caught the Police in the snares he laid for them', and used these false reports to demonstrate just how accurate and important *his* own intelligence service was to the Emperor. This was a devious and careful man: but then to survive life at the court of a dictator one needs to be. Fouché's skills as secret service chief were to set a standard never before achieved. When combined with his military intelligence service, it meant that Napoleon probably had the best national intelligence service up to that date, certainly until 1813–14.

The Napoleonic overseas military intelligence service was equally well managed. To take but one example, Fouché's secret agents were active at the Ottoman court right up to Napoleon's fall in 1814. Undercover agents like Framey and Boutin roamed far and wide on Napoleon's business in the East, collecting intelligence, distributing gold and generally acting as secret agents of French policy throughout the period of the Empire. The major activity of these agents in places like Constantinople, Alexandria and Cairo – long after France had been ejected from Egypt – was to obstruct British influence and to restore French credit; but, above all, they were to provide timely and accurate information for Paris from deep inside the Ottoman Empire.

The key to the Napoleon's military system in the field was a well-organised and run headquarters that operated according to strict staff procedures. The lynchpin in Napoleon's command post was Marshal Berthier, his chief of staff, who ran his cabinet with a dedication that sometimes seems more than Napoleon deserved. Berthier was much more than the plodding and diligent clerk Napoleon paints him as. Without his right-hand man at his side at Waterloo (Berthier either committed suicide or was murdered in Germany as he tried to rejoin his old Emperor in 1815), Napoleon failed miserably. History has many examples of 'great captains' whose stars don't seem to shine quite so brightly once deprived of their right-hand men or a good supply of secret intelligence. Even genius needs help.

Savary, the principal military intelligence officer under Berthier, ran a surprisingly comprehensive intelligence operation. From cavalry reconnaissance on the battlefield to strategic human intelligence with spies in the enemy camp, French military success was usually backed by timely and accurate intelligence. Savary's greatest coup was to recruit one of history's master spies, a young Alsatian called Charles Schulmeister. Raised in a strict Protestant household, the youthful Charles soon realised that there was far more to be gained from smuggling around Strasbourg than from the Church or schoolmastering. By 1799 Schulmeister was a well-known figure to the French garrisons on the Rhine. He needed to be. He was one of their principal suppliers of black market goods. To move his contraband, he had to know all the details of the official patrols on both banks of the Rhine and their routines. Such a bilingual, quick talking young rough soon caught the eye of Staff Colonel Savary, chief of intelligence for the region. He recruited him and from then on Schulmeister was a fully paid-up French secret agent. Savary even used Schulmeister's local knowledge of Rhine trading and of the *Schloss Ettenheim* to guide the Gendarme Squad to capture the Duke of Enghien inside Baden.

By 1804 Fouché and Savary decided to launch their new spy on a breathtakingly audacious mission. Schulmeister was provided with ample funds, servants and a coach, and 'kicked out of France', allegedly for being overheard supporting the Austrian cause against the French. Posing as a disgruntled nobleman he fled to Vienna where he set up house and offered to tell the Austrian commander-in-chief, General Mack, 'everything he knew about the French Army' as a revenge for his treatment at their hands.

It worked. Mack interviewed the 'aggrieved young aristocrat' and was taken in. Schulmeister, who seems to have been rebelling against his stern and censorious Lutheran father (and genuinely believed he was the illegitimate son of a Hungarian nobleman who had seduced his mother), so impressed the Austrian general that he was taken on as the senior intelligence adviser to the Austrian High Command! As intelligence coups go, Schulmeister and Savary's scheme takes some beating: Napoleon had actually placed a senior spy as his enemy's intelligence chief. Once in place, Schulmeister got to work, passing the whole Austrian dispositions and orders of battle back to France and, to keep the Austrians happy, producing spurious reports that the French Army was on the verge of mutiny and short of food and ammunition.

Nothing could have been further from the truth, for in the late autumn of 1805 Napoleon's *Grande Armée* was marching inexorably from the Channel ports to fall upon Austria. If Napoleon could not invade England by sea after the disaster of Trafalgar, he could at least be master of Europe on land. In disguise, Schulmeister prepared the way for his master, making the *Grande Armée*'s path straight by leading Berthier, Savary and Murat, the cavalry commander, on a secret reconnaissance of Southern Germany. The vital ground was the city of Ulm, Mack's HQ. Between them, Berthier and Schulmeister cooked up a plan to neutralise Mack's army. It was to lead to Napoleon's greatest victory.

Back in Ulm, Schulmeister fed Mack with a classic diet of 'chicken-feed', a mixture of genuine intelligence, which can be checked, disinformation and misinformation. Mack really believed that Schulmeister was a master spy and a wonderful source, with access inside the French High Command and even to Napoleon himself. He was right, but not in the way he thought. By November 1805 Savary and Berthier were ready to spring their trap. In apparent disorder they pulled back from Ulm. Lured on by Schulmeister's 'reports' of French disarray and 'British landings on the Channel coast', Mack advanced to pursue the retreating French, even dispatching Schulmeister to go forward and see what the French were up to. Schulmeister gleefully obeyed and rode off to report to Napoleon; but not before one last coup. He knew some of the Austrian officers from his smuggling days and, in a final bid to sow dissension in the Austrian ranks, he paid out massive bribes in gold to a number of key operational commanders to 'buy their delay'.

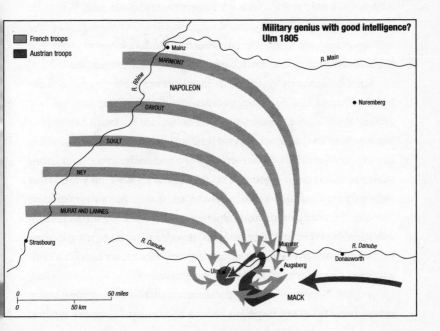

It worked. Ignoring the advice of his chief of staff that Schulmeister was not to be trusted and the army should retreat from an obvious trap, Mack advanced with 30,000 men. The French trap was sprung. Ney's 'retreating' corps suddenly turned and offered battle, locking the Austrians in from the front. Once committed to the fight, the flanking corps of Soult, Marmont and Murat's cavalry wrapped round the Austrian Army in an attack on its rear. Mack was trapped, outnumbered and outwitted. With no choice and no hope he surrendered. Napoleon was delighted with his ruse, claiming that 'Schulmeister's information was worth 40,000 men' to him.

With Mack's 30,000 troops gone, the way to Austerlitz was open. Despite this, Napoleon was curiously reluctant to attribute too much credit to his battle-winning spy. Even when Schulmeister was arrested by the vengeful Austrians the French were equivocal. When he managed to escape by bribing his guards with French gold and was eventually brought to Napoleon his reward was not the medals and honours of others. The Emperor gave him a prize of war, a captured estate in Alsace. 'The only reward for a spy is money', Napoleon said. When the Austrians finally advanced into France in 1814 they took great pains and doubtless great delight in ensuring that the Schulmeister estate was high on their target list. They blew it to bits. Schulmeister fled.

Such evidence of spies, inside intelligence, subterfuge and sheer bribery throws a different light on Napoleon's oft-trumpeted military genius. With such a combination of intelligence back-ups as a hidden hand to help the cause along, even military genius can be portrayed as merely routine. His reliance on trickery and undercover operations makes him no less of a general; on the contrary, Sun-T'zu would have rightly applauded such a master of the art of war. But some aspect of Napoleonic vanity made him reluctant to acknowledge the huge contribution intelligence and bribing his opponents made to his victories. Indeed, his own over-reliance on intelligence very nearly lured him into a disaster a year later when he invaded Prussia.

In 1806, Napoleon's unique combination of ambition, revolutionary economics and greed impelled him on to his next European feeding frenzy, this time with Prussia as his prey. Thanks mainly to a lack of good intelligence and being deceived by a false report, Napoleon got it badly wrong and was only saved from a serious setback by the skill of his 'iron marshal' Davout; for which a jealous Emperor never really forgave him. Geniuses, and especially vain ones, don't like genuine competition, especially when the truth is that it was Napoleon's own orders that were really to blame for the near debacle.

As Murat's advance cavalry pushed forward into Germany they had seized the local post office at Zeitz. Such a find of Prussian mail, plus a talkative postmaster, was a good haul, the more so when a friendly civilian sidled up to the French cavalry officer examining his find, and told him that he was an undercover French agent. He told the French that the mail was bound for the Prussian Army concentrated around the town of Erfurt. A cavalry escort promptly took the spy to Napoleon's forward headquarters, where he found Napoleon and Berthier crawling on a large map on the floor and discussing their next move. We know from his memoirs that Napoleon had a weakness for believing in intercepted postal communications and captured postmasters. He himself interrogated the 'willing agent' closely and then rapped out his orders in a typical series of rapid-fire monologues to the waiting Berthier. The French chief of staff tried to capture these sparks of genius and turn them into a series of rational movement orders and instructions for the following day for the scattered corps of Napoleon's marshals.

He should have saved his time. Napoleon's instructions to move to concentrate *west* towards Jena and Weimar were just plain wrong: half the Prussian Army was in fact sitting ten miles to Napoleon's north around Auerstadt. (See map overleaf.) To compound this error, the Prussian troops at Jena were actually pulling back out of contact. From this position, King Frederick William's men could have hammered into Napoleon's right-flanking corps, with disastrous results as the French Army stuck its neck out advancing into an empty space. The truth was that Napoleon had made the fatal mistake of relying on a single source, and an unchecked one at that, to shape his orders. The 'French spy' had deliberately passed on wrong information and suckered the 'military genius' into an incautious move. Napoleon should have checked the Zeitz spy's story more thoroughly. If he had questioned him a little more critically he would have realised that the man must have passed through Auerstadt if he had really journeyed from Jena to Zeitz. And anyone passing through Auerstadt could not have missed seeing half the Prussian Army. Napoleon, acting as his own intelligence officer, had failed the most basic test. Intelligence from a single source, and especially an unchecked one at that, is invariably a poor supporter of strategy or key political decisions, however tempting and convenient the intelligence appears to be. In fact, the more convenient the intelligence or tempting the tale, the more it needs to be double-checked for source credibility, access, accuracy and significance. As every intelligence officer knows, 'the easy way round is usually the mined way round ...'.

The result was a debacle, saved only by the extraordinary efforts of

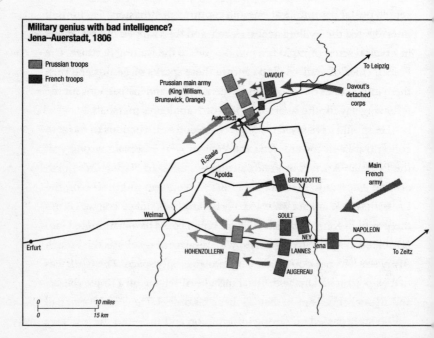

Military genius with bad intelligence?
Jena–Auerstadt, 1806

- Prussian troops
- French troops

Prussian main army
(King William,
Brunswick, Orange)

Auerstadt

DAVOUT

To Leipzig

Davout's
detached
corps

R. Saale

Apolda

BERNADOTTE

Main
French
army

Weimar

SOULT

NAPOLEON

NEY

Erfurt

HOHENZOLLERN

LANNES

Jena

To Zeitz

AUGEREAU

| 0 | 10 miles |
| 0 | 15 km |

Davout's corps to the north. As Lannes, Soult, Ney and Bernadotte pounced on the Prussian rearguard around Jena they realised early on that they were only attacking a part of the Prussian Army and a small part at that. Where was the rest? As Napoleon unleashed Murat's cavalry in a counterstroke to drive the outnumbered Prussians from the Jena battlefield, the distant rumble of guns to the north told the true story. The exposed French right-flank corps under Davout, ordered to 'outflank' the Prussians around Jena, had actually blundered into the main Prussian force around Auerstadt. Davout's heroic advance turned rapidly into Davout's heroic defence as he desperately held off Prussian attacks. As the French position weakened, despite Davout's and his soldiers' efforts as they put up the fight of their lives, the French were able to benefit from a lucky shot. The Duke of Brunswick was fatally wounded and, temporarily leaderless, the Prussians hesitated for a fatal pause in their assault. This was all a general like Davout needed. He ordered his flanking divisions to wheel inwards and begin to envelop the Prussian flank. Squeezed, outgunned and outwitted the baffled Prussians retreated, despite having a two to one superiority over Davout's isolated corps. It was a spectacular French victory and Davout had won it.

Of course, Napoleon took the credit, blaming Bernadotte for not pushing his corps north to support Davout. 'Jena' was the name of the victory he trumpeted back triumphantly to Paris. But the real victory over the Prussians was won by Davout at Auerstadt, and all the French senior officers knew it. So did Napoleon. The blunder was in fact his, and all because of bad intelligence from a single source. True to form, the Emperor of the French castigated Bernadotte and tried to keep Davout in the background from then on. The truth was, Napoleon relied heavily on intelligence's hidden help for most of his triumphs. When it was lacking, or false, his 'military genius' evaporated. It is perhaps therefore no puzzle that intelligence figures so little in Napoleon's military memoires and maxims. The myth of the great captain is eroded by any suggestion that he owed much to the help of his friends.

By 1812, Napoleon's rocket star had reached its zenith and begun its inevitable fall down to earth. Yet again, intelligence played a powerful role in his downfall. The spectacular advance of the *Grande Armée* into Russia failed for many reasons, from horses unshod with snow nails for the retreat from Moscow, to the stubborn Russian defence, trading space for time. Underpinning all these failures is the constant factor of poor intelligence. Napoleon consistently failed to inform himself of the realities of his greatest, and most disastrous, campaign. Whether it was the location of the Russian armies, the amount of logistic stocks required, or the climate, Napoleon's march to and from Moscow was effectively a blunder into the darkness, without even decent maps. His soldiers paid the price. Of the 600,000 men and 180,000 horses who massed on the 24 June across the Vistula to invade Russia, less than 58,000 survived, of which only 23,000 were French. And of all these 23,000 frozen and starving survivors who made Vilna, only 3,000 survived the winter as typhus and hunger took their dreadful toll.

Faced with such horrific losses, even Napoleon had to confess his error, admitting that 'he hadn't known that the cold struck so early in Russia', and that 'he should have ordered the retreat two weeks earlier …'. Commanding generals, even military geniuses, sometimes need more than will-power, overconfidence and inspiration to win their battles. Nothing beats good intelligence on the enemy. All successful generals quickly learn that.

Such a man was Arthur Wellesley, Britain's commander in Spain and Portugal. Since Napoleon had placed his compliant brother on the Spanish throne in 1808, the Spanish people had risen in revolt against French domination. Napoleon's ambition had, not for the first time, over-reached itself. He saw in French domination of the backward Iberian Peninsula a great chance to enforce his Berlin Decrees. These were intended to create a Continental customs union and common market, specifically designed as a Europe-wide commercial weapon to exclude British trade. Such a policy of all out economic warfare was a bold strategy. By using 'the power of the land to conquer the sea', Napoleon hoped to bring the 'nation of shopkeepers' to her knees.

He reckoned without the Spanish, who rose on 2 May 1808 against their new French overlords. At Bailen on 19 July a retreating French corps, blundering around looking for their foes, was cut off by the Spanish regular army and surrendered in humiliating circumstances. It was the first major setback for French arms since the Revolution.

The British, implacable foes of Bonaparte's France, promptly offered their support on the Iberian Peninsula. With command of the sea the British always had the strategic advantage of the whale over the elephant and the initiative it confers. They could attack almost anywhere on the perimeter of Napoleon's Empire at any time. A British expeditionary force could be landed and supplied through Lisbon to aid the Portuguese and Spanish cause. Although the first expedition was ejected ignominiously by the French at Corunna early in 1809 nonetheless the British were back by the summer and this time they stayed on. From 1809 onwards, 'the Spanish ulcer' drained off Napoleon's troops as France tried to fight a war on two fronts.

Britain's new commanding general was an old India hand, experienced in fighting the large and well-armed armies of the Mogul rulers. Unlike Napoleon, Wellesley, or the Duke of Wellington as he became after Salamanca in 1812, knew only too well the importance of intelligence and was not afraid to admit it either:

All the business of war, and indeed all the business of life, is to endeavour to find out what you don't know by what you do: that's what I call 'guessing what was on the other side of the hill'.

From the beginning of his Peninsula campaigns, Wellington was not only aware of the need for intelligence he was also fascinated by it. The discovery that he had been dispatched to fight in Portugal without being issued with any maps of the country (in 1809 the British Army's intelligence system was virtually non-existent), must have alerted him to the need for some better organisation.

For the truth was that Britain was poorly served during this period. There was no formal national intelligence organisation. The king, his prime minister and the cabinet depended on an irregular and uncoordinated diet of diplomatic observations, spies' reports – of varying quality – and the invaluable flow of commercial information from organisations such as Lloyd's shipping agents. There were also intercepted postal communications at which the British were very good, according to their rueful Continental opponents. The problem was that it was neither tasked nor coordinated. As a result the flow of national intelligence was always patchy and not to be relied upon, especially by an isolated field commander at least ten days away from Whitehall.

Only too well aware of the shortcomings of both the commander-in-chief back in Whitehall and the vagaries of the Horse Guards (as the War Office was then known) Wellington decided from the start to set up his own intelligence system in theatre. For a start he asked his brother-in-law back in London to buy some decent maps out of his own pocket and get them sent out. From then on, Wellington established a thoroughly professional, and very modern, intelligence organisation. To do this, he relied mainly on the efforts of two men: Colquhoun (pronounced Ca-hoon) Grant and George Scovell.

Grant's family was Scots aristocracy and he seems to have inherited his father's capability for hard work and integrity. Many of the Grants were soldiers and young Colquhoun naturally followed in their footsteps. Three members of the family were already colonels or generals in addition to Colquhoun, and one of them, Alexander, actually fought alongside Wellesley at Assaye. Colquhoun himself represented the best of the breed: intelligent, honest, reliable, brave, hardworking, able to communicate clearly, and with a talent for languages and adventure. He was a perfectly qualified intelligence officer.

By 1809, Grant was serving as a major in the 11th Regiment of Foot and posted to the Peninsula as part of Wellington's army. As an infantry major he fought with his regiment at Busaco in 1810. From then on he was seconded to Wellington's personal staff, following an extraordinary exploit in which he passed in uniform through the French lines to link up with Portuguese guerrillas and negotiate with their leaders to buy corn and cattle for the army. It was a remarkable feat and his successful return ensured his reputation; not as a spy but, with other officers like Somer

Cocks seconded from his regiment to Wellington's headquarters, as one of Wellington's 'exploring officers'.

Wellington's understanding of intelligence had been formed by his experiences in India. Always outnumbered, he had had to seek a qualitative advantage to ensure that his relatively small Anglo-Indian armies were not overwhelmed by the Mogul legions confronting him. Very early in his career, Britain's 'sepoy general' realised that intelligence was the ultimate force multiplier. In this he was greatly helped by the Indian subcontinent's social and cultural system of news couriers or *harkranas*. Indian life was overlayed by a network of news collectors and riders who passed news from village to village, court to court, and province to province. The beauty of the system was that a rider could go anywhere and the system could be plugged into virtually everywhere. The other great attraction was, as with any other commodity on the subcontinent, news and information could be bought. One thing that the East India Company was not short of was money. Wellington bought into the Indian news courier system from the start and reaped the benefits. To further assist him, he added a special reconnaissance unit of picked men, speaking the local languages, called the Guides. Between 1799 and 1804, Wellington could genuinely claim that he was never surprised and that he always knew where the enemy armies were, thanks to good intelligence from either the natives or his guides.

With such a background, it was inevitable that Wellington would endeavour to try and emulate a similar system in the Peninsula. While there was no network of news couriers in Spain and Portugal, there was a vast pool of would-be willing informants who hated the French and wanted to see them out. The problem was how to tap into this valuable reservoir of intelligence. His chief of staff, Sir George Murray, supplied the answer with the Peninsula's own specialist intelligence unit. In 1809 the Peninsula Corps of Guides was formed under a Captain George Scovell. Its tasks were to scout forward, collect intelligence, interrogate prisoners, and liaise with the locals 'to gain information respecting the force and movements of the enemy'.

The Guides were a success from the very beginning and by 1811, their establishment had been increased and Scovell promoted to lieutenant colonel. They roamed freely, often well forward of Wellington's army, and took great risks to collect intelligence. Their exploits became the stuff of legend and not just on the Allied side. One of their number, John Grant, was even alleged to have dined in a French officers' mess. He also wore Portuguese clothes, much to the horror of his colleagues, for if the French ever caught an exploring officer out of uniform his fate would be that of a common spy. The French devoted considerable efforts to rooting out these irritating gadflies in their midst, and the occasional capture of one of Wellington's exploring officers was trumpeted as a great victory. Their duties often placed them well behind the main French army either as 'stay behind' patrols or, even riskier, setting up agent networks behind enemy lines.

Of all the guides and exploring officers, John Grant's namesake Colquhoun Grant is perhaps the best known. His exploits would make most Hollywood adventure stories look tame. He rode deep into French-occupied Spain, and speaking fluent Spanish, was accepted by the local villagers around the hearth. More importantly, he was accepted by the leaders of the numerous guerrilla bands in the hills and caves. Around a hundred campfires, Grant and his brother officers hoovered up reports of French movements, division and battalion locations, rations and ammunition dumps and which unit was moving where. It was priceless operational-level intelligence, made even more important by the occasional haul of a French courier's saddlebags, frequently blood-stained, containing coded orders of letters between the French High Command and Paris. These lists of meaningless numbers were handed over to the exploring officers in exchange for British gold or weapons, and the precious ciphers passed back to Wellington's codebreaking expert at army headquarters.

Wellington's principal codebreaker was none other than the officer commanding the Corps of Guides, George Scovell. Scovell's talents lay not in dangerous escapades behind enemy lines but in codebreaking. He was a serious and clever man, bent on personal improvement and learning; when he could, he visited the great university libraries such as Salamanca and appears to have been fascinated by Roman ruins and the other antiquities of the Peninsula. This background of learning, allied to his fluent French and an enquiring, mathematically logical mind, made Scovell an inspired codebreaker. After 1811, he had even cracked the French 'Great Paris Cipher' and could turn the meaningless jumble of numbers and figures of the captured dispatches into lucid, clear translations. Such a treasure trove of communications intelligence gave Wellington a priceless advantage over his French opponents. His exploring officers, like Grant, were giving him good solid reports on the French dispositions and capabilities through their network of agents, long-range reconnaissance patrols and secret observation posts. Scovell could now read the enemy's *intentions* as well through their own communications. Wellington had his own 'Enigma'.

With this flow of integrated, all-source intelligence – to use the modern jargon – Wellington began, hardly surprisingly, to emerge as an ever-victorious general. Unlike Napoleon, who pretended to have some great insight or flash of genius, Wellington freely acknowledged the debt his victories owed to good intelligence, even boasting about it occasionally in dispatches to his political backers in London.

This was insecure and potentially dangerous; for if the French ever suspected that their codebook had been compromised, they would have immediately changed their ciphers. Fortunately for the British, they never seem to have realised that their security had been hopelessly compromised, and continued to use the same codes until nearly the end. For example, after the Battle of Vittoria in 1813, Napoleon's brother Joseph wrote home to Paris glumly reporting his defeat, apologising for having lost his decoding tables to the looters of the Allied army and warning Paris to change their codes in future. By then it was too late. Wellington's superlative intelligence service had rendered him a string of victories and the Battle at Vittoria was merely the latest in a depressing series of French defeats as they were driven through the Pyrenees and out of Spain.

Perhaps the most clear-cut example of the importance of Wellington's intelligence is in his victory at Salamanca. Often derided by French writers of the *la Gloire* school as a 'lucky, unimaginative, defensive general', Wellington's reputation really stands on his three great *attacking* battles: Assaye, Salamanca and Waterloo. In every case he bided his time, sometimes (as at Waterloo) soaking up heavy punishment until he judged the moment right for a devastating advance and counter-stroke. Of the three, Salamanca can best be attributed to good intelligence and is his masterpiece.

Scovell's decodes had revealed that the French Marshal Marmont was moving to join forces with King Joseph's French Army of Central Spain. If these two forces were ever allowed to link up, Wellington would be outnumbered and have no choice but to pull back. From this intelligence, Wellington knew that he had to strike while he still had the chance and decided to give battle while Marmont was on the march. The rest was accomplished by a Wellingtonian *coup d'oeil* on the battlefield, plus the skill and bravery of his soldiers, especially his cavalry commander, General le Marchant, Britain's answer to Murat, who was cut down, sword in hand, leading the final decisive charge. Intelligence may well provide the opportunity, but at the end of the day, it is the will of the commander, and the fighting abilities of the troops, that win the battles. Wellington's intelligence service was no exception to this iron rule of warfare.

That Wellington relied heavily on his intelligence service can be in no doubt. 'He was worth a whole brigade to me', he said in genuine sorrow, on hearing of Colquhoun Grant's capture by the French. He need not have worried. The ever-resourceful Scotsman was back in his headquarters within eighteen months, after a series of escapades worthy of James Bond himself. Taken to France to be handed over to Fouché's secret police to be interrogated – or much worse – Grant escaped and went on the run. Disguised as Captain O'Reilly of an Irish regiment in French service he made his way to Paris. There he made contact with anti-Napoleon groups and even managed to alert Wellington that Napoleon had taken all his available reserves to Moscow. He then obtained American papers from the French anti-Napoleon underground, before moving down the Loire to the Atlantic port of Nantes, one jump ahead of Savary's secret police, now hot on his trail. There the intrepid Grant bribed a fisherman to sail out into the Bay of Biscay to be picked up by a British man-of-war on the blockade. A French guard ship sailed up to check the fishing boat. Grant was tied to the mast and wrapped in the sail to avoid detection. Eventually he made his way back to England, courtesy of the Royal Navy. By early 1814, he was back in the Peninsula again, at Wellington's headquarters, where a relieved commander-in-chief made his legendary exploring officer head of intelligence and officer commanding the expanded Corps of Guides.

Wellington's talents as a general rested, like Napoleon's, on experience, a fine eye for ground, understanding of other men's strengths and the ability to exploit them, plus a sound understanding of logistics. Where he outstripped Napoleon was in building a comprehensive theatre-level all-source intelligence organisation that could cover almost any development. While Napoleon relied equally on spies and agents, the rival organisations they built up differed sharply in two key respects. Napoleon was obsessed with security. He was, after all, a dictator and Head of State: 'Uneasy lies the head that wears the Crown.' Napoleon's system, under both Fouché and Savary, spent as much time and effort spying on Frenchmen as it did on worrying about the Emperor's external enemies. Wellington never really had to bother with a security service; although he was forever complaining – and with good reason – about how insecure his officers were he never had to worry about treachery. The loyalty of Britons never posed a threat to him, however garrulous and indiscreet their letters home.

The second area of difference was in the organisation of their theatre-level intelligence systems on campaign. Although Napoleon's superlative light cavalry performed a not dissimilar function to Wellington's exploring officers, and both men had access to the usual clutch of lies, half-truths and perceptive analyses that pass for diplomatic intelligence, the actual organisation of intelligence in their respective headquarters differed widely. Wellington, certainly by 1814, was running a very modern all-source intelligence system. Moreover, it was an intelligence branch that would not disgrace a modern HQ. Its organisation can be summarised:

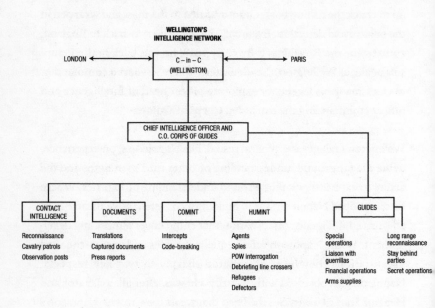

This was a very sophisticated organisation and one well in advance of anything previously seen. The irony is that no sooner had Wellington's victorious army invaded France in 1814 and Napoleon been forced into exile at Elba, than the whole apparatus was disbanded and lost for ever. A combination of incompetence in Wellington's old enemy (and *bête noire*) the Horse Guards, plus Treasury parsimony, ensured that when Wellington finally did confront Napoleon at Waterloo a year later, neither of these great captains would have the slightest idea of the other's whereabouts or intentions.

The Waterloo campaign stands as a positive monument to the blundering consequences of having no intelligence, as Blücher, Napoleon and Wellington stumbled about in the dark for four days south of Brussels. It was, as a shocked Wellington observed afterwards, 'a damn near-run thing'. If he had had his veteran Peninsula intelligence team in place, there can be little doubt whatsoever that the Waterloo campaign would have been fought very differently. For example, if Wellington had known Napoleon's location and axis of advance in time he could easily have concentrated his whole army on Blücher's right at Ligny on 16 June 1815, confronting the 90,000 men of the Emperor's *Armée du Nord* with a combined Anglo-German mass of over 150,000 troops and 250 guns, solidly blocking the road to Brussels and Napoleon's ambitions. Sadly, without the hidden hand of intelligence to guide the generals, things turned out very differently, and very bloodily, for all the combatants. While Sun-T'zu would have applauded the final victory at Waterloo, he would have been appalled at the price and the waste. Good intelligence can often save sweat, blood and lives.

The final irony is that Colquhoun Grant actually did warn Wellington of the threat before Waterloo, or at least he tried to. Recalled in 1815 by his old master to be his chief of intelligence at Brussels, Grant had managed to infiltrate back into France to make contact with his old anti-Napoleon friends in Paris. The resistance groups had good networks into Louis XVIII's, now again Napoleon's, ministries and alerted Grant that Napoleon would definitely strike up the main axis of the Charleroi road towards Brussels. Grant dispatched an urgent report back to Wellington to warn him; this was crucial and time sensitive information. But what Clausewitz called the 'friction' of war interposed in the portly form of Major General Dornberg, commanding the German cavalry screen on the border. Dornberg is alleged to have read the vital warning, grunted and sent the report back to Grant saying that in his opinion, 'on the contrary, it proved the very opposite'. By the time Colquhoun Grant discovered this piece of interfering folly it was too late. Against such stupidity, even the gods are powerless. Intelligence needs to be not just accurate, but timely too.

The French Revolution and the two decades of European war that followed revolutionised the way in which states conducted their intelligence affairs as well. Just as warfare was no longer limited, so equally was secret intelligence unleashed in all directions.

Fouché had planted the seed of domestic oppression and surveillance that would one day find its apotheosis in men like Beria and, ultimately, Pol Pot. Ironically, Fouché, once the murderous revolutionary and then the 'second richest man in France', was to survive and die of old age in his bed in 1821. (Despite Napoleon's gloomy musing from exile in St Helena, 'There are three men I should have hanged while I had the chance: Tallyrand, LaFayette and Fouché.')

The age of Revolution had also ensured that relations between states would alter too. A secret and bitter war between national intelligence services was now seen to be a perfectly acceptable undercurrent to the ancient hypocrisies of the diplomat's trade. And on the battlefield, Wellington's remarkable system of integrated, all-source military intelligence had revolutionised the conduct of operations. (Albeit temporarily for the British, who were too stupid to see what Wellington had devised and had to reinvent it a century later.) Intelligence, like so many other things, had been revolutionised by the events of 1789 to 1815. The hidden hand of intelligence would now be an indispensable tool for politicians and soldiers alike to deal with their enemies – and, when necessary, their own countrymen too.

10

The Peaceful Century?

Most intelligence reports in war are contradictory, even more are false, and most are uncertain ...

CARL VON CLAUSEWITZ, *ON WAR*

It is one of the ironies of history that the victors rarely learn the lessons of their triumph. While the defeated brood on their errors, vowing to get it right next time, the victors tend to convince themselves that the victory was mainly due to their superior moral strength, rightness of their cause, brilliance of their generals, and wisdom of their leaders. We have seen this unedifying phenomenon in our own time: the triumphant Israelis after their smashing 1967 victories over the combined Arab armies; or the British after their astonishingly swift ejection of the Argentine invaders from the Falklands in 1982. In the aftermath of victory, self-congratulation and triumphalism is the order of the day. Woe to him who dares to point out that the great victory has revealed serious flaws. The spectre at the feast is an unwelcome guest, however accurate its warnings.

Thus it was for the British after 1815. The 'Long Peace' and the memory of Britain's triumph over Napoleon's France obscured the hard facts and hard work that had underpinned Wellington's victories. Economic growth, industrialism and undreamed of prosperity coupled with complete absence of external threat encouraged an air of dreamy national pride and self-congratulation. The instruments of victory gradually ossified in the four decades after Waterloo, more monuments to the heroes of the past than fighting forces of the day. The fleet stayed firmly Nelsonic; the army remained as it had been in 1815, only much more smartly dressed. The emphasis shifted from combat power to outward show. Polishing brass and whitening decks took priority over fighting. The real instruments of victory mouldered or were discarded. Among the victims of this neglect was Wellington's intelligence system. Such folly would one day cost his heirs and successors dear.

However, these Anglo-Saxon complacencies had no place across the Channel on the continent of Europe. The turbulence of revolution had set powerful forces in motion that would gather pace as the nineteenth century unfolded. National rivalries had been sharpened. Thanks to Napoleon, German unification led by a victorious Prussia was now an unstoppable force. Italy cried out to be Italian and free of any foreign yoke. Above all, the peoples of Continental Europe were stirring to be masters of their own destinies. These were revolutionary forces indeed.

For the ancient rulers of Europe these were dangerous trends. Fortunately, help was at hand. Fouché's France and the Czar's Russia had shown them just how to deal with troublesome and restive populations. Thanks to the French Revolution the universal age of the secret police and undercover agents of government had been born. The nineteenth century may have been a time of relative tranquillity and security for the British; for the rest of Europe and across the Atlantic, for the fledgling United States of America, it would prove to be anything but peaceful.

The impact of nearly a quarter of a century of virtually continuous warfare had forced men to think deeply about the nature of war. The Enlightenment had bred a new class of thinkers and intellectuals who turned their attention to the reasons for, and consequences of, war. Men like Lafayette – and Napoleon's other bitter critic, Madame de Staël – had pondered openly on the impact of revolutions in general and more specifically on the nature of Napoleon's own dictatorship and political legitimacy. This did not make them popular. But it reflected the spirit of the age, to question and to think about 'why' and 'how'. Now for the first time, some political thinkers focused their gaze on to the very subject of warfare itself.

The two political colossi who bestrode the nineteenth century, Metternich and Bismarck, drew fundamental strategic insights from the new realities of power and control in post-Napoleonic Europe. For Metternich, the Austrian chancellor, it was the need to prevent revolution, with all its social chaos and uncertainty, at any cost. To do this he needed to control both the internal Habsburg Empire and, externally, to mark out the international playing field on which states' disputes would be settled. For Bismarck it was the cruder realisation that only power and strength mattered, both inside and outside Prussia.

They had more in common than they acknowledged. From their widely differing standpoints both these architects of 'the European Century' agreed on the need for good intelligence systems as prime agents of their political will. Both relied heavily on the secret hand of intelligence to keep their regimes secure and to win their diplomatic and battlefield victories. Above all, the national interest – as they conceived it – ruled all.

Other thinkers in the 1830s were, however, looking at a different aspect of national conflict and war. Statesmen and strategic thinkers had agonised over great political concepts for centuries, from Marius to Machiavelli. What these new nineteenth-century soldier-thinkers were writing about – effectively for the first time – was nothing less than the conduct and philosophy of war itself. Not since the Oriental thinkers of the Sui and T'ang dynasties in China or the maxims of Akbar in India had such serious thought been given to war; certainly not in Europe, 'enlightened' or not.

The two great military thinkers of the age were both soldiers who had fought in Napoleon's wars, although on different sides: Baron Antoine-Henry de Jomini, a Swiss who had fought for Napoleon, and Carl von Clausewitz, a Prussian who had fought in the 1812 campaign for the Czar. Both men can justifiably be described as that rare phenomenon, military intellectuals. Both men wrote prolifically. Jomini's monument is his *The Art of War*, Clausewitz's, his even more monumental *On War*.

Both writers exerted (and to a lesser extent, still do) a massive influence on military thinking. Both men believed that they had discovered in Napoleon's campaigns the philosopher's stone that would unravel the secrets of warfare itself. Both men sought to prove that deep within the horror, fear, smoke and confusion of battle lay a few simple semi-scientific principles that would bare great truths and could enable the thinking soldier – and the politician, too – to better guide his forces to ultimate victory. It was an ambitious undertaking. Both men were widely read. Both men's teachings were widely followed. Both men, for all their supposed thought, got intelligence badly wrong. Sun-T'zu would not have approved of either.

In this, both Jomini and Clausewitz were prisoners, as are we all, of their experience and the age in which they lived. They had observed that rare phenomenon, the all-conquering general, and had made the all too easy mistake of drawing broad generalisations from the specifics of Napoleon's triumphs. Both writers saw warfare through the narrowly focused lens of their experience of the French, a war fighting doctrine based on the *levée en masse*, or conscription, one single great leader, good staff work and finally, a decisive battle to knock out an enemy's main force. Both failed to recognise the importance of *intelligence* in this recipe for victory in war. By a massive irony, Napoleon's sheer secrecy over his reliance on intelligence misled both Jomini, and particularly Clausewitz, to underestimate its vital importance to their hero. Jomini's semi-scientific principles laid great stress on the sheer mechanics of moving armies around the battlefield and offer little more. Clausewitz's deeper and more philosophical *meisterwerk*, *On War*, attempted a much more thoughtful analysis of the political causes and origins of war and its importance; but he, too, fails to understand the primary importance of good intelligence as an indispensable aid to victory.

Clausewitz was a Prussian who had soldiered extensively during Napoleon's wars, being captured at Jena in 1806 before becoming a staff officer for the Czar in 1812. From 1818 onwards, he was director of the Berlin Staff College *(Kriegs Akademie)* where he tried to implement the ideas of his mentor von Scharnhorst, who had begun the reform of the Prussian Army after the debacle of 1806.

Clausewitz's *On War* carries roughly the same weight with military thinkers as Marx's *Das Kapital* does with communists. Both are semi-philosophical early Victorian works, dialectical in their method, and both were – certainly until the collapse of Communism discredited Marx – regarded as almost Holy Writ. Both books share yet another characteristic: very few people have actually *read* them, and certainly not in the original German. (In all fairness, they are neither of them the first books to be taken as gospels, despite being little read in the original.) Clausewitz, unlike Marx, however, has never been thoroughly discredited.

On the subject of intelligence he deserves to be. It is a topic to which he does not give due weight and both his observations and conclusions vary between the thin and the downright fallacious. In his obsession with analysing 'the nature of war', von Clausewitz makes two serious mistakes: first, he failed to recognise the vital need for material or technical superiority in warfare; secondly, he assumed that strategic deception and surprise are virtually impossible, and therefore ignored the value of intelligence. The Clausewitzian trinity of passion and violence, chance and probability, and lastly, calculation, reason and planning, take little or no account of the importance of intelligence in discovering an enemy's capabilities or intentions and, more importantly, planning for their defeat. As a result, Clausewitz's attempts to develop effective ideas to cut through the uncertainties and frictions of warfare consistently ignore the role and use of intelligence.

Effectively Clausewitz is saying that intelligence is often unreliable and so, to his tidy and pedagogic German logic, should therefore be discounted. Anyway, the great military thinker goes on, 'even if you get intelligence you can't really take the enemy by surprise.' What might possibly have been true for the early nineteenth century and the campaigns of Napoleon does not stand up to modern experience after the experiences of Pearl Harbor, Hitler's Ardennes offensive, Yom Kippur, Korea, the Six Day War, Tet, the Falklands or even al-Qaida's strike against the World Trade Center and the Pentagon. Clausewitz is just plain wrong – certainly on intelligence.

Fortunately, Clausewitz's posthumous testimony had little influence in its day, being unrecognised by most. Jomini's work, however, exerted a greater influence at the time, certainly until the American Civil War between the states revealed its limitations. In one thing, however, Clausewitz was absolutely right: war is as much 'art' as science.

The United States had long decided it had little need of intelligence as it expanded west by a mixture of immigration, land grab, diplomacy and straightforward conquest in the early 1800s. For example, when President Polk openly invaded Mexico in 1844, the US commander, General Zachary Taylor, quite happily advanced without benefit of either maps or any intelligence on the terrain or the enemy.

'We are quite in the dark', wrote Colonel Ethan Allen Hitchcock. 'The General may have information which he keeps to himself, but I know him too well to believe he does have any ...'. Attempts to storm the Mexican fortress of Monterrey without any intelligence on the stronghold resulted in excessive and unnecessary casualties. Worse, a clumsy attempt to foment a rebellion in 1846 against the Mexican leader Santa Anna by a pair of volunteer amateur spies (the expansionist New York publisher Moses Beach and his partner Jane Storms) ended in disaster, with the US spies fleeing Mexico to avoid arrest at the hands of the infuriated Mexican authorities.

Following this ignominious setback, President Polk decided to try a new tactic with a new commander. In 1847 the USA invaded Mexico from the east under General Winfield Scott. Scott was no 'rough rider' like Zac Taylor. Retracing Cortes' invasion route towards Mexico City, he appointed Ethan Allen Hitchcock as his chief intelligence officer and used trained West Point cartographers and engineers as deep reconnaissance teams to ensure the routes of advance were known and mapped. Hitchcock supplemented these long-range reconnaissance patrols by hiring a local warlord called Manuel Dominguez and his band as an irregular scout troop called, accurately enough, The Mexican Spy Company.

Perhaps surprisingly, Dominguez's spies and agent were remarkably loyal and successful. Eyeing this strange mixture of Mexican bandits and their women singing dirty songs and firing their carbines on the march, an Irish soldier wryly dubbed them 'The Forty Thieves'. The nickname stuck. The Mexican Spy Company and Scott's reconnaissance officers were, however, a great success, helping to turn a lacklustre and incompetent military expedition into an American success. It also gave a whole generation of young West Point graduates a very important lesson in the vital need for intelligence on campaign. Men like Robert E. Lee, George Meade, Pierre Beauregard and George McClellan would remember their old Mexican intelligence skills when they confronted each other across their own battlefields fifteen years later.

For Europe, military intelligence remained the stuff of theorists in the 1830s and 1840s. The real intelligence challenge and priority for the Continent's rulers was in *domestic* security and control of the population. Metternich's triumph at Vienna in 1815-16 in establishing the old pre-revolutionary Europe as a model for post-Napoleonic Europe was always a ticking political time bomb. The Congress of Vienna in 1815–16 had merely capped the explosive well of economic changes, rising nationalism and revolutionary liberal ideas unleashed by the French Revolution and its wars. What was effectively a reactionary, conservative solution to Europe's problems was always going to explode – one day. Metternich's life's work was to delay that day for as long as possible and make his new world order safe for *recht, ordnung* and the divine right of kings.

He had his work cut out. Revolution was everywhere still in the air. The French Revolution could not be ignored or forgotten. Under cover of Napoleon's wars the Spanish Colonies had torn their independence from Spain under men like Bolívar, O'Higgins and San Martín. In Spain and northern Italy, attempts at rebellion were ruthlessly crushed by the authorities. Greece was fighting for her independence from the Ottoman

Turks and, even in the autocratic Russia of Nicholas I, the 'Decembrist Revolt' of 1825 had shaken the new Czar's grip on his subjects. There was plenty of work for the internal spies and police informers to do, in every country in Europe. Intelligence was the lifeblood of domestic harmony.

The mechanics of control varied in detail from state to state, but all shared some common characteristics. There was always a small but loyal 'secret service' force with special powers under the direct control of the monarch or chancellor; secondly, regional police forces; and lastly a widely spread network of intelligence agents and informers nation-wide, but concentrating particularly on likely hotbeds of potential disaffection such as intellectuals, liberals and nationalist movements. These national networks of control and repression relied almost entirely on accurate and timely internal intelligence for their success, supple-mented by tough legislation. For example, Metternich's Carlsbad Decrees of 1819 attempted to stamp out liberal and student opposition by a programme of press censorship and by banning the works of such inflammatory and dangerously radical authors as Rousseau and Locke. Just to be sure however, Metternich doubled his domestic spy force in the aftermath of the Decrees, pushing thousands of government agents into every area of Austro-German rule where trouble might brew. Metternich was proud to sit as a spider in the middle of his wide intelligence web. He boasted of it.

In this he was far surpassed by the Russian Czar. By 1830, Nicholas I had returned Russia to a state little different from the bad old days of Ivan and Peter. At his command a special 'Third Section' of the Imperial Chancellery was set up as the Czar's personal secret political police. Under its new bureaucratic leader, Count Benckendorff, Russia's new and improved secret police began to crack down hard on likely dis-senters. University professors, students, writers, musicians, even primary school teachers learned to recognise and fear the bone-headed dead hand of the Russian secret police that would denounce a man and send him to Siberia 'just to be sure'. In Richard Deacon's words, ' … he [Czar Nicholas I] created such resentment against himself and the office of the Czar that the ultimate fate of Czardom was sealed before 1850.'

By that year the cell door had finally closed on Russia and its people. Likely revolutionaries were being hunted down by the secret police; few dared to speak out openly or write critically of the things of which they disapproved; academics and intellectuals were forbidden to travel abroad; and the villages of Siberia were beginning to fill with well-educated exiles from St Petersburg and Moscow cursing their luck – and the Czar. Underground groups spoke openly of revolution. The 'hidden hand' of the Czarist secret police had, by its own clumsiness, sown the seeds of eventual disaster. Repression, if too oppressive, merely traps and contains the explosive forces of political change and reform.

Metternich's Austro-Hungarian Empire and the German states' new confederation were never as successful as their Russian colleagues in suppressing dissent. The liberal forces stirring across the continent exploded first in France in 1830 and then again in 1832 in Belgium. Metternich cared little for these Gallic excesses. His aim was to police and control Austria's own volatile mix of eleven different national groups, to rip out any disaffection at its source and to stop the mouths of nationalist and liberal reformers. To do this he created a police state, albeit one sometimes more akin to the Keystone Cops than to the KGB. With his Director General of Imperial Police Count Sedlnitzky, Metternich's prime task was to keep dissent under control and ensure stability, not to use repression for its own sake, as in Russia.

This policy worked. For thirty years, with all its absurdities (such as sending a mother the bill for the rope with which her revolutionary inclined son had been hanged), Metternich's network of control through a spider's web of spies and intelligence agents worked to ensure relative stability throughout the Austrian Empire. This was quite an achievement in the post-Napoleonic and Revolutionary era. He also set a trend in the politics of *Mitteleuropa* that would last a long time. For the cult of denunciation, spying and informing on your neighbours sown by Metternich's world has never really gone away from those parts of Europe in which it became rooted. Günter Grass's words: 'Spies are immortal, like the poets they spy on ... sometimes poets are spies, too', about the Stasi and German reunification, might just as well apply to the sometimes Orwellian world of Metternich's Austria over a century before. They would certainly have been recognised in Gestapo headquarters, Vichy France, occupied Belgium and Bismarck's Germany. Metternich's intelligence system would eventually become the model for European domestic control.

It could not last, however. In 1848, despite all the police spies, networks of informers and censors across the Continent, Europe exploded in the 'Year of Revolutions'. The heady brew of nationalism, economic change and liberal ideas could no longer be contained. Led by a mixture of students, middle-class tradesmen, factory workers and ethnic groups, demonstrations and riots brought governments crashing down. France, the German states, Austria, Italy, Hungary and Bohemia all faced violent rebellions and dealt with them by the usual mixture of concessions and military force. Only in Britain did the great events of 1848 fail to inspire mass uprising, although in E. P. Thompson's hopeful phrase, Great Britain 'trembled on the brink of Revolution'. However, in spite of this exaggerated view of events, it did not happen.

Mass politics were far more developed in Britain than elsewhere. The economic strains of the machine-smashing Luddites and the Chartist political reformers had been slowly absorbed into the body politic over the previous two decades. London had a well-disciplined and uniformed police force. Above all, through its network of police spies and informers, the British government had good intelligence on its own domestic hotheads; and, to keep the lid on the pot, a number of these popular leaders were effectively acting as government agents to ensure that things did not get too far out of hand. The hidden hand of intelligence once more surreptitiously helped skilful leaders to make the right decisions.

The Royal Family may have quietly left London, and the government may have assembled over 100,000 men to deal with any outbreaks of mass violence for the great public meeting on Kennington Green called for April 1848. Good intelligence – the very factor that had inspired such decisions – in the end made such precautions unnecessary. More spectators than protesters turned up for the great mass meeting on Kennington Green. It rained heavily and the sodden demonstrators trudged home, leaving their 'solemn petition' to be conveyed by London cabs to the Houses of Parliament. Reading the intelligence reports from the Commissioner of the Metropolitan Police, the former Prime Minister, the Duke of Wellington, is supposed to have observed with a thin smile, nodding: 'The English are a very quiet people, eh?'

No sooner has one wave hit the shore than another breaker looms behind it. The tide of events never stops and only six years after the upheavals of 1848, Europe found itself at war, but this time it was a shooting match, not a revolution. The Crimean War's causes are among the more obscure of any conflict. It was sparked by a minor squabble between the Russian Orthodox Church and the Ottoman Turks over the holy places in Jerusalem, but its real causes can be traced to a desire to prevent Russia from gaining a warm water port at the expense of the collapsing Ottoman Empire. The threat to Constantinople and thus India – never far from Whitehall's preoccupations – plus the universal British detestation of Nicholas I's 'icy Muscovite despotism' and the Czar's oppression of his own subjects fanned public hostility towards Russia.

The final spark was a Russian invasion and an attempt to attack the Turkish fleet. Popular indignation was aroused. The mob bellowed out their jingoistic and ignorant tabloid message from the music halls of London and as the crisis wore on Britain and France both sent forces to the Black Sea to cover the Russian bases in the Crimea. By 1854 both countries had drifted, like sleeping oarsman in a rowing boat, into the rapids of a war with Russia. Domestic intelligence now took second place to the strategic and military intelligence needed to fight a major war.

The first question, rather like the Falklands affair of 128 years later, was the anguished cry that went up in Whitehall: where the hell exactly *was* the Crimea? Help was at hand, however. It came in the unlikely form of a retired officer of the Bombay Engineer Corps, and a staunch member of the Foreign Bible Society, Major Thomas Best Jervis. Jervis is one of those earnest Victorian figures whose combination of moral rectitude, energy, devotion to a multitude of worthy causes and self-belief is both astonishing and wearisome to our later generation. His obsession, as befitted a Sapper officer, was cartography and maps. His retirement in 1836 at only 39 may well have been prompted by disappointment at not being appointed Surveyor General of India. In his retirement, Major Best Jervis bombarded – there is no other word for the amount of correspondence and the multitude of topics – the government with his ideas ranging from the moral dangers to young women acting as medical assistants at sea ('instead of more suitable elderly widows') to the use of perforated zinc for windows.

One of the bees in his bonnet was, unsurprisingly, maps and mapping. In 1846, he urged Whitehall to create a 'Mapping Department' and an 'official geographer-cartographer', implying in Christopher Andrew's dry phrase that 'he was the man to do it.' Whitehall politely declined. In 1854, Jervis's moment of glory arrived. Like many enthusiasts from medal collectors to railway modellers, Major Jervis's passion was as a collector. In his case, it was maps. On holiday in Belgium he found a complete official Russian set of maps of the Crimea in a Brussels shop and, in another drawer, the Austrian General Staff map coverage of Turkey.

'Cometh the hour, cometh the map!' Back home, Jervis offered his treasure to Whitehall, now baffled by the lack of map coverage of its chosen battle zone in the Crimea, and reduced to buying school atlases in the Strand. (The British commander-in-chief, Lord Raglan, who had been one of Wellington's aides at Waterloo, was heard to remark on his departure for war that, 'Sevastopol is as great a mystery to me as to Jason and his Argonauts.') Whitehall, in the person of the Duke of Newcastle, secretary of state for war, confirmed that they did indeed want Jervis's maps, but, 'as the Budget was marked out so categorically', he could not contemplate such an outlay. However, if Major Jervis would execute the maps at his own private cost, the government would be willing to purchase from him as many copies as they might feel it desirable to obtain. Not for the last time, Whitehall was pleading lack of resources as an excuse for refusing to do anything useful in the face of a genuine national requirement.

Jervis knew exactly what to do. Whitehall had offered him an open chequebook: and in such a good cause, too! He set up his own printing business and sold thousands of copies to soldiers desperate for maps, including Britain's ally, France. Napoleon III, no less, received him officially at the Tuileries and thanked him for his efforts on behalf of France, presenting the retired Sapper major with a gold snuffbox and wishing him good fortune back in England.

It was too much. Whitehall cracked and through gritted teeth recalled Jervis to duty, appointing him director of the War Office's Topographical and Statistical Department as a lieutenant colonel. The retired major's cup of joy was full as he set to work with all that formidable energy which characterised him. (One wonders quite what a Freudian analyst would have made of Major Jervis.) By 1856, his T & S Department had produced a number of excellent maps and, as a lucrative sideline, a range of popular prints of the war, which sold like hot cakes to a credulous public, hungry for news. More importantly, Jervis hammered away at his obsession: mapping the Empire and collecting intelligence.

In the spring of 1857, Jervis died, but his legacy remains. The T & S section survived (greatly expanded) to this day as Britain's Defence Intelligence Staff. Jervis's beautifully hand-drawn lithographed maps are now collectors' items and secret satellite photography has replaced triangulation and theodolites in the DIS mapping agency. But Jervis's ideas lived on, and it is not unreasonable, certainly on grounds of continuity, to claim that this extraordinary Victorian's T & S section was the very first branch of a British Army General Staff.

Thanks to Jervis, Whitehall may have begun to collect strategic intelligence; but for the soldiers on the ground in the Crimea it was still a very different story. The British Army of the Crimea was, in Correlli Barnett's telling phrase, 'Simply the Peninsular Army taken out of the cupboard and dusted down.' Such an ad-hoc approach applied to every staff branch of the Expeditionary Force. In desperation at the lack of real, hard intelligence, Raglan's Quartermaster General Freeth had actually reissued exact copies of General Murray's intelligence orders from the Peninsula, forty years before, including such howlers as, '[Exploring officers] and Assistant Quartermasters General ... are to pay for such goods and services as are rendered in *Spanish Reals*'!

The fact was, in the long peace, the British Army had completely forgotten how to collect intelligence. The Great Duke's legacy has much to answer for. Lord Raglan himself (no foppish fool, despite his portrayal as an elderly buffoon in books and films) railed at his lack of intelligence on the enemy. The truth is that Raglan was a calculating and surprisingly sophisticated commander, who recognised the deficiencies of his command, and set out to establish an effective intelligence network. He had seen Wellington's methods in the Peninsula and at Waterloo. Like his old master, he now set out to remedy Whitehall's ineptitude and parsimony and he decided to collect his own intelligence in-theatre.

On 3 August 1854, Raglan appointed an ex-British diplomat as his official interpreter and intelligence staff officer. Charles Cattley had been born of British parents in Russia and he had risen in the Diplomatic service to become the British Vice Consul at Kertch before war broke out. He spoke Russian, understood the locals around the Black Sea and wrote good, clear reports. As such he was a positive fount of information on the Crimea and its surrounding region.

He warned Raglan of the Russians' strength and dispositions and in August 1854, he also warned Raglan and his chief of staff, Airey, about the rigours of a bad Crimean winter, 'where, if a man touched metal with his bare hand, his skin would adhere to the metal'. An amused secretary of state's response from Whitehall was to send out by courier a copy of a tourist guidebook bought in the Strand, describing the Crimea as 'mild and fine'. Not only did the British begin to fight in the Crimea without the most basic topographical intelligence, maps, but also without accurate meteorological information. The bad Crimean winter of 1854–5 would reveal just how scandalous was Whitehall's incompetence. As British soldiers died like flies of cold, hunger and disease around the besieged naval base at Sevastopol, the War Office's privatised procurement system broke down in a muddle of bureaucracy and red tape. Worse still the civilianised commissary, or military supply system, failed completely in its essential task of delivering vital stores, ammunition, food and clothing to the troops in the trenches.

The lesson of the Crimea – that economy in war is usually false economy – was relearned at a dreadful price in lives and treasure. A little intelligence, in every sense, could have avoided much misery. Cattley did his best. Renamed (for security reasons) Mr Calvert, he took over almost exactly the same job as had his illustrious predecessor Colquhoun Grant, forty years before. By the spring of 1855 he had been officially promoted to become Raglan's head of intelligence and was coordinating a human intelligence network of Russian, Greek and Turkish spies, a port watch on Russian harbours, interrogation of enemy prisoners, plus translations of captured documents and open source reports. He did it all himself. To ram home the point about reinventing the wheel, under a General Order of June 1855 a 'Corps of Guides' on Wellington's Peninsula model was re-formed under Mr Calvert. For both Raglan and his chief of intelligence it was all too late, however. Literally 'sick unto death', Raglan gave up his command and died in June 1855, a broken old man. The truth was that he had done his best in intolerable circumstances and been failed by a complacent and pennypinching Whitehall, who had starved him and his soldiers of food, ammunition, medical supplies, clothing and intelligence. Two weeks later Charles Cattley, too, was dead of cholera.

Whitehall now belatedly recognised the vital importance of intelligence, swiftly dispatching a Foreign Office official, Mr Lauder, to act as head of intelligence and chief interpreter for Raglan's replacement, General Simpson, and to take the administrative burden off his shoulders. Lord Raglan could have done with such a cooperative and 'can-do' attitude from Whitehall the year before. But it was too late. Raglan was dead of cold, fatigue and disease along with thousands of his soldiers.

By September 1855 the end was in sight. Sevastopol fell to a joint Anglo-French assault and by early 1856 the Crimean War was over: a peace treaty was signed in Paris on 30 March 1856. The war left a powerful legacy, however. The impact of photography and unsupervised press reporting had brought information on the scandalous failures of a privatised military logistic supply system into every kitchen and breakfast room in Britain. This kind of open democratic press reporting was a two-edged weapon. Russian intelligence officers (who suffered none of the social-cultural inhibitions of the aristocratic Victorian British Officer Corps who felt that: 'the gathering of knowledge by clandestine means [is] repulsive to the feelings of an English Gentleman') took great pleasure in hoovering up reports in the British press to supplement their own disguised wanderings around the British and French front lines and camps. From all this information a gleeful Czar could say, 'We have no need of spies; we have the London *Times!*'

The intelligence and other blunders of the Crimea did however have two important legacies. The British resolved to reform their whole military system. A graceful Italianate staff college was built at Camberley to educate future senior commanders and staff officers in their rough and brutal trade. Secondly, under pressure from a scornful and baying opposition in Parliament, the British government fell, 'with such a whack you could hear their heads thump as they hit the ground', as Gladstone put it.

The Crimean War could have been prevented by good intelligence; it could have been brought to a swifter and less scandalous conclusion by good intelligence; and now failures that were at root intelligence failures had brought a British government crashing down. The hidden hand of intelligence has a long reach.

11

The American Civil War

If I can deceive my friends then I can be sure of deceiving the enemy...

MAJOR GENERAL 'STONEWALL' JACKSON, CONFEDERATE STATES ARMY

Just as Metternich had stamped his mark on the first half of the nineteenth century, so too were two other men to make their indelible marks on the last half. In their own way, both Otto von Bismarck and Abraham Lincoln and their use of intelligence shaped our present-day world. While the one built the Europe of his Prussian dreams, the other sacrificed everything in order to save the Union of the United States of America; and ultimately paid for his obsession with his life.

Trouble had been brewing in North America for a long time. Long after the Civil War was over General William Sherman, one of the Union's great wartime leaders admitted in his memoirs:

> That the Civil War ... was apprehended by the leading statesmen
> of the half century preceding its outbreak is a matter of notoriety.
> General Scott told me in 1850 that this country is on the verge of
> civil war ...

Even as the war in the Crimea drew to its close, tensions between the divided states that made up the Union had been rising towards an inexorable final clash between North and South. There were two real issues, both closely related. They were states' rights over property, and the South's distinct, separate culture. Slavery was the hallmark stamped deeply on both. Abraham Lincoln was merely the human catalyst for a struggle long in the making.

Elected as an accidental president in 1860, he was a compromise candidate and with Hitler, he shared the scorn of the political establishment and sophisticated metropolitan elite of the capital, who believed that this hick provincial lawyer from the sticks would be a mere cipher, biddable to their will. Like Hitler's backers they were grievously mistaken. Like Hitler, Abraham Lincoln was also a man of unshakeable resolve. Unlike Hitler, Lincoln believed he was called by some higher moral purpose: unlike Hitler, he won. But if ever there was a living exponent of 'the triumph of the will' it was Abraham Lincoln.

From the moment of his election Lincoln faced the prospect of the dissolution of the very Union of which he had just been made Head of State. Although his votes swept the board in the North, in the seven states of the deep South he won not a single electoral college vote. Democratic legitimacy, states' rights and fears of Federal interference in Southern property and culture all combined to make the Southern states reluctantly opt to secede and then to set up their own Confederation of Southern States. Compromise proved impossible. By spring 1861, the die was cast. Confederate demands to take over Federal garrisons in the south were rebuffed and the Confederate States of America finally opened fire on Fort Sumter in Charleston Harbor. This time the Republic was at war with itself.

It was Lincoln who determined the outcome, conduct and duration of the war. Spurning negotiations, he opted for war and mobilised three quarters of a million Northern volunteers to 'crush this rebellion against Federal authority'. Viewed from the North, 'crushing this rebellion' seemed but short work. The North had a population of thirty million; the South only eight million, and half of those were black slaves. The Northern industrial heartland produced more manufactured goods in just two of its states than in the whole of the Confederacy. The huge, sprawling South had less than 10,000 miles of the new-fangled railroad; the North had three times that and with the locomotive, rolling stock and arms factories to match. Confidently, the Union moved in to crush the rebels. As a first step they marched to secure the Manassas railway junction in July 1861. Outgeneralled, outfought and outflanked by the Confederate Army, panic-stricken Union volunteers fled the field of the First Battle of Bull Run. They were only beaten back in the race to their capital by a short head by the carriages containing the picnic parties of Washington socialites, come to 'view the fun'. It was not going to be a short war after all, and certainly no 'fun'. The next four years would see the grimmest and most bloody war in American history, as nearly three quarters of a million men died while American sought to slay American.

From the start, both sides realised the importance of intelligence. The long crisis of the 1850s had spawned numerous secret societies and conspiracies on both sides, the most notorious being John Brown's attempted seizure of the Union armoury at Harper's Ferry on 16

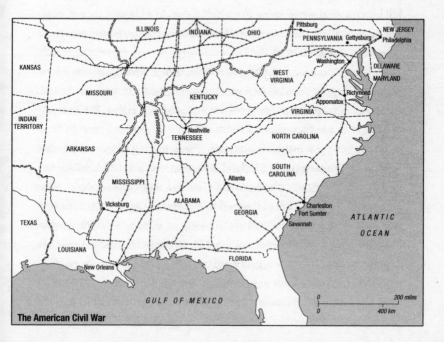

The American Civil War

October 1859. The proximity of the combatants, a very open press and the porous 'border' between North and South ensured that intelligence, intrigue and spies would play a notable role in the conflict, as they tend to do in most civil wars. Both sides therefore already had rudimentary intelligence and espionage underground networks in place from the beginning. Both sides learned the hard way the value of timely, accurate battlefield intelligence, although it was the increasingly professional and experienced Union Army that eventually began to develop a recognisable military intelligence system from 1863 onwards.

Part of the Union's problem was Lincoln's sheer lack of military experience. His short attachment to the army during the Black Hawk rising of 1832 compared ill with George Washington's years of campaigning with the British Army on the French Canadian frontier. Washington had known from the start about the value of good intelligence. Lincoln had to learn the hard way. His first choice as chief intelligence officer was a detective, Alan Pinkerton. Pinkerton had used his men to guard the president-elect and uncover an alleged assassination plot to kill him on a railway joining from Baltimore. In a classic piece of political cronyism, by mid 1861 President Lincoln had hired the con-man-cum-detective as chief of the US secret service, with powers to match.

It was an unusual, but understandable, choice. Pinkerton was a Scot, born in Glasgow in 1819. As a young man he had run with the radical Chartists, demanding political reform and workers' rights, like so many of his Clydeside successors. Eventually the authorities began to close in on the young Scottish revolutionary, and, fearing betrayal by police spies, Alan Pinkerton fled Scotland with a price on his head, sailing to a new life in America as a barrel-maker (he was originally apprenticed as a cooper) in 1842. There, steeped in conspiracy and with an understanding of the secret world and a liking of it, too, Alan Pinkerton, poacher turned gamekeeper, founded Pinkerton's Detective Agency to supply security and intelligence services to a consortium of railroad companies. It turned out to be a lucrative trade for the ex-barrel-maker from the Gorbals. His undercover work eventually brought him to the attention of the Republic's new president, who had first met Pinkerton when the young Lincoln had been working as an attorney for the Illinois Central Railroad line.

Pinkerton's style as an undercover intelligence operator was based on two clear policies: first, get access to the senior man with the money; second, never underestimate or underplay the threat. Indeed, wherever possible, inflate it. If his agency's badge was a never-sleeping eye, then its motto should have been, 'An insecure employer is a paying employer.' Pinkerton's appointment as chief of Lincoln's secret service was the finest contract he could have hoped for, and right at the heart of Washington tax dollars. Money, prestige and power now fell into Pinkerton's hands through his proximity to the President. All he had to do was prove that he really was catching Confederate spies and secondly, provide the Union with good solid intelligence. Like the detective he was, Pinkerton concentrated on spies and spying. It was what he knew.

From the start Pinkerton was confronted by a security panic in the North. By no means everyone agreed with President Lincoln's stand. The jails of Maryland in particular were overflowing with dissident Northerners or security suspects who had been identified by censorship or by daring to speak out openly. Treachery was in the air on all sides. Even the police chief and magistrates of Baltimore were flung into prison for sedition when they protested against the war. The ace detective set to work with a will.

Pinkerton's comfortable billet hunting down traitors from Washington took a nasty jolt when General McClellan, commander of the Union Army of the Potomac, insisted that E. J. Allen (as Pinkerton soon styled himself for cover) accompany his army into the field. Despite his protestations, the great detective found himself wrenched from his cosy Washington office. Alan Pinkerton was about to become a *military* intelligence officer. But then, as a professional, he should have realised that, in war, there is really no other kind.

Pinkerton had two basic tasks: intelligence and security. For the first, he was lucky enough to have a number of first-rate agents already planted deep in Confederate territory. For the second he was greatly helped by an easy capture of an openly Confederate Washington socialite, Mrs Rose Greenhow. Rose Greenhow's career was a classic example of the old poster of the beautiful blonde surrounded by garrulous officers, keen to impress: 'Keep mum! She's not dumb!' Mrs Greenhow had been deliberately left behind in Washington on secession in order to run a Confederate spy ring. Alerted at a Washington reception by loose-tongued Federal officers talking about McClellan's intended advance on Manassas, she fired off an urgent warning in a pre-arranged code to the Confederates at Richmond to alert them to the Union advance. After the Confederate victory of the First Battle of Bull Run in 1861, President Jefferson Davis openly wrote of 'his debt' to his Washington socialite spy. McClellan bitterly complained that she must have heard his orders before even he received them.

It was no great feat of detective work therefore for Pinkerton to put Rose Greenhow under observation. Surveillance was not easy. Her salon-cum-drawing-room was on the first floor. Pinkerton's resourceful team formed a human pyramid, enabling the agent to listen at the open window. This unusual approach to discreet clandestine surveillance brought the vital evidence of treachery, in the form of an incriminating conversation overheard in snatches by the uneasy top man of the acrobatic undercover agents. Rose Greenhow was arrested by Union police and carted off to jail to await trial as a Confederate spy. Pinkerton and his team then 'staked out' the Greenhow household for the rest of the day to identify and lift any of her contacts. Alas, the watchers in the bushes and those searching her house saw no one. Rose Greenhow's eight-year-old daughter admitted years later that she had climbed a tree by the front gate and was shouting to passers-by: 'Mother's been arrested!' Unsurprisingly, there were no more visitors to the Greenhow residence for the rest of the day.

Pinkerton's own spy rings in the South enjoyed as much success as his counter-espionage efforts in the North at first, thanks to a remarkable Federal undercover operator, Timothy Webster, a New York policeman recruited by Pinkerton before the war. Webster had been a key figure in the Pinkerton Agency's uncovering of the Baltimore Railway plot to assassinate President-elect Lincoln in 1860. (Whether he was a genuine guard or an agent provocateur remains a moot point; many Americans still regard the Great Baltimore Train plot as a put up job by Pinkerton to ingratiate himself with the new, and nervous, president.)

Webster set himself up in Baltimore once the war broke out, freely spending money in the local bars and shops and openly bad-mouthing the Union cause. Soon he was welcomed among the Confederate sympathisers, even having a fistfight with a fellow member of the secret Confederate 'Knights of Liberty' who claimed to have recognised Webster as a Yankee policeman. 'That's a damn' lie', shouted Webster and he launched himself at his accuser who produced a knife. Webster's response was to hold a cocked six-shooter to his accuser's head and invite him to apologise, or else. Faced with such a compelling argument the hapless accuser grudgingly admitted that he might just have made a mistake. Southern honour was satisfied and now, fully accepted by the Confederate underground, Webster began to run dangerous spying missions for them, bringing valuable 'intelligence' from the Union at some risk to himself. His stock rose.

In fact, Pinkerton's man was a classic double agent. The 'intelligence' from the North that Webster was passing over was 'chicken-feed'. In reality he was spying for the Union and reporting *against* the Confederacy. His exploits soon allowed him easy access, even to the Confederate War Minister's office. Judah P. Benjamin was, like most politicians, careless of security, leaving secret papers openly on his desk. A keen-eyed Webster was able to see much that should have been kept secret from prying eyes and reported accordingly. On one occasion, he sent Pinkerton a thirty-seven-page report of the Confederates' military dispositions and plans as well as a treasure trove of information on blockade-runners and commercial intelligence.

Such high visibility espionage is always a dangerous game. Eventually such a blatant rebel sympathiser and line-crosser was bound to come to grief. Sure enough, Federal officers arrested Webster on suspicion of being a *Confederate* spy and flung him into jail. A delighted Pinkerton arranged for Webster to 'escape' by leaping from a wagon while being driven to Fort McHenry for questioning. Such an exploit inevitably strengthened his cover story. His triumphant return to the South merely buttressed Webster's reputation as a 'good ol' boy' and his access to Confederate secrets was even easier. His prestige had never been higher, on both sides.

Fate now intervened to curtail the extraordinary career of the Union's ace spy. Back again in Richmond, this time accompanied by a Mrs Hattie Lawson (also a Pinkerton agent), Webster became seriously ill. His anxious Union spymasters became concerned when they heard no word from their best agent. What could have happened to him? Two Britons also working for Pinkerton volunteered to go to Richmond and try to find out why no reports had been received from Webster.

It was a fatal – and stupid – mistake. For both Scully and Lewis, the two Britons, had been working as interrogators for Pinkerton's counter-espionage and security service in the North. Their faces were well known to Confederate sympathisers as Federal security men. Their arrival at the Spotswood Hotel (where Mrs Lawson was nursing a debt-ridden Webster) was quickly noted and they were arrested by the Confederate police. Under questioning as spies the two Pinkerton men broke. The threat of the noose encouraged some desperate plea-bargaining. Scully implicated Webster as his Federal undercover contact at the hotel. The sick man was dragged from his bed and arraigned as a Yankee spy. He denied it indignantly. On trial for their lives, Scully and Lewis turned 'State's evidence' and pointed the finger at Webster as the real spy. They were just messengers. As British citizens, Pinkerton's two security men could not be hanged; but Webster could as a Yankee spy and a traitor to the Confederate cause. On 29 April 1862, Timothy Webster, the Union's ace spy went to the gallows betrayed by his master's inexcusable incompetence and haste for an answer from an agent trying to operate under deep cover.

With the loss of his top agent and McClellan's fall from favour, Alan Pinkerton's star also waned. His detective exploits had always owed as much to good public relations as to intelligence work. The regime of the warrior in the field was not his kind of environment and the strict demands of military reporting gave Pinkerton's talents for 'conning' his clients little chance to flourish. When McClellan fell from favour, so too did the Glasgow con-man.

He was replaced by Lafayette Baker, who had made his name as Sam Munson and whose exploits had paralleled Pinkerton's rise to power. Sam Munson had been a field agent and a successful spy, even being arrested and questioned by the Confederate leader Jefferson Davis. Baker was no con-man and he took a firm and more professional grip on the North's intelligence apparatus. As effectively chief of counter-intelligence for Secretary of State Seward and Secretary of War Stanton, Baker's powers were wide-ranging. His ruthlessness was legendary and for the rest of the war he led the National Detective Bureau, hunting down Confederate spies and plotters. With Pinkerton and Webster gone, and Baker now back in Washington, other Federal agents, such as the heroically bearded Phil Henson – he sported a six-foot beard – and the remarkable Miss Elizabeth van Lew, took up the underground war for the Union.

The Confederacy had its share of espionage triumphs, too. One of the most remarkable was a CSA officer using the cover name of Captain Coleman. Hiding among a contraband expedition in Tennessee he and Sam Davis, his courier, were arrested with a group of civilian smugglers. They were searched and Coleman's secret dispatches discovered on Davis. While the rest of the group sprawled on the ground under guard, Davis was questioned. 'Where's your chief?' demanded the Federal officer. 'You must have met him. You're carrying his papers. Where is he?' Stubbornly, Sam Davis refused to answer.

The questioning changed tack. Davis was reminded that he would swing if he didn't tell the truth. *He* was the spy unless he would tell the Union officers where his boss, the notorious spy, Coleman, was. Davis played dumb. Only ten yards away in a ferment of anxiety, Coleman was sitting and hearing the whole conversation. A single word, a mere nod, would have betrayed him and saved Sam Davis's life. Davis, however, never let on, stoutly denying everything. The infuriated Union soldiers hanged him as a spy and a relieved Coleman escaped to spy another day, thanks to his colleague's bravery. (When, much later, the

Union scout master, General Dodge, learned of this remarkable story of how his chief adversary had slipped through his fingers, he contributed to the memorial being erected in Nashville to Sam Davis, the Confederate hero.)

The South's most famous agent, however, was a woman called, appropriately enough, Belle Boyd. When civil war broke out in 1861, she was 18 and with her family a staunch supporter of the Confederacy. So much so that when an invading Yankee detail attempted to raise the Stars and Stripes over her Virginia home, she first remonstrated with the sergeant in charge and then, 'him not seein' any sense', she drew a pistol and shot him. This vehement expression of Belle's loyalties seems to have done her no harm; in the words of one writer: 'martial law drew a protective arm of "justifiable homicide" over a Virginia belle not yet 18, whose trigger finger had so convincingly reached the age of consent.'

From then on, this intrepid southern belle ran what was effectively a one-woman spy service for the Virginia Confederacy, on 23 May 1862 actually dashing onto the battlefield of Front Royal under a hail of fire to warn General 'Stonewall' Jackson that three undetected Union columns were about to fall on his outnumbered force.

Eventually, like most amateurs, Belle's enthusiasm overcame her judgement and she handed a secret message destined for the Confederacy to a Union soldier who just happened to be wearing a grey uniform at the time, begging him to deliver it safely to his superiors. The soldier did just that and handed the incriminating letter direct to his officers in Washington. Agent Cridge of the Federal security service ('a mean, grizzled, repulsive creature' according to Miss Boyd) was immune to Belle Boyd's crinolined charm and bore her off to a Washington prison, where Pinkerton himself interrogated her. However, this redoubtable young woman managed to pull the wool over the eyes of Lincoln's 'ace detective' and bluffed her way out of jail, only to be caught some months later by Lafayette Baker. This time she was held.

Belle Boyd's story, unlike poor Sam Davis's, has a happier ending. After her release in 1864 she met a US naval officer, Sam Hardinge, who apparently took one look at this redoubtable young woman and resigned his commission to make the rebel belle Mrs Hardinge. Alas, even then there was no storybook ending. The Union authorities threw Belle's new Yankee husband into prison for his romantic impulse, where sadly he died. The beautiful Belle, ace rebel spy, was forced to dine out on her exploits ever afterwards.

As with so many wars, it is the stories of espionage exploits that tend to dominate the secret history of intelligence. Men like Lafayette Baker, who as part of his Sam Munson legend, spied on the Confederacy by roaming around as an itinerant photographer – although he never had any plates in his camera – and the Union's Pauline Cushman, who narrowly evaded execution when General Rosecrans' advancing vanguard forced her Confederate firing squad to run for their lives, excite our imagination. But in truth, these heroic exploits on the fringe of a bitter civil war are mere sideshows.

A much more bitter underground intelligence was being waged in Liverpool, of all places. The Confederate's chief European intelligence agent, Jim Bulloch, used the English Mersey harbour as his base from which to wage economic warfare on behalf of the CSA's naval chief, Stephen Mallory. His task was straightforward: to buy vessels capable of beating the Union Navy's blockade of Confederate ports. This savage economic and naval war was as important to the South's survival as any of the battles taking place along the rivers in the west or the stand off across the Potomac. The Yankee blockade could starve the South of raw materials within a year. To survive, Bulloch had to buy arms and vital stores in Europe, then get them safely across the Atlantic to Charleston or Savannah. As an ex-naval officer, Bulloch was a good choice. He and his army counterpart Captain Huse bought up guns, ships and ammunition all over Europe, dodging the attentions of British police, Austrian informers and Union agents desperately trying to stop the Confederate's arms supply at source.

The chief architect for the Union in this commercial struggle was the US ambassador to Belgium, the rich and elegant Henry S. Sanford. From his Brussels office, Sanford orchestrated what amounted to a Union

'Ministry of Economic Warfare' based in Europe and devoted to identifying arms supplies, clothing and warlike stores in factories, buying them up before the Confederates wherever possible by the simple expedient of offering to pay more. He bribed clerks, managers and journalists, especially in France. Stocks of key raw materials, such as saltpetre, used for gunpowder, were bought at source to prevent Bulloch's rebel purchasing agents laying hands on them. By 1862, a genuine economic war between Union and Confederate undercover agents was raging across Europe. This economic and commercial struggle on neutral territory inevitably turned into a propaganda war as well. Parisian journalists were bribed to write stories that supported the Northern cause and 'knocked' the Confederacy. Sanford even tried to buy up one Paris newspaper, and when that was refused by Washington, offered to set up a news bureau in Europe to pump out Union propaganda. Not to be outdone, the Confederacy sent their own news agent called Henry Hotze to set up a pro-Southern newspaper in London, called *The Index*.

The key to this economic and propaganda warfare was always delivery. The European sinews of war had to cross the Atlantic to get to a Confederate harbour. With over £2,000,000 worth of goods sitting on the dockside in Europe, the weakest link in the chain was always ships to deliver the cargoes to the Confederacy. Ambassador Sanford's chief agent, a detective called Pollakey, tried to bribe ships' crews, buy up their cargoes, even to induce sailors to mutiny on behalf of the Union in exchange for Yankee gold. It was a never-ending game of cat and mouse between North and South, mainly waged around Liverpool and Britain's west coast. In its way, it was as intense an economic battle as any of the U-boat campaigns of the twentieth century, and for the South, just as vital for national survival. In the 'European front' of a secret war by any means possible, anything went.

At one point, Sanford even tried to enlist Garibaldi, the unifier of Italy, for the Union, both as a European figurehead for the cause and as a general in the Union Army. As a morale-boost and as a symbol it could have been an inspired blow in the Union's propaganda war. Unfortunately great men are not so easy to control. Italy's proud 'man of destiny' insisted on being made commander-in-chief of *all* the Union forces and on the immediate freeing of all slaves as preconditions to helping the Yankee cause. When Ambassador Sanford explained that such powers were *ultra vires* for a mere minister to Belgium (only the President of the US had the legal authority) Garibaldi haughtily declined the Union's offer.

As the Southern commerce raiders, built at British yards, and stuffed full of British goods, slipped out of British ports to harry Northern shipping, the Union's patience ran out. In August 1863, with the CSS *Alabama* running wild at sea and two of the new ironclad battleships on the stocks for the Southern Navy at what was to become the Cammell-Laird shipyard, the Union minister-ambassador in London, Charles Adams, wrote to Lord John Russell threatening war.

The British had already had enough, however. With secret agents like Pollakey, Dudley, Bulloch and literally hundreds of spies and informers causing mayhem along Britain's western seaboard and pressure from the City of London's golden square mile to back the winner, it was time to call a halt. Anyway, the news of Gettysburg the previous month had clearly shown which way the wind was blowing, however many Confederate 'Stars and Bars' flags were flying over Liverpool. The British government impounded the two ironclads and gradually, in a reflection of events 3,000 miles away across the Atlantic, the South's underground propaganda and commercial war in Europe withered and died.

As the American Civil War drew to its climactic denouement, an observable trend, common to all protracted wars, began to take root. The intelligence efforts on both sides became more professional and more ordered. The Union began to set up a proper Bureau of Military Intelligence and the South embarked on a campaign of sabotage masterminded by an undercover operations command. Of the two, the North's efforts bore more fruit. The South's, however, were more spectacular and carry overtones of some of today's terrorist attacks. By summer 1864, running short of supplies, beaten on several battlefields and with time running out, the Confederate leadership was desperate. They turned to a desperate remedy to split the Union and to weaken the North's resolve: terror attacks well away from the battlefront and a political campaign to exploit the war-weariness and unrest in the North.

They were not the first. In March 1864, the Union had itself launched an abortive behind-the-lines undercover mission against Richmond in an attempt to 'decapitate' the Confederacy and promote rapid regime change by assassinating President Davis. Colonel Ulric Dahlgren's mission failed and he was killed by a Confederate ambush. But when a wave of sabotage and bank raids spread in cities along the Canadian border from Chicago to Vermont, it was obvious that Confederate irregulars in Canada were launching well-coordinated attacks from neutral soil. Attempts were even made to disrupt the 1864 presidential election. The whole campaign culminated in a fire-bombing terror assault on New York on 25 November 1864 in order to, in Confederate Colonel Robert Martin's words, 'give the people a scare, if nothing else', and in an echo of the Union's scorched earth policy in the south, 'let the government at Washington know that burning houses in the south might find a counterpart in the north …'.

In all, the Southern special operations team lit twenty-two fires that night in New York City. However, despite the panic at the time, these Confederate behind-the-lines special operations had little real impact on the North's ability to fight (or on the outcome of the war) merely tying down about 50,000 Union lines-of-communications troops as guards and security details in the final year of fighting.

The North's contribution to intelligence was more profound, if less dramatic. By 1863, the Union Army of the Potomac was disgruntled, badly organised and licking its wounds after the debacle of Fredericksburg. Its new commander, General Joseph E. Hooker, was if nothing else an organiser. One of his first moves was to set up a proper headquarters staff, and 'set the paperwork straight'. In the words of his chief of staff, Daniel Butterfield, 'we're almost as ignorant of the enemy as if they'd bin in China …'. Under the army's provost marshal, a new 'secret service' intelligence and security organisation was formed. It was to revolutionise the Union Army's battle-winning potential and lead to Lee's defeat at Gettysburg later that year. The North's Bureau of Military

Information (BMI) was nothing less than the first real military intelligence staff. Jomini would have been delighted. At last one of his theories – an ordered 'General Staff' approach to the organisation of war – was being put into practice. Halleck, the Union's commander-in-chief may have had a hand in these innovations. A dedicated student of Jomini's works (he even read his books while in the field) he believed that organisation and method were the keys to success in war. He was nearly right.

The chief of this new staff branch was a New York lawyer, now in uniform, Colonel George Sharpe. Sharpe was only too well aware of the importance of good intelligence. He had watched professionals like the Confederate General 'Stonewall' Jackson run rings around the Union Army in the earlier days of the war, especially in the Shenandoah Valley in 1862. He knew that Jackson had possessed the most basic of all intelligence's secret weapons: good maps and guides. He put together a completely new kind of organisation that drew together all the elements of an intelligence agency. While his boss, the white-haired 'preacher figure' of Provost Marshal Patrick rounded up all the spies and deserters he could lay his hands on – and there were many – and cracked down hard on the Union's security (which was appalling), Sharpe concentrated on the intelligence staff work. His organisation was almost an echo of Wellington's in the Peninsula, half a century before. The BMI contained a 'scouting' wing of nearly 200 roving spies and scouts, a captured document office, telegraph interceptors, codebreakers, prisoner of war interrogators and even, for the first time in a major war, an aerial reconnaissance cell.

The Union had used balloons from the start. A Mr Thaddeus Lowe had demonstrated in 1861, that at 1,000 feet, a man in a balloon could see deep into rebel territory. Unfortunately, this first balloon could only use Washington's town gas supply, which restricted its mobility: it had to be near the town gasometer. The idea caught on, however, and by 1862–3, balloon intelligence was an important factor at the Battle of Fair Oaks, with Lowe's balloons providing regular accurate intelligence reports to the Union commanders on the Confederates' dispositions, even forcing them to adopt early camouflage measures.

Lowe even invented the aircraft carrier. He converted a coal barge to tow a balloon aloft. His great ballooning rival, John la Mountain, went one better: he used a converted tug to launch free hydrogen-fuelled balloons over the rebel lines. The Prussian General Staff observers of 'this amateur war' were so impressed with these technical developments that they sent an observer out to America to report on the military potential of balloons. His name was Count Ferdinand von Zeppelin.

Sharpe's BMI took the raw information from all its sources, from Confederate open-source newspapers to decoded signals intelligence from the telegraph, and presented Hooker with probably the best and most accurate order of battle intelligence of the war. There is, however, an unfortunate truth that is often overlooked, that intelligence in itself is not a self-sustaining art form. Intelligence exists only to inform others and is a service for decision makers. It is how the good intelligence is used that is the key. Intelligence by itself cannot win battles.

For example, one of the all-time classics of this universal truth about intelligence comes from the American Civil War. Just before the bloody clash at Antietam in September 1862, two Union soldiers discovered an envelope containing cigars. The cigars were wrapped in a secret copy of Robert E. Lee's Special Order No. 191: his detailed orders for the invasion of Maryland. McClellan, the Union commander, failed to use this priceless intelligence coup, and in a disastrous bumbling battle, was defeated by the weaker Confederate force, even though he had a complete copy of their battle plan in his hand. Timely, accurate intelligence exists for no other purpose than to enable decision makers to do the right thing.

In this case, General Hooker consistently failed to make good use of the regular intelligence summaries being handed to him on a plate by the diligent Colonel Sharpe. At Chancellorsville, he ignored the timely and accurate warnings of his intelligence staff. Sharpe's BMI persisted in its efforts, even alerting Hooker to the fact that Lee was on the march into the North as early as 27 May 1863, long before Gettysburg. Hooker dithered.

His opponent Robert E. Lee did not. As high summer unfolded he pushed swiftly on into Pennsylvania pursued by the surprised Army of the Potomac, now led by General George Meade. Between 1 and 3 July 1863 the two armies clashed at Gettysburg. What many people forget is the decisive contribution of intelligence to the outcome of this, the decisive battle of the Civil War. It was lack of intelligence that sucked Lee into the battle: his dashing cavalry commander Jeb Stuart let him down badly. Ordered to push across the Blue Ridge Mountains and locate any enemy forces on Lee's flank, instead Stuart took the Confederate cavalry off on a dashing, but pointless, *chevauchée* deep into Union territory, leaving Lee completely blind at a critical moment. Abandoned by his cavalry eyes and lacking vital information on the presence of the enemy, the Confederate commander pushed a whole corps across the mountains into the small town of Gettysburg to find out what was going on, just as Meade's leading Union units blundered into the town from the other side. In a rolling encounter battle, Lee's soldiers battered themselves to death against a desperate Union defence, until after three days of savage fighting both sides felt themselves on the brink of exhaustion.

It was now that intelligence tipped the balance between victory and defeat. George Meade was made of sterner stuff than his timid or pedestrian predecessors. He made the historic decision to keep the Army of the Potomac in its defensive positions overlooking Gettysburg, and not to withdraw on the third day of the battle, on the strength of accurate intelligence provided by Sharpe on 3 July of the state of Lee's shattered army. The BMI changed history. The Union Army stood their ground, leaving the Army of Northern Virginia short of ammunition and, having lost nearly a third of its men, to limp back to the South and final defeat.

Meade's successor, Grant, took the Union's intelligence process even further. From his experience in the western theatre of operations, Grant well understood the importance of intelligence. The one time store owner and unsuccessful farmer may have failed at every occupation he had tried before the war but he was a military commander of the highest order and knew exactly what a good intelligence service could do for a commanding general. He seized the Army of the

Potomac by the scruff of the neck, strengthened the role of the BMI, promoted Sharpe to brigadier-general and reinforced its operations. While in the west, Grant had become aware of the value of unconventional operations as well. A redoubtable ex-slave called Harriet Tubman had organised an intelligence service consisting of former slaves to infiltrate the Confederate lines. Once mingling freely in the South, Tubman's ring had collected intelligence and even located Confederate mines blocking the river routes, leaving one Southern officer to remark ruefully: 'The enemy seems ... to have been well guided by persons thoroughly acquainted with the river and country ...'.

Grant determined that his new command and the BMI would pursue all possible intelligence operations. The Union was helped enormously by his ability to take advantage of a long running spy ring, a remarkable penetration operation running deep inside Richmond itself. Try as they might, the Confederate's security police could never break what turned out to be the most effective espionage network of the whole Civil War. Its leader was an eccentric spinster called Elizabeth van Lew. Colonel Sharpe himself paid tribute to this unlikely superspy's success: 'The greater portion (of our intelligence) from Richmond in its collection ... and its transmission, we owed to the intelligence and devotion of Miss van Lew.'

Her neighbours in Richmond regarded Miss van Lew as eccentric at best and unhinged at worst. 'Crazy Bett' was an open and vociferous abolitionist and had long since freed her own black slaves. In this she was not alone in the South, but it was always an expensive gesture. Slaves cost money. From the start, she openly refused on principle to support the South's stand. Where other women sewed and knitted 'for the boys in the Army', Elizabeth van Lew poured scorn on the cause and confined her good works to visiting the sick and wounded, including the Federal prisoners of war. Armed with prison visiting permits signed by General Winder, the CSA chief of security, or even on one occasion Confederate Secretary of War Benjamin himself, Crazy Bett was able to collect a vast amount of raw information on everything the Union prisoners of war had seen behind Confederate lines. Perhaps more remarkably, she was able to fuse this information with her own observations around Richmond, and the indiscretions of Confederate officers, and send it back to the North by a complicated series of Negro couriers 'runnin' errands for Miss Bett'. These enciphered messages hidden in dummy eggs and servants' frocks were never intercepted.

This complicated system of cut outs in her courier system enabled Miss van Lew to keep up a steady flow of high-grade intelligence for most of the war. Her greatest coup was to get one of her Negress helpers, Mary Bowser, into the Confederate White House as a waitress at President Davis's own table, where every indiscretion or revelation was promptly relayed back to Miss Bett. This remarkable woman even hid Union fugitives on the run in a secret room concealed behind a chest of drawers in her attic. By 1864, Elizabeth van Lew's house had become the nerve centre of the biggest spy ring in the South, with sub-agents in the Confederate Army and Navy headquarters, food and ammunition suppliers, the Confederate White House and links with a railway network to record and report all train movements. It was a formidable achievement and an extremely risky one at that.

Despite numerous scares and close shaves, Elizabeth van Lew survived the Civil War. However, her help for the North meant that she spent the rest of her days as a social pariah. Hated and ostracised by her Richmond neighbours, she was abandoned by the North. An ungrateful Congress refused to vote her any money for her efforts and, after Grant's death, she passed her last years in poverty and alone; a sad end to a genuine master spy who ran an extraordinarily successful undercover operation.

The final shot of the American Civil War may also have been an undercover operation, perhaps even the last shot in the locker of the Confederate secret service. We will probably never know the truth now, but when John Wilkes Booth fired the fatal shot into President Lincoln's head at Ford's Theatre, it had all the hallmarks of a conspiracy. There is a sizable body of circumstantial evidence to indicate that Booth was far from a 'lone gunman, acting alone'. President Lincoln's murder may well have been a belated retaliation for the abortive Union Dahlgren raid (see page 228) and its botched assassination attempt on President Davis. Lafayette Baker always claimed the Wilkes murder was a Confederate plot. Whatever the truth behind the shot, it ended the most explosive episode in America's history, as violently as it had begun. There is a dreadful irony behind the murder of the architect of the bloodiest struggle in American history. Despite his clear wish for magnanimity in victory, Lincoln's war ended up by finally killing him, too.

America's Civil War left behind a bitter legacy that still casts a shadow over the South today. It also left a legacy, unheeded at the time, both in European war ministries and staff colleges, who tended to regard the American War as some kind of curious military aberration, and failed to learn its many lessons. This failure to learn its lessons was not just confined to the Europeans. In the US itself, although Grant and Sharpe's Bureau of Military Information had demonstrated just how a good intelligence organisation can mould events and change history, it was not wanted once the fighting was over. Like Washington's achievements of the Revolutionary War and Wellington's intelligence staff in the Peninsula, America's first intelligence staff was promptly forgotten, even by its creators. It was a costly mistake.

One day the United States of America would have to reinvent a decent intelligence organisation all over again.

12

The Great Architect

I am particularly proud to have a spy in
all the important civil and military services
of a country, without ever having one
discovered ...

WILHELM STIEBER

Lincoln's co-architect in shaping the second half of the nineteenth
century was the Prussian Chancellor, Otto von Bismarck. In the same
year that the American Civil War burst into flame, William I succeeded
his half-mad brother as the 'All Highest', the King of Prussia. In 1861,
he appointed Helmuth von Moltke as chief of the General Staff and
Otto von Bismarck as Minister President, effectively prime minister. It
was a fateful choice and one that was to prove a formidable combination
with far-reaching consequences, not just for the people of Prussia, but
also for the whole world. For Otto von Bismarck had a dream: the
creation of Germany as a single unified state under Prussian leadership. His dream was to come true. One day it would father a nightmare
of dreadful proportions.

To achieve his goals, Bismarck had a very clear idea of what kind
of Germany he wanted and a clear road map of how to get there. Like
his fellow German Nietzsche, Bismarck worshipped strength, and
strength alone. But Bismarck was no abstract philosopher. For him the

ideas of the *übermensch* were very real. He saw the world in concrete terms: 'The importance of a state is measured by the number of soldiers it can put into the field.' His Germany was going to be strong. To do this would require a degree of ruthlessness not seen in Europe affairs since Napoleon's day, where any policy of deceit or force would be justified without reference to morality provided it was in the national interest. Bismarck called it 'realpolitik'.

His fellow appointee, Helmuth von Moltke, the general destined to turn Bismarck's goals into reality, had no problems with either Bismarck's aspirations or his methods of execution. The only book that had ever really influenced him was Clausewitz's *On War*. Moltke's doctrine for Prussia mirrored von Bismarck's: military and diplomatic strength, and a close relationship between war and politics. This combination of von Clausewitz and Nietzsche, strategic thinker and philosopher, plus von Moltke and Bismarck, soldier and politician, was to prove a deadly quartet of German thought and action.

The two Prussians did, however, differ in one important area: intelligence. For von Moltke (a man so dour that it was alleged he was only seen to smile twice: once on hearing that a certain Polish fortress was impregnable; the second time on learning that his mother-in-law had just died), intelligence was a regulated General Staff activity, carried out by proper Prussian staff officers in a disciplined and orderly manner. Unfortunately, intelligence is rarely like that, as Bismarck had long recognised. For Bismarck had his own intelligence system and one with a talented and efficient spymaster at its heart. Moreover, he was an intelligence officer of considerable cunning, intelligence and had the priceless advantage of having no scruples whatsoever.

Born in Saxony in 1818, Wilhelm Stieber was destined by his father to go into the Church. Theology bored him, however, and in 1841 he graduated in law. His father promptly disowned him and at 23 the young man set up a criminal practice in Berlin, where he soon gained a reputation as a defender of radical political activists and other anti-government clients. Stieber encouraged them to believe he shared their political views. Soon he became the 'attorney of choice' for the disaffected and radicals, of whom Berlin had many in the years before the revolutions of 1848. Stieber was hard working, cheap, sympathised with their cause, and had an unusually good track record of acquittals. His clients would have been horrified to learn the truth: Stieber was, in fact, acting as a police spy, tasked with identifying political agitators and revolutionaries on behalf of the government. His acquittal rate was boosted by his inside knowledge of the prosecution's case as he was also editor of the Berlin police journal and a confidante of the Berlin Police.

Stieber was singularly unscrupulous. In 1845, he secretly denounced his wife's uncle, Schoffel, to the Berlin police. What makes this particular betrayal so despicable is that it was Stieber himself who had talked the man into embracing the idea of a socialist revolution in the first place. Once the arrest had been made, it was Stieber who denounced it most passionately and as a result was elected to the Underground Revolutionary Council. Somewhere in the years 1846 to 1848, Stieber took the final decision that would mould his life. Leadership of the revolution guaranteed little. Leadership of the forces of law and order on the other hand, guaranteed money, a career and promotion. Stieber opted for the State, not the revolution. He became a full time police undercover agent.

As the ferment boiled in the years before the explosion of 1848, Stieber was never busier, the classic psychological traitor: a man with no morals and a foot in both camps. At heart, however, Stieber, like von Moltke and Bismarck, believed in power, strength and order. His moment came as the rioting revolutionaries tore through Berlin in 1848. King Frederick William IV was mobbed and trapped in his coach in Dorotheen Strasse, by hostile protesters. One of the 'dangerous radicals' stepped from the crowd and bundled the terrified king into a doorway. The crowd saw one of their leaders apparently manhandling the king himself and shouting at the royal ear. In fact, Stieber was whispering, 'It's all right, Your Majesty. You are under the protection of Stieber, and Stieber's men. No harm will come to you.' He then allowed the shaken King of Prussia to drive on. Stieber's career was assured. Two years later the grateful monarch made Stieber *Polizeirath*, commissioner of police for Berlin, as a reward. (Much later it transpired that Stieber himself may have engineered this particular riot, and actually paid police informants to 'threaten' the king, with a view to getting some kind of preferment from the half-mad monarch.)

By 1852, Stieber was in Paris and London, this time on Russian business, travelling under the cover name of Schmidt and claiming to be the editor of a radical journal dedicated to reprinting the new theories of socialism being expounded by a dangerous revolutionary called Karl Marx. The radical German exiles were completely fooled by the earnest lawyer from Saxony and cooperated with their newfound friend. On his return to Berlin, Stieber promptly filed an arrest list identifying all the known radical revolutionaries whose identities he had learned from the exiles abroad. To ram home the point, he published an open attack on the 'Marxist Threat', including a list of all identified 'suspects'. After the king, Stieber was now one of the most powerful men in the land. He was also one of the least liked or trusted.

In 1855, Prussia rewarded him with the sack. King Frederick William's addled wits finally failed him completely and the half-demented monarch was put 'into care'. His successor as regent was his brother who clearly believed that his predecessor's appointment of a man like Stieber as *Polizeirath* was a manifold and clear proof that he had gone mad. Stieber was dismissed.

Thirteen years of arrogance and ruthlessness now came home to roost. Stieber's enemies – and they were many – closed in for the kill, remembering the midnight knock, the arbitrary arrests and brutal police interrogations, and brought him to trial indicted for exceeding his authority. Stieber's defence was effectively to throw down the gauntlet to his accusers. Everything he had done, he claimed, had been done on the orders of the king or his governing council. He had only acted as directed by them. *Befehl ist Befehl* – orders are orders – he claimed. To challenge his defence would have meant condemning Prussia's king or worse, dragging him out of his asylum as a witness for the prosecution in open court. This was not a prospect to which the court looked forward to with any great relish. The case collapsed.

However, Stieber's career as a Berlin lawyer was over. He was ordered by King William I to get out of Berlin while he still could, and to stay out. Stieber now an exile himself fled to Russia. There he had friends. He had hushed up a scandal involving a senior Russian diplomat while *Polizeirath* in Berlin. St Petersburg owed him a favour he insisted.

In St Petersburg Stieber was reluctantly put in charge of reorganising the Russian Foreign Office's counter-intelligence department, an unusual accolade for a foreign national. Stieber continued his old trade, spying for Germany and at the same time completely reorganising the Russians' overseas secret service. The dossiers of his time in London and Paris – which he had thoughtfully remembered to bring with him – undoubtedly helped to convince any doubters of his loyalty to the anti-communist and anti-revolutionary cause. His arrival in Russia was also timely, as Czar Alexander II had just come to terms with the idea that the growing band of revolutionaries and agitators were really out to kill him and, not surprisingly, security and security intelligence were high on Russia's list of priorities. Assassination plots tend to concentrate powerful men's minds. The 'Third Section' of the Czarist Chancellery was reinstituted and the Department of the Protection of the State took over the responsibility for the secret police or Ochrana. Stieber himself was, as far as we know, given little opportunity to access this new internal *apparat*. However, his contribution to penetrating the *external* network of Russian exiles and disaffected émigrés abroad was an important step forward in establishing what we nowadays think of as Moscow Centre's spy rings.

He set out to suborn, blackmail, threaten or buy the services of the Russian émigrés, especially those in London and Paris, and to force them to spy on their colleagues and, when necessary, act as agent provocateurs for the Russian secret service. Stieber's boss saw where this secret nonsense might all lead to one day, uncannily prophesying the later misgivings of CIA Agent James Jesus Angleton, who memorably described counter-intelligence as a 'wilderness of mirrors'. Russia's ambassador in London, Count Schuvaloff, wrote of Stieber's methods:

> There is no end to this game of spies ... you set the criminal exiles
> to spy on the Radicals, and then, to be quite sure, you need to find
> spies to watch the criminals - and it has even happened that a
> criminal is spying on the very Radical who has been selected by
> one of my attachés to spy on the criminal ... the fact that this
> happens at all is surely an indication of how such madness can
> spread.

If Wilhelm Stieber had read this he would surely have nodded in recognition of his methods: wheels within wheels. The Russian secret service owes him a big debt to this day.

By 1863 he was back. A newspaper proprietor had introduced Stieber to Bismarck and Stieber had warned the Prussian minister of a plot to kill him. The aristocratic Bismarck may well have despised the *parvenu* Saxon lawyer but Bismarck's task was to recognise talent and to use talent, not make social judgements. Stieber, hungry for office, power and recognition, was begging to be used by a man like Bismarck. Thus began one of the secret powerhouses of the nineteenth century as Stieber became Bismarck's 'sleuth-hound' for the next twenty years. The 'Prince of spies' and the 'Chief to 40,000 spies' (some of the nicknames given to Stieber by admirers and enemies alike) began to carve out a spying career that would, to a very great degree, set the agenda for modern espionage, if not a complete intelligence service. Stieber provided both for his Prussian masters.

Stieber's methods were by and large despicable by the standards of his day, and even by our more amoral age's mores, he comes across as a deeply unpleasant, two-faced and corrupting creature. The Prussian nobility loathed him with a deep and passionate dislike. Bismarck tolerated and protected the chief of his 'Central Intelligence Bureau' because Stieber got results. Stieber achieved these results through three main avenues, none of them new, but never really before combined. The heart of his empire was a massive network of underground informants ('the 40,000 spies') from which reports and dossiers flowed on the internal situation in Prussia. Secondly, he conducted extremely detailed reconnaissance and spying missions (which he, unusually for a spy-master, undertook himself) on Bismarck's diplomatic 'targets'. Last but not least, he analysed and combined all this material into comprehensive secret all-source intelligence reports for Bismarck and von Moltke. It was a tour de force and Prussia's – and Bismarck's – success owes as much to Stieber's clear intelligence reports as to any great diplomatic 'genius' on the part of the Iron Chancellor.

Stieber took his orders direct from Bismarck. For his master's first great coup, the invasion of Schlezwig-Holstein in 1864, he provided basic target briefs from his agents in 'Danish-occupied north Germany'. The Prussian Army easily brushed aside the tiny Danish garrisons to seize their new territories. Defeated, Denmark was treated surprisingly gently by Bismarck. His experiment in realpolitik had worked. He now turned his 'massive shaggy head' towards the only possible rival for leadership of a German-speaking hegemony: Austria. But first he needed intelligence on Prussia's next victim. For that he turned to Stieber.

Stieber's solution was, to say the least, hands on. The chief of Prussia's secret police dressed up as an itinerant pedlar and roamed Austria and Bohemia in a horse and cart. During much of the summer of 1865, Stieber became a familiar sight clip-clopping along the dusty roads of Bohemia, stopping at towns and villages, talking to the locals and always happy to sell his goods to any Austrian units on manouevres or exercise. Stieber's wares were well chosen and popular. For the villagers he sold religious trinkets and pictures of saints; to the soldiers, especially the rich young Austrian officers, he peddled a more interesting line in pornographic pictures. By the time he returned to Berlin, he was able to draw up a highly detailed report on Bismarck and von Moltke's planned invasion routes towards Vienna. Roads, bridges, defensive positions, weapons, morale, discipline, food, ammunition and tactics were all minutely analysed for strengths and weaknesses. On seeing the report even von Moltke was startled at the wealth of detail and the precision of the intelligence. In particular, Stieber's minutely accurate military maps made planning the invasion a straightforward series of pre-planned moves for the General Staff.

The stage was now set. France was neutralised by a typically Stieberesque ploy. One of his Polish agents was ordered to fire at the Russian Czar as he processed through Paris with Napoleon III, but to ensure that he missed. The 'assassin' was duly arrested and put on trial. A sympathetic French jury – almost certainly bribed by Stieber's agents – then acquitted the young man, much to Russian fury. Relations cooled. With Russia and France neutralised, and Britain indifferent, Bismarck was free to provoke his war with Austria.

It was all over in seven weeks. Using the new railways and the telegraph to mobilise the Prussian legions and to envelop the Austrians, von Moltke's armies closed in along Stieber's well-reconnoitred routes to surround the Austrian Army at Sadowa. Armed with their new 'needle guns' – rifles accurate out to 300 yards or more – the Prussian infantry ripped the musket-armed Austrians to shreds. In the fighting around Königgratz-Sadowa, the Austrians lost 44,000 men to the Prussian's 9,000. It was a decisive defeat. In three weeks, the Prussian armies were at the gates of Vienna and the Austrian Emperor had sued for peace. Thanks to Stieber's intelligence the Prussian Army had changed the balance of power in Europe for ever.

Bismarck now looked to France. A nervous Napoleon III, alarmed by Prussia's victories and her increased power, tried to placate the German Chancellor. Bismarck brushed these overtures away. He did not 'give tips' as to a servant. He was set on what the British ambassador to Berlin called, accurately enough, *une certaine politique de brigandage*. Yet again Prussia's implacable chancellor set Stieber loose on his next victim to spy out the land.

For this new expedition against France Stieber was accompanied by his two principal lieutenants Zernicki and Kaltenbach. Zernicki was a good socialiser with all the courtesy and charm of the Polish aristocracy. Kaltenbach, on the other hand, was a cold-blooded exploiter and plotter. Between them they made a formidable team and established what was, up to then, probably the most comprehensive intelligence and espionage system ever seen. While Stieber travelled as a Greek entrepreneur looking to invest in French industry (backed by a large bag of gold), his two acolytes quietly hired dozens of whores and distributed them around the French garrison towns of the frontier. To supplement these rough front-line troops, the Prussians added a thousand young women 'of good upbringing', to act as servants and chambermaids in French officers' messes, smart hotels and the residences of local prefects, mayors, deputies, etc. As if such a spy network was not enough, Stieber got permission from Bismarck to recruit several thousand farm labourers to help the French farmers with their harvest.

This vast network, estimated by Prussian sources at 35,000 strong at its peak, was controlled by a selected group of retired German officers who set up businesses in key military garrisons at Paris, Lille, Vincennes, Strasbourg, Bordeaux, Lyons and Marseilles. They and their 'young captains', posing as clerks, gathered in the individual reports from a huge number of 'dead letter boxes' and dispatched them in cipher to regional controllers set up by Stieber at Brussels, Geneva and Lausanne. It was a prodigious undertaking, controlled directly by Stieber himself. He controlled the operation by arriving in the area disguised as the Greek on business where he would, with Kaltenbach and Zernicki, collect any reports, pay off his agents and assess the situation for himself. For nearly two years Stieber's intelligence network collected every possible detail on France's military preparedness. His farmhands even counted all the cattle so that the invaders would know exactly how much beef would be available to reduce their supply chains. The world had seen nothing like it.

Of course, operations on such a scale could not go completely undetected. The French Military Attaché in Berlin warned time and again that Prussia was collecting intelligence in France and preparing for war. A languid Napoleon III ignored Baron Stoffel's prescient warnings, ignoring the entreaties of his senior military advisers that France was in danger, and leading the commander of the Strasbourg garrison, General Ducrot, to complain bitterly: 'It is exasperating that nobody provides the Army with the means of knowing what our military neighbours are doing.'

In the summer of 1870, Bismarck struck. Stieber had brought back over three trunk-loads of documents and compiled over 1,650 separate intelligence reports on every possible aspect of the invasion of France, from up-to-date maps to the locations of draught horses. Von Moltke's armies could not have asked for more. All that remained was a *casus belli*, which Gallic intemperance provided after Bismarck deliberately published a misleading version of a high-level telegram from the Prussian king. This 'red rag to the Gallic bull' provoked the very reaction Bismarck sought. The French unwisely declared war on Prussia and her German allies, the thing that Bismarck and von Moltke were praying for. Von Moltke was asleep when an aide woke him with the news of war. German army legend has it that von Moltke grunted, sat up and said: 'Go to the Planning Bureau's files. Take out Secret Folio number 1. Then follow the instructions and tell the Branch Chiefs to report to me in the morning', before going back to sleep, leaving his subordinate to put the fruits of Stieber's meticulous intelligence reports into action.

Unusually, as the invading Prussians swung into Eastern France they were accompanied by Prussia's intelligence chief and his two lieutenants. In key towns and villages they would ride in, arrest a Frenchman or woman and drag them off to the garrison headquarters. If there was any resistance, they were brutally handcuffed, beaten or flogged. Then, having safely collected and rescued his secret agents from under the very noses of the locals, Stieber's round up would move on. Meanwhile, mysterious chalk marks appeared on doors and trees all over the invasion area. Stieber's agents, like an army of gypsies, had marked up the area for the advancing Prussians: how many horses were hidden on a farm, where the food and hay was, how big the potential billet was. It was an intelligence triumph by an army of undercover sympathisers. Less creditable was Stieber's treatment of suspected French spies. In a deliberate policy of *schrechligkeit* (frightfulness) he ordered any potential spies executed even to women and children watching German columns march by. The terrified French hid, but such ruthlessness, although it may have scared off French spies or partisans, was to sow a bitter legacy of hate for the future.

Despite his success – or perhaps because of it – Stieber was deeply unpopular with the senior officers of the Prussian Army. Jealous of his influence with Bismarck, despising him for his techniques of blackmail and eavesdropping, the *junkers* of the Prussian General Staff treated Stieber with all the icy aristocratic disdain of the 'real soldier' for the 'cheap little spy'. At Falquemont one night during the 1870 campaign, their dislike boiled over as Stieber demanded credit for the Prussian triumph and a Prussian general snubbed the 'little Saxon spy'. It was a very public humiliation and an explosive moment, calmed only by Bismarck striding over, coffee cup in hand, to shake Stieber's hand and personally congratulate him on his contribution to victory. The icy tension dissolved. Stieber had been publicly acknowledged by Bismarck himself, in front of Prussia's victorious generals. The *junkers*, however, like all their class eagle-eyed to every social nuance, smiled secretly at each other. They had noticed that Otto von Bismarck had clasped the Saxon spy's hand with his *left* hand. In the closed network of the Prussian aristocracy, this was a deadly insult. The chancellor's accolade was ambiguous and really counted for naught. This ghastly little man, who knew far too much about their own foibles and little indiscretions, was still a social pariah. Honour was satisfied.

Stieber's finest hour came in the moment of victory. A small army of Prussian spies, estimated at least 3,000 and probably more, turned out to welcome the victorious King William and to cheer his triumphant entry into Paris for his declaration in the Hall of Mirrors at Versailles as the first 'Kaiser' or Emperor of the Second Reich – the United German Empire of Friederich Barbarossa, now recreated at last. Many French spectators joined in, well paid by Stieber to demonstrate their joy at their conquerors. It was a publicity masterpiece of which Dr Goebbels would have approved.

Perhaps Stieber's greatest individual coup and a clear demonstration of his methods came after the war. The French peace commissioner came to Versailles to help draw up the peace treaty. Bismarck ordered Stieber to find out what instructions Ambassador Favre had been given. When Favre got off the train he was met by a carriage, driven unbeknownst to him, by Zernicki, Stieber's Polish agent this time dressed up as a coachman. They drove to 3 Boulevard du Rois, which had been set up as a luxury diplomatic residence. It was, in fact, the headquarters in France of the Prussian secret service. At the door the ambassador was met by a liveried servant who attended to Favre's every need with discretion, courtesy and silent efficiency. It was Stieber himself, in disguise. When Bismarck later sat across the table to negotiate with Minister Favre, he had before him a full brief and intelligence report, prepared by Stieber. It was a copy of the detailed secret instructions from the French government to their emissary, which the 'servant' had copied from the ambassador's portfolio of papers while the visitor was in the bathroom. Unsurprisingly, Bismarck was able to score yet another diplomatic triumph.

After the war, Stieber returned to Berlin as chief of Bismarck's secret police. There he refined his methods still further, setting up a high-class bordello in Berlin called the Green House, staffed by a carefully selected group of his agents and patronised by foreign diplomats, German aristocracy and senior officers. Soon Stieber was extracting a high price from the Green House's clients by the most loathsome means. His recruited whores – both male and female – soon made him aware of their high-born clients' likes and dislikes, especially individual perversions. Armed with this insider's knowledge of sexual habits and illicit liaisons Stieber was now able to blackmail much of Berlin society and a number of important foreign visitors too. The cream of Berlin may not accept him socially, but he could ensure that they would fear him.

Stieber may have had over twenty decorations for his contribution to Bismarck's dream of a united powerful Germany but he never gained the social acceptance he craved. His dream of acceptance by the upper echelons of German society did, however, finally come true in 1892. When he died a huge crowd of nobility came to the funeral and followed his coffin. At the time it was noticed that the mourners were unusually cheerful. One Berlin wag commented wryly that, 'the reason that so many toffs came to the funeral was because they wanted to confirm that Stieber really was dead.'

Stieber's legacy lives on to this day. He was the first national intelligence chief to use agents to monitor and control the press, the banks, business and industry. His collection of comprehensive military intelligence ensured Prussia's victory on the battlefield. He devised the idea of a 'fifth column' in place before an invasion long before Franco. He regularised mass postal censorship and used it to spy on both the army and the population, and to enhance his own power. His Central Information Bureau virtually invented modern 'psyops' – psychological warfare designed to raise the morale of his own troops and population by publicising enemy blunders, bad news and casualties and to weaken the enemy by bad news. There can be no doubt that Stieber's contribution to intelligence has been immense. His techniques poisoned the atmosphere throughout Europe, demonstrated the power of intelligence, created a spy fever that is with us to this day, and helped to set the international climate for the Great War of 1914–18. Stieber's achievement on behalf of Bismarck, Prussia and modern intelligence is awesome.

He and the devil must have much to discuss.

13

Imperial Echoes

So 'ere's to you Fuzzy Wuzzy at your 'ome
in the Soudan, You're a poor benighted
'eathen but a first class fightin' man!

RUDYARD KIPLING

Stieber's achievements, for good or ill, changed the nature of intelligence for ever. From being the private plaything of kings, ministers and generals, intelligence now became part of the bureaucratic fabric of the nation state, both in peace and war. Intelligence was no longer part of some private world but was recognised as part of the political military mainstream in every developed capital.

Different countries handled this in different ways. From the Fall of Sedan in 1870 to the outbreak of the Great War in 1914, the French and Germans were locked in a bitter undercover espionage war almost without respite, which culminated in the disgraceful public pillorying of an innocent French officer, Alfred Dreyfus, by a nation deeply divided by spy fever. Austria, alarmed by Prussian ambition overhauled her intelligence services although her selected chief of counter-intelligence Redl was eventually to fall prey to Stieber's blackmail techniques, this time wielded by the Russian secret service just before the First World War. Redl's treason would cost the Austrian Army over 300,000 casualties in the first great attacks of the 1914–18 War. Thanks to their blackmail of the secret homosexual, the Russians knew everything. Redl shot himself.

The British, true to their social and cultural climate of the time, relied on amateurs. Their post-Crimean reforms, which were running out of steam a decade on, received a jolt from the salutary lessons of the Franco-Prussian War. Spy fever gripped the British in their turn, first the professionals and then, during 1906–14, the population at large. There were two obsessions for the British: the worry about Ireland and the worry about the now united Germany. At first Ireland dominated.

Irish underground revolutionary groups had flourished from 1798, all piously clinging to the hope that 'England's difficulty will be Ireland's opportunity'. First America, then Revolutionary France was hailed as a possible *deus ex machina*. Alas for the Irish cause, both proved broken reeds and English control from Dublin Castle efficiently penetrated the Irish Volunteers and Fenians through a series of well-polished secret service operations. By the 1860s the Fenians had taken firm root among the émigré Irish expatriates in cities like Boston and New York. Grievances about the Great Potato Famine lost nothing in the telling (although how – or why – the British were supposed to have infected Ireland's potato crop in 1848 has never been made clear to this day) and inflamed the émigrés. In 1866 the Fenians mounted a half-baked raid on British Canada to set up an Irish government in exile, and were repulsed with 300 casualties.

Watching this strange affair with a mixture of disbelief and incomprehension was an ex-US cavalry major called Thomas Beach. Within two years Beach, now calling himself Henri le Caron, was Britain's chief agent inside the Irish Republican Army in America and helping to run its not particularly secret affairs. At this time relations with the USA were cool. Britain had been neutral during the Civil War and had, if anything, favoured the South, the losing side. President Andrew Johnson was now repaying Britain by siding with the Irish cause.

By 1870 the Irish Republican Army was planning another invasion of Canada and President Andrew Johnson openly told 'le Caron' (now Inspector General of the Irish Revolutionary Forces) that the USA would turn a blind eye to any adventures along the Canadian border by the

Irish. Beach reported all this faithfully back to London, and, when Ulysses Grant took over as president in 1868, he made sure that the new Head of State and the US authorities were well informed of the Hibernian troublemakers in their midst. The US authorities moved in on the Fenian armed gangs and nipped yet another incipient invasion in the bud. But Beach could not stop the tide of history, however clearly he reported on it.

Fenian violence had bubbled to the surface in England and Irish home rule was high on the political agenda. Indeed, by 1880 it was top of Gladstone's political agenda in Britain. Efforts such as the Home Rule League of 1873 looked for a peaceful solution. Fenian activists and extreme Irish nationalists encouraged a solution by any means, preferably more violent. In America, in Churchill's phrase, 'The hatred of American [Irish] Immigrants for their unforgotten oppressors' added fuel to the fire. Terrorism broke out in Ireland.

The Irish Question now became a top intelligence priority in both Dublin and in Westminster. Beach in America and the undercover operations of the secret service in Ireland did everything in their power to uncover and to hamper the plans of the Irish Republicans in whatever militant form they were emerging. London itself tried desperately to resolve the crisis as its Metropolitan Police Force tried to stamp out a Fenian bombing campaign while the Royal Irish Constabulary clamped down hard on terrorism across the water. The murder of Lord Frederick Cavendish, chief secretary for Ireland, in Dublin's Phoenix Park in 1882 was the last straw. London set up a Special Commissioner of Police to deal with a wave of Fenian dynamite bombings. The Special Irish Branch – Britain's political police – was formed to cope with Irish terrorism. In America, Beach was warning of more terrorism to come and reporting on the 'Dynamitards', Irish-Americans smuggling explosives into England. A vicious little undercover intelligence war broke out as events were rapidly moving to a head.

In the end, it was the public blackening of the Irish Republicans' political figurehead that demolished the Republicans' cause. Their leading politician, Charles Stuart Parnell, had been triumphantly buoyed up in 1887 by the publication of a letter (which had all the hallmarks of a forgery) in which he appeared to support the Irish terrorists. Parnell denied it, denouncing it as a crude forgery and went to court. Government lawyers later confirmed that it had been forged by a drunken Welsh journalist called Piggott. Was the Piggott-Parnell letter a British secret service plot? It has all the characteristics of a clumsy piece of disinformation and 'spin' gone badly wrong. Beach was in no doubt that Parnell was a secret backer of terrorism, but the Government Commission had vindicated Ireland's leader. Parnell's stock had never been higher. All Ireland – and many Englishmen – now looked to him as the leader who could take Ireland into a looser and more harmonious relationship with England.

Alas, it was not to be. Within eighteen months, Parnell was disgraced, revealed as co-respondent in a highly publicised divorce case suddenly brought by a Captain O'Shea. The fact that the affair had been going on for ten years and that Parnell and Mrs O'Shea had been openly living together made little difference. British middle-class opinion and the popular press of the day suffered one of their fits of moral hypocrisy, acting as if none of them had ever enjoyed an extra-marital liaison or been indiscreet. The Nonconformist wing of Gladstone's governing Liberal party tut-tutted sanctimoniously. Catholic opinion in Ireland and America was outraged. Parnell fell heavily into disgrace, taking with him for a generation the hopes of an independent Ireland. For the 'Ultras' of the British Establishment the timing could not have been better. Almost overnight, with Parnell's disgrace, the home rule issue became ever more problematic on the political agenda. Within a year Parnell was dead. It was all very convenient. The whole thing was, almost certainly, a British secret service undercover operation.

Such diversions, although novel enough to the British, were old hat to the undercover intelligence warriors of the Continent. By the last quarter of the 1800s, spying was commonplace. Spies were expected at every major function. Spies in their turn expected police surveillance at every hotel or salon. Stieber and his methods were accepted unquestioningly.

Into this tangle of intrigue stepped the ample figure of Henri Opper de Blowitz, one of the very few men to outwit Stieber in his own backyard. In 1878, de Blowitz was dispatched as *The Times* correspondent in Berlin to cover the Congress of Berlin, Bismarck's diplomatic masterstroke to emphasise Prussia's new pre-eminence. It was all intended to be highly secret and Stieber's security men went to great lengths to keep it that way. Yet, despite all their precautions, every morning in London, *The Times* published a full account of the previous day's proceedings. Stieber's surveillance teams began to concentrate on the affable bon viveur, following his every move. To their bewilderment, the sleuth-hounds found nothing to report. De Blowitz ambled around Berlin, not going anywhere near the conference and apparently not meeting any of the delegates, although he certainly seemed to eat well. Eventually, on the day after the conference concluded, *The Times* delivered its Berlin correspondent's coup: the publication of the complete – and supposedly highly secret – text of the final Berlin Treaty itself. Bismarck and Stieber were beside themselves. The rest of Europe was equally baffled but amused.

The trick came out later. Opper de Blowitz had suborned one of the delegates at the conference. Every lunchtime they dined at the same restaurant, albeit sitting far apart and never communicating. Every day they separately retrieved their coats and hats after lunch and went about their separate business. The trick was that de Blowitz's accomplice inside the congress hall wore an identical hat to the journalist. All they did was take the 'wrong' hat: the delegate's hat, now jauntily cocked on *The Times* man's head, contained a detailed report of Congress's progress. The hat exchange trick had been carried out under the very noses of the Prussian security police, who had never suspected a thing. It was – and still remains – a classic example of the espionage agent's tradecraft in communicating with a case officer undetected under the gaze of hostile surveillance.

It also demonstrates how spy fever, even for journalists, was taking hold in the new industrial urban society of late nineteenth-century Europe. Where once intelligence had been the tool, and the toy, of kings and councillors, now it was part of mainstream political life. An increasingly literate population was becoming more aware of the role of intelligence as the nation states of Bismarckian Europe nervously jockeyed for position as the century drew to its close. Almost inevitably, the public interest focused primarily on espionage and spies with all the risks, derring-do and drama of their breed, rather than on intelligence; a trend and misunderstanding that persists to this day in the James Bond genre. Human intelligence ('humint') is merely one source, one way of collecting information. It matters not. To a credulous public demanding amusement and diversion, spies equal intelligence.

Nowhere was this growing trend so clearly observed as in Britain. France had experienced Fouché; Middle Europe, Metternich; and the new Germany had Stieber and all his works. Russia had, of course, known little else other than spies and secrets for all her frigid and terror-struck existence. But for the British, intelligence burst upon the scene as a new idea in the wave of recriminations and reforms that followed the Crimean War and Bismarck's brutal reordering of Europe. The Irish had virtually encouraged the growth of an undercover political police and the War Office had gradually assembled a specific branch, the Military Intelligence Division that evolved out of Major Best's Topographical and Statistical Department. 'British Intelligence' was beginning to demonstrate a recognisable organisation.

Inevitably, given the cultural and social climate of the day, Britain's military intelligence department attracted bright adventurous young officers who combined their staff and analytical function with the actual collection of material. Thus a Captain Tulloch of the Military Intelligence Branch found that his shooting trip to Egypt and his fishing holiday in Belgium yielded not only good solid intelligence reports for the War Office, but it also paid his expenses. Combining a cheap holiday with business is always congenial, and the idea of the enthusiastic amateur as intelligence collector took firm root among the British Establishment.

Tulloch later opted for a walking holiday in the West Country to assess possible enemy invasion beaches. He was not alone, discovering on checking out of his final hotel that a German attaché had been making a similar exploration on behalf of his own government the summer before. Tulloch's reaction was disappointment: 'We might have done it together ...'.

Such amateur collection methods, when combined with a sound database, were surprisingly successful. By the end of the nineteenth century, the intelligence department of the War Office boasted over 40,000 books and journals and was busy collecting a mass of information on foreign countries and their armed forces by a daily open-source collection effort. Such clerkish work was not universally popular with the bright young sparks of the later Victorian army, although one of them later recorded:

> The reputation, however, I got, back in my battalion was that
> I spent my time in cutting out ... pictures from *La Vie Parisienne*
> and sticking them on a screen while my hard-worked brother
> officers were doing my duty.

Gleichen's rueful comment echoes that of an earlier generation. Sixty years before, Wellington's invaluable exploring officers had been treated equally coolly by their peers in their regiments, who felt (and voiced) the general army view that these amateur intelligence officers had merely been gadding about and avoiding 'real soldiering' while they had been doing all the really hard stuff. Not every senior officer agreed. Lord Kitchener, whose face was to adorn the famous recruiting poster of 1914, first made his name as an early 'Lawrence of Arabia', exploring deep into the Egyptian desert wearing Arab clothing and escorted by twenty sworn Arab 'brothers', and should this band of cut-throats fail to protect, a bottle of lethal poison. Kitchener had once been present when the local Arabs caught, and tortured, a spy. He had no intention of such horrors ever befalling him.

Part of this amateur-adventurer approach, for the British at least, came about because of the demands of Empire. The expanding requirements for information of colonial exploitation needed a constant supply of information from around the globe. Such colonial intelligence was not confined to Britain. France, Germany, Belgium and the growing United States all took a keen interest in the new territories they seized and colonised as the age of imperial colonialism spread across the globe. Lack of intelligence and cultural arrogance exacted a heavy price from the unwary, even in land grabbing colonial battles against 'savages', as Custer discovered to his regiment's cost at the Battle of Little Big Horn in 1876, and the Italians at Adowa in 1896, where the 'primitive savages' cut well-armed but mapless European forces to ribbons. Such colonial disasters were in fact *intelligence* disasters at heart. Even the failure to rescue General Gordon from Khartoum in 1885, which brought the British government down, was stripped to its essentials, an intelligence failure. (The rescue force did not know just how close the besieged Gordon was to defeat, and arrived only sixty hours too late to save the cut off colonial hero and his men.)

Even when colonial commanders possessed first-class intelligence, however, they risked defeat if caught, outnumbered and unprepared, by well-armed native enemies. The classic example of this was the disastrous British expedition in 1879 to suppress the Zulus in Southern Africa. Most people, whose knowledge is restricted to the film *Zulu*, assume that the British took to the field against King Cetewayo's Zulu nation in ignorance of their foe. Nothing could be further from the truth. Before Chelmsford's columns set out to invade the Transvaal one of his intelligence staff, Bernard Fynney, had compiled a complete Zulu order of battle, supplementing it with an accurate description of how the Zulus fought, plus a list of key personalities, including a list of the '100 most wanted'. Chelmsford was, rightly, impressed and issued this accurate intelligence briefing, with an up-to-date map, to every company commander in his force. In Donald Morris's words, 'No expeditionary force ever started a native war so well informed about its enemy.' Moreover, Chelmsford was so confident of victory that he is on record as saying: 'My only fear is that the Zulu will not fight ...'.

Sadly, for the men of the 24th Foot, the South Wales Borderers, Chelmsford's column commander then made two fatal mistakes. He discounted the first-class intelligence and, like his commander-in-chief, he underestimated his enemy. Secondly, he failed to push out picquets and sentries to warn him of an enemy approach. Such military liberties were unlikely to go unpunished by the experienced officers of the well-organised and disciplined Zulu Army. The British lost 52 officers and 1,277 men at Isandhlwana, their greatest loss of life since the Crimean War. Even given good intelligence, commanders and decision-makers always have the final responsibility for how they use it.

Fynney, Chelmsford's intelligence officer, was, in fact, a 'political', one of Britain's civilian army of colonial civil servants dealing directly with the 'natives' and reporting back to the colonial seat of government or to London. These political agents waged their own intelligence war for nearly a century on the Northern Frontier of India from Afghanistan to Tibet, in what Kipling called the 'great game'. Daring and adventurous Russian and British officers tangled with each other and the native tribes 'east of Constantinople', in an underground struggle for influence and control over the high mountain passes and border approaches to India. Its alleged romance has caught the imagination of generations ever since, from Kipling to today's BBC news correspondents. Equally, generations of soldiers with a more practical approach to their duties have learned to detest the cold, arid miseries of the North-West Frontier and to respect their murderous and hardy opponents, who one British officer memorably described as 'hard and fast buggers who wipe their arses with rocks and will cut your balls off if they capture you.' To which one of his surprised audience was heard to mutter, 'Well, if that's true, then that's certainly useful intelligence!'

The Boy's Own myth of the 'great game' was fostered by men like Baden-Powell, founder of the Boy Scout movement, who spent some time on the North-West Frontier having what he described as 'some jolly larks' before graduating to pottering around the Mediterranean, drawing pictures of fortifications disguised as butterflies. Reflecting his time and his caste, he wrote, 'The best spies are unpaid men doing it for the love of the thing', and memorably, 'For anyone who is tired of life, the thrilling life of a spy should be the finest recuperation.' (One wonders quite what William Buckley, the CIA Beirut station chief murdered by Hezbollah, would have made of such a remark as he lay chained to the water pipes in his filthy underground prison.) With attitudes like these, it was inevitable that the British would lock on to the cult of amateur espionage as being synonymous with intelligence, and such attitudes would cast a long shadow.

Across the Channel, harsher disciplines prevailed. Stieber's legacy of distrust and deceit pervaded diplomatic exchanges at every level. Above all, it poisoned relations between Germany and France. The most notorious case of all was *l'affaire* Dreyfus. It was to become the worst political scandal in modern French history, as its repercussions brought the French Army and society into turmoil. Its sour recriminations still evoke strong responses in French society to this day. It had all the hallmarks of Stieber's methods. This time the evil genius was not German but French, and there were many accomplices to help him.

Alfred Dreyfus was an artillery officer. He was felt by his rating officers to be a bumptious officer on the make, and he was unpopular with both his fellow officers and his superiors. He was also a Jew, the first ever to become a member of the General Staff. In September 1894, he was called to the office of the CGS, asked to draft a letter and then arrested and imprisoned on the grounds that 'his handwriting was that of a known spy for the Germans.' Dreyfus was court-martialled and, on the evidence of a suborned handwriting expert, duly convicted of passing top secret plans to the Germans. A stunned Dreyfus was led away, weakly protesting, and locked up.

Not everyone was convinced. The governor of the military prison who took Dreyfus in exclaimed on hearing the sentence, 'Dreyfus is as innocent as I am!' More importantly, so did Georges Picquart, the head of the General Staff's *Deuxième Bureau* (GH2). Picquart noticed that Dreyfus could never have had access to the operational plan that he was alleged to have sold to the Germans. So who could have?

Picquart began to analyse those who really had had access. He found a document between a Captain Ferdinand Esterhazy of the French Operational Plans Branch, and Colonel Schwartzkoppen, the German attaché, who allegedly received the secret plans from Dreyfus. In August

1895 Picquart, believing he had uncovered the real spy, took his evidence to the chief of staff. To his astonishment, Picquart was treated like a leper and bundled out of the General Staff, accused of lying and possibly being a spy himself. He was relieved of his post and sent to a distant colonial appointment in Tunisia. Dreyfus was sent to a living death on Devil's Island and a Major Henry (a close friend of Esterhazy's) was put in as head of the *Deuxième Bureau*. When Picquart complained, he was arrested in his turn. It was clear by now that nothing must be allowed to undermine the reputation of the General Staff. It was the fatal point in institutional judgements at which evidence falls short and where blind fanaticism and obsession take over, whatever the cost to innocent individuals. The scandal erupted into the papers, with Emile Zola thundering 'I accuse!' against the army high command and the government. He was arrested too and had to flee France.

It took ten long years to clear the sorry case up and then only in the teeth of a massive conspiracy and cover up by the French General Staff, who appeared to believe that better any number of innocent Jewish officers went to Devil's Island than aristocratic French officers were found to be passing secret plans to German intelligence. By 1903, after a long battle in the courts, which revealed that much of the evidence to keep Dreyfus in jail had been forged by the French Army or the French intelligence service to protect their reputations, Dreyfus and Picquart were freed. Henry, Esterhazy's friend, confessed to being part of the scandal and cut his own throat. Esterhazy, the guilty spy, did not cut his own throat: he wrote a best-selling book about his experiences. Schwartzkoppen the German attaché who had been the cause of the whole affair went on to fight in the Great War. On his death bed Esterhazy's agent handler's last words were reputed to have been, 'Tell them that Dreyfus was innocent!'

The whole affair split the French nation, its intelligence services and the French Army from top to bottom. Its scars even carried deep into the First World War. Joffre, the French commander-in-chief in 1914 was a compromise candidate because the minister of war refused to accept an aristocratic Catholic candidate from the General Staff in the post. They could not be trusted. It was not a good way for France's army to go into the 'war to end wars'. Once again the secret hand of intelligence had poisoned the well and influenced great events.

As the European powers began that long drift towards war, they openly spied on each other's preparations and intelligence was such an obvious priority in international relations as to be almost unworthy of note or comment. Spy fever took hold. The occasional outrage or scandal broke the surface as one of the new breed of military attachés exceeded his orders or was caught doing what he was paid to do: spying on the host country. Russian attachés were notoriously blatant in their activities. Men like Zantiewitz in Vienna and Michelsen and Barazov in Berlin were all forced to return to St Petersburg as *persona non grata*, expelled by their weary hosts for what is euphemistically referred to as 'activities inconsistent with their diplomatic status', i.e. spying, bribing and blackmailing host nation nationals. The KGB and GRU invented little that was new for Russia.

Russia's secret service did not, however, confine itself to mere Continental adventures. During one of Gladstone's great moral crusades about Turkish atrocities in the Balkans the Ochrana seems to have tried to set up and frame the British Prime Minister himself using a beautiful woman as the bait. Gladstone enjoyed a reputation of saving 'fallen women'. Prostitution was open, rife and a blight in nearly every late nineteenth-century city, where the pressures of rapid urbanisation, population growth and poverty exerted their malign influence on women. 'Vice' and 'fallen women' loomed large on the social reformers' agenda. Gladstone took a close interest in the topic; too close, say the cynics. The Ochrana and the Russian Foreign Office were interested in this strange English politician who liked to roam the streets at night, consorting with prostitutes, if only for the privilege of attempting to save their immortal souls.

The Russians had already used one of their specially recruited female agents, Anna Popova, in Washington DC to infiltrate the Irish American Fenians and stir up trouble for Britain after the American Civil War. She turned out to be a mine of useful information. Thomas Beach had spotted the Russian activity and reported it back to London, but St Petersburg decided not to act and the explosive possibilities of an Ochrana-IRA link withered. The Russians did not forget, however, the tip off from Popova about Gladstone's 'predilections'. As relations between Britain and Russia grew worse in the late 1870s, the Russians began to re-examine the benefits of putting the bite on a British prime minister. At best – unlikely though it was – they might recruit a high level spy through blackmail. At the very least they could see an excellent opportunity of exposing the high-minded British premier as a moralising humbug and hypocrite. Whatever happened, the British government and its interests would be damaged. It was an enticing diplomatic opportunity to discredit the most senior British politician, busy advocating British interference in Russia's Balkan backyard.

St Petersburg selected another suitably moralising individual as their chosen instrument. Olga Novikoff was in her late thirties and an attractive woman by any standards. She had a reputation as a political activist in Russia, espousing the cause of Christian morality to bring good to the world through enlightened political reform. Not without cause, St Petersburg reasoned that such a bait would be irresistible to Gladstone. They were spot on. The delightful Olga's ecumenical ideas about uniting Orthodox and Anglican Christianity brought them together and a correspondence began followed by discreet meetings and stimulating mutual talks. What really transpired remains unclear, although Olga claimed that Gladstone had, after a meeting on 'the Eastern Question' at St James' Hall, escorted her to Claridges Hotel 'on his arm'. Her main role in the end seems, however, not to have been to compromise Gladstone but rather to pump him for information on British policy and attitudes. In this she appears to have been largely successful. Despite his cries of moral outrage at the atrocities of the *bashi-bazouks* in the Balkans, the still uncompromised Gladstone, the great orator, failed to rally the British people to intervene in the Russian-Turkish war of 1878. As an 'agent of influence' Olga Novikoff may have exerted a leverage we remain ignorant of: whether she seduced Gladstone is questionable. What we do know is that someone served

Russian interests behind the scenes extremely well in London between 1876 and 1878. The hidden hand of intelligence had yet again manipulated great events.

Russia's overseas intelligence coups were not being repeated inside the Czar's empire, however. Although many Russian exiles had drifted back home they had not found their native land any more welcoming to their radical views on democracy, social reform and liberty. On the contrary Russia's reorganised internal secret police began to hound the reformers more and more. Gradually opposition and dissent, even of the most liberal and democratic elements, was driven underground. More ominously, the secret police's block-headed tactics drove the liberals into the camp of the extreme radicals and nihilists. The killing of General Trepoff, the chief of police in St Petersburg by a Vera Zassulich in 1878 (and her subsequent acquittal by a sympathetic jury) signposted a possible way ahead: the assassination of key figures.

This was a dangerous shift in tactics. Thanks to the secret police, the nihilists, revolutionaries and liberals now all shared a common policy, effectively of open war against Russia's ruling elite. This desperate underground struggle was to be waged all over Europe for the next forty years. The culmination of this campaign of assassination came in 1879 with the 'sentencing' of the Czar of All the Russias to death at an underground meeting of the Council of the Truth and Freedom Society. Attempts were made on Alexander's life. The Czar, however, led a seemingly charmed existence although the repressive hand of a reorganised Ochrana fell ever more heavily on the plotters. A new head of the secret police, General Melikoff, reorganised the government's anti-revolutionary troops and intensified the intelligence offensive against the revolutionaries.

It was to no avail. Ignoring Melikoff's warnings not to travel, on 1 March 1881 Czar Alexander's sledge travelled once too often down the Malaya Sadowa Street and into a well-prepared ambush of multiple bombs. The murder of the Czar of all the Russias changed everything. Yet again the secret police and Ochrana were reorganised. New generals were appointed and, to confront the growing threat from espionage, sabotage and subversion, Russia's security service gradually became the most potent force in Russian internal politics and a political power to be reckoned with in its own right. By the end of the century, the Ochrana had evolved into a recognisably modern intelligence service with intelligence and counter-intelligence arms, codebreakers and all the paraphernalia of a modern secret service that continues to this day. To ensure its hold on the population it now controlled a mass army of underground informers and spent a fortune in taxes collecting information on behalf of the State. The Ochrana mirrored the role of East Germany's MfS almost exactly as it locked into its secret intelligence war against its own people.

Treachery, betrayal and deceit became the hallmarks of this secret war as men like Ieono Azeff spied on the émigré revolutionaries on behalf of the government, but at the same time engineered the murder of his own secret policeman boss 'to establish his true revolutionary credentials' with the revolutionaries! Azeff's organising of the secret police chief Plehve's killing foreshadowed a darker new century: General Plehve was a Jew and Azeff hated Jews. As a Jew, explained Azeff, his boss, even if head of the secret police, was 'expendable'.

Britain on its little island was mercifully spared the complexities of fighting an underground war against a sizable minority of its educated elite like Russia, or preparing for a revenge war against any single arch-enemy like France. Political intelligence was mainly confined to Irish dreamers and keeping hotheaded asylum-seekers and anarchists who flocked to London under control. Russia's wars were not going to be fought out in London's streets. Overseas, the Pax Britannica ensured no foreign threat.

It took the impact of South African farmers descended from Dutch settlers to move Britain's intelligence services on into the new century. The Boer War and the growing threat from German economic and military power did the rest. As a result, by 1914 Britain too had all the basic intelligence and security apparatus of a modern state: a fully developed Military Intelligence department, an internal security service to supplement the secret political police, and a new external Secret Intelligence Service.

The 1899–1902 Boer War had some important outcomes for late Victorian Britain. First, it revealed how disliked and isolated Britain was abroad; secondly it encouraged reform of Britain's defences and national security policies; last, but not least, it demonstrated exactly what a military intelligence organisation was capable of. By 1903, Britain had acquired a complete all-source intelligence system to fight the Boers.

It had been a painful process. The Boers had shot the initial clumsy British attacks to ribbons, not unlike the colonial Americans on Bunker Hill. Unlike Bunker Hill, at the Modder River, the Boers soundly thrashed the British regulars. In the inevitable wave of recriminations, lack of intelligence was blamed. Under the microscope of a Royal Commission, however, it emerged that on the contrary, early British commanders in South Africa were probably supplied with the clearest, most accurate intelligence on both the Orange Free State and the Transvaal. It became apparent that while the Boers spent £170,000 annually on intelligence, Sir John Ardagh's military intelligence staff in the War Office had been allotted just £100 and never more than ten officers. He himself condemned the leadership on the ground in South Africa once the war had started pointing out tartly to the later Royal Commission that, 'it was only the action of the Boers in scattering all their forces ... which saved us', hardly a ringing endorsement from Britain's Director of Military Intelligence. In the words of the editor of *The Times*: 'I would have been ashamed to have sent [*Times*] correspondents anywhere, or even a commercial traveller, with the sums of money they were given.' The first commander of the British forces in South Africa, General Sir Redvers Buller, actually sent his intelligence-briefing package back to Whitehall, explaining that he 'knew everything there was to know about South Africa.'

Despite these setbacks at home, the British rapidly developed a comprehensive Field Intelligence Department on the ground in South Africa. With the experienced and intelligence-minded Kitchener in charge, Colonel G. R. Henderson soon organised a modern intelligence staff with 'embedded' intelligence officers at all levels on all unit staffs. From native tracker-scouts with advanced units, to semi-civilian codebreakers back at GHQ, by 1902–3 the British had devised as efficient an intelligence system as was possible; far better than the Boers, despite their advantage of fighting in their own backyard.

The native black scouts caused the British problems. The Boers in particular detested them, regarding British policy as politically danger-ous. Some British officers shared these views. One scouting officer wrote:

> The boys were a curious mixture – Kaffirs, Basutos, half-caste Hottentots and one evil-eyed Bushman ... of course, most of these boys should never have been enlisted; further, we ought never to have armed the Kaffirs during the war. They were the Boers' servants ... to employ them as soldiers was to break down the tradition and the rule which had enabled the white man to conquer and occupy South Africa ... The worst of the business was that no quarter was shown by either Boer to armed Kaffir or by armed Kaffir to Boer ...

These misgivings are confirmed in a remarkable letter from a Captain Smith of the Orange Free State Artillery to the British com-mander at Morreesburg, which clearly warns that in future, 'Any black "scouts", armed or unarmed, will be treated according to our decided decision [sic].' Captain Smith calls it a 'disgrace' for the British to use armed blacks, ending, 'in future, we are obliged to shoot the so-called scouts.' The roots of South Africa's political problems go back a long way and for many Afrikaners, it was the British who let the genie out of the bottle.

Wars attract adventurers, and the freebooting world of 'scouting' soon attracted a number of unlikely characters. One such individual was an American called Fred Burnham. A native of Minnesota, his earliest memory was of an Indian massacre at New Ulm by Red Cloud and his band. With such a childhood, he gravitated towards tracking and by 1893 was panning for gold in South Africa's Matabeleland. In the clashes with the native Matabele, Burnham met Baden-Powell and established a reputation as a scout and tracker. By 1900 the American was recalled from the Klondike to South Africa by Lord Roberts himself and seconded to the new Field Intelligence Department as a senior scout leader in the British service.

On daring long-range reconnaissance patrols deep into Boer lines Burnham's reputation was confirmed. Captured three times, he escaped every time and in a final act of daring after yet another Boer ambush he crawled out from under his dead horse (having lain doggo for twenty-four hours) to place a sabotage charge on a Boer bridge. After two days crawling across the Veldt to evade the now alert and enraged Boers, Burnham escaped back to British lines. For his exploits, this remarkable American was invited to dinner by Queen Victoria, commissioned as a major in the British Army and awarded the DSO by King Edward VII.

By the end of the South African war, the British had put together a thoroughly professional Military Intelligence Department in South Africa. Signals intelligence teams were reading Boer telegraph codes and cracking their ciphers. Human sources were being intercepted, and prisoners of war being skilfully interrogated. A balloon section was even experimenting with aerial reconnaissance. Translators scanned captured Afrikaans documents. Letters home were censored and a thriving counter-intelligence section was busy blocking security leaks and hunting down Boer spies. A Royal Engineers map and printing section was pumping out vital intelligence to all levels of command, while specially selected officers providing accurate and timely briefs to Kitchener's general headquarters, and its planning staff. It was all very modern. By 1903, Britain had acquired, almost by accident, the best intelligence system in her history, staffed by now experienced battle-hardened intelligence professionals.

In 1904, the whole careful edifice was demolished and disbanded. Yet again the British government was 'cutting costs'. Yet again, intelligence was to suffer from the thrifty eye of its 'humble servants' in Whitehall and the Treasury, keen to save every penny and determined to spend as many of the taxpayers' pounds as was necessary to do so in order to demonstrate their sense of economy. The Empire could do without an intelligence service in 1904.

Events were soon to alter that.

14

Into the Abyss

If ever there is another war it will come out of some damned silly thing in the Balkans...

OTTO VON BISMARCK

The loss of Britain's best intelligence service in 1904 was not a complete disaster. Colonel Henderson, who had headed the Field Intelligence Department in South Africa, wrote a complete pamphlet on intelligence organisation and doctrine – the British Army's first. It became the intelligence 'Bible'.

Despite the commonly held – but quite mistaken – view that the senior leadership of the British Army did little apart from 'huntin', shootin' and fishin'' before the Great War, Colonel Henderson's handbook appears to have been the source of a number of highly professional training courses for intelligence staff officers in Edwardian times. For example, the Eastern Command staff intelligence courses run in 1908 and 1909 appear to have been extremely well organised. Their syllabi would not have disgraced any modern military intelligence training course and the programme seems to an expert modern eye to have been both rigorous and thorough.

What makes the record of these highly professional intelligence courses particularly interesting is the name of the energetic and highly competent officer who organised and ran them: Colonel Aylmer Hunter-Weston, an officer whose name has become synonymous with incompetency, who was one of the 'butchers and bunglers' of the Great War at both Gallipoli and on the Western Front. The contrast between the thoroughly professional staff officer of 1909 and the supposedly incompetent butcher of 1915–17 is a subject that bears closer examination. It would be an admirable topic for one of the many ambitious academic researchers looking to make themselves a name by uncovering the real story of the First World War as historical fact, rather than the emotional literary outpourings of shocked young public school boys thrust into the brutal furnace of industrial warfare. If nothing else, we may learn something about the way the historical record of the Great War has been 'spun' over the years to promote one particular point of view rather than the objective truth. From the evidence of the War Office record it is quite clear that the British military establishment of the early 1900s was deeply interested in professionalism, reform and improvement.

The War Office absorbed most of the lessons so painfully learned in South Africa, at least into its planning cycle. A general staff was formed on the Continental model. Perhaps most important of all, many of Britain's senior commanders were now experienced intelligence officers themselves, to a degree never seen before or, it must be said, since. Men like Kitchener, Grierson, Colonel Edmunds, Henry Wilson, 'Wullie' Robertson, Count Gleichen and, of course, Henderson himself had all done intelligence work in the 'great game'. All knew the value of intelligence in war. Even if the organisation had been disbanded, they knew what was required and, more importantly, they knew how to recreate it. As all were to have an influence over the early days of the Great War in 1914, this knowledge alone would prove to be a vital pool of expertise.

Typical of this breed of intelligence officer was a future chief of the Imperial General Staff in 1940, Lord Ironside, who, as part of the War Office's policy of 'keeping an eye on the Boers and their sympathisers' after the South African war actually enlisted under cover as a Boer auxiliary in the German Army, controlling South West Africa.

Ironside spoke both fluent German and Afrikaans and carried this extraordinary deception through, even gaining a German Army campaign medal. He later took delight in wearing the German decoration when being presented to a startled Chancellor Hitler in 1938.

The idea that the Britain of pre-1914 went to war unprepared and unprofessional is therefore wholly wrong. The pace of life may have been more languid and the social round more demanding, but people took their responsibilities seriously. The mixture of the lessons of South Africa and the first real 'Revolution in Military Affairs' (RMA) was breathtaking in its accelerated change. This first RMA between 1860 and 1914 was perhaps the most dramatic change in military – and civilian – life ever seen. It was certainly the most concentrated period of upheaval ever recorded in most people's lives and society at large. Everywhere change and progress were in the air: industrial, medical, technical, scientific and social. The age saw an explosion of growth in almost every field. The military was not immune.

For example, Admiral Jellicoe, Britain's naval commander at Jutland in 1916 had gone to sea in the age of sail, and trained by climbing up the masts of wooden warships. By 1916 he commanded a fleet of 20,000-ton battleships, made of steel armour, driven by oil-fired turbines, and equipped with radio, electric power and 15-inch guns that could shoot nearly 20 miles and were laid by primitive fire-control analogue calculator-computers. The so-called RMA of our modern computer age is 'old hat' indeed, compared with the pace of technological change our Victorian forebears had to absorb from a completely non-technological educational background.

Looming above all, though, was the spectre of Germany and German expansion. With such sobering new influences, plus the excitement of a new era and the new century, reforming zeal was everywhere in the air in Britain in the first decade of the twentieth century. In politics, in the armed forces and inevitably, given the spy fever of the early 1900s, among those responsible for Britain's non-existent intelligence services. The principal driving force behind Britain's mania of the early twentieth century was the sense of what has been well described as 'imperial frailty' and isolation after the Boer War, plus the unlikely figure of William le Queux, whom we met in Chapter 1.

Le Queux was not the only prophet of imperial doom at the hands of the cunning Germans, however. German spies under the bed plotting the downfall of honest Britons were very much part of the Edwardian landscape and not just among gullible middle-class newspaper readers either. By 1908, Brussels had even become an open market place for spies, international agents and intelligence. Genuine, and sometimes not so genuine, 'information bureaus' openly advertised and contracted to provide intelligence on a wide range of subjects, from the commercial formula for a new foot powder to the plans of a nearby fortress on the Belgian frontier. The upshot was that by 1906–10, the idea that Britain was riddled with a huge army of undercover German spies posing as waiters, barbers and commercial travellers was accepted as gospel by many otherwise intelligent people. Stieber's malignant successes had not been forgotten. When added to fears of Germany's blatantly anti-British naval programme and German commercial penetration of British markets, it all added up to a major threat to Britain from the Kaiser's Germany. The idea that Germany was one day planning to invade the British Isles seemed only too believable. It took firm hold on public imagination and, more significantly, among a number of key opinion formers.

Having identified that there really was a problem, Whitehall now decided 'something must be done'. By 1908 serious senior officers in the War Office had added their influential voices to newspaper clamour, lobbying for defence against enemy espionage, real or imagined. In 1909, Britain's Committee for Imperial Defence set up a sub-committee to examine the great spying saga with Colonel James Edmonds of War Office counter-intelligence as its star witness to outline the real facts. Mere facts were not going to sway the opinions of Whitehall, however, given the public mood of the time. The truth was, real facts about 'German spies' were actually few and far between. Such German espionage as there was in Britain was poorly organised and mainly concerned with naval targets, not military or invasion matters.

Undeterred by such unwelcome truths, the Committee of Imperial Defence listened solemnly to a catalogue of half-truths, fantasies, rumours and downright lies about German intelligence activities in Britain from Edmonds, journalists, 'interested persons' and the public. Then, equally solemnly, it advised that Britain needed some new organisation to keep itself informed about espionage and to 'accurately determine its objectives'.

As a result, in August 1909, an obscure captain of the South Staffordshire Regiment who had a facility for languages (and who happened to be Colonel Edmond's right-hand man in the War Office's intelligence department) was appointed as the head of MI5, Britain's domestic security service. Vernon Kell, bureaucratic empire builder extraordinary, was to cling on to his post for another thirty-one years until the summer of 1940 when Winston Churchill was to summarily dismiss him in the shadow of a real German invasion scare. Ironically, it was Churchill who gave Kell's tiny organisation its first real support. As a grandstanding home secretary in the pre-First World War era, it was Churchill who supplied the legislation that enabled Kell to expand his 'office and one clerk' into a major bureaucratic organ of State security linked into every police station, dockyard and factory in the land, and able to intercept mail at will.

Armed with these powers Kell was remarkably successful. In the last hours before war, he ordered police throughout the country to lift twenty-one of the known twenty-two German agents he had identified. (The twenty-second was in Germany on leave.) This MI5 coup totally disabled the German intelligence network in Britain for the rest of the war. Britain's pre-war spy fever may have been exaggerated and farcical. It did, however, indirectly lead to the very result it advocated: the complete eradication of German spies in England.

Kell's counterpart of the War Office's Special Intelligence Bureau was an ex-naval Commander called Mansfield Cumming, who had been invalided out of the Royal Navy in 1885. Since his retirement he had dabbled in some undercover intelligence trips abroad for the Naval Intelligence Department and was still loosely employed by the navy as a superintendent of Southampton's boom defences. In 1912 he was appointed as head of the Special Intelligence Section, the new overseas arm of Britain's Secret Service Bureau.

Given his background and Britain's strategic priorities at the time it is hardly surprising that Cumming concentrated mainly on providing naval intelligence from his agents abroad. A loose network of commercial travellers, Lloyd's agents and shipping clerks sent back accurate reports on German naval progress, which were promptly relayed to Cumming's principal customer, the Naval Intelligence Department.

We know a little about Cumming's activities from one of his failures. In 1912, German security rolled up a network based around the shipyards and docks at Bremen and put Schulz, a naturalised Briton, and an engineer called Hippisch on trial along with the rest of the British naval spy ring. The Schulz network had been collecting the naval architect's plans for new German warships and passing them 'to the English Intelligence Office'. Hippisch went down for twelve years.

Cumming's great problem was that he never quite knew who his boss was, certainly in the early years of the Secret Service Bureau. As a naval officer his allegiance was instinctively towards the Admiralty (who were, after all, his main customers and who had the power to make or break him). He was not funded by the Admiralty, however. The War Office and the Foreign Office both had major claims on his department and both still dabbled in their own peculiar brands of intelligence. While the diplomatic reports and telegrams of the Foreign Office posed little threat to Cumming's branch, the same could not be said for the activities of the War Office. The cult of the 'enthusiastic amateur' still pervaded the thinking of many young officers. A minor swarm of British holidaymakers looking suspiciously like British Army officers on leave appear to have spent many cheerful hours wandering around Germany in the golden summers before 1914, happily collecting whatever intelligence they could discover. It was 'capital sport'.

It was also diplomatically troublesome. Even the Royal Navy was not immune to such amateur nonsense and in 1910 a Captain Trench of the Royal Marine Light Infantry and a Lieutenant Brandon of the Royal Navy were sentenced to four years 'fortress detention' in Germany for spying. More serious was the escapade of Captain Bertrand Stewart of the West Kent Yeomanry. In August 1911, at the height of a diplomatic crisis over Agadir, he was arrested after being lured to Bremen dockyard by a German double agent. Put on trial *in camera* before the Supreme Court of the German Empire in January 1912 for espionage Stewart cut a lonely figure. The German press pilloried him as one of the breed of 'gentleman spies'. The German newspapers described him as:

> ... belonging to that numerous set of people in England who although having a regular profession only require to devote a part of their life to it and lead a versatile life in hunting and other sporting pleasures.

This time the court was more severe. Stewart was sentenced to three and a half years' imprisonment in the forbidding fortress of Glatz. His incarceration was marred by his unfortunately ill-tempered remarks about German courts and justice. Any chance of a pardon was ruled out. Stewart was finally released as an act of clemency on the occasion of King George V's state visit to Berlin in May 1913, together with Trench and Brandon. An embarrassed War Office clamped down on any future amateur spying expeditions, but it was too late. The summer of 1914 was to bring its own crisis.

The First World War was the first technological war where for the first time men manned machines and machine fought machine. The wooden warships of past ages had relied on muscle power and the elements. Like all wars, the Great War brought about dramatic changes. War has always been the greatest catalyst for change in human history. For good or ill, war accelerates development whether it is a boon to humanity – such as blood transfusions – or a curse, such as poison gases. War changes things. Nowhere is this more manifest than in the field of technology. Build a better mousetrap and the customers will buy it. Build a better machine gun and the world will beat a path to your door, cheque book in hand.

In 1878 Alexander Graham Bell's 'telephone' had reached London. Added to the growing network of terrestrial and submarine cables it meant that the communications age had begun. Telegraph cable could squirt messages at up to 400 words a minute around the world. Codes protected traffic, both commercial and governmental. It was all very modern. To this burgeoning growth industry, in 1896 a young man called Guglielmo Marconi brought his own new invention: a wireless transmitting device. First trialled in London (the centre of the world shipping trade), by 1897 Marconi's Wireless Telegraph and Signal Company was transmitting over the horizon, and by 1899 the Royal Navy, seriously interested in such a development for obvious reasons, was backing a naval trial between warships 75 miles apart. The radio age had arrived.

The problem with radio is that transmissions can be compared with the ripples that flow out from a pebble in a pool. Except in certain specialised applications radio transmissions can be identified and listened to by anyone with a suitable receiver tuned to the right wavelength. Not for nothing security officers from the start have quoted the crude truth, 'transmission is treason'. As early as 1903 a leading academic pointed out:

> Submarine Cable will be for a long time pre-eminent for the purpose
> of long distance telegraphy. It is manifest that wireless ... cannot
> compete in secrecy.

Despite this obvious drawback Marconi's invention prospered. The arrest of Dr Crippen and his girlfriend Ethel le Neve at sea in 1910, thanks to wireless, was an advertising coup worth millions for Marconi's products. By 1914, the Royal Navy (like the Germans, the French and the Americans) relied on wireless to control its ships all over the world. Even before the outbreak of war, the possibility of jamming messages or, worse, 'wireless spying' – listening to transmissions – had been raised by either the Committee of Imperial Defence or the popular press. The age of signals intelligence had arrived. One newspaper wrote:

Of the many forms of espionage adopted by the Germans, the use of wireless telegraphy was one that ... promised many profitable results to the enemy.

By the war's first winter of 1914 the British were busy building large wireless aerials at Abbeville and later St Pol, and intercepting German radio transmissions. Signals intelligence ('sigint') had gone to war and unknown to the Allies, it had already scored its first victory. As early as August 1914 the invading Russian armies in East Prussia had been smashed and driven back by Hindenburg and Ludendorff at the fighting between Tannenberg and the Masurian Lakes. Thanks to the German Army's interception of Russian radio messages, many *en clair*, the High Command was able to redeploy the German corps south to catch the garrulous and unsuspecting Russians in a massive pincer movement. The Russians were enveloped and overwhelmed. By 30 August 1914 they had lost 130,000 men, plus 92,000 prisoners and 400 guns and the shocked survivors were stumbling back to the Russian frontier in disorder. General Samsonov committed suicide. It was a disaster, and it was mainly due to the first use of signals intelligence in war. Hindenburg and Ludendorff were fêted as national heroes and great military commanders in the mould of Blücher, Scharnhorst and von Moltke. The truth was more prosaic. Radio intercepts had let them know exactly where their enemy was and what he was going to do next. It is quite hard to lose in such circumstances. But not many people knew that. The German duo took the credit.

On the Western Front a very different scenario was unravelling. As the German Schlieffen Plan ran like a juggernaut through Belgium and swung south towards Paris and the Marne, French officers expressed surprise at both the direction and mass of the German advance. Nothing could be more deceptive. The truth was that France's *Deuxième Bureau* had acquired knowledge of von Schlieffen's great plan years before. The troubled French High command, finding such reports incredible and unpalatable, ignored the well-assessed reports of their own intelligence. In Douglas Porch's biting condemnation:

... one can only conclude that if von Moltke had walked into the French War Ministry and dropped the Schlieffen Plan on Joffre's desk it would have made little difference. Intelligence in French planning was simply irrelevant.

More grievously for the French they were ill informed about the Belgians' preparations for war, assuming, quite wrongly, that Belgium was too heavily fortified for any swift German advance to succeed. They were badly wrong. The German great guns and their borrowed Austro-Hungarian howitzers soon smashed the Liège forts like so many cracked walnuts and opened up Belgium to the invaders. The German armies flooded through, delayed but not halted.

The French also miscalculated badly over the German dispositions and locations when they ordered the great French advance into the Eiffel, Alsace and Lorraine in August 1914. Plan XVII depended on good intelligence. The French treated it as a parade march to the front and virtually ignored the enemy. But war is a two-sided phenomenon and enemies can surprise. Taken in mass ambush by the German defenders, the French in their Napoleonic formations were massacred. They lost 300,000 men before 1 September 1914, including many irreplaceable professional officers and NCOs. (By 31 December 1914, the French Army had suffered one million casualties, with 300,000 dead – the same number as British casualties during the whole of the Second World War.) Good intelligence on the frontiers could have saved many lives. The debacle prompted swift action. By the end of August, the French were collecting intelligence very assiduously on their enemy. It was the wireless listening station on the Eiffel Tower that brought the news that von Kluck was heading south to the Marne.

The British had little reason to be smug. Although General Henderson's plan to revitalise military intelligence had swung into action when the British went to war on 4 August 1914, Rome was certainly not going to be built – or trained and equipped – in a day. No field intelligence organisation existed for the British Expeditionary Force (BEF). The result was that as the British cavalry clattered forward to contact from Mons on 21 August they were advancing blind. Napoleon and Wellington had been thus served, often better. The results were predictable. The British advance guards and von Kluck's cavalry blundered into each other outside Mons. If the British were surprised ('The information you have acquired ... appears to be ... exaggerated. It is probable that only mounted troops, perhaps supported by (Light Infantry) battalions, are in your immediate neighbourhood', wrote General Sir Henry Wilson of the cavalry reconnaissance reports of von Kluck's massive First Army), then so were the Germans, believing the British to be still on the dockside at Boulogne. 'Am I surrounded by dolts?' shouted the Kaiser on learning that the BEF was deployed and fighting his advancing troops and not still mobilising, 'Have we no spies in England?'

Even an attempt by the newly arrived Royal Flying Corps (RFC) was a waste of time. The first aerial reconnaissance of the war revealed massed German columns marching south-west from Brussels. The British commander-in-chief expressed polite interest to the youthful aircrew, then ignored the critical intelligence they had brought him. 'It must be very confusing for you up there, my boy', said Sir John French. Three days later, French's staff had changed its tune. 'A magnificent air report was received ...' wrote Macdonough, the BEF's chief intelligence officer on 3 September. Intelligence from aerial reconnaissance turned out to be a crucial factor in the events around the Marne and the stopping of the German tide. Aircraft were now acting as the cavalry of old had acted. Aircraft were now the eyes of the commander, enabling him to keep his 'contact intelligence' up to date and to discover exactly where his enemy was and what he was up to.

From being the commander's eyes, aircraft swiftly became useful platforms for other payloads besides eyeballs. It was but a short step to using photography to lay hard facts before doubting generals and headquarters' staffs. A photograph can be worth a thousand words. In fact, the RFC had done some amazing pioneering work in this area well before 1914. In the last two summers before the outbreak of war they had used cameras extensively over Salisbury Plain, culminating in some excellent quality pictures of Southampton Docks photographed from

5,000 feet in 1913 and *developed in the air*. This kind of near real-time photographic intelligence would revolutionise warfare.

The first real use of aerial photography was to improve mapping for the troops and for the artillery. Once the fighting masses sank into the static lines of trenches along the whole Western Front accurate maps could be produced showing enemy trenches, defences, artillery locations and railheads.

Overseas this mapping role was even more important. Great trackless wastes in Palestine and Mesopotamia could be plotted (the last good series of Palestine maps had been produced by Kitchener as a young intelligence officer thirty years before) and maps issued to everyone who needed one. It is worth remembering, as Marlborough, Napoleon, Wellington and Grant all admitted, intelligence in the first instance is always a good, accurate map. Aerial photography's contribution grew as the war progressed. Men like Brabazon worked with the French to invent new cameras suitable for use in the air. The quality grew to such an extent that by 1917 Haig himself was enthusing over the RFC's aerial intelligence:

> Our photographs now show distinctly the 'shell holes' which the
> enemy has formed into 'strong points'. The paths made by men
> walking in the rear of those occupied first got our attention ...

This kind of detail was crucial because by far the most important task of aerial reconnaissance was spotting for the guns. In an artillery war, the role of artillery intelligence was to grow and grow. Both at sea and on land the role of the aeroplane as an intelligence collector and then as a weapons platform expanded beyond anyone's imagination in the four short years from autumn 1914 to 1918. One index of this expansion is that in 1914 aerial photography only existed in the hands of a few enthusiasts. By 1918, the British had processed over half a million aerial photographs for intelligence purposes. It is an interesting parallel with our own day. Today's satellites may be new, but their development and use have paralleled almost exactly the growth and roles of that other 'aerial platform' from the real RMA, the aeroplane.

The technical possibilities of the aeroplane even extended to wireless. It is an astonishing fact that as early as the winter of 1914 the first wireless equipped aeroplanes were taking to the air to test their use for artillery spotting. Photography may have been overlooked at first, but from the very start, it was obvious that this Great War was going to be a wireless war. Wires and cables, secure though they were to interception, were just too vulnerable. For example, on the 5 August 1914, the British cableship *Teleconia* winched up the Germans' submarine cable linking the Kaiser's Reich with the rest of the world and cut it. From now on Germany would have to rely on wireless or neutral friends to talk to the outside world. Britain's Naval Intelligence Division, soon joined by a dedicated group of private radio enthusiasts, listened to Berlin and Bremen's increasing radio traffic with bewilderment. It was all in code. Even a supposedly secret German code book which Cumming's secret service had bought in Brussels before the war turned out to be useless. It was a fake. Cumming had been 'sold a pup'.

The British then had – or so they claimed – a stroke of good luck. In rapid succession they acquired all the key German naval code books. The full story of this remarkable series of coincidences has never been fully explained. By a combination of hard work, recruiting clever academics from civilian life and ensuring that the First Sea Lord (Churchill) was kept 'on-side' the Naval Intelligence Division's intercept and code-breaking staff now became a war winner. Its director, Admiral 'Blinker' Hall (so-called because he blinked a lot) put his growing team of code-breakers into Room 40 of the Old Admiralty Building, and 'Room 40' was the name that stuck.

Room 40 was remarkably successful. For the rest of the war, the Naval siginters kept a tight surveillance on the German High Seas Fleet at all times. In this they were aided, in the early days, by the Germans' assumption that their low-powered sets could not be intercepted from a range of more than 80 kilometres. The German operators chattered away, often not even in code, and across the North Sea Room 40 hoovered it all up. As a result, British naval intelligence was always one step ahead of its opposition and provided the fleet with accurate and timely intelligence. Unfortunately, the rigid caste distinction between operations and intelligence sometimes led to some very basic blunders, the classic being before the potentially decisive clash at Jutland. The senior operations officer asked Room 40 what and where was the High Seas Fleet's (HSF) commander's radio call-sign; Room 40 accurately reported: 'DK; at Wilhelmshaven.' They did not inform the Ops Room that the call sign had been transferred ashore. The Ops Room failed to ask the question to which they really wanted an answer: 'Where is the German High Seas Fleet?' As a result, and thinking that the HSF was still in port, the Admiralty ops room failed to get the Grand Fleet to sea in time to cut off Scheer at Jutland, and misled both Jellicoe and Beatty once they had sailed.

Partly as a result of this sort of nonsense, caused primarily by the Operations Division's lofty insistence that they be shown only the original decrypts without comment, the navy changed its staff intelligence procedures. Originally it had been felt that the comprehension and significance of raw intelligence on ships was a matter for 'salt horses', experienced sea-going royal naval officers alone, not for a bunch of long-haired civilian academics and a pretty rum bunch at that. In May 1917, Room 40 was reorganised into Naval Intelligence Division 25 and encouraged to send *full* intelligence reports in future, complete with context, interpretation and assessments to the naval ops staff. The results were dramatic. Operations and intelligence began working in harmony at a critical time for Britain. The U-boat campaign was at its height and the arrival of accurate intelligence reports, plus the newly introduced convoy system, finally broke the back of the German submarine effort, at a time when Britain's reserve food stocks were down to a mere six or seven weeks.

Room 40's greatest success was to change both the nature of the war and the nature of the world. Thanks to their efforts, British intelligence was able to show the United States of America where her real enemy was, and pave the way for America's entry in Europe's war.

Once their submarine cable had been cut off, the Germans had to rely on others for telegrams. Sweden was neutral and obligingly pro-German and so the Swedes let the German government use Swedish cable and the Swedish telegraph service to send diplomatic telegrams out to its embassies and consulates worldwide. This cable route went through the UK, and the British, after an initial diplomatic protest to the Swedes, decided to let the German diptels flow, for then Room 40 could read them. This so-called 'Swedish roundabout' suddenly produced pay dirt on 17 January 1917, when a Room 40 codebreaker handed Blinker Hall an intercepted German telegram.

Even Hall must have stopped blinking and stared at what he read. The telegram was nothing less than a set of instructions from the German Foreign Minister Zimmerman to the German ambassador in Mexico City to let him know that the Kaiser's Germany was about to start unrestricted submarine warfare against the British. This diplomatic bombshell would affect US shipping, too. It also instructed the ambassador to offer Mexico an alliance with Germany on the promise that Berlin could offer 'an understanding ... that Mexico is to reconquer the lost territory in Texas, New Mexico and Arizona.'

Hall sat on this diplomatically explosive document for over two weeks, presumably in the hope that America might be provoked without any action on his part. The Germans began their submarine campaign, while Hall obtained a copy of the actual telegram that had been delivered to the Germans in Mexico City to supplement his intercepted copy. The problem now was how to tell the world of the Germans' plans and, more importantly, how *not* to let the world know how the British had found out.

One of the perennial problems with intelligence is the difficulty of using it. Where a single source is the obvious provider of intelligence, then to disclose it will blow the source. If you realise someone is listening to your phone calls, you put the phone down and use another. Action on highly secret signals intelligence is always a problem. In such a case, the best solution is to pretend it has been found elsewhere before passing it on. United Nations 'intelligence' (or operations information – the UN will not tolerate intelligence gathering on its member states) officers usually become remarkably adept at spotting perceptive and well-informed newspaper articles in the world's press. The uncanny ability of such UN officers to spot exactly the right article and choose only those which seem to reflect real events accurately is frequently a source of admiring, if cynical, praise from experienced diplomats. They have a pretty shrewd idea whose hidden hand is steering the exact selection of such open source 'secrets'. Signals intelligence like every other sensitive secret needs to be masked by a bodyguard of lies whenever possible to protect the source.

Thus it was for Blinker Hall. To allow Britain's Foreign Office to present the Zimmerman telegram to the Americans would give the game away immediately that Britain was intercepting 'neutral' Sweden's telegraphic traffic, and, worse still, had cracked the German and Swedish codes. Then the Germans would change their codes and the flow of perfectly good intelligence would be cut off. It might take months or years to break the new codes. His 'insurance' copy of the Mexican version of the telegram provided the solution. When the Americans were handed the formal copy of the offending telegram, they were told that it had been obtained by an agent in Mexico. To British astonishment, Germany confirmed this deceit. Zimmerman admitted that the telegram was no forgery. Berlin ordered Mexico to burn all compromising material as 'indications suggest that the treachery was committed in Mexico'. The American press jumped on the bandwagon, claiming that a copy of Zimmerman's telegram had actually been stolen by patriotic Americans, or found in a diplomat's trunk. It was a fine old muddle and Hall had successfully muddied the waters to conceal his true source. On 2 April 1917 an indignant President briefed the Congress and called for war. On the 6th the USA declared war on an unrepentant Germany. Hall's Room 40 had started the USA down the road that would lead to superpower status. Yet again, intelligence's secret pulling of the strings behind the scenes had changed the world for ever.

Not all the intelligence successes of this new technical war were on the side of the Allies. Older disciplines still prevailed and the espionage war waged as hotly as the one in the trenches. The human intelligence networks of spies and undercover agents set up by the British and French in occupied Belgium and neutral Holland in particular, were frequently penetrated and rolled up by the vigilant (and ruthless) German counter-intelligence service. Count Nicolai, the head of the German secret service, ran one 'crack' agent in London, Jules Silber. Although he was a German national, Silber spoke English like an Englishman and had served with the British in the Boer War. In 1914, he was in New York and did a 'walk-in' on the German Embassy, offering his services as an intelligence agent and a German patriot. When he disembarked at Liverpool Silber was welcomed as an Englishman and with his 'excellent German', his past record and contacts, quickly found a job as a British postal censor in London.

For the rest of the war this extraordinarily brave man lived in the heart of the enemy capital soaking up all the information he could, and relaying it back to Germany through neutral capitals by post. He had access to all the censor's stamps and seals, so he could personally 'authenticate' his own reports with stolen 'Cleared by the Censor' stamps. He took the added precaution of never mixing his official post with his undercover activities, never having any contact with German agents and keeping himself to himself. This resourceful man avoided conscription through his 'reserved occupation' and avoided promotion out of the censors' work room by making himself deliberately ill through drugs. Silber was never suspected – let alone detected – as a German agent by Kell's MI5 or Thompson's vigilant Special Branch. It must have been four years of endless strain, but Silber survived the war. He even received a glowing testimonial letter from the Director of Military Intelligence, thanking him for: 'the pressure [censorship] has enabled us to exert on the enemy, or of the part it played in winning the war', and ending, 'There is no lack of appreciation of the importance of the work to which you have given your services.' In 1925, Silber quietly left England and returned to Germany. There he wrote his memoirs. Vernon Kell at MI5, we can be sure, bought one of the first copies.

The First World War was the first truly 'world' war. Its experience affected virtually every family in Europe and many others around the globe. Survival itself was at risk and not just from enemy action. The war's grim struggle pulled down half the political structures of Europe and ushered in the world we now recognise. What it also ushered in was the total commitment of national effort to winning the war. This in its turn extended to intelligence in all its forms. From prisoners on the battlefield to spying on civilian agitators in factories back home, all possible intelligence resources were mobilised to ensure victory. The new technical intelligence techniques merely made intelligence more capable and more in demand as part of the total struggle of a society at war.

What this total struggle also brought about was a recognition that 'society' was at war with itself. The gaping social divisions of pre-1914 Europe had fostered great resentments throughout the Continent as the French socialist Jaurés had seen only too clearly. Anarchism, nihilism, socialism and Marxism had all found sympathetic roots in the urban slums of Europe's cities. Red Revolution had been in the air everywhere when Europe had embraced its violent destiny in 1914. The outbreak of war had merely postponed an explosion temporarily and the war's devastating progress had only accelerated a much greater one.

The immutable law 'that war is the greatest agent for change' now took its iron grip on Europe. Not, as Marx and Engels had hoped and anticipated, in the teeming slums of Manchester or Mannheim, but in backward Moscow, or more specifically, St Petersburg. In 1917, the Red Revolution had struck down Russia from her war and now threatened all Europe with the Bolsheviks' creed. Intelligence was going to have much to do in the peace that followed.

15

The Red Peril

There is only one eternally true
legend ... that of Judas.

JOSEF DZHUGASHVILI, KNOWN AS STALIN

The Bolshevik Revolution of October 1917 swept Russia out of the
Great War and ushered in a new era, albeit one that had been brewing
a long time. Raised in secrecy and maturing under decades of conspiracy in their long-running struggle with the Czar's secret police, Russia's
new rulers were quite frankly incapable of seeing the world as anything
else than an undercover war of conspiracy, espionage and plots. All
Russia's new leadership had spent their lives deeply immersed in a
culture of secrecy and risk. Many of them had been exiled, or worse.
In such an environment, paranoia thrives and the secret police had
become as much part of the universe as the mountains and the trees.

Not all the Bolsheviks' links with the Ochrana were as the secret
police's prey. Sometimes the hunted slipped into the role of hunters.
Even the Party's general secretary, the Georgian known as Stalin, had a
surprisingly equivocal relationship with the Bolshevik Party's supposedly
deadly foes. Stalin's links with the Ochrana were confused to put it
mildly. As Josef Georgi, before the Great War he had been a well-known
face in London's Continental Café, near the Communist Club off Queen
Charlotte Street.

He was even alleged to be involved with the 'anarchist' gang of

'Peter the Painter' who supposedly perished during a siege in a burning house in Sydney Street in 1911, in a hail of bullets from British Guardsmen called in by the Home Secretary Winston Churchill. The Russian anarchists had tried to raid a jeweller's shop, allegedly been caught in the act, opened fire on the police and then been trapped in the Sydney Street house. (The mysterious Peter seems in fact to have been quietly allowed to escape by the police, having performed his undercover duty to his masters in the Ochrana and the British Secret Service. It remains a murky tale.) Such bizarre gun battles seemed to have little place on the streets of Edwardian London, but it was no more bizarre than Stalin living in London. Was he an Ochrana agent? Certainly the Ochrana files list him in his real name as Josef Dzhugashvili and show him on the books of their 'Foreign Agency' in 1909. Unlikely though it may seem, Comrade Stalin had been a spy for the Czar's secret police.

With such a background of double-dealing, it was almost inevitable that Russia's new government would automatically slip into confrontation and hostilities with the non-communist nations from the start. It was equally inevitable that the Bolshevik leaders would seek to subvert her non-communist neighbours in the name of the People's Revolution. Britain in particular eyed the new Russia askance. The Czar's armies had tied down nearly half a million men from Imperial Germany's army on the Eastern Front. Should the new Russia make a separate peace with Germany then Hindenburg and Ludendorff would have another eighty divisions to unleash against the war-weary British and the mutinous French armies on the Western Front. For the Allied leadership it was a stomach-churning prospect.

Attempts to keep Russia in the war failed and the Bolsheviks quite literally sneered with contempt at such suggestions. From the very beginning, the West, and Britain in particular, were effectively at war with a Bolshevik Russia dedicated to exporting revolution and the overthrow of capitalist governments everywhere. At first it was military intervention by the Western powers in support of the White Russians. When the latter's cause weakened and war-weariness at home brought the troops back from Murmansk the clash between communist and capitalist nations became and remained an intelligence war in a classic Clausewitzian exercise of 'diplomacy by other means'. Quite how diplomatic a British attempt was to 'out' Lenin and Trotsky in 1917 and 1918 as 'secret agents of the German High Command' was supposed to benefit Britain's war effort remains a moot point. The attempt to smear the new Red leadership failed, but all is fair in intelligence and propaganda. Such clumsy moves were to set the agenda between Britain and the USSR for many years to come.

The tone of relations between Britain and Bolshevik Russia was also hampered by the person of the Czar and his family. Nicholas II was a cousin of King George of Great Britain and his incarceration in 'rebel' Bolshevik hands remained a bone of contention on both a political and personal level between the two countries. Could the Czar and his people be rescued? British intelligence set out to find out. When this came to the attention of David Lloyd George, Britain's Prime Minister, he flatly forbade any rescue attempt. A radical politician to his finger tips, Lloyd George was smelling unrest and whispers of Red Revolution in Britain in 1918, and wanted no part in importing Bolshevik Russia's problems or bringing autocratic Russian monarchs into Buckingham Palace, even as guests.

Balked by his 'dictatorial' prime minister, King George V embarked on an attempt to rescue his imprisoned cousin behind the British government's back and by secretly using sympathetic intelligence officers. It was a desperate scheme, but King George was desperate. In spring 1918, he invited Colonel Richard Meinertzhagen of Military Operations 2 (which specialised in undercover operations) to the palace and outlined a rescue plan using a covert operations team in Siberia, plus RAF aeroplanes flying up the Trans-Siberian railway. Also present at the meeting was Trenchard, a personal friend of Meinertzhagen and the king, and founder of the RAF. Unlikely as it may seem the meeting at Buckingham Palace undoubtedly took place and a plot was hatched on the authority of the king to rescue the Czar of all the Russias and his family from imprisonment in Russia.

By the end of June 1918, the plot was ready. The two British special operations officers, Captain Digby-Jones and Major Joll, had infiltrated Ekaterinburg and a Captain Poole of the new RAF was also in the area. On the evening of 1 July, the team moved in for the rescue attempt. Meinertzhagen's secret diary records that 'success was not complete. The Czar and Czarina were "too closely guarded"'. However, according to Major Alley, the head of Military Intelligence's Russian section, 'one of the women was known to have gone missing'. In the event only one of the Romanov children was rescued, flown out to the east down the Trans-Siberian railway line to be spirited away by the cruiser HMS *Suffolk*, stationed at Vladivostok. From there, the mysterious princess disappears.

So, curiously, does Prince Arthur of Connaught, who happened to be on an unusually timed special visit to Japan at the exact dates of Meinertzhagen's undercover operation. All the evidence points to a carefully orchestrated exchange of 'baggage' between HMS *Suffolk* and a Japanese warship, followed by the hasty sailing of Prince Arthur of Connaught to Vancouver on a 'surprise visit' to Canada. Much more significantly, Meinertzhagen's wife, Armorel, was in Canada at the time. Shipping records reveal that Mrs Armorel Meinertzhagen disembarked from the Canadian Pacific ship SS *Corsican* at London on 8 August 1918. She brought back a 22-year-old 'Canadian' woman called Marguerite Lindsay. Also disembarking was a Miss Henrietta Crawford, 'a principal matron at the War Office' who had been in Canada at the time for reasons unknown.

Marguerite Lindsay did not exist. There is no record of any 22-year-old Canadian of that name. The address in London was a cover address. The young woman disappears from history. All Meinertzhagen's official documents have either been filleted or disappeared, some of them taken away personally by the king's private office. The historical record in the PRO and National Archive has been completely obliterated. The only record we have is in Meinertzhagen's diary, Major Alley's report and the events themselves.

That something did happen that night in Ekaterinburg is not in doubt. Witnesses speak of shooting and uproar on the night of 1 July and three days later all the Czar's guard-force was either arrested or removed, to be replaced with a dedicated Communist unit of professional soldiers. Astonishing as it may appear, it seems that Colonel Richard Meinertzhagen and British Military Intelligence actually did rescue one of the Romanov daughters, the Grand Duchess Tatiana, in July 1918, and smuggled her secretly into Britain on the orders of the king of England, in defiance of his own prime minister. She allegedly died in 1926 at Lydd.

The trail of evidence is circumstantial but compelling. Why was Meinertzhagen's wife suddenly in Vancouver with a matron from the War Office? Why was Prince Arthur of Connaught suddenly asked at short notice to present the Japanese Emperor with an official British honour just at this time and then why did he 'pop across to Canada'? This is unregal behaviour even by the standards of today, let alone the stuffy protocol-conscious days of 1918. Who was the mysterious Marguerite Lindsay and why was Meinertzhagen's wife escorting her with an official matron from the War Office? Meinertzhagen's diary contains no lies anywhere else as far as we can tell, so why should he invent such a story? Why was a mere colonel lauded and showered with honours after the war? There are many questions to be answered: but good intelligence operations should always remain secret: especially private ones mounted behind the prime minister's back.

Such intelligence exploits were never going to endear the British to the Bolshevik government in Russia, and it is not surprising that relations remained cool, if not downright hostile, between the two countries in the years immediately after the Great War. Churchill's great plans for an expedition to crush the Reds petered out as Britain withdrew from Russia. At home, a surly army awaiting demobilisation mutinied 'twenty times a week', waiting to join an even surlier work force, crippled by class war, strikes and unrest. The mood in Britain, as with Russia and Germany, was revolutionary. The Red Menace was very real in 1919. Angry soldiers gutted Luton's town hall and invaded the War Office in Whitehall. Unrest grew and a frightened Cabinet actually ordered the Guards Brigade to march down Whitehall in full battle order with bayonets fixed, as a show of strength and a threat to any would-be rioters. Calls for strikes and mass action grew and the national mood in a 'land fit for heroes' was one of discontent and class struggle. War was again demonstrating its power to change whole societies.

For Russia's new secret service, now reorganised under the Bolsheviks as the Cheka, the chance to foment trouble among the capitalists was too good to miss. The 'class struggle' of the workers in Britain's industrialised slums was basic Marxist doctrine, and the International Workers' Revolution needed encouragement from its proletarian allies in Moscow. The Cheka, under its new leader Dzerzhinsky (a secret policeman so indoctrinated by the ideals of the Communist Revolution that he even ordered the execution of his own mother), and the agents of international revolution moved in to exploit the workers' struggle in Britain. If the British and their intelligence services could interfere in Russian affairs, then the Cheka and its successor, the GPU, could return the compliment in Britain. An intelligence war was breaking out between the wartime allies.

Counter-intelligence in Britain was still the province of Kell's MI5. Kell, now a Whitehall major general with a staff of over 850, had come a long way from the 'one desk and one clerk' of ten years before. With the help of the Special Branch, Britain's security service and political police, the British were now running a domestic intelligence service of a high order, and it wasn't looking for spies, either. Fouché and Stieber would have instantly recognised (and approved of) this new obsession with internal control. The raft of Britain's 'emergency' wartime laws also helped: many of which, like the pre-war Official Secrets Acts and the 1915 licensing laws to close pubs and bars, were just too convenient for Whitehall to repeal at the end of the war and remain with us to this day.

By 1918, the threat of subversion at home was the order of the day. To supplement their intelligence collection roles, Kell and Thompson, the head of the Special Branch (SB) of the police, were not above an effective 'dirty tricks' department. One example shows both the subtlety and cleverness of their techniques. In Coventry, a SB agent 'let slip' in a striking workers' pub, that he had arrived to serve government conscription notices, 'but only on strikers'. Those actually at work would be exempt. By Monday, the strike was over and the workers back at their 'vital war work'.

Both Kell and Thompson were in agreement that the Red Menace was desperately serious. A general strike on Clydeside in 1919 was seen as the beginning of a British revolution and tanks and troops were stood by. King George V genuinely feared the worst. Bolshevik agitators and the Comintern's financial support from Russia stirred the pot, pressing for violent revolution. For their part, British would-be revolutionaries were establishing regular links with and taking money from Moscow's Bolsheviks. Anglo-Soviet relations were at an all time low.

To add to Kell's troubles Ireland had finally burst into flame, its long-delayed war for independence from Britain causing even more work for the British hard-pressed security services. Any idea of a return to the pre-war calm of a country without a security service was unthinkable. The threat was real and highly visible. Kell and Thompson did not have to urge this policy on a sceptical Establishment. Alarmed Cabinet ministers, viewing the latest Room 40 – now remodelled as the Government Code and Cipher School – intercepts of Soviet intentions and Bolshevik mischief needed little convincing of 'the threat'. The Reds stood condemned with every secret cable and telegram the British intercepted.

Events exploded in 1924 with the publication of an intercepted letter from Zinoviev, head of the Comintern to the British Communist Party (CPGB). The letter openly called for a British armed revolution. Its leaking and publication in British newspapers undoubtedly contributed to the socialist Labour Party losing the general election. Ramsay MacDonald's Labour government had been contemplating signing a trade agreement with the Soviets. The Zinoviev letter changed all that and the Conservative Party came back into power.

The whole Zinoviev affair remains a mystery to this day. Many believe that the letter was a forgery, engineered by Britain's intelligence services to 'fix' a dangerously radical government. If it really was a forgery then the culprits may have been a group of White Russians based in Berlin. However, the motive for such an act by them seems unclear: they had little to gain. On the other hand, the British Establishment of 1924, thoroughly alarmed at what they regarded as a well nigh Bolshevik government in power and what looked like an imminent rising of the working class, had every reason to blacken the Bolshevik cause and their 'Red friends' in Britain. Behind the scenes some very manipulative string pulling appears to have been going on.

We know that the Zinoviev letter was in the hands of the Foreign Office and the SIS on 10 October 1924. Within a few days an unknown called Thurn was passing the letter round Whitehall and on the instructions of Blinker Hall and the new head of MI6-SIS Sinclair, sold his copy for £7,500 from Conservative Party funds. Prime Minister Ramsey MacDonald's specific instructions to the Foreign Office on 23 October that no action was to be taken until the letter had been authenticated were simply ignored. By the 24th the permanent undersecretary at the Foreign Office, Sir Eyre Crowe, had very publicly sent the letter to the Russian Embassy demanding an explanation and Conservative Central Office promptly passed the letter to the *Daily Mail* for publication. By next day the story was all over all the newspapers – just four days before the voters went to the polls. Labour lost the election.

The truth is that the Zinoviev letter was little different from the tone and content of many other intercepted inflammatory Russian messages. There is ample reason to believe it might well have been genuine, although the MI6-SIS almost certainly orchestrated its leak to a newspaper. Its effect on Anglo-Soviet relations however was disastrous. Diplomatic ties were broken off. The hidden hand of intelligence had struck once more.

Three years later, diplomatic uproar erupted again, when in 1927 the Special Branch raided the London Office of ARCOS, a Russian trading front and an undoubted nest of Russian subversion. Nearly a quarter of a million documents were impounded but little real evidence was uncovered of any Russian espionage. In desperation, ministers produced intercepted communications to prove their case against ARCOS and waved them openly in Parliament; here was the clear proof of the Russians' perfidy.

It was a serious mistake. These could only have come from one source. The Soviets swiftly changed their codes to use one-time pads and opted for reliance on illegal agents in future. Britain's decoders were suddenly in the dark. Intelligence on Soviet Russia dried up. The Soviets on the other hand, now wary of front organisations and secret telegrams, turned to 'illegals', and illegals from within the British Establishment. They looked to Cambridge University and rebellious adventurous youth as their next source of penetration agents to collect intelligence and influence British policy. The Reds' intelligence war against Britain went even deeper underground.

By the 1930s, a new menace was beginning to intrude, at first no bigger than a cloud on a sunny day, but gradually beginning to fill the sky. As if Bolshevik communism was not enough to contend with at a time of economic and social unrest, fascism was now becoming a force to be reckoned with, and not just with Mosley's Blackshirts at home either. The uniformed political parties of Soviet Russia, Italy and now Germany, posed a completely new threat with their clearly stated territorial ambitions and growing armed forces to match. As the 1930s unravelled, the threat of war loomed on every side: in Manchuria, Abyssinia, the Rhineland, Spain and Czechoslovakia. All over the world, alarmed governments turned to their intelligence services, most of which had been allowed to run down, and demanded answers on 'the threat'.

Nowhere was this more clearly seen than in the USA. American national intelligence was almost non-existent. A Military Intelligence Division had been formed in 1885, but as it consisted of one officer and one clerk, its impact had not been profound. By the outbreak of the Spanish-American war in 1898, it was, however, well prepared enough to issue a comprehensive intelligence brief on Cuba urging caution because of the climate. President McKinley took his intelligence chief's advice and delayed the invasion, although the war secretary publicly censured the MID chief, Colonel Wagner, for his caution shouting, 'I'll see you never get promoted in the Army in future!' Sometimes being the bearer of unpalatable intelligence can be career threatening, as many a diplomat and civil servant can testify. We may never know what corrupt political deal lay behind Secretary Alger's desire to see young Americans get killed.

One man who took this on board was an army captain, called Ralph van Deman. He joined the MID in the year of Colonel Wagner's imperial bollocking by the secretary of war. From then on van Deman tried single-handedly to keep American military intelligence alive as a staff branch. It was a tall order. General Franklin Bell, no friend of van Deman, had deliberately reorganised 'G-2' (the intelligence branch of the General Staff) as a mere information office at the US War College. By 1915, van Deman was the only officer keeping any real intelligence records in the US. When 'Black Jack' Pershing and his American Expeditionary Force sailed for France in 1917 they did so without any intelligence organisation or staff. Van Deman remonstrated with the chief of staff of the army, who told him that an intelligence organisation was unnecessary and ordered him not to raise the matter again, and 'especially not with the Secretary of War'. Van Deman ignored the order, briefed his civilian friends – who in turn briefed the politicians – and within forty-eight hours he was being interviewed by the secretary and appointed as the first head of the US Military Intelligence Branch.

By the end of the Great War, van Deman's US 'MI' had expanded and this time was not disbanded. One office had been especially successful: MI8, the US's code and cipher branch. Its head was a Captain Herbert Yardley, who by 1921 was cracking and reading Japanese diplomatic codes. In peacetime, the majority of these were of interest to the State Department rather than soldiers. In May 1929, Henry Stimson, the new secretary of state, saw his first intercepts of decoded Japanese. In the words of an observer, Bill Friedman, 'Stimson's reaction was violent ... on learning how the material was obtained he ... declared it would cease immediately ... he gave instructions that the necessary fund would be withdrawn at once.' Stimson characterised the whole process as unethical and added, in a famous line: 'Gentlemen do not read each other's mail.' Yardley was out of a job.

America in 1929 had no Official Secrets Act. Yardley, who appears to have already betrayed his country by passing secrets to the Japanese for money, took his treachery to the marketplace and began writing a book called *The American Black Chamber*, revealing just how American signals intelligence worked and how cleverly he had broken the Japanese codes. The book was a bestseller, particularly in Japan. The Japanese promptly changed their codes – which should have surprised no one – and an embarrassed US government hastened to legislate a secrecy law through Congress. It was not American intelligence's finest hour.

By 1934, even America was having to take intelligence seriously from, if not the Red Menace, then from the Yellow one rising on the other side of the Pacific. It was impossible not to be aware of the war clouds threatening from 1931 onwards. No one took the gathering Fascist storm clouds more seriously than France. Their *Service de Renseignements* (SR) had been watching German rearmament with growing alarm and warning anyone who would listen of the growing threat from France's powerful and belligerent Nazi neighbour. The problem was that in the early 1930s no one believed the SR reports and particularly the military intelligence warnings of German rearmament. Ambassadors and the Quai d'Orsay far preferred the witty and often brilliant analyses of diplomats abroad to the dry and uncomfortable truths of military intelligence reporting on German rearmament. Incredible as it may seem, there was no formal method of disseminating regular intelligence reports to ministers. Most dangerous of all, French politicians were allowed to alter any intelligence they did get to suit their own political requirements. Intelligence was, 'Interpreted or tailored in ways to fit most snugly with the predispositions of French generals and politicians.' (This may even have been a subconscious process: the French civil servants of the day would not be the first – or the last – to try and please their masters in power.)

Whatever the reason, the result was that Paris was effectively in denial. Even a senior intelligence analyst commented, after a visit to

Berlin in 1938, 'I discovered a new world, about which I had had reports from the SR, yet which I did not believe until now.' Faced with this blank wall of incomprehension, the *Deuxième Bureau* redoubled its efforts to glean good intelligence on German intentions and had a stroke of luck.

A member of Germany's *Forschungsamt*, the code and cipher branch of German intelligence, asked discreetly if he could meet the *decryptement* head of the SR. French codebreaking, once the envy of the world, had fallen sadly behind since the end of the Great War. Poor security, the closure of the codebreaking school at Versailles and stupidities such as using the same formal diplomatic phrase ('J'ai l'honneur de vous …') to begin diplomatic messages had made Paris's communications an open book to the outside world. So, despite initial suspicion, the French decided to see if they had anything to gain from such an unlikely offer. They struck pay dirt.

Their new agent was none other than a young German called Hans-Thilo Schmidt who spied for France from 1931 to 1939. Codenamed Agent Asche, Schmidt worked in the Germans' most secret code and codebreaking office and he opened up the secrets of the German Enigma coding machine. He also handed over operating manuals, keying instructions, old key settings and explained how the whole new Enigma system worked. This was useful, but not for the French who did not have an Enigma machine and, even if they had, it would have remained just that – an enigma. They still could not make it work.

The Poles, however, had been forging ahead using an impressive mixture of theft, 'reverse engineering', mathematical logic, commercial purchases and sheer brain power to unravel the secrets of the undecipherable Enigma. Armed with material supplied by the baffled French from Agent Asche, the Poles began to break down the Germans supposedly uncrackable code machine. By 1938, Polish intelligence had discovered exactly how to recreate Enigma's key settings on its three electrical rotors. It was a tour de force. But in September 1938, disaster struck. The Germans changed their operating procedures and began to reset their security codes daily, by using a self-selected random key of any three letters. It would take months to crack the new system.

By January 1939 it was obvious to all which way the wind was blowing in Europe and the Poles needed friends, badly. In desperation, the Poles turned to the French and British for help. At a specially arranged secret conference to exchange information the three nations' delegates were open, but not *too* open. The Poles forgot to mention that they had actually developed a primitive computer called a 'Bombe' to solve the permutations of the Enigma's key settings. The British in their turn forgot to disclose that they had begun to see into some low-level Enigmas from the Kondorlegion traffic in Spain, where German 'volunteers' were helping Franco. By June 1939 all deceits were swept away. With war imminent and Poland at risk from Hitler's Germany, two key members of Britain's GC & CS, now moved to Bletchley Park, flew to Warsaw and met the anxious Poles. On 24 July 1939 Major Gwido Langer, head of the Polish Cryptological and Cipher Section, revealed everything the doomed Poles knew and handed over working copies of the latest Enigma machines they had manufactured for themselves, offering a copy each to London and to Paris.

On 16 August 1939, just three weeks before Hitler invaded Poland, the British received a working Enigma with extra plug board settings and Polish cribs on how to make it work. For the first time the British – and later their American allies – would be able to see into the mind of the German High Command. Thanks to the Poles, intelligence had provided a war-winner.

As Europe went to war for the second time in twenty-five years, the intelligence war was, perhaps for the first time ever, fully staffed and ready from the start. In 1939 there was no doubt on any side that good intelligence would be crucial to victory. Both sides took it seriously. This time it was the Germans who scored the first intelligence coup. The Venlo incident was not only a huge embarrassment to Britain's MI6-SIS but showed that the 1939 intelligence war was going to be waged without kid gloves.

In November 1939, Neville Chamberlain's Britain was locked into what was known as the Phoney War along the Western Front and Chamberlain still harboured hopes of some kind of a deal with 'sensible, moderate Germans'. The Germans in their turn were well aware of Chamberlain's desperate wish for peace at almost any price. They decided to offer the British just what they hoped to find. Walter Schellenburg, a dedicated Nazi and a senior officer of the *Sicherhiets Dienst* (SD), was personally briefed by Hitler to offer the British a deal they could not resist.

SIS-MI6 had two high level British officers stationed in neutral Holland, a Captain Payne-Best and Major Stevens. The bait was a carefully controlled approach on behalf of a mysterious group of 'sensible, moderate Germans'. A Dr Fischer, made contact with Payne-Best. The German said he was a dissident Catholic German who had fled the Reich to escape the Nazis, and who claimed to be in touch with anti-Hitler groups inside Germany. Payne-Best was suspicious. He was an experienced intelligence officer. He had been heavily involved in British intelligence in Holland in the First World War and he didn't like the 'smell' of Fischer, or his alleged 'dissidents' back in the Fatherland.

But SIS in London insisted he follow up. It was an important chance to make contact with the 'anti-Nazi underground'. As a result and against his better judgement Payne-Best got sucked into what was really an elaborate sting planned by the SD. As the 'anti-Hitler plot' developed both Payne-Best and Stevens slowly became convinced and agreed with London that it probably was not a trap. Arrangements were made for a face-to-face meeting at Venlo, just inside the Dutch frontier, with the leaders of 'the conspiracy'. Payne-Best briefed the head of Dutch Intelligence, who in turn allocated an English-speaking Dutch officer, Lieutenant Klop, to assist these hypersensitive negotiations and keep den Haag in the picture.

The pace intensified. SIS arranged for Stevens to hand over a brand new and very secret MI6 Mk XV radio to communicate direct with the conspirators. The leader of the coup was apparently none other than one General von Wietersheim of the German High Command. His 'aides' met Payne-Best and Stevens on the frontier to discuss terms for a face-to-face meeting with the general. In reality, Hauptmann von Seidlitz and Leutnant Grosch were junior SD officers. Reports flew back to England. Both the Foreign Office and SIS dismissed any lingering doubts and pressed the two intelligence officers for action.

Accordingly, Payne-Best and Stevens went back for another meeting, this time with Schellenburg himself, posing as a Major Schemmel and accompanied by a Colonel Martini, alleged to be one of the conspirators. 'What are the British terms for peace?' he demanded. Back home, it went to Chamberlain, the Cabinet was consulted and both the British government and SIS headquarters urged the two SIS officers to meet up with the 'loyal Germans' and talk directly to General von Wietersheim as soon as possible. A meeting was arranged at Venlo on the border. The general didn't turn up. 'Perhaps tomorrow', signalled the 'German underground'. For three days the two MI6-SIS senior operators in the Netherlands made their rendezvous on the German border at the same time and the same place waiting for their vital contact.

On 9 November, Klop, Payne-Best and Stevens got out of their car and settled down for a coffee at a carefully chosen café just inside the border post at Venlo to await the general's arrival. Instead, on the German side a black saloon car suddenly accelerated towards the customs post and crashed through the barrier. An SS-SD snatch squad was hanging on the running board, guns at the ready. Lieutenant Klop pulled out his own pistol but was promptly shot down. Payne-Best and Stevens were swiftly sandbagged and dragged along with the dying Dutchman into the car, which raced back the few metres to Germany. Silence settled over the border crossing and the Dutch bystanders ran to stare across the frontier at the dissappearing car and a platoon of German border guards.

The German propaganda coup was immense. Although they had deliberately squandered the chance to play a long double game with the British, the short-term gains were solid enough. The British were exposed and duped; SIS's carefully constructed European networks were swiftly rolled up as they were exposed or fled (Payne-Best and Stevens both talked). Holland's 'neutrality' was shown to be a sham. SIS London sent plaintive signals asking the 'conspirators' if the 'generals' in the conspiracy were still at Schellenburg's headquarters and were they safe? At Schellenburg's SD headquarters they must have been rolling in the aisles: days afterwards the stupid British Secret Service still hadn't cottoned on to the fact that the whole thing was a charade and a German secret service sting to fool the British. Eventually even the SD got tired of its game and signalled back:

> Negotiations for any length of time with conceited and silly people are tedious. You will understand therefore that we are giving them up. You are hereby bidden a hearty farewell by your affectionate German opposition.
>
> *[Signed] The Gestapo*

Britain's first major intelligence operation of the war had been a disaster. Not only had they been made to look fools but the whole of SIS Europe must now be assumed to be compromised. To rub salt in the wound, the British secret service had also handed over a brand new copy of their latest classified radio set with all its codes and instructions. It was not SIS's – or Britain's – finest hour by a long way. Payne-Best and Stevens rotted in a German concentration camp for nearly six years.

Schellenburg got an Iron Cross, First Class, from a grinning Hitler's hands. As an undercover agent for German Army intelligence in the years after the Great War ex-Corporal Hitler knew a thing or two about special operations.

16
Total War

The essence of war is violence and ...
moderation in war is imbecility.

THOMAS BABINGTON MACAULAY

The Second World War was the first total war. It started with the
Japanese invasion of Manchuria in 1931 and, for the next fourteen years,
spread all over the world. From 1939 to 1945 it was a truly global war, its
mayhem only ending with the detonation of two of the new American
atom bombs over Japan in August 1945. Crushed and deterred by the
awesome power unleashed upon Hiroshima and Nagasaki, the Japanese
government bowed to the unthinkable and surrendered. The Second
Great War cost the lives of twenty-four million servicemen of all sides,
plus up to another forty million civilians who died from bombing, forced
labour, extermination camps or disease. It was without doubt the bloodiest war in human history.

From the very start it was obvious to all the combatants that intelligence was going to be vital in this new struggle. It was also blindingly
obvious that this war would need more than just human intelligence and
old-fashioned spies to provide that intelligence. The Second World War
was the first war in which technical intelligence would prove to be a crucial
element in victory. It was also the first war in which unconventional operations and guerrilla war were incorporated as an integral part of fighting
operations on a major scale. It was also a total intelligence war.

At the beginning the Allied effort was hampered by more traditional Anglo-French suspicions. France had endured a turbulent and troubled decade in the 1930s. Faction and anti-war attitudes spilled over into the Phoney War, with many Frenchmen (including those in high places) convinced that 'Britain was prepared to sell France out' and, 'Britain would fight to the last Frenchman'. It was a demoralised France that noted secret British Foreign Office plans for Reichsmarschall Goering to fly to Britain in the week before the war, and wondered why. In this climate, French espionage reports that the Duke of Windsor was to be driven to Hannover and declared Emperor of all the Germans seemed credible and lent weight to their innate suspicions of *perfide Albion*.

Such ambiguous Foreign Office machinations inevitably inspired quite reasonable distrust in France as to just what Britain's war aims were. Such misgivings should have been swept away by the first British moves of the war that demonstrated that whatever pre-emptive cringe or continued appeasements the 'Old Gang' of Westminster and Whitehall were contemplating British forces at least took the idea of fighting seriously. In the very first intelligence moves of the war, MI5 repeated its tactics of 1914 and was keeping a close look out for any German spies. One in particular, an Abwehr agent, a Welshman called Arthur Owens, was well known to MI5 and looked as if he could be dangerous. Kell arranged for the Special Branch to lift him. On 4 September, Owens was arrested and interrogated.

What happened next was the stuff of legend and would bear a rich harvest for Britain's counter-intelligence service. Owens offered his MI5 interrogators a deal: in exchange for not going on trial, he agreed to send back false intelligence to his Abwehr controllers in Hamburg. Soon Agent Snow was chattering away to the Abwehr on his 'secret' radio. This was the first seed of what would later grow into the Double Cross radio game (*funkspiel*) that would turn the Abwehr inside out and leave MI5 controlling virtually every German spy reporting from Great Britain. Agent Snow was eventually allowed to meet his Abwehr controllers in still-neutral Holland, accompanied by an ex-Swansea policeman posing as a Welsh Nationalist bomber, supposedly recruited by Owens. His real task was grim. Inspector Williams had not only to sell himself to the Germans as a fanatical Welsh revolutionary but the retired policeman also had to ensure that Owens was discouraged from redefecting back to the Abwehr – permanently if necessary. The Germans were convinced and Inspector Williams safely ushered his charge back to Britain clutching instructions and a new Abwehr code book to send his messages to Germany. The radio game began.

From then on what became the Double Cross committee system grew into a full-blown Whitehall operation. It worked beautifully. After the fall of France in June 1940, the Germans began to send agents into Britain, instructing them to make contact with 'Johnny' (Snow and Owens) their 'master spy in England'. As the agents landed, they were picked up. If a civilian had seen them they were usually very publicly tried and then hanged. If they had not been spotted, the startled German spies would be dumped in an interrogation room with a cup of tea. There they were given a simple choice: cooperate with MI5 and Whitehall's Double Cross committee by sending messages from a warm cell with three square meals a day plus regular outings – or hang as a spy. It wasn't a tough choice for most of the captured men.

Only one German agent is thought to have escaped the British security net undetected. A Dutch national, Jan ter Braak – probably not his real name – landed undetected by parachute in November 1940 north of London and took rooms in Cambridge. He told his landlady that he had escaped from Dunkirk with the British Expeditionary Force when it fled from the Continent in June. Little else is known about ter Braak except that he claimed to be a Dutch journalist and that he was found with a bullet in his brain in an air raid shelter in Spring 1941. His secret Abwehr radio had never been used. The mystery appears never to have been explained and suicide appears the most likely explanation; or was it?

By the end of the war, the Double Cross committee system had run about 120 German agents. Of these, about a third were run as valued long-term assets. One of the most famous was a Yugoslav, Dusko

Popov, known wryly by his MI5 codename 'Tricycle' – Popov enjoyed sharing his bed with two women at a time if he got the chance.

Popov had been recruited on the Continent by the Abwehr to spy on Britain. On his arrival at Christmas 1940, he promptly approached the British authorities and told all. The British checked him out, found that the Yugoslav was genuine and bore little love for Hitler's Germany. They promptly took him up on his offer and recruited him to play back to the Abwehr. This Tricycle did with great success. Popov was delighted to cooperate; the Germans were delighted by the content of his fake intelligence reports from England. Everyone was happy. So much so, that Popov was ordered by his German controllers to go to America and set up his spy network there, including checking on some details of Pearl Harbor; the British encouraged him to go – as their man. Popov duly flew by Clipper flying boat from neutral Lisbon and, once in Washington, presented himself to the FBI as ordered.

Popov's alleged meeting with J. Edgar Hoover was a disaster. Hoover had been alerted by the British to Popov's louche lifestyle. J. Edgar Hoover didn't like the British and he certainly didn't like 'perverts'. (They may have made him uncomfortable about his own secret urges.) 'The dirty Nazi spy' was placed under surveillance by the FBI and given little or no cooperation by the US, who refused to provide even credible 'chicken-feed'. Hoover was running his own very secret double-cross operations against Nazi Germany by this time and these British distractions were the last thing he wanted. The FBI ensured that Popov was not allowed to travel anywhere near Hawaii and Hoover never bothered to follow up this unusual interest – to put it mildly – by Berlin in an American *Pacific* fleet base. He certainly never bothered to inform either US Navy Intelligence or Pearl Harbor. This was FBI business. Later in December the USA would pay a high price for J. Edgar Hoover's inertia, bureaucratic ambitions and prejudices as the Japanese made their devastating surprise strike against Pearl Harbor.

Hoover's crimes were not just of omission, however. In the summer of 1942, the FBI's director made the cold-blooded decision to cash in on a bungled German sabotage operation. He succeeded, and six

German agents went to the electric chair amid a blaze of publicity. The result was that by August 1942 Dusko Popov, contemplating the burning headlines in the US newspapers ('Hoover's Latest Triumph' and 'Nazi Spies Go to the Chair!'), must have felt a distinct touch of unease. Faced with a dangerous monster like J. Edgar Hoover as a potential adversary, Tricycle's scalp might well be the next to hang on the FBI director's belt. It is therefore not surprising that in 1943 Popov returned to England and picked up with his Hamburg controller – and MI5 – where he had left off.

This time his brief was to concentrate on the double-cross system's real coup, the deception plans for D-Day. This huge fraud, called Operation Fortitude completely fooled the Germans about the place and timing of Operation Overlord. One of the double-cross agents, Garbo, actually stopped the German armoured reserves moving in on Normandy, signalling that the Normandy bridgehead was just a huge diversion and the real landings would be in the Pas de Calais. Hitler was impressed with his trusted agent's radio messages. He ordered the divisions around Calais to stay put and awarded the agent an Iron Cross (Second Class) by radio. The British and American deception staffs cracked open the champagne.

The British were not the only ones who could play *Funkspielen*. In 1941, the Germans bagged an agent of N (Netherlands) Section of Britain's Special Operations Executive (SOE). Under duress, Lauwers, the captured operator, agreed to send a fake message back to his controllers in London. He knew that if he left out his secret security check from his Morse-code message, London would realise that he had fallen into German hands. London did no such thing.

Instead, it ignored its own signals security rules and parachuted in another agent, who fell straight into the waiting arms of Major Giskes of the Abwehr office in Holland. The embittered agent, convinced that there must be a German spy back in SOE London, talked to his captors. A delighted Giskes and the Abwehr now began to build up a complete profile of N Section and opened a radio dialogue with London, pretending to be N Section's 'Dutch network'. London was ecstatic.

They had established a spy network in enemy occupied Holland. They had, but it was German.

In return for his 'hard work on the ground', Giskes and his colleagues were now regularly supplied with whatever they asked for, be it gold, weapons, fresh codes and an occasional new agent, startled to discover his reception committee at the landing zone was German. The German cells began to fill up with SOE's Dutchmen captured as soon as they landed. In vain Lauwers omitted his radio security checks. No one back in SOE's N Section in London took the slightest notice of signals clearly marked 'Security check missing!' Even when the Germans put their own operator on the Morse Key, claiming that Lauwers had recruited a Dutch helper because he had 'sprained his wrist', London signalled back saying, 'Don't forget to instruct him in the secret security check.' Professor M. R. D. Foot in his official history of SOE, wrote plaintively: 'How monumentally stupid can a staff officer be?' The answer is: very.

The Abwehr continued with their 'England *spiel*' for three years. Every effort to warn London failed. Even when two of the captured Dutch agents escaped and fled to Spain to get back to England and warn N Section, the inventive Giskes came up with a master-stroke. He 'warned' London that two of the Dutch network had 'betrayed them to the Gestapo' and disappeared. When the two brave Dutchmen finally reached London they were promptly locked up in jail as turncoats and traitors, their protestations unheeded.

By early 1944, it was clear even to N Section in London that something was wrong, even if it was too stupid to realise just what it was. Giskes put the knife in with a final mocking telegram sent appropriately enough on 1 April 1944, All Fools Day, thanking N Section for their 'long and successful cooperation' with the Abwehr and assuring them that would be 'received with the same care and attention as those they had sent before'.

Most of the Dutch prisoners were shot, although Lauwers survived the war. Operation North Pole was over, a triumph for German counter-intelligence. They had even been able to fund the whole operation – and make a small profit – with the gold and banknotes obligingly dispatched by London. Although Giskes' scam was essentially a double agent bluff, it was different from previous double operations, relying as it did on technical devices – in this case, radio – to make it work. Technical intelligence was now as important as traditional spying.

This emphasis on things technical was reinforced in November 1939, when the British received an astounding espionage windfall. Someone left seven typewritten pages on the windowsill of the British Consulate in Oslo, containing an amazing wealth of technical detail on German weapon research programmes. The mysterious packet was ostensibly from 'a German Scientist who wishes you well' and included information on rocket developments and a little box containing a glass vacuum tube for a prototype anti-aircraft proximity fuse. True to form Whitehall assumed that it was all a hoax or a plant. But some of the details rang true. The Oslo Report mentioned Peenemunde for the first time and tied it in with the Wehrmacht's rocket experiments. This was all news to Whitehall; but the information about Rechlin, the Luftwaffe Experimental Base, tallied with known intelligence and the details of German anti-aircraft detection radars seemed accurate enough. In 1939 Whitehall decided to wait and see, just in case the Oslo Report was a plant. As events turned out it was not a plant, and German technical developments matched the capabilities predicted by Oslo's anonymous author fairly precisely. Someone, and someone with access to Germany's top military secrets, was trying to do the British a favour right from the start of the war.

The first recipient of the Oslo Report was a young scientist called R.V. Jones. Jones was an untypical civil servant in the 1930s, having an open mind and a great desire to get things done. In the stuffy atmosphere of pre-war Whitehall, this was often a disadvantage. His other great attribute was a genuine sense of fun, which sometimes got him into trouble with his superiors or the victims of his practical jokes. Although they were never malicious, on one famous occasion he nearly induced a non-scientific colleague, who had been having trouble with his telephone, to try lowering it into a bucket of water, 'to test the circuit'. At the last minute he stopped him.

As a new discipline, technical intelligence inevitably tended to attract some unusual characters to the ponderous committee rooms of Whitehall. One of the more bizarre was a Major Freddie Wintle of the Royal Dragoons, Jones's Army colleague seconded to work in Air Intelligence. The young scientist and the monocled older cavalry officer got on well until Wintle showed just a little too much character. Ordered to rejoin his regiment in the dark days of the fall of France in the summer of 1940, he refused, saying that as an ex-instructor at France's *Ecole de Guerre*, he felt he would make a better contribution to the crisis as a liaison officer to the French Army. The director of Air Intelligence then unwisely called Wintle a coward.

This was a serious mistake to a cavalry officer of Wintle's generation. Major Wintle promptly pulled out his service revolver and threatened to blow the Air Commodore's brains out. The white-faced chief of Air Intelligence duly had Wintle arrested, sent to the Tower of London – the nearest military prison for officers – and court-martialled.

His court martial descended into farce. He cheerfully confirmed that he had indeed told the Air Commodore that 'he and all his kind should be shot', and agreed that he had said that most senior officers were useless, 'especially some Ministers'. To explain his point, and to the court's embarrassment and the journalists' delight, he then produced a list of those who he felt were particularly useless, and exactly why he had come to this measured view of his masters' courage and convictions. He then proceeded to read out those who he felt were letting the country down, and why. The judge advocate general intervened hastily and dropped the charge. When asked why he had said that his eyesight was not good enough for active service, the redoubtable Wintle removed his monocle and pointed out that he was blind in his right eye from a wound sustained during the Great War. Wintle cheerfully admitted that he had fooled the Air Commodore just as he had been fooling the army doctors for years. The court moved hastily on.

To the final charge, the court martial asked Wintle if he had intended to intimidate the Air Commodore when he pulled his pistol, to which Wintle replied that, 'from experience, he didn't think it possible to intimidate the Air Commodore, and all his type.' Asked what type he meant, Wintle swore that it would have been a pointless exercise as all 'that type' could do on being confronted by a genuine threat was 'to take up a pen and write someone a minute about it, even if the building was on fire.'

To stifled laughter, the court moved swiftly on to its verdict. Clearly the army could not tolerate such absolutely disgraceful behaviour towards a senior RAF officer. Major Wintle was duly found guilty and given a severe reprimand. But one cannot escape the feeling that the court's members were busy stuffing their handkerchiefs into their mouths to stop laughing as they passed sentence. Freddie Wintle was rapidly posted out of Air Intelligence.

With free-thinking characters like Jones and Wintle as technical intelligence officers and a stream of bright civilian academics flooding into the codebreaking centre at Bletchley Park, it was clear that, whatever else happened, the Second World War's other great difference to all previous wars was that the brightest and the best were being recruited into intelligence – certainly in Britain. Technical intelligence, not spies, would rule.

The real interface between technical intelligence and spying is codebreaking, which is really only spying on enemy communications. A host of TV documentaries, books and films have portrayed Britain's codebreaking centre at Bletchley Park, (Station X) as the great codebreaking Enigma story and no more. Signals intelligence is in reality much more than that. It involves several clear activities of which codebreaking is merely one. Signals intelligence is actually a number of separate activities involving intercepting radio signals, 'direction finding' to identify their location, technical analysis of the radio concerned, traffic analysis to establish the pattern and identities of who is talking to whom, reading the signal, or, if you can't read the message, trying to decipher and break the enemy's code.

The final activity (often forgotten by oversimplified TV dramas) is using the stuff; which means getting the intelligence, in conditions of maximum secrecy, to the individual decision-maker who has to act on the intelligence in time to make a difference. The codebreakers, clever and important though they undoubtedly are, are only a small cog in a very large intelligence machine and it is a mistake to overlook the contribution of traffic analysis or direction finding. For example, the German Air Defenders of the Reich *always* knew when a big air raid was on its way by the chatter as the USAF and RAF aircrews tested their radios before taking off; simple stuff, but vital intelligence. Codebreaking, however, tends to get all the glory from signals intelligence. It is customary to portray the British as the worldbeaters at this in the Second World War. Indeed they were, but they were not the only ones. The activities of the Americans and Germans are worthy of note, too. German skill and codebreaking success between 1939 and 1944 cost many Allied lives, even if such intelligence triumphs have failed to inspire any big-budget Hollywood productions.

The German B-Dienst (Beobachtung/Observation) was an extremely efficient and successful organisation. At the start of the war it quickly broke the British and Allied Merchant Ships code (BAMS) and began to steer Admiral Dönitz's U-boats towards the Allied convoys. As these were obligingly codenamed by their ports (e.g. HX equalled Halifax) and their cargoes it was relatively straightforward for the German codebreakers at the Kriegsmarine High Command's own version of Bletchley Park to plot the convoys' courses and their likely locations. Long before the war their ace codebreaker Wilhelm Tranow had been cracking British naval codes. He had started in the Great War and by 1932 he had unbuttoned the whole of the British government's telegraph code. By 1939 his skill and encyclopedic knowledge of the Royal Navy and all its ships was acknowledged as invaluable to German intelligence. As head of the English Language Section (Radio Reconnaissance Branch) of the Kriegsmarine's Naval Communications Service, Tranow proved to be a very capable and dangerous enemy indeed. With this kind of expertise and the forty-four German signals intelligence listening posts all over Europe, the B-Dienst under Tranow was into British naval secrets from the start of the war.

By early 1943 the by now experienced and skilful German naval analysts could predict the most probable diversions and convoy tactics of HQ Western Approaches with chilling accuracy. Even when Dönitz's staff misjudged, they could invariably rely on British naval communications traffic to correct any mistakes on the vast chess board of the North Atlantic and reroute the Wolf Packs to pick up the slow-moving Atlantic convoys and begin their depredations.

And what a feast of targets the U-boats had in the first three years of the war! By the time the British changed their naval codes and tactics and began to beat the U-boats in May 1943, Dönitz's submarine fleet and the Luftwaffe's few long-range bombers had sunk 3,505 Allied ships, killed 38,000 sailors and sent something like 25 million tons of shipping and their vital cargoes to the bottom, and all mainly due to weak British naval codes. Despite Enigma and Hollywood's glamorous movies, real professionals should never forget that codebreaking intelligence can break both ways. The German codebreakers and intelligence analysts were certainly – at the tactical and operational level – every bit as skilful and dangerous as their British counterparts.

German codebreaking success had another extraordinary coup in the autumn of 1940. Reading the BAMS code, the B-Dienst was interested to note that a fast liner, the MV *Automedon*, had been routed on a solo fast passage to the Far East on a special mission. The *Automedon* was in fact carrying a unique cargo of new codes, courier mail and classified 'most secret' correspondence for Malaya. The B-Dienst quickly informed the Kreigsmarine and in November 1940 the *Automedon* was stopped and captured by the disguised German surface raider *Atlantis*, deep in the Indian Ocean. On board was a treasure trove of British secret documents, including a new set of BAMS codes.

The German skipper duly put in at 'neutral' Japan and handed over his invaluable haul to the German Embassy. They obligingly shared their windfall with General Tojo and the Japanese. Japanese military planners must have been encouraged to read the British War Cabinet's gloomy prognostications in a series of 'most secret' letters for 'C.-in-C. Malaya's eyes only', basically telling him the good news, 'You're on your own if the Japs try anything.' 'The Japs' duly noted this useful intelligence and treated it as a green light to do just that, trying – and succeeding – to invade Malaya a year later. It was a triumph for the B-Dienst and a disaster for British interests in the Far East.

While (so far as we know) Germany never replicated Bletchley Park's cracking of enemy top-level codes, this kind of strategic success was also achieved by the Americans completely independently of the British. In March 1939 the Japanese brought in their own version of an Enigma encoding machine and began to use a new high-level enciphering system called 'Purple'. Within eighteen months, the US Army's Signals Intelligence Service (SIS – not to be confused with the British MI6-Secret Intelligence Service) had broken the Purple code with a team under their top codebreaker William Friedman. Despite Secretary Stimson's refusal to countenance signals intelligence in 1929, the US Army had quietly set up its own signals intelligence organisation and kept it going throughout the 1930s. It was staffed by a high grade and very dedicated cipher staff. Friedman called his team 'Magicians' and the name stuck. Appropriately enough 'Magic' became the code word for intelligence from the Purple coded messages, and the American's Magic paralleled Britain's Enigma throughout the war and was to be the source of a number of American naval triumphs in the Pacific.

America's greatest signals intelligence coup was in their use of 'sigint' to trap the Japanese aircraft carrier fleet off Midway in the summer of 1942. Although in the end it was as always the heroism of the fighting men who sent four of the Japanese Imperial Navy's priceless aircraft carriers to the bottom in one afternoon, it had been intelligence in general and 'sigint' in all its forms that had placed them into position. Without the courage of the US Navy's aircrew there would have been no victory: but without US Naval Intelligence there would have been no battle. Once the commander has decided what to do based on the intelligence received it is all down to the battle he chooses to fight: and once battle is joined it is all down to the warriors.

Midway was the turning point of the Pacific War and as vital to the history of the world as the great battle at Kursk on the Eastern Front a year later. The battles of Kursk and Midway decided the Second World War. Both relied for their victory on the hidden hand of intelligence to guide their commanders' hands to victory. In July 1943 Kursk was the key battle of the war on the Eastern Front and effectively sealed the Wehrmacht's fate. After Kursk Hitler was always on the defensive, only delaying the inevitable as the Red Army assaulted his forces again and again with overwhelming might and increasing skill until they burst into his Berlin bunker in May 1945.

Kursk started in April 1943 as Operation Zitadelle, the Germans' great plan to pinch out the Kursk pocket and to break through once more to drive the Russians back in headlong retreat. Hitler confessed: 'it made me sick to my stomach to think about it.' He was wise, for the Soviets knew about it from the start. The Russian victory at Kursk was only made possible by the oldest and sometimes the very best intelligence of all: human intelligence. The Russians had a high-grade spy in the heart of the German camp and he told them everything.

We now know from the uncovered KGB archives that from 1941 onwards there was a high level Soviet spy at the very top of the Nazi war machine. His codename was Werther. Via a network of radio operators and couriers based in Switzerland (which included a Liverpudlian, Alexander Foote) the spy Werther betrayed every German operation in Eastern Europe, sending battle plans, details of the Nazi military strategy, tank positions, endless sets of numbers, and details of the weaknesses of German army positions. This Swiss spy network, called the Lucy Ring, sent over 2,300 messages to Moscow between 1941 and 1945 of which a fifth came from Werther. The CIA has managed to decrypt all or some of 332 messages in all. Werther's information was so important it was marked 'for Stalin's eyes only' and went immediately to Stalin personally. Though he never knew who Werther was, Stalin eventually trusted him completely, basing his battle plans on the information received.

Werther was prolific, answering (sometimes on the same day)

detailed lists of questions from the Russians, and giving away the most sensitive secrets of the Third Reich. His intelligence was crucial to the outcome of the war in the East: despite their better tanks, generals and soldiers, from late 1942 onwards the Wehrmacht was outmanoeuvred every time. In Hitler's own words, 'It was almost as if they knew we were coming'. They did.

Astonishingly, there is a very real possibility that Werther could have been linked with none other than Martin Bormann, Hitler's deputy. Despite the enormity of this claim, the facts and the circumstantial evidence deserve closer examination. Whoever he was, Werther's clandestine work changed the course of history and defines the world we live in today. Without his treachery, the Germans would – almost certainly – have defeated the Russians by 1942–3 and the final outcome of the Second World War would have been very different. Throughout his entire spying career, spanning 1941–5, Werther's identity was only known to one member of the ring, a woman called Rachel Dubendorfer. All the other principal characters in the Lucy spy ring have long been unmasked as Soviet agents. Many of the key players in the story were women – or used women's names.

The ring was named after Rudolf Rossler (codenamed Lucy), a German journalist, based in Switzerland. As well as the mysterious Werther his ring also ran several other major spies high up in the Nazi command. This network was set up by a Russian woman, Maria Poliakova (Gisela) in Switzerland in the 1930s, before she returned to Moscow to become controller of what became known as the *Rote Kapelle*, the 'Red Orchestra' of Soviet spy rings in Europe. The most important figure was Rachel Dubendorfer (Sissy), an untidy neurotic who alone knew the identity of Werther and – despite relentless pressure – refused to reveal the name of her source.

Alongside these three 'women' were three men: Alexander Foote, a Liverpudlian wireless operator and dedicated Communist who had fought with the Republicans in Spain in the 1930s; Alexander Rado (Dora) the administrator of the ring; and Leopold Trepper, who was a Soviet triple agent throughout most of the war. Bormann's role remains an enigma: but one possible motivation is that of all the Nazi leadership only Martin Bormann seems to have really believed in the other half of the National Socialist Party's creed: he was a life-long socialist.

After Rudolf Hess's defection on a fool's errand to Scotland in 1941, Martin Bormann became more powerful than any of the other Nazi satraps surrounding the Führer, primarily through his role as the trusted secretary of the National Socialist Party. As the war went on and as Hitler became more deranged (largely through Parkinson's Disease and the bizarre concoctions of drugs given to him by his doctors), he began to rely increasingly on his trusted aide Bormann. He alone controlled access to the Führer and was the only one allowed to issue orders in his name. No one knows if Bormann first made contact with Rachel Dubendorfer, but the radio material began to flow in 1941. Werther's warnings about Operation Barbarossa were included among the 103 separate reports given to the Soviet leader of Hitler's plans to invade Russia – warnings which Stalin ignored.

He was not to make the same mistake again. The flow of top-grade intelligence from the heart of the German war machine continued and initially it was so good that Stalin believed it was a German trap. But then, in mid 1942, in all the chaos of conflicting intelligence and imminent defeat, Stalin decided to trust in Werther. By the late summer of 1942 it was clear that Werther's reports were pure gold. Instead of fighting the Wehrmacht at every opportunity – and losing – by summer 1942 Stalin had opted for a strategic trap, and one that would win the war. The Red Army was ordered to give ground and retreat to lure the Germans deep into Russian territory, starting at Stalingrad. In autumn 1942, Stalin's trap began to close. Once the Germans had reached Stalingrad they were exhausted. For the first time in months, on the banks of the Don, the Wehrmacht suddenly ran into heavy resistance. By the end of 1942 von Paulus's German 6th Army was cut off and in deep trouble.

Werther's spying career might all have ended there, at Christmas 1942. A message from Moscow Centre to Rachel Dubendorfer ('Werther is to state clearly how many replacement divisions in all are being formed from recruits by 1 January. Reply urgent') was intercepted by German intelligence, who now knew they had a major spy in their midst. But as Hitler's triumphant German divisions had swept all before them deep into Russia by the end of 1942, one spy was an irrelevance in the euphoria of victory. Even with the disaster of Stalingrad looming over them, the German High Command ignored the warning and the alarm bells went unheard.

Back home, OKW had devised a new plan to ensure that no detail or decision was missed at the daily *Führerkonferenz*. Stenographers should in future attend every Führer meeting and keep detailed notes so that Hitler's brilliance could be recorded for posterity. The moment the new secretaries started work (often producing five hundred typewritten pages a day) the level of detail given to the Lucy group soared. Suddenly Stalin was receiving detailed discussions from Werther of who said what in Hitler's daily war conferences *on the very day they took place*, and long before the orders had been sent out in Enigma code to the frontline German commanders in the field and the waiting codebreakers of Bletchley Park. We now know that there were only two recipients of these stenographers' draft transcripts: Martin Bormann, Hitler's closest day-to-day confidante, and the senior communications officer in OKW.

As his confidence grew, Stalin grew bolder, often sending Werther dozens of highly detailed questions such as, 'What is the current position of the 11th and 18th armoured divisions and the 25th mobile division that were previously engaged in the Bryansk-Bolkhov sector?' and, more damning still, 'What is the attitude of the Senior Military officers in the Führer HQ to the latest order? Who is for and who is against?' Only someone with access to the daily conferences could possibly have known that level of detailed discussion. Werther was now providing war-winning intelligence on every subject dear to Hitler's heart, and often on the very day it was discussed. Claims that the Lucy Ring was some kind of British front to conceal Bletchley Park's Enigma 'sigint' simply don't stand up. The Lucy Ring was passing crucial and accurate intelligence direct to Moscow long before Bletchley Park had deciphered it and before many *German commanders* had even received it.

Kursk was Werther's most dramatic success. The 'greatest tank battle in history' was the hinge moment of the Second World War on land. It was a battle, which all things being equal, the Germans expected to win. They had 900,000 men, 2,700 tanks and 10,000 artillery pieces plus the element of surprise – or so they thought. But Werther had warned the Russians. Knowing every last detail of Hitler's 1943 offensive plan for Zitadelle, Stalin mustered 1.3 million soldiers, 3,444 tanks and 19,000 artillery pieces in no less than *eight* separate defensive lines exactly facing the Wehrmacht's planned thrust lines. In all, an astonishing 40 per cent of the Red Army was moved into place to ambush the German onslaught when it came. With the precise and detailed German operational orders in their hands the Red Army laid 400,000 mines to channel their attackers into a lethal crossfire from pre-placed anti-tank guns. Thanks to Werther's intelligence, the Red Army's deadly trap destroyed a year's production of German tanks, guns and planes. Kursk broke the Wehrmacht in the East once and for all and opened the door to the Soviet drive that would end two years later in the ruins of Berlin.

The Germans had been defeated not by Russian brilliance but by the single-minded treachery of the greatest spy of modern times, whoever it was. Only one man in Hitler's headquarters ever had the opportunity to access all the intelligence reported to Stalin over the period in question: the Führer's faithful Nazi Party secretary, Martin Bormann. The evidence is compelling. Werther could well have been Martin Bormann, possibly the greatest spy of the twentieth century.

Bormann was last seen amid the burning ruins of Hitler's bunker in Berlin as the vengeful soldiers of the Red Army closed in for the kill on the 1 May 1945. Along with Fritz Kolbe, Alan Dulles' master spy inside the Reich's Foreign Ministry (who spied for OSS with in the hope of seeing Hitler out of power) the mysterious Werther stands as one of the great secret influences of the Second World War. Sometimes there is no substitute for a really good spy. Even signals intelligence, with all its wartime triumphs can never be steered to tell you exactly what you want to know. For all its risks and fallibility, human intelligence is absolutely necessary and has been at all times and in all ages.

Lacking any Werther in the Japanese camp, America relied heavily on 'sigint'. America's reliance on this to win victories in the Pacific was as vital as any of the British achievements in the Atlantic. Whenever 'sigint' went wrong or was absent then the US warriors had to take their chance like anyone else. In the summer of 1942 the American signals intelligence stations lost their ability to break into the Japanese Navy's JN 25 code. As a result suddenly the US Navy was blind to Japanese fleet movements.

The price for losing the intelligence war even for a short period was heavy. In late 1942 Japanese hit-and-run warships began to sink American supply ships and their escorts in 'the slot', a narrow passage off Guadalcanal Island, while the Americans were trying to make vital resupply runs to their embattled US Marines ashore. By early August 1942 so many ships had gone to the bottom that it was nicknamed Ironbottom Sound.

On the night of 9 August an Allied cruiser squadron moved in to protect the resupply convoy and was surprised by a Japanese naval ambush. In the dark the fighting was confused. The Americans had primitive radar to help them, but the Japanese had been exercising using just such cruiser squadron night actions for years. Sweeping down on both sides of the baffled Allied ships, much as Nelson had done at Aboukir Bay a century and a half before, the Japanese Navy blasted their confused opponents at short range in the dark. Their well-practised tactics and superb Long Lance torpedoes overwhelmed the Allied cruisers in a confused night mêlée, sending all four Allied cruisers to the bottom. The loss of the USS *Vincennes, Quincy, Astoria* and the Royal Australian Navy's *Canberra* off Savo Island was a devastating reminder of Japanese naval capabilities and the worst defeat in US naval history. It was also a powerful incentive to the US and intelligence staff to break into the new version of Japan's JN 25 code. Good intelligence was the key to victory it seemed: Admiral Halsey said so forcefully.

The US codebreakers redoubled their efforts. By the spring of 1943 they had succeeded and in doing so were able to inflict a crushing blow both to the Japanese forces in the Solomons and to the morale of the whole Japanese Navy, when they ambushed and killed the Japanese commander-in-chief. The commander of the Combined Fleet was Admiral Yamamoto. Yamamoto was a national hero to the Imperial Japanese Navy and to his countrymen. It was he who had planned and executed the stunning victory over the Americans at Pearl Harbor and his reputation stood high as a charismatic and popular admiral. Not for nothing was he sometimes referred to as the 'Japanese Nelson'. In April 1943 he planned a combined inspection and morale-building tour of the Japanese positions in the Solomons. The necessary signals were sent out to warn the garrisons of the great man's itinerary. It was a mistake. Yet again transmission would prove to be treason.

The US Navy's siginters intercepted and read the Japanese traffic with interest before passing Yamamoto's itinerary to Admiral Halsey. Admiral Halsey took a more robust view of fighting than his illustrious predecessor the Duke of Wellington, who at Waterloo memorably refused to turn his artillery on a dangerously exposed Napoleon, saying 'it is not the duty of Commanders in Chief to engage in fighting one another.' No such honourable eighteenth-century nonsense was going to stay the US admiral's hand when presented with the opportunity to get rid of Japan's most important war leader in the Pacific. (Halsey is alleged to have said, 'Let's try and kill the bastard!')

He ordered an interception by long-range P-38 Lightning fighters flying from Guadalcanal as a reception committee. In a well-timed aerial ambush eighteen Lightnings dived on Yamamoto's lumbering 'Betty' long-range bomber transport as it began its final approach to Bougainville Island nearly 400 miles north of Guadalcanal. Taken totally by surprise, the escorting Zero fighters failed to protect their charge and the unarmoured fuel tanks of the Betty caught fire as the bomber dived for the ground. It was too late. The burning aircraft ploughed into the jungle from 2,000 feet, killing all on board. Yamamoto was found sitting dead in the wreckage, his sword between his knees. 'There was only one Yamamoto', mourned a fellow admiral. His talents would be sorely missed by the Japanese in the months ahead. The intrepid P-38 pilots might have done the business – but it was intelligence's hidden hand that put them there to make their kill. It was an intelligence coup of the highest magnitude.

'Sigint's' other great contribution to the American victory in the Pacific was the US Navy's uncanny ability to place one of their long-range submarines into the path of any Japanese transport or warship that happened to come along. It was the US Navy's submarines that made the Japanese island empire in the Pacific wither on the vine in 1944 and 1945. In their own undersea battle of the Pacific, ComSub-Pac's boats caused three times more damage than ever Dönitz's men were able to achieve in the Atlantic. The answer was simple: the Americans knew exactly where their targets were. And it was the Americans' Magic and their signals intelligence that made it so.

This development was so important that when President Roosevelt and Prime Minister Churchill met in August 1941 for the first ever Allied 'Council of War' on board HMS *Prince of Wales* to sign the vague press release known to history as the Atlantic Charter, one of their key agreements was to exchange intelligence. A Magic decoding machine was actually handed to the British to take back to Bletchley Park; ironically, the one destined for Pearl Harbor. The US-UK special relationship began on that day. At its heart, from the start, has been intelligence. It has remained there ever since.

As HMS *Prince of Wales* sailed back to Britain from Canada (it sailed at high speed through the middle of a convoy so that the sailors could cheer a 'gratified' Churchill) it also bore an agreement to exchange US-UK technical intelligence as well. At the working level this included many of Britain's radar secrets. Britain had been a pioneer in radar or 'radio echo locating'. It had been noted for a long time that the presence of an aeroplane near radio transmitter masts affected the transmission in some way. In 1935, an obscure scientist called Watson-Watt at the Radio Research Establishment had been asked to see if he could devise a 'radio wave death ray'. Watson-Watt dryly pointed out that the power demands of such a death ray were beyond his limited talents but noted that radio waves did tend to bounce back off solid objects. The French, for example, were experimenting with an 'anti-iceberg radio detection beam' for their new liner *Normandie*. Perhaps the idea could be adapted to use radio waves to detect ships or even incoming aircraft?

A worried British Air Ministry, obsessed with the prevalent ideas of massed air raids on London in any future war, poured money and other resources into the project. It went well. By 1939 the British had built a chain of crude air defence radar-locating stations along their south and east coasts. German intelligence was well aware of the existence of these 'Chain Home' stations; their 200-foot lattice towers were impossible to disguise. Germany's problem was what on earth were they for? The Germans had invented their own radar system quite separately and it bore no resemblance to these curious radio towers. So puzzled were they by them that in 1939, in the last days of peace, they sent their airship *Graf Zeppelin* cruising up the east coast of Britain to see if German Air Intelligence could collect any signals. They came away baffled. The towers were apparently silent. In a particularly devious stroke, the cunning British had switched them off.

The truth was that the two countries had adopted completely different approaches and completely different radars. The British radar development scientists' motto was 'second best tomorrow'. They knew that the Germans had some very precise, high-tech systems. When the battleship *Graf Spee* was scuttled in Montevideo Harbour in December 1939 the first thing the British discovered was a gunnery control radar antenna on the top of the mast, set up for the 80cm wavelength. British radars were crude by comparison. Where Germany stressed accuracy, Britain went for range. The result was a curious intelligence impasse. The Germans with their excellent radars (despite Watson-Watt's self-publicising claim to have invented radar) thought that British radar was a long way behind their own, particularly after the capture of a few crude experimental sets among the litter of the British Army's discarded equipment on the Dunkirk beaches. The British, who were secretly sharing their 'wonderful new radar technology' with the US Navy below the counter from 1940 onwards, refused to believe that the Germans even had locating radar. As late as 24 February 1941, Britain's Air Ministry called a meeting, 'to discuss the existence of German radar'. It was not exactly British intelligence's finest hour. The Oslo Report was beginning to be vindicated and revealing itself to be only too true, its secrets unveiled one by one.

What was going on was the birth of a completely new kind of intelligence: electronic intelligence. As the war progressed it would begin to dominate the battle as the combatants struggled to keep a technical superiority over the enemy's weapons, especially in the air. Air combat, particularly at night, was becoming a competition between machines and their technical aids. Not for nothing was radar sometimes called an 'instrument of darkness'. Technical superiority was the key to success in this new battlefield. It could be devastating. When the British fire-bombed Hamburg on 23–24 July 1943, they used 'window' (chaff) to jam the German radar for the very first time; tiny strips of Christmas decoration tinfoil cut to the length of German radar frequencies. The German radar defences were completely fooled and blinded. British Bomber Command lost only 1½ per cent of their planes – 12 aircraft out of 791, Hamburg was burnt out by a firestorm, and the USAF's daylight raids added to the historic port's misery as the combined bomber offensive tried to rip the heart out of Nazi Germany.

The key to winning this technical battle was intelligence. It would have been useless for Bomber Command to drop the wrong kind of tinfoil strips over German radars. The British had to know the correct frequencies and wavelengths. The effect of this battle for technical knowledge was to force military operations to carry out special operations for the sole purpose of collecting intelligence. Just as cavalry patrols in Napoleon's time and snatch patrols in the First World War's trenches had tried to bag a live prisoner for interrogation, so by the Second World War some highly dangerous operations were launched solely to collect crucial technical intelligence.

The raid on Bruneval is a classic. British intelligence needed to know the technical details of the Germans' radars. Coastal defence radar tends to be near the coast and so, on the night of 27 February 1942, the newly raised British Parachute Regiment dropped in to steal a German 'Wurzburg' radar and spirit it home across the Channel.

The raid succeeded brilliantly. The British not only stole key equipment from the radar but also captured its disconsolate operator (who had fallen over a cliff in his efforts to escape and been 'rescued' by the Paras). From the wealth of information obtained, British technical intelligence was now able to advise the British bomber squadrons how best to defeat the Germans' air defence system.

They were less successful with their own bombers' radars. As the war progressed, and the aerial battle became more and more a struggle of machine against machine in the dark, RAF bombers were fitted with increasingly technical aids. One was 'H2S', a radar that scanned the ground and could spot features on the ground through fog and cloud. Another was a radar detector called Monica that swept the area behind a bomber searching for the presence of prowling night fighters sneaking up on the bombers. The problem was that both Monica and H2S *transmitted* radar beams. 'Transmission is treason', and so it proved once again, this time for the hapless RAF crews. After the war, the Germans happily admitted that their own radar warning stations in *Berlin* could sometimes spot bomber's H2S radars being switched while the RAF bombers were still over Britain. Monica was even worse. The Germans had checked the mysterious rearward-looking radar devices on shot-down RAF bombers and identified the frequency. It was then child's play to fit a simple receiver tuned to Monica's characteristics in the front of the Luftwaffe's night fighters. From then on using Monica was the equivalent of shining a bright light backwards in the darkness to guide the delighted German night-fighter crews to their lumbering targets, plump with high explosives and high-octane petrol. Bomber Command losses rose dramatically until a captured German night fighter was tested. The boffins discovered that while flying over London they could 'see' a RAF Monica set on a bomber flying 50 miles away over Bristol. Monica was effectively a beacon on which German night fighters could home. Monica was removed – rapidly – and from then on, H2S was used only in ten second bursts.

This constant technical struggle to collect intelligence in the air, and at sea against the U-boats, often called for as much heroism as any 'combat operation'. For example, in December 1942 a slow and almost obsolescent twin-engined Wellington was sent out on a raid as 'electronic bait' on an intelligence-gathering mission. It was crewed by a specialist crew of radar and radio specialists and its role was to identify the German night fighters' radar characteristics in the air and in action. To say that this 'ferret' mission was dangerous is a grave understatement of the risks involved. To carry out their mission the bomber and its crew had to wait to be attacked by a German night fighter.

It was. Pumping out its radar signals like a bat hunting a moth, a Junkers 88 night fighter homed in on the Wellington. The aircrew recorded the transmissions coming in on the 490 mhz wavelength and signalled the details back home just before a storm of cannon shells lashed the bomber. Again and again the night fighter pounced, trying to close with the Wellington which twisted and turned in the night sky, all the time collecting the Germans' radar signatures. It was an epic battle. The RAF rear gunner drove the German off until he was himself hit and put out of action. Four of the Wellington's crew of six were seriously wounded. After no less than eleven separate firing passes the night fighter eventually disappeared into the darkness and the crippled electronic collector limped back to England to ditch in the sea off the coast at Deal. It had, despite its loss, succeeded in collecting the vital intelligence on exactly how German night fighters' radar worked. Medals were distributed among a very gallant aircrew when they came out of hospital. Any doubts about the capabilities of the German night fighters were finally resolved when a Junkers 88, complete with its brand new Lichenstein radar suite and crew defected to RAF Dyce near Aberdeen in May 1944. Secret Service officers whisked the cheerful Germans away to an unknown destination while the technical intelligence experts fell on their trophy to gorge on its secrets.

The other great source of technical intelligence was the 'old-fashioned' method of photography. By the Second World War, aerial photography techniques were well developed. It had been a crucial factor over the trenches in the First World War and both sides used it extensively from the start in the Second. By 1939 the Germans were using specially adapted Junkers 86 to fly at nearly 40,000 feet to spy on both the Soviet Union and the Western Allies. In Britain the RAF developed high performance Spitfires and Mosquitoes to collect intelligence from high over Germany and occupied Europe.

Aerial photography has two main uses: to look for enemy activity, and secondly to check on the success of operations, such as bombing raids. Like all photography it could be deceived – the British in particular providing lots of false 'evidence' around Dover and Kent in the spring of 1944 to fool the Germans that fake wooden oil depots and dummy rubber tanks were really a huge army waiting to invade at Calais. But when combined with other sources, aerial reconnaissance paid big dividends. One of the classic technical intelligence operators of the Second World War was the saga of the German rockets and flying bombs. It demonstrates just how important intelligence is from *all* sources.

The story started, as do so many intelligence sagas, with a piece of straightforward espionage or human intelligence. The Oslo Report had said that the Germans were experimenting with rockets at a place called Peenemunde off the Baltic coast. The Polish underground corroborated this; strange things were happening around Stettin, and stranger 'things with fiery tails' were flying over the sea. Enigma further corroborated the tale, noting that the German Army was calling on the German High Command for greater anti-aircraft protection of their vital research installation at Peenemunde. A key radar unit was to be dispatched to give help. The Danish resistance smuggled pictures back to England of a mysterious pilotless 'flying bomb' that had crashed on Bornholm Island. Eventually a keen-eyed photographic interpreter spotted a tiny 'aeroplane' on a launch pad at Peenemunde. It was the V1. It was a classic story of photographic intelligence and sharp, attractive young WRAF officers.

The real intelligence coup was, however, much more subtle. Technical Intelligence (Air) and the British Secret Service under the everpersistent Jones had decided to track the Enigma signals traffic of two key Luftwaffe experimental radar companies to see just what they were protecting and watching. In the autumn of 1943, sure enough, up popped one of the special electronic companies, now posted out on the Baltic coast. More interestingly, it was transmitting its readings of a 'small trials aircraft ... flying out to sea at about 400 mph.' Although encoded, Enigma by this stage of the war was often an open book and the Germans' readings of the 'little rocket's' height, speed and course were all faithfully checked by the Allied intelligence staff. By now thoroughly alerted to the danger, the RAF was ordered to fly a special photo-recce mission precisely to capture Peenemunde's V1 on camera. Constance Babington-Smith's 'discovery' of the V1 on her film at the RAF Photographic Interpretation (PI) Establishment at Medmenham should therefore be seen in a different light. Her great PI 'coup' turns out to be nothing more than visual confirmation of something already well known and suspected from other intelligence. Photo recce and aerial pictures are often like that.

The V2 rocket saga was not dissimilar. Driven out of Peenemunde by the devastating Bomber Command raid of August 1943, the Germans relocated their rocket trials to the Polish Baltic coast, far from prying eyes and far from Allied bombers. By the spring of 1944, they were active again and the Polish underground reported that a 'big new rocket' was being developed using liquid fuel. Signals intelligence supported the story. An off-course German rocket fell in Sweden and the British offered to buy the wreckage in exchange for Spitfire fighters. The 'neutral' Swedes, who by now knew exactly who was going to win the war and which side their bread was buttered, duly obliged. The final clincher was the discovery of a fired V2, which splashed down in a Polish marsh and was snatched from under the very noses of the German search party by the underground Polish Home Army. The RAF flew a Dakota out to land in a muddy Polish field to retrieve the vital surviving rocket parts. After much argument (and many bruised egos) in Whitehall, a combination of brave spies, codebreaking and technical intelligence had discovered the truth about the V2. It wasn't as bad as they had feared.

The British had been preparing to evacuate a million people from London to avoid a hail of '10-ton rocket bombs'. It turned out from the technical specification of the rocket parts that the new missiles could not support a payload of more than one ton: bad enough, but bearable and certainly no worse than the earlier Blitz. London could take it. The evacuation plans were quietly shelved, but a new operation was planned for autumn 1944 to push on into Holland. The aim was to get across the Rhine and to drive the Germans out of V2 missile range. The advance would be towards a little town called Arnhem. Once again, intelligence's hidden hand had altered history's strategic priorities. Technology was now driving the conduct of war.

As the Second World War drew to its close science and technology were about to bequeath their next boon to mankind. The diligent mathematicians, physicists and chemists who had given humanity high explosives, blood transfusions, poison gas, radar, computers, penicillin and chemical nerve agents now looked to a new weapon to end war. They invented the atom bomb. In doing so they ensured that the wartime allies against Hitler would one day confront each other in a new kind of war, this time driven by intelligence, not fighting. For in the atom bomb lay the seeds of a new kind of warfare and a new war.

17

New Instruments of War

The conventional army loses if it does not win: but the guerrilla wins as long as he doesn't lose ...

HENRY KISSINGER

It was his very inability to prosecute a 'hot' war in the summer of 1940 that prompted Churchill to order a campaign of limited and unconventional warfare. With the British Army defeated and driven ignominiously from the Continent the only way to fight the Germans, apart from a largely ineffective bomber force, was by irregular warfare aimed at irritating, not defeating, Hitler's triumphant legions. With Churchill's memories of the depredations of the Boer commandos of his youth still fresh in his memory, 'Set Europe ablaze!' the old warhorse trumpeted to a bemused Dalton in July 1940. Thus the Special Operations Executive (SOE) was born. It took over the existing chunks of the War Office and MI6-SIS that were concerned with irregular warfare and sabotage, and set itself up in Baker Street in London to oversee a new theatre of operations: unconventional warfare. Whitehall, startled by the Nazi onslaught in Europe and suspicious of any redistribution of responsibilities and power, looked at this boisterous new cuckoo in the government nest with some distaste and set about clipping its wings.

Irregular war was by no means new in 1940. The Spanish uprising against the French usurpation of their land in 1808 has given us the word 'guerrilla' (literally 'little war'), to describe the campaign waged by irregular Spanish bands hiding in the hills, living rough and attacking isolated French outposts. The French called them bandits and terrorists; the Spanish called them self-sacrificing patriots or freedom fighters. It is an ambiguity that lives on today in the Middle East as Israelis and Arabs jockey for the moral high ground in their interminable struggle over Palestine's land and the ear of world public opinion. Such irregular war is not new in the region. In the First World War, Lawrence of Arabia had waged a successful sabotage campaign against the Turks using Bedouin irregulars in Palestine and Arabia in 1917–18. The Irish Republican Army had emulated his style of hit-and-run warfare to drive the British out between 1919 and 1922, before falling out among themselves. Emigrating Jews had formed terror gangs (or protection squads – it depended whose side you were on) as they bought or fought their way into Palestine and Judea in the 1930s. Irregular warfare had a strong and cost-effective track record as a means of 'prosecuting politics by any other means'.

The Germans were the first to set up special operations forces as

The myth of Nazi special forces

" Of course at the moment it's still just a suspicion." 31.iii.41

regular units. In 1939 the Abwehr raised a special service unit at Brandenburg specialising in intelligence gathering, sabotage and 'direct action'. They were nicknamed the 'Brandenburgers' and the name stuck. German special forces had led the way for the Wehrmacht's blitzkriegs, seizing key points and bridges, blocking roads and rivers and securing valuable installations. At Eban Emael in May 1940 specially trained German airborne assault engineers landed their gliders directly on top of the Belgian fortress in a daring *coup de main*. The success of these specially selected elite troops encouraged others to emulate them.

The British were particularly taken with the idea. It seemed a cheap and cost-effective way of waging war, an idea that happened to chime nicely with British strategic thinking between the wars, desperate to avoid the mass casualties of the trenches on the Western Front. The indirect approach appeared to offer an alternative to the grim realities of battlefield attrition, as well as being a quick solution. Such ideas have always been attractive to those who sit at Whitehall's desks. Small raids are quicker to mount than Armoured Corps' attacks. Above all it seemed *cheap*: and under the sacred mantra of 'saving the Treasury money', Whitehall's Mandarins have always favoured the cheap solution, however much it eventually costs the taxpayers from their pockets or their lives.

SOE's task from the War Cabinet was clearly spelled out in its charter: it was to coordinate all sabotage and subversion against the enemy overseas. From the start, it banged into closed bureaucratic doors. Implicit in its brief was an awkward overlap with the newly formed Political Warfare Executive (PWE) over propaganda and its closely linked activity, subversion. PWE had started life as an offshoot of the Foreign Office in 1938 tasked with 'discreet' propaganda and had only been harnessed into the traces with SOE when the latter was formed. It was never an ideal solution: the two organisations had very different roles, and when PWE went its own way in 1941, both parties heaved a sigh of relief. Similarly and much more seriously, SOE was always bound to tread on MI6-SIS's toes over intelligence collection unless there was well nigh superhuman cooperation and good relations on all sides. There wasn't. To add to this poisonous climate of bureaucratic

ill will SOE struggled to deal with the Armed Services on whose cooperation it relied heavily, whether for supplying suitable recruits, or getting
the use of ships or aeroplanes. It was hard to parachute into occupied
France without an RAF aeroplane. From the start SOE ran into problems
from both without and within.

The trouble was that SOE was two separate services under one
organisation. One half provided the administrative back up while the
operations abroad were run by individual country sections. This made
for great security; it also meant that any operational bungle or incompetence could be trapped unseen and fester (as happened with Operation
North Pole, the Germans' radio game in Holland) with grave results.
SOE was certainly, compared with the other secret services, very security
conscious, with the same individuals frequently using several different
working names. This sometimes confused the Germans; more often
than not it just irritated Whitehall.

At first the British intelligence war was confined mainly to subversion and propaganda. It would take time to set up sabotage and resistance networks overseas. The Germans, on the other hand, had a head
start. Dr Goebbels, the master of 'the big lie', used the radio to wear
down the defeated British. Lord Haw Haw's (Lesley Joyce) mocking
tones on the radio spelled out German triumphs, derided British follies
and offered a vision of inevitable German victory. It didn't work –
Britons were more amused than convinced. Later, British and American
subversion was to prove far more subtle and much more successful than
Lord Haw Haw's crude brand of propaganda and mockery.

War by propaganda was by no means new. In the Great War, both
sides had unleashed crude news campaigns to vilify the other and to
justify their actions to their own populations and the rest of the world.
In 1914 the Germans had come off second-best in this new form of
warfare for two reasons. First, they had laid themselves open to criticism by their offensive campaign. France had not invaded Germany;
nor had gallant little Belgium advanced on Berlin. Germany was not
unreasonably seen as the aggressor, and there was nothing to pretend
otherwise, however much the domestic propaganda of the Kaiser's

Reich tried to smear the French and British. Germany was waging an aggressive war of conquest. Encircled she might claim to be; but she had attacked her neighbours, not the other way round.

The second reason was quite straightforward and owed much to Stieber and all his works. The invading German armies in Belgium had behaved extremely badly. The stark General Staff doctrine of *schrecklichkeit* had much to answer for. Whatever excuses were made at the time, and have been made since, German soldiers did undoubtedly commit atrocities. These were a gift to Allied propaganda. Babies may not have been 'spitted on brutal German bayonets' as Britain's yellow press gleefully claimed, but over 3,000 innocent Belgians were killed by the Kaiser's men, and the great University of Louvain and its irreplaceable medieval library was deliberately torched by the Germans to make a point to the locals.

There could be no denying of such actions. The Germans *did* resort to terror to cow their occupied territories. 'News management' and 'spin' was therefore spawned in the 'great moral crusade' of the First World War. The belated arrival of the United States in 1917 merely reinforced this trend towards ideology and propaganda as additions to the moral armoury. From being 'just a war', the Great War became, certainly for President Wilson and his fellow Americans, some kind of sacred moral crusade to 'make the world safe for democracy', a trend which shows little sign of diminishing to this day. In democracies it seems that crude national interest always has to be dressed up in morality, if nothing else to assuage any qualms voters may have. As a later British Prime Minister was to find out in the joint US-UK attack on Saddam Hussein's Iraq in 2003, it is a policy that can backfire with momentous consequences.

By 1939 things had evolved. Goebbels's potent brand of spin and lies, dressing up black as white to promote his premier's 'party line' and present facts as the Nazi government wanted them to be, not as they were, had had a profound effect on governmental news management during the 1930s. The media was now recognised as a powerful tool to influence public and world opinion, particularly since the advent of wireless and cinema. It also showed how the clever and cunning could manipulate the masses through these new forms of communication.

What was also crystal clear was that propaganda, government spin and intelligence were indissolubly linked and an invaluable tool for controlling public opinion. They could also be carefully monitored and assessed. In wartime, intelligence and propaganda now came together to constitute a new form of warfare – psychological operations (psyops) – to influence the opposition's will to fight. It was a new aspect of total war, with no less than three target audiences: the public at home, the enemy and world opinion. The British, in particular, threw themselves into this new form of bloodless combat with relish and, it must be said, with considerable imagination and flair. Nor for them the sturdy exaggerations and hyperbole of Soviet propaganda, with its Stakhanovite absurdities, let alone the crude 'big lies' of Dr Goebbels. The British had much more subtle plans for their new attack on the enemy population, and, by and large, they were extremely effective.

Intelligence's contribution was to identify weak areas, suggest lines of attack, and monitor success. Thanks to Enigma and well-placed human sources, the impact of these psyops offensives could be tracked. The results were interesting; psyops worked, at least on a certain level. If it did not set Europeans ablaze against their new Nazi overlords it certainly got their attention. By 1941 PWE and SOE had gone their separate ways: PWE would concentrate on psyops and subversion while SOE concentrated on 'direct action'.

PWE's 'black' propaganda operations were the most damaging to the Axis cause. Led by a newspaper correspondent, Sefton Delmer, from a scruffy collection of huts near Milton Keynes not far from Bletchley Park, PWE broadcasts were imaginative, to say the least. Sefton Delmer's greatest coups were against Nazi Germany. He had been brought up in Berlin and knew the Nazi leaders personally before the war. His German language broadcasts carried extraordinary weight, particularly in the last three years of the war when many young German soldiers began to realise that German defeat was inevitable. Delmer played on their homesickness and sentimentality with a light but poignant touch.

Real German news was easy to come by. British Intelligence had captured a *Deutsches Nachtrichtenburo* (DNB) *Hell-Schreiber*, the German Propaganda Ministry's unclassified teleprinter, so Delmer was able to receive every Nazi official news release and propaganda declaration coming out of the Propaganda Ministry in Berlin. He often got the Nazi news bulletins before the German commanders in the field received them and could turn news round quickly as a propaganda tool. By mixing this German news with known British intelligence from captured prisoner of war interrogations, PWE's propaganda programmes were right up to the minute with the latest slang and gossip from deep inside Hitler's Germany. Radio stations like *Soldatensender Calais,* for soldiers in France, and *Deutsche Kurzwellensender Atlantik* were aimed specifically at homesick and frightened German soldiers and U-boat crews in the West. Thanks to skilful editorial control and subtle mixing of truth with propaganda, Delmer's broadcasts undoubtedly had an impact on German morale.

Delmer discovered early that truth is the best propaganda and earned a grudging accolade from none other than Dr Goebbels, who wrote in his diary:

> Soldatensender Calais ... which uses the same wavelengths as Radio Deutschland – when the latter is off the air during air raids – gave us something to worry about. The station does a very clever job of propaganda and from what is put on the air one can gather that the English know exactly what they have destroyed in Berlin and what they have not ...

Delmer realised from his newspaper days that the surest way to get people to listen to his propaganda station was to be as crude and shocking as possible. He knew, as does every tabloid editor, that by 'denouncing' vice he would invariably secure a large circulation among those who wanted to read about such a wicked – but entertaining – topic. Delmer's masterpiece was a station calling itself 'GS1' (Gustav Siegfried Eins) where *Der Chef* (the Boss) a foul-mouthed 'patriotic German' reigned supreme. This extraordinary creation claimed to be the voice of an 'underground group of loyal patriotic Germans' who had severe misgivings about both the conduct of the war and especially the leadership of the Nazi Party. *Der Chef* – in reality a German journalist called Peter Seckelmann who had fled to England in 1937 – managed to blacken the name of virtually every Nazi leader with his foul-mouthed rants against the British and Americans under the guise of 'encouraging' his fellow Germans to fight on.

His first broadcast was in May 1941 just after Hitler's deputy Hess had flown to Britain, allegedly to try and convince Churchill not to fight on once Germany had invaded Russia.

Hess, although he never knew it, seems to have been the victim of a spectacularly successful British deception operation. SOE's 'SO1' Section had created a mythical 'British Peace Party' (allegedly a group of aristocrats headed by King George VI himself) who secretly wanted to end the war with Germany at any cost. Lured by this false bait, and wanting any excuse to turn East and fall upon Soviet Russia, Hitler and Hess were only too willing to believe such an elaborate hoax. Hess was despatched in a Messerschmitt 110 long range fighter to fly to Britain to meet the Duke of Kent and the Duke of Hamilton of the fake British Peace Party to negotiate a separate peace. It was a catastrophic mistake by the German political leadership. The Fuhrer's deputy – or someone who claimed to be Rudolph Hess – fell straight into the waiting arms of MI5. It was a propaganda gift for the British. It was PWE's great chance. *Der Chef*'s Prussian upper-class Junker voice barked out for the first time to his 'fellow Nazis':

> ... this fellow Hess ... he was a good comrade of ours in the old
> days of the FrieKorps. But, like the rest of this clique of
> meglomaniacs and parlour Bolsheviks who call themselves our
> leaders, he's simply got no guts in a crisis ... at the first sign of
> trouble he flies off with a bag of quack pills and a white flag ...
> to throw himself - and you and me too - at the mercy of that
> flat-footed bastard of a drunken old Jew Churchill! Eh?! *And* he
> completely overlooks that he carries the Reich's most precious

secrets in his head, all of which the f*****g British will suck out of
him like drinking Berlin Weissbier!

As this kind of language and tone reflected almost precisely
what many Germans – and particularly the higher echelons of the
Wehrmacht – were saying behind closed doors about Hitler and the
Nazi leadership, this was devastating stuff. And it was effective: Delmer's
close links with the Combined Services Detailed Interrogation Centre
allowed him not only to collect up-to-date intelligence from newly
captured prisoners of war on what real Germans were saying but it also
enabled him to monitor the success of GS1's tirades.

'OK!' *Der Chef* would rave, 'So we are short of rations and the gas
supply lines to the Fatherland have been cut for good. But we can still
fight on, can't we?' His military audience, nervously contemplating
their dwindling stocks of petrol, would begin to contemplate the
wisdom of pulling back closer to Germany. Such classic lines as:

The f*****g Allies are lying to us again as usual, *lieber freunde*!
Ignore their ***** propaganda. The RAF didn't drop one bomb on
Berlin last night! Ignore the lying ****s! They're ***** filth! I have
it on absolute authority that their so-called big air raid was on
Munich, not Berlin!

could be guaranteed to leave any Bavarians in his audience stirring
uneasily and wondering just how things really were going with the folks
back home in Munich.

Not everyone was happy with this kind of approach. One of
Churchill's ministers in the wartime coalition, the ardent Christian
Socialist Sir Stafford Cripps (teetotal, vegetarian and the worst example
of prissy moral rectitude so prevalent among many upper-class British
intellectuals of the 1920s and 1930s), complained bitterly about the style
and language of Delmer's broadcasts. His utopian Christian Socialist
view of the New Jerusalem did not encompass such outrageous
language, even to fight a tyranny as vicious as Hitler's Nazi Germany. On
one occasion, waving one particularly fruity GS1 script that went into

considerable detail about just what a well-known German admiral was supposed to have done in a bed with four sailors and his mistress, he stammered pathetically to the foreign secretary: 'If this is the kind of stuff that's needed to win the war, then I'd j-j-jolly well rather lose it!'

Fortunately total war's unremitting demands superseded the delicate sensibilities of such do-gooders. More robust counsels prevailed. Britain chose not to lose the war merely to appease Stafford Cripps's overactive personal opinions about what was right or wrong for his fellow countrymen's delicate sexual sensibilities. Despite Cripps's wails about 'this beastly pornographic organ!' Delmer's GS1 went on from strength to strength and proved the value of PWE's unusual contribution to the British war effort.

Der Chef's 'sad demise' in October 1943 was a dramatic triumph. In mid broadcast he 'was arrested by the Gestapo' and never heard from again. Unfortunately, in one of the cock-ups so easily made in broadcasting, an overenthusiastic technician in the Milton Keynes black studio broadcast the recorded episode again a couple of days later by mistake, leaving some very puzzled listeners.

Perhaps the most concrete accomplishment of Delmer's transmitters was in expediting the Italians to quit the Axis in 1943. To encourage an Italian surrender, a mysterious 'Radio Leghorn' began to urge fellow Italians to give up, as the war was over. The radio broadcasts allegedly came from a disgruntled group of patriotic Italian naval officers and ratings on board their cruiser in Leghorn (Livorno) harbour. In fact the whole scam was run by the British broadcasting from Milton Keynes, using sympathetic Italian prisoners of war who just wanted to get home. Guided by PWE's intelligence section, the 'secret broadcasting station in Livorno harbour' eventually gave out the exact instructions as to how the Italian fleet could end their war peacefully. Next day, the Italian fleet sailed to Malta to surrender to Admiral Cunningham, to the fury of the Germans.

PWE's role was clear-cut, but part of the problem with this 'new instrument of war', as Churchill saw SOE and the irregular warfare campaign, was that SOE's charter masked a number of inherent contraditions. Intelligence collection, for example, should be a discreet, quiet war that ought to stay well hidden. By and large, successful spies do not advertise and codebreakers certainly never do. It puts them out of business.

Direct sabotage unlike intelligence is, however, a very public display of enemy action. It is hard to conceal a wrecked train or a factory going up in flames. Sabotage and intelligence collection are not totally irreconcilable, but they do need careful control if they are to work in harness. In the fevered atmosphere of 1940, there was little careful control and much pressure to 'do something'. Spy mania and rumours of a Fifth Column gripped the British public's imagination. It was, it seemed, the only possible explanation for the rapid collapse of France and the Low Countries. 'Aliens' were interned. Cartoons of hairy Nazi paratroopers disguised as nuns dominated the popular press. (See page 328.) It was not a good time for a serious philosophical debate about the balance of priorities between intelligence, subversion and sabotage. The result was that as the irregular war progressed sometimes the cracks began to show, and particularly between SOE and MI6-SIS.

From 1941 onwards, a positive plethora of special units was springing up. In addition to SOE's newly trained sabotage teams in England a Long Range Desert Group (LRDG) was beginning to push deep behind Axis lines in the Western Desert. To add to this rash of new 'Special Forces' a young Guards officer, David Stirling, was forming a new unit called the Special Air Service to hit the enemy when and where he least expected it. Not to be outdone, the Royal Navy raised its own special force of Royal Marines to form the Special Boat Squadron for amphibious sabotage and coastal close reconnaissance, which duplicated many of the duties of the Small Scale Raiding Force, an offshoot of SOE. Everyone wanted to get in on the action. Special units proliferated on every side.

Therein lay the real problem of Special Forces. Many professional soldiers felt that creaming off the best and brightest from line units into elite units, to carry out pinprick attacks for intelligence, however high profile, was a serious mistake, and diluted the overall quality of the mainstream fighting forces. Better, they argued, to raise the standards of existing units to that of any elite forces than to remove the brightest and most adventurous from the frontline. Orde Wingate did just this with his Chindits – regular units trained to carry out very special and hazardous tasks behind Japanese lines in Burma – before he died in a plane crash. Special Forces represented a real problem for both armies and for the intelligence services.

Part of the problem lay not just in the very natural urge to 'do something' and get at the enemy's throat, but also in the nature of bureaucracy and power of all regimes. Once Special Forces became an accepted part of the armoury of modern warfare, the struggle to control such politically high profile assets became intense. Where men of power can dispense resources and patronage, ambitious underlings will seize their chance for advancement. Special Forces represented a fast track to preferment for many. In the end the 'specialists' won the day, not only in the British but the American Services, too.

The American Office of Strategic Services (OSS) mirrored SOE's experience when America finally joined the fighting. The OSS's Special Operations Division ran intelligence and sabotage missions in Europe, Africa and the Far East by 1945. Wherever brave men and women are willing to risk their necks in search of adventure then hard faced calculating puppet masters will be happy to pull the strings. America was no exception and under 'Wild Bill' Donovan the OSS flourished from its headquarters in Grosvenor Street, London. While the British and the exiled Europeans tried to set Europe ablaze, the Americans concentrated mainly on North Africa and Italy. By the end of the Second World War Donovan's 'Oh So Secret' (often referred to sarcastically as 'Oh So Social!') organisation was running agents in Burma and China, and by 1945 had also placed over two hundred OSS agents – mainly war-weary ex-prisoners of war – back under cover inside Nazi Germany itself. In an ominous indicator of future trouble to come they had even encouraged and rearmed an indigenous resistance group in French Indo-China: its leader was a tough and cunning anti-Japanese guerrilla leader called Ho Chi Minh.

Some of the special operations carried out by these small irregular Special Forces' units were extremely successful not only in their mission but also in their wider effect. When two SOE operatives kidnapped a German divisional commander on Crete in the spring of 1944, they not only removed the garrison's commander from under the Germans' noses, a propaganda coup in itself, but they also got every German on the island jumpy and looking over his shoulder for weeks. A little terror, as the Comintern had proved on so many occasions, echoes for a long time. (Ironically, the German general in question was deeply unpopular with his staff, who allegedly toasted his captors!)

Not all SOE's direct actions ended so cheerfully. The arrival of *Reichsprotektor* Heydrich in Czechoslovakia in late 1941 boded ill for the occupied Czechs. Heydrich's star had risen dramatically in the Nazi firmament since Venlo. He meant to keep it there and the wretched Czechs suffered under his lash. He reckoned without the long arm of the Czechs in exile. The head of the Czech intelligence service had escaped the Nazis in 1938. Now in London, Moravec planned a special operations coup to kill Heydrich. Two volunteers were trained by SOE and parachuted back to their country. On 27 May 1942, Jan Kubis and Josef Gabcik ambushed Heydrich's car on a hairpin bend on its way to the office. Gabcik's Sten gun (a cheap and unreliable British sub-machine gun) jammed. An infuriated Heydrich leapt out, pistol in hand, to arrest Gabcik just as Kubis's hastily thrown grenade exploded behind him. Heydrich went down, mortally wounded by grenade splinters and the debris of the gutter blown deep into his abdomen. In an age before penicillin, he was doomed, despite the efforts of Germany's best doctors.

Heydrich lingered and died, leaving the SS to exact a terrible revenge. Gabcik and Kubis were betrayed for money by a fellow Czech, hunted down and, after an epic gun battle in the crypt of a church, turned their last rounds on themselves. Thwarted of their prey, the Nazi stormtroopers went on the rampage, killing Czechs 'like *berserkers*' at random and razing two villages, Lidice and Lezaky, literally to the ground. In this orgy of revenge and killing over 5,000 innocent Czechs were executed across the country by their maddened occupiers. It was a heavy price for one German *Reichsprotektor*.

The Germans themselves were heavily into their own Special Forces operation in the summer of 1942, which in its small way was to end every bit as bloodily as the assassination of Heydrich, thanks to the duplicity and ambition of J. Edgar Hoover, the head of the FBI. America's own puppet master was to commit an act of blatant cruelty and self-serving ambition that fully justifies the FBI leader's reputation as a truly evil man. In the summer of 1942 J. Edgar Hoover deliberately conspired to send two men to the electric chair.

The idea for Operation Pastorius grew out of a successful Irish Republican Army campaign to sabotage the British war effort in 1939. Fanatical Republican terrorists, ever mindful of their old motto 'England's difficulty is Ireland's opportunity', embarked on an extended campaign of terror bombings on the mainland, attacking a variety of targets ranging from power stations to shops in the West End and even bombs in left luggage offices and pillar boxes. The German intelligence service under Admiral Wilhelm Canaris was impressed. In 1939 his Abwehr established links with the IRA with the aim of steering the Irish terrorists towards targets that would benefit Hitler's war effort. A radio was provided to help communications, and arms and explosives were shipped to the IRA to aid 'the cause'.

At first everything went well for the Germans. In a spectacular detonation the Royal Ordnance Factory at Waltham Abbey in Essex blew up in January 1940 killing five and injuring thirty more. Irish terrorists were held responsible. The IRA's sabotage campaign suddenly looked like being a real threat. However, behind the scenes the angry British began to turn the screw. Once Churchill came to power in the summer of 1940 things changed. With a German invasion looming Britain's new and aggressive Prime Minister had to neutralise any threats from the Irish Republic and diplomatic niceties were dispensable in a crisis. It was made very clear to the Irish President that 'England' was not prepared for 'neutral' Ireland to be used as a terrorist base to help the Nazis attack the British mainland: de Valera had better crack down, or else His

Majesty's government would take whatever action it felt was necessary.

De Valera, however, had his own problems with the IRA. It was, as ever, riven by internal factions, leadership struggles and arguments about what to do next. There were those within the IRA that even regarded de Valera as a traitor to the true cause, wanting to come after him and his government in Dublin and rule Ireland themselves. Not only that, most Catholic Irishmen and women were deeply anti-Nazi and antipathetic to the excesses and brutalities of Hitler's Germany. Many sympathised with the fate of Hitler's latest victim, Catholic Poland. Hitler's minions meddling in Ireland spelled nothing but danger for de Valera and the men in Dublin. A powerful and well-armed IRA was the last thing the Irish government wanted in 1940.

Dublin moved to distance itself from the IRA and the terror gang's activities faded, much to the Abwehr's disappointment. De Valera's hatred of England was only suppressed, however, not abandoned. His 'neutrality' continued to regularly run foul of Churchill and the British throughout the war and the Irish premier stayed friendly with Hitler's regime to the end. De Valera even sent a diplomatic 'Irish message of condolence' on hearing of the Nazi leader's death amid the ruins and defeat of the Berlin Bunker in 1945 – one of only two countries in the world to do so. But his fellow Irishmen's sabotaging adventures had sown a seed in the Third Reich. If the British war effort could no longer be targeted in alert wartime England, then it could certainly be hit and hurt at the source of many of its weapons: peacetime USA.

From the autumn of 1940 onwards a wave of unexplained fires and accidental explosions swept the north-eastern United States. There was even a mysterious fire in the US Navy building in Washington. All the incidents seemed to be related to the war effort or production. The most spectacular was an attack on the Hercules Explosives Factory in New Jersey, which killed fifty-two people and was heard 8 miles away. All these incidents were explained away by Hoover and the FBI as 'accidents' despite the 'Teutonic efficiency' of the wave of sabotage (which is how one newspaper described the attacks). Even the discovery and dismissal of three 'pro-Nazi workmen' at the Liquidometer

Manufacturing plant, where the production of tubing for aircraft systems was being interrupted by a series of mishaps on the production line and wildcat strikes, was glossed over by J. Edgar Hoover and his less than vigilant FBI. The truth was that Canaris's Irish and IRA protégés were striking against Britain by sabotaging her American arms suppliers inside continental USA and making Hoover and his FBI look increasingly incompetent and impotent.

In early 1942, with the USA now as an open enemy of the Reich, Canaris decided to step up this successful campaign by attacking American production at source with his own dedicated Abwehr sabotage teams. If the Germans could wreck the electricity supply for aluminium factories and the railway moving coal, then Berlin's economic warfare analysts estimated it could put US arms production back six to eight months. Under the direction of a German-American called Walter Kappe (who had been a member of the Bund, the American-Nazi League before the war) in June 1942 Operation Pastorius was launched with the aim of attacking and sabotaging key industrial bottlenecks in the US. It was fatally compromised from the beginning.

Once the first four-man sabotage team from Germany was ashore from U-202 on Long Island on 13 June 1942 one of its members, Georg Dasch, promptly made his way to Washington and turned himself and the rest of his team in to the FBI. For Dasch was no dedicated Nazi spy. As he tipped a briefcase containing $84,000 in cash onto the floor in front of the goggle-eyed FBI agents he cheerfully admitted that he and another member of the team, Ernst Burger, had intended to turn themselves over to the authorities and work for the Americans the moment they arrived. It was a mistake.

Hoover promptly ordered a security clamp down and while the obliging Dasch and Burger cheerfully told their new American friends from the FBI everything they knew, the FBI boss plotted to make capital for himself out of this priceless gift of free intelligence. Their cover blown by the obliging Dasch, the remaining Pastorius saboteurs were swiftly rounded up and put behind bars. So too, to his surprise, was Dasch. Suddenly placed in 'protective custody' in a prison cell he began to have misgivings. The first inkling of what Hoover was planning became clear when the puzzled Dasch saw a copy of the *New York Times* with his own picture, released on Hoover's orders, blazoned across the front page underneath the banner headline 'Captured Nazi Spy'.

Hoover's reputation had been under attack for some time. His links with the Mafia and suspiciously well-funded own lifestyle, plus the FBI's dismal track record in stopping spies and saboteurs were attracting criticism on Capitol Hill and in the newspapers. Hoover was now going to use Dasch and the Operation Pastorius team in a cold-blooded if not criminal conspiracy to salvage his own reputation. In July, Dasch and his fellow saboteurs were put on trial for their lives charged with capital crimes. In vain Dasch complained that he had told the FBI everything, and that it was *he* who had tipped off Hoover and the FBI about the whole plan as soon as he landed. In a closed court Dasch was tipped the wink by the US Attorney General, Hoover and their stooge 'defence' lawyer that if he just pleaded guilty to all charges then his identity as the traitor who had betrayed the Germans could be kept secret. Once the trial was over he would be quickly smuggled out after a few months once the story had died away. He had 'Hoover and the President's word on it'. Plead guilty and all would be well. Foolishly Georg Dasch and Ernst Burger did just that. To their horror both were sentenced to death along with the rest of their Operation Pastorius co-conspirators by a secret military court.

On 8 August 1942 six members of the Pastorius sabotage team were fried alive in the Washington DC's district jail electric chair. Only Dasch and Burger were spared. They received a last minute reprieve from the President of the USA and only because Franklin Delano Roosevelt had little love for Hoover or his methods. On reviewing the confirmation transcripts of the trial he had spotted that Dasch and Burger had actually given themselves up voluntarily to the FBI and told them everything – a point that his own attorney general and J. Edgar Hoover hadn't thought important enough to flag up for the President's attention. He therefore refused to confirm their death sentence, much to Hoover's fury and despite his urgings that they should go to the chair, too. Hoover wanted Dasch out of the way: he was the only one who knew the real truth about the 'FBI's great coup'.

Instead the two Germans were thrown into an American jail to rot while J. Edgar Hoover's personal publicity machine went into overdrive. The FBI produced a lengthy press release praising their great leader to the eyeballs and trumpeting the Bureau's flair, efficiency and expertise. Dasch was, according to the FBI, just another 'dirty little Nazi spy' apprehended by the great leader's genius. America's security was in the safe hands of the FBI as long as it was led by the indomitable figure of J. Edgar Hoover, ace spy catcher.

The credulous American wartime media swallowed this load of self-glorifying nonsense whole. While a furious Hitler berated Canaris back in Berlin, Hoover lapped up a wave of public adulation. The only men who could tell the truth about his cynical manipulations were safely banged up in jail. It was only after the war that the truth came out and by then it was far too late. In 1948 Dasch and Burger were pardoned and released from prison and deported from America in conditions of great secrecy by the FBI. J. Edgar Hoover said privately that he would rather have seen them executed with the others. The FBI's puppet master had yet again proved himself a truly cynical and corrupt individual, and one who would go to any lengths to protect his reputation.

The German Special Forces tried their luck at assassination attempts as well as sabotage. In July 1944, they tried to kill Stalin in a little known mission called Operation Zeppelin. The plan was to land a Special Forces long-distance plane at night close to Moscow and detach a motorcycle husband and wife team of anti-communist Russians to drive into the city and assassinate the Soviet leader. The operation went wrong from the start when the pathfinder team of Brandenburgers was captured on landing. The huge Arado 232 was fired at as it came in to land and diverted to its secondary landing site at Karmonovo to the east where it crash-landed and caught fire. Major Tavrin and Lieutenant Shilova drove off towards Moscow and the Arado's crew went on the run. The two Russians were eventually stopped at a roadblock on the outskirts of Moscow, where the Soviet sentry checked their forged documents (which were excellent) but claimed to be puzzled by the fact that the pair were dry despite the heavy summer rain. The Soviet version is that the suspicious sentry called his officer and the pair were arrested, never to be heard of again, along with the 428,000 roubles and 116 forged documents and passes provided by the Sicherheits Dienst. The German controllers got just one radio message from the Arado aircrew, on the run somewhere east of Smolensk, the following day saying, 'Aircraft crashed on landing. All crew members uninjured. Crew split up into two groups to try and break through to west.' None of the Operation Zeppelin team was ever heard from again although some accounts claim that the aircrew lay up in hiding until after the war. This seems unlikely, but the men of KG200 were hardy souls. To the cynical intelligence operator the whole affair screams of betrayal from start to finish. Operation Zeppelin was a brave, almost desperate, attempt and was at the very limits between foolhardiness and courage. Special operations require very special people.

The dedication and professionalism of SOE's two Czechs and the German Brandenburgers might be thought to be the standard expected of operators in the world of undercover warfare. It was not always so. In France, the SOE's PROSPER intelligence and sabotage network betrayed itself by regularly gossiping in English in a Paris restaurant. Unsurprisingly, the members were rounded up and arrested. However, such crass amateurism was far from usual or general. SOE's men and women were generally as professional as they could be: their lives depended on it. They were also extremely resourceful when required to be.

One even invented a new method of prosecuting irregular warfare, what Professor M. R. D. Foot, the official historian of SOE, accurately calls 'blackmail-sabotage'. Harry Ree (nicknamed César) was active in the Franche-Comte area in 1943. Noticing that a recent RAF raid on the Peugeot factory at Souchex, which was making tank parts for the Nazis, had caused extensive damage and killed a number of Frenchmen without actually stopping production, Ree made the factory manager an offer he could not refuse. The RAF were obviously going to come back and obliterate the factory at some time, were they not? Ree pressed his point: would it not be better for all concerned if the plant was put out of action by a single discreetly placed bomb against just one essential machine and then the RAF would not have to come back? The Manager was nervous but doubtful. To prove his credentials, Ree arranged for a code message to be played on the BBC confirming his offer. The manager took the hint; no point in getting a lot of Frenchmen killed and the whole factory wrecked.

A foreman personally took Ree to the key machine where they laid a bomb in a workman's haversack before retiring to the local café. The bomb exploded, the factory stopped turning out tank parts for the Nazi war effort and all the workers went home unscathed. It was, without doubt, a very intelligent and elegant way for SOE to carry out Churchill's directive to 'Set Europe ablaze!' History does not record whether the factory manager received a medal from de Gaulle after the war. He deserved one.

This kind of economic warfare – for that is what disrupting Nazi Germany's war effort was – could be mounted from the other end of the economic scale too. Cutting off production was valuable, but how much better to go for the *supply* side and cut off the raw materials at source?

The loss of Malaya in early 1942 had been a grievous blow to the British and American war economies. Rubber and tin were in short supply. At this point, a retired rubber smuggler offered his services to SOE. Walter Fletcher was a half Austrian naturalised Briton and chairman of a rubber broking firm based in London. He claimed he could get rubber out of Sumatra – for a price, naturally. SOE was interested, despite a recruiter's assessment that said: 'He [Fletcher] is not exactly the person to be trusted with the private means of an orphan or widow.' The American Board of Economic Warfare supported the project and duly set up a below-the-counter black market for rubber in the Dutch East Indies. Alarm bells should have rung when Fletcher insisted that the Allies pay over the odds for any rubber, but his point was valid: black markets are driven by demand and the risks from Japanese reprisals would be fatal for the suppliers if they were ever caught.

The British treasury put up £100,000 and the US $100,000 to fund

Fletcher's rubber plan. He went to work in Northern Australia, but only three and a half tons of rubber could be collected. The problems of moving rubber in small dhows under the very noses of the Japanese were just too difficult. Undeterred Fletcher turned his entrepreneurial gaze to other commercial opportunities. He set up an Economic Warfare Unit on behalf of SOE in India and began negotiations to smuggle quinine for the American forces in Guadalcanal, who were dropping like flies with malaria, and to sell rubber to Chang Kai Shek's Nationalist Army in China. The negotiations were lengthy and the results few. All the time he was spending SOE's money, 'bribing the big boys'.

Eventually, under pressure from an outraged committee in Whitehall, SOE tried to pull the plug. Fletcher then played his ace. By dealing with the Chinese warlords and speculating on the black market he explained, he had discovered that he was now potentially a first-class source of really good intelligence. SOE was baffled, but Fletcher's fairy godmother appeared in the unlikely pin-striped form of HM Treasury. 'Sir Humphrey' pointed out that Chinese Nationalist dollars were in very short supply in these dark difficult days of war. A guaranteed and plentiful *cheap* source of Chinese Nationalist dollars would help them enormously in paying their bills for the war (at the *official* rate of exchange, of course) to the Chinese Nationalists. They would be *very* interested in black market Chinese dollars: the more the merrier. A bemused SOE had to agree and Fletcher went to work. For the retired rubber trader it must have been like the good old days in the City of London, but this time HM Treasury was putting up the capital.

Fletcher was diligent, to say the least. By 1945 he was selling diamonds from de Beers, Omega watches, cigarettes, pearls, medical drugs and who knows what else, on behalf of HMG and SOE to the Chinese Nationalist warlords – who were paying well over the odds and in useful Chinese national dollars for such hard to come by commodities. The biggest profit centre of Operation Remorse as the project was named was without doubt the currency speculation. Under Fletcher's entrepreneurial eye, SOE's 'rubber swindle' grew into a vast financial trading empire all over the Far East and a very real economic force in the area. It was 'the biggest financial black market in history', and it was all funded by the British Treasury in the middle of a world war. By the end of 1945, Fletcher's 'little rubber smuggling scheme' had made a profit on SOE's books of £77 million – equivalent to just under a billion pounds sterling at 2004 prices. It was a most decidedly irregular operation of war. But then total war's demands are total and extend to the humblest commodities like Swiss Rolex watches, South African rubies and unwanted Chinese dollars.

This kind of economic warfare against the supply of vital goods and materials was always closely linked to intelligence, because intelligence was invariably the first to spot emerging enemy weaknesses or emerging enemy threats from their demands for certain commodities. It was Enigma that confirmed what the Ministry of Economic Warfare had been saying for years, that Nazi Germany's modern war fighting capacity was totally dependent upon oil. Only when intelligence forced the Allied 'Bomber Barons' to go for oil targets (with the RAF's Air Marshal Harris grumbling about 'panacea targets') did the oil squeeze really begin to choke off the Nazi war economy. Many people are unaware that German arms production reached its peak only *seven* months before the war ended, with more tanks, guns and planes built in September 1944 than in any other month. The Germans' real problem was that they couldn't move their newly built weapons, let alone train their pilots, for lack of oil and petrol.

It was intelligence that alerted the Allied war leaders to German demand for another vital commodity and one with much more ominous implications: 'heavy water'. Heavy water is basic H_2O with an added molecule to make it D_2O (deuterium oxide). It is expensive to manufacture and has only one real commercial use. It can control an atomic pile; and an atomic pile is essential to build an atom bomb. The international scientific community had known about nuclear energy and its potential for years. The idea of an atomic bomb had been postulated and argued over since the late 1930s. Scientists are no different from any other group of academics, endlessly putting forward and arguing for their own pet theories and rubbishing those of their colleagues. The Hegelian dialectic is alive and well thriving in the groves of Academe. The work of physicists like Szilard, Fermi, Hahn and Strassman was therefore well known among the international scientific community when the pressures of life in Hitler's Germany forced many eminent scientists to flee to Britain and America in the late 1930s. However scientifically brilliant they might be, Jews were not welcome in the Nazis' paradise. Two of these refugees, Frisch and Peierls worked in London and, with French theoretical physicists, discovered that by manufacturing an artificial element, plutonium, an atom bomb was a theoretical possibility.

In 1940 Albert Einstein, the most famous physicist of his time, was persuaded by his colleagues to write to President Roosevelt to urge him to start a research programme into an atomic bomb. Roosevelt ignored the idea. It was too expensive and the USA had little need for speculative wonder weapons. By the end of 1941, however, the picture had changed dramatically. The United States was at war after the devastating attack on Pearl Harbor, and British intelligence had discovered that the Germans were stepping up their production of heavy water. The source of this report was a Norwegian scientist who was smuggled across the North Sea to Britain where he corroborated his evidence. The intelligence jigsaw was looking threatening. Werner Heisenberg's Atomic Research Group at the Berlin Physics Institute were known to be working on a nuclear programme; the industrial giant I. G. Farben had been trying to buy up heavy water on the open market and now the occupied Norwegian Hydro Plant at Rjukan had been ordered to step up its production for the Reich. It looked as if the Germans were on to something. There could only be one possible explanation at the start of 1942: Nazi Germany was developing an atom bomb for Hitler.

The British intelligence services and SOE were ordered to find out the truth and to sabotage the project at any cost. A Norwegian operation smuggled out of Norway the foreman of the Morsk hydro plant where the heavy water was being processed who bravely volunteered to parachute back into Norway to collect intelligence for the sabotage operation. (Foreman Skinarland was understandably nervous about jumping out of a foreign aeroplane over a glacier in the dark, and the pilot had to 'stooge around' for twenty minutes while the Norwegian summoned up the courage to finally leap out into the night.) The foreman's intelligence, however, was spot on and an SOE pathfinder team of well-trained Norwegians led by Jens Poulssen, parachuted into occupied Norway on 18 October 1942 to set up a landing zone for British commandos from Combined Operations. It was a typical 1942 Combined Operations mission: poorly trained and, like the Dieppe raid, an organised disaster. On 19 November 1942, Operation Freshman failed completely. Either the glider missed the beacon, crashed or was shot down. All the commandos were either killed by the crash-landing, or by the Germans. SOE told the Norwegian pathfinder team camped in the mountains to stay in place and wait for a second assault team, this time of Norwegian parachutists who would 'parachute in soon'.

Despite intensive German cordon and search operations and intensive security sweeps Poulssen's waiting team on the glacier (now codenamed Swallow) stuck it out in the open throughout Christmas 1942. They had no food, were living rough in the mountains in a Norwegian winter, eating moss and shooting the occasional reindeer to survive. It was an extraordinary feat of endurance. *Three months* after they had first set out, Swallow finally learned that the new assault team were on their way in February 1943. Poulssen's men set up their beacon and waited. True to form the RAF dropped the 'Gunnerside' assault group nearly 30 miles from the drop zone. After a week's searching for each other in the mountains, the two groups finally met up by accidentally bumping into each other in the woods, and moved in to attack the heavy water plant on 27 February 1943.

The attack was a complete success. The Norwegian foreman's intelligence had been completely accurate and the attack group went straight to the heavy water store, placed their charges and disappeared into the night. The muffled 'thuds' of the explosions in the concrete sheds brought only a curious and perfunctory torch flash from the German guard house. The SOE teams split up and made their escape, some to Sweden 250 miles away over the mountains, others to stay behind, observe and report. Next day all hell broke loose as the Germans swept the area with a whole division of 12,000 ski patrols, but by then the saboteurs were well away and all the vital heavy water had run off into the drains.

Despite this setback, the Germans persisted. Heavy water was essential to their war effort and by August 1943 they were back in production. A USAF bombing raid by 150 B-17s only put twelve bombs (out of the 400 tons dropped) on the Rjukan factory. It did, however, finally convince the Germans that the time had come to pull all the heavy water and all the high concentration plant machinery back to safer premises in the Fatherland. SS troops guarded the move in conditions of intense security as two rail tanker-wagons of the precious heavy water were rolled onto a lakeside ferry to start the journey back to Berlin.

The Germans had not reckoned on the determination of SOE's Norwegians, however. Knut Hankelid had dropped in with the Gunnerside group on 23 February 1943 and had stayed behind to keep reporting on intelligence developments over the heavy water project. He realised that this was his last chance. On 20 February 1944, Hankelid bluffed his way onto the lake ferry and planted a home-made bomb, based on his SOE training, using an alarm clock as the timer. He also remembered his other sabotage lessons because he placed it well below the waterline in the very bows of the ship and timed it to go off after the ferry had sailed. Sure enough at exactly 1100 next morning and halfway across the lake, Hankelid's improvised explosive device of 20 lbs of plastic explosive blew out the forepeak of the ferry which promptly began to go down by the bows. The propellers were lifted high out of the water and the helpless craft stood on her nose as the heavy water tankers crashed into the lake before she finally sank. With the ferry heading to the bottom of a Norwegian lake went Hitler's last real hopes of ever building an atom bomb. It was an SOE triumph of brave men, determination, and endurance, and all steered by good intelligence.

If ever there was a case for claiming that intelligence changed the world then the thwarting of a Nazi nuclear device must rank very high indeed. For in the secrets of the atomic bomb and in the risks of a nuclear-armed world lay the seeds of the most dangerous conflict the world had ever seen – the Cold War.

18
Cold War - Intelligence War

The only way to win an atomic war is to make damn' sure one never starts.

GENERAL OMAR BRADLEY

The Cold War was the first true intelligence war. The diabolical trinity of total war, Churchill's 'new instruments of war' and nuclear weapons meant that full-scale war as a tool of national policy was far too risky to hazard. The great strategic thinker Clausewitz was confounded.

The great powers instead must prepare for war but not allow it to happen under any circumstances. Instead governments were devoting all their energies to finding out what the opposition was up to. For the first time intelligence meant 'operations'. Submarines jockeying for position under the Arctic ice cap were collecting intelligence; aircraft streaking towards alerted coastal radar stations were collecting intelligence; and British Marines dressed incongruously as fishermen watching Soviet intelligence agents also pretending to be fishermen were all collecting intelligence on one another.

The reason was simple. The whole point of the nuclear-armed stand-off between the Soviet Union and her satellites, and America and the NATO Alliance was to know exactly what the other side had in terms of weapons and capabilities and secondly, to discover the enemy's intentions. The Cold War was an intelligence war. In this it changed the nature of war. The spectrum of violence still encompassed the whole range of man's brutality towards man but now with an added dimension. Total war in an atomic age meant mutually assured destruction; therefore a new form of 'prosecuting politics by other means' had dropped into the equation of conflict, since no one really wants to be destroyed, especially politicians. Now, hovering, poised on the brink of Armageddon, the protagonists elected just to spy on every aspect of each other as they jockeyed for advantage.

This new clash of superpowers has rewritten our understanding of war. The idea of warfare as being some brutal clash of arms and action needs to be revised. War used to be about doing and killing: 'breaking things and hurting people'. At the nuclear end of the spectrum of violence this is no longer desirable nor is it true. Competition between nuclear-armed superpowers is about keeping an eye on the opposition.

Intellectual activity in the Cold War replaced the brutally physical ordeal of battle in a number of key conflict scenarios. It was an important spectrum shift in the whole business of international relations and in military responses to international conflict. When two duellists hold cocked and loaded pistols to each other's heads, the temptation *not* to fire is strong. The temptation to find out just what one's opponent is thinking is equally powerful. You might need to fire first. Suddenly, across the centuries, Sun-T'zu's aphorism rings true: 'To subdue the enemy without fighting is the highest point of skill.' It should have been adopted as the key strategic motto of the Cold War.

The first frosts of the Cold War came early. In Soviet Russia the Bolsheviks had been bred in conspiracy and come to power through intrigue. Surrounded by enemies of the Revolution from the very beginning they could no more conceive of international relations with their neighbours without espionage than they could believe that the Communist cause might be wrong. Espionage was a vital tool of Soviet foreign policy right from the start. The conspiracies of foreign spies and agents swiftly replaced the Ochrana of the Czar as the enemy of the Revolution. Events such as British intervention in Soviet Russia in 1919 and the bungling attempts of the Comintern to export the Revolution merely confirmed the paranoia and prejudices of a lifetime of conspiracy among the Bolshevik leaders. The blunt truth was that Lenin and his colleagues were only content when locked in mortal combat with the enemies of the Revolution, whether inside or outside their new Russia. Not to have had external foes on which to heap abuse and blame would in truth have been a serious embarrassment for the leaders of the fledgling USSR in the 1920s and 1930s. 'Animal Farm' needed its Snowball, whether as a capitalist or as a defector from the great cause of the People's Revolution. Lenin and particularly Stalin, struck back vigorously at their foes, real and imagined. Where once the Party penetrated and spied on their oppressors in the Czar's secret police, now they deployed their secret skills against the enemies of the Revolution in the West. The Cold War had begun.

The ARCOS debacle of 1927 (see page 291) was followed by a number of serious Soviet intelligence failures. Idealistic Party workers like Wilf Macartney, who was jailed for passing RAF secrets in 1928, were no use for long-term espionage. The GPU-KGB tried a new approach. Realising that the 'comrades' of the Western Communist Parties were only too well known to the authorities, they adopted a much safer tactic to recruit spies and agents of Communism. The emphasis shifted to non-communists who might be sympathetic to the cause.

In the early 1930s there was a genuine feeling, particularly on the left-liberal wing of political thought, that Stalin's Russia was somehow better and more moral than the unfettered capitalism of the West which had just brought about the Wall Street Crash and the worst economic crisis in recorded history. Idealists really believed that Russia was involved in a great and noble social experiment. Western intellectuals (who should have known better) somehow missed the dark side of the Bolsheviks' own version of the noble experiment: State communism. The massacres of the land-owning peasants, the Kulaks, the great famine in the Ukraine and the murderous purges of those Bolsheviks who disagreed with Stalin were somehow overlooked as the gullible intelligentsia allowed themselves to ooh and aah over 'triumphs of socialist planning' on their guided tours in Russia. H. G. Wells was enraptured; Beatrice Webb, on a carefully controlled visit to a new collective farm full of happy peasants and workers, hissed to her husband, Sydney: 'You see! It works; it works!' Faced with such credulous acceptance of Stalin's cynical propaganda by these iconic godheads of the Fabian left, it is little surprise that a number of young men at Cambridge, idealistic and wary of their parents' generation and its lost causes thought that communism was a good thing.

The story of Burgess, Philby, Maclean, Cairncross and Blunt has been told many times already. What is often not stressed is the impact of their sexual preferences on their treachery. Many were associated with a closed society at Cambridge called 'The Apostles'. Together they enjoyed the freedom of university life, clear of the fetters and bonds of parental control. One of the freedoms in which some of them could revel was the ability to indulge their homosexuality. In the 1930s, homosexuality was a crime, and had to be kept secret. This frisson of sexual conspiracy and secrecy from an uncomprehending and hostile world undoubtedly bred a hothouse climate in which other more dangerous conspiratorial secrets could be encouraged to flourish.

Guy Burgess was the link man of the original Cambridge group. He was a hard-drinking, superficially clever show off, witty in conversation and an incorrigibly promiscuous homosexual. According to the Group's British based Soviet handling officer Yuri Modin: 'It was Burgess who recruited Blunt and so on down the line'. Other members of the Cambridge Conspiracy joined later: Leo Long and Alan Nunn May. Burgess and 'Kim' Philby were the first recruits to the ring, probably in 1933. The GPU-Cheka, now renamed the NKVD, were incredibly patient with their new espionage assets. They took a long view, sometimes not requiring anything from their new agents for years as they tried to 'grow' these potentially vital assets in place. Philby was first groomed in Vienna, where he married a Communist agent who was on the run from the police. (Philby was decidedly not homosexual.) 'Litzi' Friedmann was a devoted Communist and therefore a *very* dangerous wife for a Soviet agent. She soon faded from view, leaving Philby to follow a glittering career in MI6-SIS. The other members of the ring did the same in their chosen fields.

It must be stressed that the NKVD's spy ring was no group of gullible intellectuals or 'useful idiots'. These young men knew exactly what they were doing and exactly where they were going. While Burgess struggled to settle down in the BBC in London, his colleagues started to climb the Establishment's rungs; Blunt in the rarefied world of art and high culture, and Maclean and Cairncross in the Foreign Office. At the same time all were working to improve their access both to potential recruits to the cause but more importantly to British secrets.

The defining moment for the 'idealistic' spies of the Cambridge conspiracy came in August 1939 when Ribbentrop and Molotov signed their Russian-German Non-Aggression pact. From then on, any pretence that the Cambridge spies were working for some great moral cause went out of the window. There have been few agreements so cynical and as redolent of self-interest and realpolitik as the Ribbentrop-Molotov Treaty and its brutal carving up of innocent Poland. Suddenly Nazi Hitler was now Communist Stalin's sworn ally and bosom friend. However, the intellectual gymnastics required to surmount this ideological obstacle posed no problem to the agile minds of Cambridge men from Trinity. By claiming that they were working for the *Comintern's* interests (and not the USSR) they could salve their consciences. The truth is that Burgess, Philby and MacLean hated their own society and fellow countrymen so much that they were prepared to sell their soul to the Devil – for that is what the Cambridge traitors did. Besides, as many a spy has found, it was too late to turn back. They were doing very nicely out of spying for the Revolution: and there was always a threat of blackmail or exposure in the background if they didn't carry on cooperating with the Soviet Union. The Famous Five spied on, for Moscow and for glorious Comrade Stalin – whatever deceits they may have practised on themselves.

They were phenomenally successful. The Cambridge Ring finally penetrated the innermost secrets of the British State and provided Moscow with virtually every secret known to the British. Cairncross worked directly for Lord Hankey who was effectively Churchill's Controller of Secret Services; Leo Long sold out Bletchley Park's Enigma secrets; Donald Maclean was First Secretary of the British Embassy in the USA and betrayed all things Anglo-American; Anthony Blunt was spying on MI5; and Kim Philby was running the Iberian Desk inside MI6-SIS. So successful were they that at times Moscow Centre found it difficult to process, let alone believe, the sheer mass of material being forwarded by their spy ring.

By 1945 some inkling of the scale of Soviet espionage began to dawn on the Americans. They became aware of the existence of heavily coded Soviet traffic from within the US, obviously related to espionage. No one could read it at the time, so it was collected and filed away for that rainy day when someone might be able to read it. It was code-named Venona and it proved to be a ticking bombshell.

The Venona story starts with the capture of half burnt NKVD code books by Finnish siginters as they advanced with the Germans in 1941. The Soviet victory of 1945 forced the Finnish intelligence experts to flee to supposedly neutral Sweden and re-establish their operations there, a fact soon known to and accessed by Western codebreakers. The real breakthrough came in late 1945, when it gradually became clear that the Soviets had foolishly reprinted 70,000 individual pages of the supposedly one-time cipher pads in the summer panics of 1942. Armed with the possibilities opened by this careless duplication of ciphers and the revelations of defectors like Gouzenko and Petrov, British and American cryptanalysts were able to slowly and painstakingly reconstruct the secret Soviet cables from the US between 1943 and 1948. To their surprise, they discovered that their wartime ally had devoted as much effort to spying on them as Hitler.

Venona casts a light that illuminates many of the mysteries of the time. Philby, Burgess and Maclean, Blunt, the 'martyred' but very guilty Rosenbergs, even Harry Hopkins, President Roosevelt's closest confidante, stood unmasked unequivocally as Soviet agents. The only pity is that it was all uncovered so slowly and after the damage was done. Even Bletchley Park was penetrated. In the early 1950s, a GRU copy of an original Ultra decrypt was decoded to show that someone had been passing Ultra secrets direct to Stalin as early as 1941. Only by 1964 did it

USSR

████

Reissue(T1108)

From: NEW YORK

To: MOSCOW

No: 976

11 July 19**44**

To VIKTOR[i].

Your no. 2686[a]. PODRYaDChIK[ii] has not shown up for the last two meetings. Advise when he left and if possible a further description of him and also the cover-name by which our worker was known to PODRYaDChIK.

No. 550

Please give instructions to the COUNTRYSIDE[DEREVNYa][iii] to buy two cameras and send them to TYRE[iv] by the first post. You allowed one camera for ANTENNA[v]. The second is needed for the work of the Office[KONTORA][vi] The cameras find their way to the COUNTRYSIDE from Germany and cost 200 dollars. There are no cameras in TYRE. Inform us of your instructions.

With a view to reducing the time required for the receipt and handing back of RELE's[vii] materials we consider it would be a good thing to make it his job to photograph his own materials and bring to TYRE only undeveloped films. For this purpose we want to pass on to him STUKACh's[viii] old camera. The camera

[17 groups unrecoverable]

Note: [a] Not available.
Comments:
    [i]   VIKTOR: Lt. Gen. P. M. FITIN.
    [ii]   PODRYaDChIK: i.e. CONTRACTOR, Alexander SAFFIAN.
    [iii] COUNTRYSIDE: Mexico.
    [iv]   TYRE: NEW YORK CITY.
    [v]   ANTENNA: Julius ROSENBERG.
    [vi]   KONTORA: The local MGB organ or residency.
    [vii] RELE: i.e. RELAY, possibly Morton SOBELL.
    [viii] STUKACh: i.e. INFORMER, Joseph KATZ.

13 June 1975

VENONA: A decoded Soviet message implicating the Rosenbergs

become clear that the culprit was Leo Long of MI14, one of Stalin's large stable of treacherous Britons. Venona proves that the Famous Five of British traitors turns out to be a gross underestimate. There were many others, too. Although it is normal to speak of the Famous Five, the NKVD spy ring of the late 1930s was much bigger. According to Nigel West there were at least thirty-three active British agents spying for Stalin. A few were openly communist but most were only vaguely linked with the great and the good 'liberal-left' intellectual establishment of the 1940s.

One of those unmasked was Professor J. B. S. Haldane ('intelligentsia'), another the Hon. Ivor Montagu ('nobility'). A third traitor 'reservist', a Royal Artillery colonel, wounded in the Dunkirk campaign and seconded to the Ministry of Supply in the autumn of 1940, remains unknown. It would be interesting to know his true identity and, more important, where he ended up.

Venona also revealed an important penetration and betrayal of the Manhattan Project – the US-UK effort to develop the atomic bomb. Operation Enormoz (the GRU's choice of codenames seems to have been peculiarly overconfident) stripped the programme of its secrets wholesale at a time when even the FBI was unaware of its existence. (J. Edgar Hoover only discovered the atomic bomb project by accident; one of his surveillance teams tracked an NKVD officer recruiting Americans and asked just what the Russian was spying on.) We can only guess at the reactions of the Venona codebreakers on 20 December 1946, as they finally stared at the clear text of a secret cable to Moscow Centre that revealed America's greatest wartime secret – a list of the names and details of all the top Allied scientists and locations involved in the bomb programme and sent in December 1944. No wonder Stalin had been so matter-of-fact when told officially about the bomb at Potsdam; he probably knew more about its details than the US President.

Venona makes quite clear that Soviet wartime penetration of the USA went far, from the office of the president down to the San Francisco waterfront. Senator McCarthy may have had a real case when he began his investigations later in the 1950s, whatever his methods; the

CPUSA figures large in these pages. But Roosevelt, with the ever-present Harry Hopkins (Agent A19) murmuring treason in his ear, would have none of it. In 1944–5, Uncle Joe Stalin and the Soviets could do no wrong.

Many of those outed by Venona, particularly the 'intellectuals' and those who should have known better, who claimed to have been 'working for peace' in 1940 turn out not to have been the clever but misguided idealists that they would have us believe. Anyone who could spy for Stalin after he had concluded a solemn alliance with Hitler in the summer of 1939, could have had no illusions about an 'anti-Fascist crusade'. The truth is that many of the British traitors revealed by the Venona decrypts just hated their own country so much, that they could even blind themselves to the excesses of Stalin's Russia.

Incredible as the Soviet spy ring was in the West, it was eclipsed by another Russian espionage success. This was targeted against Japan and rested on the shoulders of just one man. Rarely can that unreliable and erratic commodity 'human intelligence' have been as successful as in the work of Richard Sorge. Sorge served in the Kaiser's army in the Great War. After the war the half German, half Russian wounded ex-serviceman became a communist and volunteered to spy for the Soviet Union. By 1927, the GPU realised that they had a valuable asset. Sorge, masquerading as a loyal German – which he was by birth – began to build a solid cover as an international newspaper correspondent. By 1938, after a spell in Britain and the USA he ended up in Japan as Tokyo correspondent of the highly respected *Frankfurter Zeitung*.

The Axis between militaristic Japan and Nazi Germany in the late 1930s was strong. Sorge was accepted everywhere and befriended an American communist working in the Far East, called Agnes Smedley based at Shanghai. Smedley, the China correspondent of the *Frankfurter Zeitung*, was an avid worker for the Communist Revolution and was busy setting up communist cells in China on behalf of the NKVD. She took Sorge under her wing and introduced him to her friend and fellow communist, a Japanese called Hozumi Ozaki who worked directly for the Japanese Prime Minister and had complete access to his office.

As Sorge was the Tokyo correspondent for the most prestigious

German newspaper of the day he now had access to both the Nazi embassy and to Japan's highest level of policy thinking. It was formidable access for a spy and Sorge pumped back his reports to Moscow. When the 'German' newspaperman began to get interviews with the Japanese General Staff and even the Imperial Household his stock soared still further. By 1939 he was running a tightly controlled network whose tentacles could reveal any Japanese secret. Sorge's espionage made two immense contributions to Stalin's USSR. One Stalin believed, the other he ignored.

Sorge's first contribution was over Khalkin-Ghol. The Battle of Khalkin-Ghol is unknown to most Westerners but it was one of the most decisive battles of the twentieth century. In August 1939 the Japanese, prospecting for new sources of raw materials for their war economy tried to probe north out of Manchuria and seize a major chunk of the Siberian–Mongolian border. The Soviet Union's Siberian Army under an unknown general called Zhukov stopped them and in an epic battle threw them back into Manchuria with very heavy losses.

Sorge had warned his controllers in Moscow of the Japanese plans for Khalkin-Ghol. As a result the Red Army were well prepared for the Japanese Kwantung Army's onslaught. Following this complete setback in Manchuria, the Japanese then made the fateful decision to go south, not north. If they could not get the raw materials they so desperately needed in Central Asia then they would have to strike south and seize the tin, oil and rubber of Malaya and the Philippines. It was a historic geostrategic decision that would lead to Pearl Harbor and America's war in the Pacific. It was Sorge's intelligence that actually lit the powder trail that would detonate on 7 December 1941.

Sorge's next great intelligence coup was not so well received by Comrade Stalin. Through his contacts in the German Embassy he learned the secrets of Operation Barbarossa, Hitler's plan to invade the USSR in June 1941. Sorge quickly signalled the Red Army's 4th Bureau in Moscow and awaited more instructions. They never arrived. 'Preposterous!' shouted Stalin on being briefed. 'That little shit Sorge has got himself a woman and a nice cosy set up in Tokyo. He's just feathering his own nest. It's rubbish!' The fact that his fear of a Nazi invasion had forced Stalin into insisting that only intelligence that showed the Germans were *not* going to invade the USSR was true, may have clouded his view of dissenting Sorge's report. Truth is often unwelcome, especially to dictators. When Sorge eventually learned of Stalin's reaction the Communist spy wept in his Japanese mistress's arms. He could not accept that Stalin wouldn't believe his warning that the Germans were coming. Sorge should have realised that those in power, and especially dictators, don't like being contradicted.

Just four months after the Wehrmacht crashed into the USSR, Richard Sorge, Stalin's master spy, was arrested by the Tekko, Japan's secret police. He had been caught almost by accident on a sweep among communist sympathisers as the Tokyo Special Higher Police rolled up a number of Communist cells. He was interrogated and, despite one British diplomat's observation that, 'the stupidity of the Japanese Police is only exceeded by their brutality' Sorge appears not to have been tortured. Eventually on 25 October 1941 Stalin's master spy cracked, admitting to his Japanese questioner (who by now had got access to the Kempei Tai (Military Police) records) 'I have been a member of the Comintern since 1925.' He was tried before the Tokyo district court on 29 September 1943. The delay was caused by the famously impartial nature of the Japanese court system: even in the middle of a war with an enemy agent, the prosecuting judges considered themselves independent of Tojo's government, and took their instructions only from the Imperial Household.

Sorge's case went to appeal and it was not until 7 November 1944 that Richard Sorge finally went to the gallows along with his principal Japanese agent, Ozaki. Stalin refused to lift a finger to save one of communism's most dedicated spies. Sorge's devoted Japanese mistress Hanako had a ring made from his gold teeth that she wore to the grave.

In 1964, Richard Sorge, the Soviet spy who gave his life for Stalin and the Communist cause was finally commemorated – on a postage stamp. His legacy lives on in a different way, however. It was Sorge's intelligence during 1939–40 that Japan was turning south after Khalkin-Ghol that enabled Stalin to redeploy his Far East and Siberia divisions to face the USSR's western borders. That historic decision based on Richard Sorge's intelligence helped to stop Hitler's Panzers at the gates of Moscow in the dark days of December 1941 and changed the world.

The Soviet espionage offensive was not just concerned with Japan, Nazi Germany and the 'Great Patriotic War'. To the secret service, the intelligence war was a seamless affair serving the Soviet Union in war or peace. They had not given up any of their pre-war targets just because they were now allies against Hitler: capitalism was still capitalism. By 1942–3 their intelligence networks in Britain and the USA were already reporting a mysterious American project to build a giant bomb that would unsettle any post-war balance of power once Germany was defeated. The Soviet spy rings were tasked to find out the secrets of the atom bomb from their wartime allies. A total intelligence war – which is how Stalin's Soviet Union viewed their world – made no distinction between friend and foe. All were fair game for Moscow Centre.

From the very beginning the Soviets penetrated the Manhattan Project, as the atomic bomb project was known. American writers tend to blame the leaks on 'foreign scientists' working on the project. This is untrue. The Soviets were first tipped off by one of the Cambridge spies, John Cairncross, who worked for Lord Hankey, Churchill's intelligence and security coordinator, as early as 1941. Even the project leader, Robert Oppenheimer is not above suspicion; his name also figures as Agent 'Star' in the KGB files. The truth is that the Soviets made a massive effort to glean the secrets of the atomic bomb. Not for nothing did they codename the Manhatten Project 'Enormoz'. From scientists like Klaus Fuchs at Los Alamos, to researchers like Alan Nunn May and Bruno Pentecorvo in Canada, the whole project was as insecure and as full of holes, certainly as far as Moscow was concerned, as a Swiss cheese. If that were not enough, another Cambridge spy, Donald Maclean, was in Washington as the Anglo-American atomic weapons programme coordinator. All reported back direct to Lavrenty Beria, Stalin's chief of the NKVD-KGB, coordinator of the intelligence war against the West.

If the Cold War started anywhere it started well before the Potsdam

Conference of 1945, or Churchill's 'iron curtain' speech of 1946. The Cold War was alive and kicking from midsummer 1944 onwards, and nuclear weapons were the battlefield over which it would be fought. The truth is that the Soviets knew almost everything; far more than the Germans ever did. Yuri Modin, who was the handler based in the UK of the Cambridge spies, actually wrote in his memoirs of the time, 'I can confirm that we in the USSR knew absolutely everything about the technical and political aspects of atomic bomb development'. A special section was set up in the NKVD to do nothing but handle atomic espionage and to accelerate the Soviet nuclear weapons programme.

Perhaps because of this America's new president was surprised and taken aback when he first revealed the existence of a 'new weapon of unusual destructive force' to Stalin at Potsdam in July 1945. The Soviet leader just nodded and grunted, leaving the baffled Truman to move on to the next item on the agenda. The truth is that Stalin knew more about the details of the atomic bomb than did Truman or any of his staff.

Details of the Soviets' spying did much to poison the already deep wells of distrust between the allies after the war. As cooperation broke down and in Churchill's words, 'an iron curtain descended from Stettin in the north, to Trieste in the south', more evidence surfaced of the Soviets' espionage against their wartime allies. A defector called Gouzenko fled the Soviet Embassy in Ottawa (where he was the NKVD's cipher clerk) in 1946. His revelations to the RCMP and the decrypts of the Venona signals intelligence traffic would begin a trail that would eventually lead to a round up of many of the key players in the NKVD's 1940s great spy apparatus. The damage they had done, however, really was *'enormoz'*. The result was that the post 1945 world looked out on a new form of warfare, a 'Cold War'.

Any doubts about the Soviets' post-war intentions had been clarified by their 1948 blockade of the Allied half of Berlin. The world realised that the wartime allies now stood bitterly opposed to each other. Political, ideological, economic and military differences divided them deeply. A new world war seemed highly likely, if not inevitable.

From the Berlin Airlift onwards, both sides began to prepare for a final clash of arms. For America and the West, it meant that the 'peace dividend' was actually rearmament to protect capitalism. For the Soviet Union, it meant that an arms race was on to acquire nuclear weapons and make the world safe for Communism. Both sides set to, to spy on each other by every means possible. The Cold War became an intelligence war.

The detonation of the first Soviet atom bomb on 29 August 1949 shocked the West. Its development had been accelerated by the generous and informative contributions of Klaus Fuchs, a German refugee from Hitler, whose spying from his post-war appointment as head of theoretical physics at Britain's AWE at Harwell saved the USSR many thousands of hours and many millions of roubles. His reward on being caught was fourteen years' imprisonment, but it was too late. The Soviets now had the vital information needed to manufacture their own atom bomb. Tension, already high between East and West, finally exploded on 25 June 1950 when Communist North Korea invaded its non-communist neighbours having first cleared the attack with Stalin and Mao Tse Tung. The South Koreans were driven back and saved only by the intervention of UN forces. It was the first real shooting war between the Cold War power blocks.

The Korean War revealed an ugly new development. By and large, in the previous wars of the twentieth century, captured enemy prisoners had been treated correctly under the Geneva Convention, with the exception of the Nazi-Soviet fighting on the Eastern front and those who had the misfortune to fall into the hands of the Japanese. In Korea, Allied prisoners of war could expect no such consideration. On the contrary, ill treatment and brutal interrogation were now applied as deliberate weapons of war to brainwash enemy prisoners. The hardened Turkish prisoners of war spat in the faces of their captors, and suffered the consequences. The less robust American prisoners died like flies in the Communist prison camps of North Korea.

The Communists' methods went deeper than mere brainwashing in some cases. The North Koreans and Chinese were also briefed to talent spot among the prisoners of war, looking for potential recruits for the KGB once the war was over. We will never know how many prisoners were approached to act as agents and refused to drink from the Communist cup. What we do know is that one British national did offer to spy for the Communists. George Blake had been interned along with all the British Embassy staff in Seoul when the North invaded. But Blake was no ordinary Consular official: he was an MI6-SIS officer and on his release in 1953 came back on the Trans-Siberian Railway through Russia. Here he met his KGB handler and from that moment on became a long term Soviet asset at the heart of Britain's secret services. When he was finally caught and jailed (on evidence supplied by a defector to the CIA) his sentence reflected the extent of his treason. The judge gave him forty-two years, supposedly one year for every British agent he had betrayed. Sadly Blake never served out his punishment, being sprung in a daring escape in 1966 and fleeing to Moscow to eke out his life in the small and dismal community of ex-Soviet spies living on their memories in the Russian capital.

Eventually the war on the Korean peninsula settled down to a stalemate of trench warfare, but the international temperature had been raised to new limits. The big intelligence problem for the West was getting access into the closed society of Soviet Russia. Stalin's Moscow was, to put it mildly, a hostile environment for intelligence operators and even the occasional good human intelligence source, such as the Russian-Canadian (Gideon) who spied as a KGB double agent for the RCMP in the early 1950s (and then suddenly disappeared on a 'routine consultation' in Moscow in 1952) soon dried up. Anyway, it was not enough. More intelligence was needed, much more.

The West turned to technology to address the intelligence deficiency. The 'Cold Air War' had begun as early as September 1946, when the USAF had trundled elderly B-17 bombers and DC-3s around Europe trying to spot any unusual Soviet radar emissions. They soon found them. In 1947, a DC-3, flying above clouds over Soviet East Germany, was nearly blown out of the sky by very accurate anti-aircraft fire. The shaken aircrew reported that it could only have been radar controlled.

The Soviets had radar. By the time of the Korean War, 'ferret flights' to collect electronic intelligence were commonplace. They were also potentially very dangerous. Even the neutral Swedes suffered. A DC-3 collecting radar emissions over the Baltic was shot down by Soviet MiGs despite being over international waters. The message was clear.

Despite this, the Americans and British persisted, sending specially equipped aircraft to sniff out intelligence on the periphery of the USSR and to photograph anything of interest. Attempts to overfly the Soviet Union tended to stir up a hornet's nest of fighter interceptors looking for blood. There was another danger, too, and one not often briefed to the reconnaissance aircrew in the early days. Since the mysterious disappearance of a specially equipped PB4 flying boat in April 1950 the Americans suspected that the Soviets were hanging on to any captured airmen. They just disappeared into the Communist Gulag. This was not an encouraging prospect for the aircrew manning the specialised recce probes into Soviet airspace.

By 1954, the US was desperate. Rumours of new MiG fighters and Soviet bombers under construction prompted a deliberate flight over Archangel and Murmansk to see and photograph what was on the runways of the Soviet Air Forces main bases in the north, especially any long-range bombers. The aircraft selected was one of the new six-jet RB-47s, capable of flying too high for the Russian MiG-15s. The RB-47 penetrated Soviet territory over Murmansk, collected masses of radar data and good photographs as it flew south-east towards Archangel, then headed west for the Finnish border and safety.

The reconnaissance jet had been over Soviet airspace for about fifteen minutes when the first MiG-15s appeared, well below the RB-47, cruising at over 40,000 feet. They quickly fell behind. However, as it turned west and put its nose down to head for home, the RB-47 crew got a nasty shock. Coming up at them was a flight of the new MiG-17s, which bore in to attack from astern at 38,000 feet. The RB-47's tail gun kept them partly at bay but the Stratojet was damaged in the MiG-17s' firing passes. Leaking fuel and losing height, the USAF aircraft was only saved by crossing into Finnish airspace, at which point the MiGs broke for home.

The RB-47 staggered back to RAF Fairford with the help of a 'wet tow' – semi-permanently plugged into one of the KC-97 tankers waiting to see them home. It had been a near run thing; but at least the USAF now knew about the characteristics and deployments of the Soviet's new fighter among the mass of other intelligence they had collected.

As a result of these dangerous overflights, and driven by the need to acquire intelligence on the Soviet's latest weapon developments, in 1955 President Eisenhower actually proposed a joint 'open skies' policy for the USA and USSR in a bid to lower the international tension. A year later the Soviet Union rejected the idea out of hand. The vital Western overflights would have to continue, but this time using something different as an aerial intelligence collector. The USA decided to build a special intelligence collection aeroplane.

The U2, designed by Kelly Johnson and built at Lockheed's secret Skunk Works in California, was essentially a motorised glider able to float high above the earth on the edge of the atmosphere with a payload of high-resolution cameras and electronic warfare sensors. Its strange mixture of metal, balsa-wood and plastic construction meant that it was remarkably light and its powerful J79 engine meant that it could climb like a lift on take off. At 65,000 feet and more above the Soviet Union, from 1956 onwards the U2, or 'Black Lady', could collect intelligence out of the reach of the Soviet PVO-Strany, or Air Defence organisation. Despite Soviet protests the intelligence overflights continued, and the U2s earned their money, revealing that Western intelligence estimates of Soviet bomber strengths had been seriously exaggerated. The intelligence was gold dust and the U2s were invulnerable, even if they infuriated the Soviets.

By 1960, new threats were emerging. The launch of the Russian Sputnik in October 1957 had shocked the West. Could the USSR have developed the world's first Intercontinental Ballistic Missiles (ICBMs)? Where the 'bomber gap' had been seriously discredited, had it now been replaced by a new and very real 'missile gap'? The CIA was tasked to find out. A Major Gary Powers of the USAF ('sheep dipped' to be a civilian contractor) was tasked to fly a U2 over the Soviet Union from

Peshawar in Pakistan to Bodo in Norway. On the way he would overfly the possible new ICBM bases at Plesetzk and Tyuratam. It was a crucial overflight, for later that month Presidents Eisenhower and Khrushchev were due to meet for a vital summit meeting designed to lease East–West Cold War tensions.

Something went horribly wrong. The U2 had a very narrow operating envelope at altitude. Ten knots too fast and the plane's structure begins to break up; ten knots too slow and it will stall and fall out of the sky. For safety at 70,000 feet pilots have to rely on the autopilot. Boredom is the biggest problem on a nine hours flight in a nice warm cockpit, on the dark edge of a black stratosphere, with only the hiss of breathing in their ears. It was not unknown for U2 pilots to read a book or sing, to keep awake.

The Russians had detected the Black Lady as soon as it crossed their border and were tracking it on their radar screens as the U2 cruised

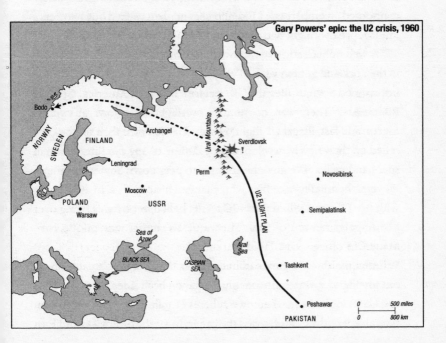

Gary Powers' epic: the U2 crisis, 1960

north-west behind the Urals. MiG interceptors struggled for height and frustrated, fell away far below. Powers sailed on serenely. What happened next remains a mystery. According to Powers a SAM-2 Guideline missile suddenly detonated nearby and blew off part of the U2's tail. The U2 began to fall out of the sky. Powers waited until he was nearer the ground and then parachuted to safety.

At the enquiry years later the CIA debriefers asked the same questions over and over: had Gary Powers fallen asleep? Had the autopilot failed and brought the plane lower? The SAM-2 Guideline's ceiling was only 63,000 feet and Powers should have been nearer 70,000. Whatever the truth, Powers had made three huge mistakes on his intelligence flight across Russia. He had failed to operate the U2's self-destruct mechanism, thereby giving the USSR a present – albeit as a monster jigsaw – of a top-secret aeroplane and all its equipment. Secondly, his failure to kill himself with the poison needle so thoughtfully provided by the CIA meant that the KGB interrogators could now put him to the question. And last, but no means least, his failure had wrecked the Paris Summit. (Khrushchev confronted an embarrassed Eisenhower and then walked out.) Powers's intelligence overflight had made the Cold War worse, not better.

A well-publicised Soviet show trial followed. Powers 'confessed all' in the dock and got ten years. Two years later he was exchanged for the imprisoned Soviets' illegal KGB *'rezident'* in North America, Colonel Rudolf Abel. There were no more U2 overflights after Powers's twenty-fourth, and last, illegal U2 flight over the USSR. From then on the USA relied on their newly developed programme of spy satellites flying in space and well above any one country to peer down Soviet chimneys. Powers, the intelligence flier who changed history, died in 1977 along with his TV crew, when the NBC traffic helicopter he was flying over Los Angeles ran out of fuel. The inquest's verdict was 'pilot error'. Many CIA officers said, 'Told you so!'

After the abortive Paris summit of 1960, the Cold War became an all-out intelligence war, quite openly waged on both sides. Both the USA and USSR looked after their own spheres of influence and went to considerable lengths to embarrass the other. In 1961, the Soviets and East

German government even walled off the whole of East Germany with a border fence designed to keep the West out and to keep their own people in. The USSR openly supported Castro's Communist revolution in Cuba and relished the USA's failure in the abortive 'Bay of Pigs' invasion by US-trained Cuban exiles. With a now friendly Socialist country only 90 miles from Miami the temptation for Khrushchev, the ebullient Soviet leader, to exploit the 'romantic Revolution' was just too great, and in autumn 1962 he over-reached himself and precipitated the greatest crisis of the Cold War. The Russians started secretly to ship nuclear missiles into Cuba to threaten America.

It was signals intelligence that first alerted the Americans to this new threat. At the time America was being sucked into Vietnam and disturbing signals about 'Russian rockets in Cuba' were just a distraction. To clear up the issue, President Kennedy ordered photographic intelligence sorties over the island. In June 1962, four U2 overflights showed that the Soviets were building anti-aircraft missile emplacements on the island. Why? The US stepped up its recce flights. By 29 August it was clear that something big was going on. Soviet bombers and high performance fighters were identified on new Cuban airbases. The CIA ordered maximum effort to find out the truth. Their top agent in Moscow, Colonel Oleg Penkowsky, alerted them that Khrushchev was serious and courting trouble. Finally on 14 October 1962 the USAF and CIA air photographs identified Soviet nuclear missiles on Cuba.

The shock in Washington was profound. By 19 October, the US had declared a military alert and by the 22nd, the American military was on a war footing. B-52 bombers were kept in the air ready for nuclear war, and Cuba was blockaded by the US Navy. Castro, probably in bravado, ordered one of his new SAM-2 missiles to fire at the American overflights and actually hit a U2, downing it into the sea with its pilot. The Cuban President called on Khrushchev to be ready to go to war. Khrushchev temporised: hotheads like Castro had little place in a life or death debate about nuclear Armageddon between the grown-ups. What was needed was diplomatic and accurate intelligence and quickly too, while behind the scenes Khrushchev and Kennedy tried to hammer out a face-saving diplomatic solution as Soviet merchant ships on the high seas ploughed on towards Cuba and the waiting US warships. Confrontation seemed inevitable. The world held its breath. By 20 November, it was all over. Soviet ships turned back and the Russians began to remove their rockets from Cuba. The US removed its Jupiter missiles from Turkey. The whole world breathed a sigh of relief. The Cuban missile crisis was accelerated by intelligence and it was intelligence that ultimately solved it. In the long history of the Cold War, nothing came as close to turning it into a genuine nuclear holocaust.

One feature of the crisis was the emergence of the US Navy as a major player in the dangerous game of deterrence. On 2 October 1962, at the height of the crisis, the navy realised that Soviet submarines were trying to run the blockade. It is relatively straightforward to stop a surface vessel and order it to heave to. Submarines are a different matter. The US Navy knew that they had to interdict the Soviet boats. The question was, how? They couldn't attack them: that would have meant war. Under direct orders from the Pentagon, US destroyers, submarines and aircraft began to track the Soviets' Foxtrot-class submarines and try to signal them to stop. This involved throwing small practice depth charges (PDCs) overboard 'to get their attention ...'.

Hearing the explosions, pandemonium broke out in the Soviet submarines. They had been at sea for weeks; the crews were tired, frightened and very jumpy. The clang of American depth bombs – even practice ones – from above was the last straw. On at least two of the Soviet boats the captains prepared to fire nuclear torpedoes at the American ships. On Submarine B-130 the skipper actually ordered the nuclear tube to be loaded, then watched with satisfaction as his political officer wet himself and fainted with fright. Captain Nikolai Shumkov of the Red Banner Fleet grunted and ordered the nuclear torpedo (which was fifteen times the size of the Hiroshima bomb) unloaded. 'Just testing', he told his stunned control room, adding that he had no intention of using the torpedo, 'because we would all go up with it if we fired. Agreed?' His wide-eyed officers dumbly nodded their heads in agreement with their 'ballsy captain'.

On board Submarine B-59 on 27 October, a 'totally exhausted' Captain Valentin Savitsky, 'unable to establish communications with Moscow', became furious and ordered the nuclear torpedo to be brought to battle readiness. This was almost certainly a gesture and a bluff by Savitsky, because intelligence in this most critical of the Cold War clashes had failed both sides. The Americans had no idea that any of the Soviet submarines even had nuclear torpedoes. The Americans in their turn had orders to release full size nuclear depth charges if attacked. Nuclear war could easily have broken out during the Cuban Missile Crisis: not as part of some Dr Strangelove-like exchange of ICBM's but at sea, and almost by accident, merely as a very low-level tactical exchange between surface ships and submarines crewed by exhausted and frightened men. That is the really frightening aspect of those terrifying days in the autumn of 1962.

By November the crisis was over. Both sides – and the rest of the world – were shaken by the experience of Cuba. NATO and the Warsaw Pact both redoubled their efforts to control nuclear weapons and monitor any future crises. Intelligence now became the driving force of the Cold War at every level, but particularly the strategic. For by the late 1960s, a clear triad of deterrence was emerging and a real balance of terror. It was a situation not unlike the little old lady who seizes her dentist's tes-° ticles as the drill approaches her mouth and says, sweetly, 'Now, we aren't going to hurt each other, young man, are we?' This triad of ICBMs, bombers and submarine-launched nuclear missiles was to ensure that for the last twenty years of the Cold War, no one got hurt.

The only shooting battlefields between the two sides were proxy wars (like Vietnam and Afghanistan) fought by their clients or allies, or at sea, both above and below the waves. Cuba set the precedent: it was at sea that the Cold War was played out most dangerously between the two sides as fully armed warships manoeuvred to collect intelligence on each other. What started out as a few specially equipped fishing vessels pretending to be part of the Soviet fishing fleet but spying on the West soon escalated into a full time specialisation in most navies. Exercising their rights of innocent passage on the high seas ships could shadow each other's battle fleets without interference or sit off the coast in international waters and collect electronic and any other intelligence. By the 1950s the Americans too had begun to convert old merchant-men into auxiliary technical reconnaissance ships to match the Soviets' 'spy trawlers' as the intelligence war went to sea.

These intelligence-collecting ships quickly proved their value. It was a US Auxiliary AGER spy ship that first alerted the Americans to the presence of nuclear missiles in Cuba in 1962. The Pentagon testi-fied at the later Congressional hearings:

> Electronic intelligence acquired by surface ships led to the photographic intelligence from aircraft - that's what gave us the indisputable evidence of the installation of Soviet Missiles in Cuba.

After this success the US AGER fleet was expanded and a new class of smaller vessels was planned. Collecting Cold War intelligence was never a risk free occupation. Tragedy struck during the Arab-Israeli war of 1967 when the intelligence collector USS *Liberty* was cruising off the Egyptian-Israeli coast in international waters. Without any warning Israeli aircraft and torpedo boats carried out a sustained attack that culminated in machine-gunning survivors and which killed forty-three Americans. Israel claimed 'it was all just a mistake'; President Lyndon B. Johnson accepted this lame explanation, despite all the evidence, and a US Navy court of enquiry found as it was ordered to do so by the President. Espionage on the high seas did have its dangers after all – if not from her enemies, then certainly from America's 'friends'.

Undeterred, the US stepped up its intelligence collection efforts at sea as their new class of smaller intelligence auxiliaries put to sea. In early 1968 the USS *Palm Beach* was deployed into the Atlantic and the USS *Pueblo* set off for the Pacific and the coast of North Korea. On 23 January 1968 the *Pueblo* was loitering 15 miles off the port of Wonsan when North Korean gunboats attacked the ship in international waters and boarded her. They took the crew of eighty-three prisoner and captured the US Navy's complete signals intelligence operation: men, machines and documentation. On board the *Pueblo* was the intelligence equiva-

lent of the American Crown Jewels. Among the booty were several
KW-7 encryption machines.

The KW-7 machines were the Americans' worldwide naval communications system, used like the German Enigma machine to automatically code and decode messages. As soon as it was known that the
Pueblo's crypto-machines were compromised, voices were raised in the
National Security Agency (NSA, the US code and cipher agency) at Fort
Meade, Maryland, about the possible dangers of compromise and advocating its replacement with the new KW-84. The US Navy and the other
services hotly resisted any change of coding machine on two grounds:
first, without the daily one time key settings the machines were deaf
and dumb, just big teleprinters. Secondly, the cost of replacing the thousands of coding machines in US service all over the world because one
machine had fallen into enemy hands would be exorbitant.

The crucial argument was the access to the American's key settings;
these were the real secrets, not the machines. As long as the daily top
secret one time cipher key lists used to 'set' the KW-7 machines were
kept safe, the communications traffic would still be secure. Dissenting
voices that said, 'Yes; but if the Soviets ever do get our cipher keys as
well we will be hopelessly compromised', were ignored or passed over
for promotion. Anyway, how could the Soviets ever get access to the
key lists for all the different services for every single day? It just couldn't
be done.

The Soviets did it, however. The weak Cold War link was not signals
intelligence but human intelligence: good old-fashioned espionage.
The most vulnerable link in the American classified materials
system was the access to the daily key lists by their custodian officers.
These specially selected and vetted men and women received the NSA
code key lists in sealed, tamper-proof packets from the top secret code
materials printing works at Fort Meade. They then stored them in their
classified safes, only opening the daily packets under control of a
witness in order to 'fill' the KW-7's electronic brains with that day's
codes. If the Soviets could ever get on to the distribution list for the
key lists and put them into their captured machines, then they would

be able to read the whole of the US's classified traffic worldwide.

About a month after the capture of the USS *Pueblo*, a US Navy key list custodian calling himself John Harper walked into the Soviet Embassy in Washington and calmly offered to spy for the Russians. His real name was Chief Warrant Officer John A. Walker US Navy, and he was the custodian of all the code word top secret classified materials for CINCLANT, the US Atlantic Fleet's naval base at Norfolk Virginia. To prove his credentials he showed the KGB officer his US Navy ID card and gave him a copy of a month's key lists in advance. In return he wanted money, lots of money. He knew exactly what he was doing and what it was worth. The amazed Russians bundled this intelligence equivalent of Santa Claus out the back of the embassy in disguise and set up a regular monthly income for their wonderful new benefactor.

Within six months Walker's treachery had become a regular commercial exchange. The KGB even slipped Walker a specially built rotor detector for the new KL-47 series of American machines that could detect and read encoded rotor settings automatically. Their scientists had developed it from the KW-7 machines captured on the *Pueblo* and from those lost in Vietnam. The Russians assured Walker that they were prepared to pay handsomely for any cryptographic materials that he could supply. It was possibly the greatest cryptographic intelligence coup ever.

For the next seven years until he retired in 1976, Walker set up what amounted to an organised cryptographic spy business inside the US Navy. Philby, Burgess and MacLean paled into insignificance against this deepest new treachery carried out purely for money. Walker was a living example of the 'capitalist-materialist ethic'. His partners in the business were his son Michael Walker on board the nuclear carrier USS *Nimitz*, his brother Lieutenant Commander Michael Walker, his wife Barbara and his chief 'supplier' Senior Radio Technician Arthur Whitworth. All were paid 'by results' by John Walker's pyramid selling operation from Russian-supplied funds. By the time his estranged wife turned him in to the FBI in 1985 Walker and his family business had effectively compromised almost every single US Navy secret transmission for fifteen years. His spy ring had even betrayed some of the US Navy's most secret signals of all, those controlling the sub-surface Cold War.

Cold War submarine espionage became as dangerous as any game of blind man's buff that is played in the cold darkness of the oceans between 13,000-ton steel blind monsters. Despite the risks both sides constantly harassed and shadowed their submarine counterparts trying to collect the vital intelligence needed in case of war. What sound did they make? How fast were they? How deep could they dive? What were their operating zones and how did they make contact? For thirty years, all over the world, an unseen submarine war was fought out, both sides jockeying for information. On one occasion one of the new Soviet titanium hulled 'Alpha' class high-speed nuclear subs squirted at an impossible depth at 40 knots, directly underneath the US Atlantic Fleet, before drawing away into the distance, leaving shocked US sonar operators tearing their headsets off and staring at each other in disbelief. It was like Formula 1 racing, played with huge machines in the dark, underwater. Underwater collisions were not uncommon. Above all, with nuclear boats that could stay underwater for months the cat and mouse game called for endurance. On one epic mission, the USS *Lapon* stayed at battle stations and tracked an unsuspecting Soviet missile submarine for *forty-seven days*.

Anyone unfortunate enough to get in the way risked being sucked in. For example, in the submarine choke point of the Irish Sea there were literally scores of incidents where fishing boats suddenly found 'something big' caught in their nets and accelerating faster than any fish. Wise fishermen cursed, and quickly cut their nets. Fishermen with a big investment in their boats were often too slow. Whatever was in their nets dragged them under. Over 150 seamen drowned in unexplained 'accidents' in the Irish Sea between 1973 and 1993. When the Irish FV *Sheralga* was dragged in 1982, the Americans denied any knowledge, the Russians refused to comment, and the Admiralty haughtily declared that 'none of HM submarines were in the area of the tragedy at the time in question'. The explanation was shattered when an Isle of Man family, out for the day in a boat from Peel, produced a holiday snap of HM Submarine *Porpoise* on the surface near Irish fishing vessels just hours before the incident.

Apart from the obvious surveillance submarine operations, the Cold War produced some activities normally associated with more conventional espionage, but underwater. Submarines actually tapped into undersea cables or dropped off special pods to collect signals intelligence and, almost unbelievably, sometimes divers would swim close enough to slow-moving submarines to take photographs of key features like propellers, torpedo tubes and sonar arrays. It was a dangerous business, trying to collect intelligence in the dark in the deep. On one occasion the USS *Tantoa* got too close to a Soviet submarine, *Black Lila*, which turned and rammed the US boat. Both sides thought the other had been sunk in the collision, and reported accordingly. Neither was, although both were damaged, and the incident was hushed up by both sides. The British Royal Navy's submarines, which at one time were the quietest in the world, even tried to probe inside Soviet fleet bases, but very slowly and quietly. The sheer invisibility of submarines still encourages navies to chance their arm collecting vital underwater intelligence. Whatever populations and newspapers may say, the silent intelligence struggle still remains the last front of the Cold War.

The rest of that curious struggle is now history, fading as the world adjusted to its new world order after the collapse of Communism and the tearing down of the Berlin Wall in the 1990s. As that final symbol of the Cold War disappeared, so a flood of dammed-up secrets began to pour out from the East. It made astonishing reading in the West on two levels. No one had ever realised just how great an effort the Eastern Bloc had put into collecting intelligence over the previous forty years. That no one had an inkling of it, however, shows just how much effort the Communist countries had put into collecting intelligence on and controlling their own populations. Richelieu, Fouché, Stieber and the various Czars' efforts paled into insignificance when compared with the Eastern Bloc's efforts, and none more so than the revelations of Markus Wolf, for thirty years head of East Germany's Ministry of State Security (MfS).

With true German system and efficiency Wolf and his political masters had built up a society that was effectively a huge prison. To call the DDR a police state is no hyperbole. Wolf's Germany stood as a model of State Communism. It was the nearest thing to *Nineteen Eighty-Four* we have ever seen. The MfS had 91,000 full-time secret police and intelligence officers and 170,000 'associates', or collaborators. Out of a population of only 17 million people, about a quarter of a million East Germans spied for the MfS. In addition, the Kripo (criminal police) had 30,000 paid long-term informers. As these all turned over at about 10 per cent a year, it meant that by the time the Berlin Wall came down, the majority of East Germans were either spying for, or had at some time spied for, East Germany's intelligence and security service. The MfS had total control of society: ministries, borders, factories, schools, universities, police, diplomats and, of course, all visitors. In addition, Wolf ran 20,000 spies in the West. By the 1980s the MfS had identified new threats which they felt were 'decomposing' the Communist purity of DDR society – skinheads, Jehovah's Witnesses, the churches and any ecology-minded 'greens'. All were targeted by the Stasi.

In his interrogations with German BfV and BND (Germany's equivalent to MI5 and MI6) officers after unification, Wolf cheerfully admitted to his methods. He ran 4,000 operational intelligence operations every year and their aim was to: 'destroy and neutralise "perceived threats"'. It was always better to attack targeted individuals' reputations and jobs, and break up families through a series of elaborate campaigns than to publicly pillory them and offer a platform for any opposition.

The Stasi's day-to-day activities were very wide and even extended to managing the comprehensive State sports doping programme as well as a special Office for the Protection of the State Economy. This latter did not just spy and steal overseas commercial secrets, but also kept a close eye on 'sabotage' of the economy, which, in a Communist state's command-based economy meant only one thing: corruption and black marketeering. Britain had suffered a much milder form of this particular infection in the semi-Stalinist period immediately after the Second World War. George Orwell's *Nineteen Eighty-Four* accurately portrays the world of shortages, black market goods and unobtainable luxuries that was 1948 Britain struggling to survive after a war that had bankrupted her and her economy. The DDR was like that *all the time*. A totally planned economy means total control, and total control means that there will inevitably be rule-breakers prepared to pay extra for things in demand and people prepared to get them, for a price. It is impossible to control people's wishes. The Stasi tried.

The Stasi policed the economy, taxing imported luxuries, prosecuting theft from factories and ensuring that favoured government employees always got the best. It is almost impossible for us to grasp the full extent of the Stasi's grip on DDR at every level. Its six million files on 'individuals of Security interest' give some indication of its reach and all-seeing eye. Wolf himself was unrepentant. At home in the DDR, he had done exactly what was required of him by his political masters; no more and no less. He could hardly be accused of 'doing his job too well.' He was even more proud of his intelligence efforts overseas.

When the CIA bought the Stasi's complete microfilmed records in 1992 (either from the KGB or a disgruntled ex-DDR employee), the officers at Langley were amazed at what they read. The computerised MfS databases were especially interesting. The Stasi had completely penetrated virtually the whole of West German society from the Chancellor's office down to junior non-commissioned officers working on NATO bases. West German intelligence officers invited by the CIA as part of Operation Rosenholz to share this feast of information at Langley must have paled on reading that the BND had harboured two spies in their midst for nearly twenty years. Alfred Spuhler worked in Communist Countries Analysis Branch and Gabriel Gast in the agency's USSR Division. Operation Rosenholz also helpfully revealed that the German security service (BfV) was not immune either. The deputy director of the BfV, Klaus Kuron, had been in the Stasi's pay since 1982. Worst affected of all by the Stasi's 'long cold finger' was the military security service, the MAD: Colonel Joachim Krause, its deputy chief, had been a Stasi spy from 1973 until he died at the helm in 1988.

Embarrassment at these espionage disasters was not just confined to the Germans.

While the Stasi was never able to penetrate its principal target, the nuclear targeting and operational processes at the military Supreme Headquarters Allied Powers Europe (SHAPE) at Mons in Belgium, someone else did. One Friday in 1981 a Dutch Air Force officer called Avner Smit working in intelligence plans walked into the Warsaw Pact ground forces intelligence office and expressed an interest in the extensive files on Soviet tank development. At the time the identity and characteristics of new Soviet tanks were the number one intelligence priority for NATO's ground forces.

'This looks very interesting work', Smit said, looking at the secret intelligence photographs of the new tanks provided by the US and UK. 'Do you mind if I check it with some work we are doing in Intel Plans?' The Ground Forces desk officer saw no objection and the 'secret' file was duly signed out to the Dutchman in Plans; unusual, but perfectly reasonable between intelligence offices within the secure Intel area. The need to know principle applied – just.

When the file had not reappeared after the weekend, the alert desk officer in Ground Forces told a colleague in the Current Intelligence Branch. It turned out that Smit had been asking lots of questions about tanks and borrowing 'interesting' files from him too, on Soviet tanks and Ground Forces – strange behaviour for an Air Force officer, whose specialty was long-term plans. Interested, and now slightly alarmed, the two intelligence officers alerted the SHAPE security officer. A suggestion that some spurious intelligence be pumped into the system – a so-called dye stain operation to see where it came out – was hastily rejected by the security office. In NATO the first priority was never to embarrass another member nation, whatever the possible benefits. A subsequent undercover security operation, between SHAPE, the SHAPE security office and the Marechaussee (the highly efficient Dutch Military Police) caught the Royal Netherlands Air Force officer red-handed in the act of stealing NATO secrets. He was duly tried and sentenced by a Dutch court for espionage on behalf of a foreign power – *Israel*.

It transpired that the Israelis were more interested than most in the gun and armour on any new Soviet tanks. What the USSR built today, the Arab armies might acquire tomorrow. Smit's beautiful Jewish wife, Dalia, was the clue; it had been noticed that she had gone to extraordinary lengths to make friends with a number of influential officers in SHAPE, including most of the 'Command Group' and the senior intelligence staff. She had made particular efforts to ingratiate herself with the US suppliers of hard 'codeword' (above top secret) intelligence. Dalia Smit was in fact an undercover Mossad agent and had been Smit's handler, and his link with Tel Aviv. Any lingering doubts were dispelled when Avner Smit came out of jail. He and the beautiful Dalia promptly emigrated to Israel, where both restarted their real careers: working for Mossad.

NATO and the US did not come out of the Stasi's clutches unscathed either. The DDR scored some notable intelligence successes at NATO's headquarters in Brussels. A massive flood of intelligence and documents poured back to East Berlin from the Stasi spies operating inside the NATO building. The Director of Operations' personal assistant was Stasi agent 'Bordeaux' according to the Rosenholz files. Ursula Lorenzen accessed every single NATO war plan for the Stasi until she defected in 1979. A Belgian secretary codenamed Michelle spied directly from the secretary general's office until 1980. Worst of all, agent 'Topas' (Reiner Rupp), after many attempts finally got himself a NATO civilian job in the Economics Directorate of NATO headquarters. From there he sent back regular reports on every meeting of NATO's top-level Defence Planning Council, every summit and (as part of his job, he drew regular duty in NATO's cosmic top secret Operations Situation Centre) on exact procedures for every eventuality in emergency and war. There were dozens of other Stasi agents in both NATO and the NATO countries. The Vienna agent alone sent 800 documents a month to Berlin during the arms control talks held there.

All this information was passed by the Stasi straight back to Moscow. As a result, in Bernd Schaefer's words, 'NATO Defense Planning in Brussels was absolutely transparent for Moscow for years.' The paradox of all this intelligence activity was that it was, in the words of the old pre-war Communist spy-recruiters, 'working for peace'. For example, Reiner Rupp (Topas) was specifically briefed to warn East Berlin of any NATO surprise first strike. He was even given a special signalling device. His intelligence that NATO had no such contingency plan and no first strike plans must have caused eyebrows to knit in the Kremlin. If nothing else, it made the Warsaw Pact question their intelligence assessments of NATO's intentions, especially at key moments of the Cold War like cruise missiles deployments when tensions rose on both sides.

Markus Wolf reinforced the point. 'The man without a face' was absolutely clear. To him his intelligence activities had been for the good. He and his Stasi team, fighting on what he and the Russians called the invisible front, had actually saved the world. Their intelligence activities had prevented the nuclear confrontation that had terrorised the world since 1949:

> Generally speaking we reaffirmed that the purpose of our intelligence service (maybe of all the services) was to prevent surprises – above all, military surprises – against one's own country or one's own alliance. That was the main job; that's the way we formulated our functions, and that's the way I saw it ...
>
> I'm pretty sure that the intelligence services on the whole, and the spies both in the east and the west, tended towards a more realistic assessment of the balance of power than that of politicians and military leaders; so that actions, or even adventurous actions which could easily have led to an escalation [of tension] or even to a war, would have been desisted from. So, yes, I do claim that my unit contributed to our having had the longest peacetime in modern European history. I feel I can justly say so ...

As Markus Wolf reviewed his life's work, it is not unreasonable to suggest that, for all its confrontations and spy scares, it really was intelligence that prevented the Cold War from becoming a nuclear Hot War. The age of the greatest battle of all – an exchange of thermonuclear tipped missiles – may possibly be over.

Smaller battles loom.

19

The Globalisation of Terror

We have slain a large dragon ... but we live now in a jungle filled with a bewildering variety of poisonous snakes ...

JAMES WOOLSEY, EX-DIRECTOR, CIA

As Westerners we are obsessed with battles. Napoleon and the Duke of Wellington have much to answer for. While the crushing defeat of the French Emperor at Waterloo was the final blow to the old European order and ushered in a new century of British power, industrial growth and German reunification, the Battle of Waterloo also resulted in a very dangerous misunderstanding in Western minds: the myth of the great, decisive battle.

The idea that warfare should be waged primarily through a decisive head-to-head clash on the battlefield is one of great antiquity. But it is by no means the only way for men to fight. For the weak and ruthless, sometimes the stiletto in the back has been the only way to attack powerful enemies. Terrorism is as old as time and its attacks on the innocent, rich and powerful have a long and bloody history. The modern-day notion that it is a new phenomenon is therefore misplaced. The idea that terrorism is somehow not a legitimate weapon for 'furthering policy by violent means' is quite simply wrong.

There are two main kinds of terrorism: terror tactics and terrorism itself. They are quite separate things. Terror tactics are deliberately horrific acts of mass terror, designed to cow whole populations or armies, and have been used throughout recorded history as adjuncts to normal, conventional warfare. For example, by massacring a whole population or the particularly stubborn garrison of a captured city (as Wellington allowed his maddened Redcoats to do at Badajoz in Spain in 1812), the message is sent out to future foes: don't resist too strongly, or this will happen to you. Genghis Khan, with his mounds of skulls, stands as the arch-practitioner of such a brutal policy of waging war, but he was by no means the first national leader – or the last – to indulge in savage psychological operations. Terror has always been the lifeblood of tyranny. Sometimes mass terror has even been turned against a regime's own people. The French, Russian, Chinese and Cambodian people have all been on the receiving end of a *domestic* terror meted out by their own government, determined to control its own citizens by quite simply terrorising them.

Terrorism as we understand it today, however, means something quite different. It now means an act of specific violence aimed at a target audience to obtain some political advantage. The phrase 'armed propaganda' is entirely accurate. Terror attacks are not intended to destroy an enemy's capacity to wage war, but are meant to communicate a clear threat, whether in pursuit of a grievance or to warn enemies off. The aim is always to frighten, but at the same time send a message to three key constituencies: the enemy, the domestic population, and lastly, to foreign audiences. As Lenin said: 'Kill one – frighten ten thousand.' Unlike normal warfare, *advertising the message* is as important for modern terrorists as the actual violence itself. It is the oxygen of publicity that has helped modern terrorism to become 'politics by other means'. Clausewitz would have approved. The truth is, like it or not, terrorism is now recognised as just another part of mankind's brutal spectrum of resolving disputes, and a very cost effective one, for the determined terrorist.

Terrorism boiled to the surface in the nineteenth century. Of course it had been around in various forms for centuries. Jewish fanatics called the *Sicarii* plunged curved knives into the backs of off-duty legionnaires in the back alleys of Jerusalem during the Roman occupation of first-century Palestine, and political murder has always been with us, as Guy Fawkes's 1605 Gunpowder Plot demonstrates. Closer to our own time the *Thuggees* of India, with their murderous strangling attacks on travellers in the name of their bloodthirsty goddess Kali, and the brutal way the Mafia traditionally held sway in Sicily are examples of historic terrorism in action, dominating whole populations by the use of fear as a weapon.

It was during the Industrial Revolution, however, that the terrorist gained three invaluable new tools: accurate, quick loading firearms, reliable explosives, and a political theory. The usefulness of the first two developments as practical aids to destruction by criminals or terrorists is obvious. The last point, the 'political blueprint', emerged from *Risorgimento* Italy and Czarist Russia. In the last half of the nineteenth century a number of revolutionary groups began to target politicians and officials in an attempt to bring down the State by a deliberate campaign to assassinate and terrorise its functionaries. And therein lies the true message of political terrorism – at heart it is an attack on the power of the State, for the terrorist seeks *power*. They are invariably hoping to attain the power to order other people's lives and imprint their own view of the world on their neighbours. Very few terrorist movements actually achieve this goal: only the African National Congress and the Jewish Stern and Irgun terror gangs have really succeeded in living memory in attaining the terrorist Nirvana of seizing full political power. Most other terrorist groups have had to settle for much less – grabbing public attention or headlines, or gaining recognition and building up support for their cause.

What is also striking about terrorism is how small the terrorist 'army' usually is. Terrorism is rarely a mass movement. The PIRA and ETA (the Basque separatist movement in northern Spain) illustrate the point. In both cases no more than 10 per cent of the population – if that – are active for the terrorists' cause: yet, despite this, the terrorists have ended up dictating the agenda and swaying events, even though they are in a massive minority. Terrorism has had an impact out of all proportion to the numbers involved – it is profoundly undemocratic.

Almost by definition terrorism is nearly always committed by an obsessed minority, trying to impose their will on other people. The terrorists' belief in their cause and their will to succeed, allied to the refusal of their enemies to use major armed force against them, has usually carried the day for the determined terrorist since the end of the Second World War. This reinforces the paradox of terrorism. For these deadly minorities to survive, let alone thrive, they need to be operating in a relatively benign environment. Terrorism can only hope to flourish in a climate *where they can get away with it*. This is what distinguishes it from guerrilla warfare. For example, Resistance attacks on the Germans in occupied France were intended to weaken the Nazi war machine, not wring obscure political concessions from the Vichy government or the German governor in Paris.

Very rarely does the hothouse plant of terrorism survive if confronted by the icy blast of an equally determined opponent. There was very little terrorism in Stalin's USSR, or in Hitler's Nazi Germany. The reason was simple: the totalitarian State would kill any dissidents they caught without a second thought, and probably all their friends and family as well. Most people were more scared of State terror and reprisals than anything else. The PIRA would not have lasted three months in Pol Pot's Cambodia during Year Zero. Terrorists invariably rely on their enemies' weakness and concessions to a much greater extent than they or the general public care to admit. An 'asymmetric response' by the authorities is almost a requirement for terrorism's success.

Terrorism's impact today owes its notoriety to three main factors which have combined to put the subject on the front page of every newspaper. First, there has been a tradition of successful political violence since the end of the Second World War. Secondly, the spread and sophistication of modern media have carried terrorists' messages more widely than they themselves could ever have hoped – in some cases the media have become virtually accomplices of the suppliers of 'big stories for the newsroom'. Lastly, the technical potential of new weapons has offered the terrorist new and undreamed of ways to break things and hurt people.

The success of terrorism as a weapon or tactic in the latter half of the twentieth century has been dramatic. Since 1945 it has quite clearly worked. The straws were in the wind immediately after the First World War, when the Irish Republicans hounded the British out of Ireland by a deliberate campaign of murder and terror. By 1921, the British, sickened by the prospect of a bloody and open-ended campaign and with war-weary voters at home, gave up the struggle with the Home Rulers and quit, leaving the Unionist rump of Ulster to fight it out as a separate province in the North. Terrorism by a minority of determined killers had worked.

Two very clear indicators of the way in which terrorist wars would be fought in the future marked the IRA's early struggle. There was a deliberately targeted campaign of murders and atrocities against noncombatants on both sides; and it was blindingly obvious that it was intelligence that drove the war. For example, in 1919 in a series of spectacular coups the IRA murdered undercover British intelligence officers and Special Branch police officers as prime targets. From the very start the terrorists' war was an *intelligence* war and the IRA's leader Michael Collins fought it as just that. For their part, the British authorities realised early that intelligence was the only tool to prevent terrorism succeeding, because the terrorist will always have the initiative. No amount of passively guarding vulnerable buildings or flooding towns with soldiers and policemen will deter the determined terrorist working in the shadows and hiding in the crowd. The terrorist can always get through, if not to strike at the well-guarded symbols of authority, then at some less well protected target. For the truth is that to the terrorist with murder in his or her heart, Society itself is the true target – not just its visible manifestations.

The British with their long history of colonial warfare swiftly adapted to the vicious realities of undercover war, employing virtually the same methods of intelligence that had proved so successful on the North-West Frontier. In the words of Field Marshal Montgomery:

In many ways this war (against the IRA) was far worse than the
Great War .... It developed into a murder campaign in which,
in the end, the soldiers became very skilful and more than held
their own ...

The success of the anti-colonial movement which succeeded in
hounding the British out of Ireland in the 1920s, plus the successes of
the irregular tactics of the resistance movements and organisations like
SOE, alerted new groups with a grievance after the Second World War
to the possibilities offered by guerrilla warfare and terror attacks. The
Jewish Zionists fought an openly terrorist campaign to evict the UN
mandate and the indigenous inhabitants from Palestine. (It is one of
the curiosities of history that Israel's present day government now
condemns Palestinian terrorists for using the very methods that the
Israeli terror gangs used in 1945–8 to take over Palestine and consolidate their own rule.) Suddenly terrorism was everywhere, usually in
the guise of an anti-colonialist struggle. From Malaya to Vietnam and
from Cyprus to Algeria guerrilla and terrorist wars marked the three
decades after the Second World War. The most successful campaign of
all was the Viet Cong's bid to seize and take over South Vietnam. With
a clear political aim, and veering between guerrilla and terrorist tactics
as the opportunity demanded, the North Vietnamese and their backers
eventually wore down the resistance of American domestic opinion
until the global superpower finally quit the battlefield in sheer war-
weariness, leaving their South Vietnamese allies to their fate. By a
massive irony it was the 'War of the Flea' which actually characterised
warfare and conflict during the military stand-off we call the Cold War,
not set piece battles, as the long running struggles in Northern Ireland,
South America and the Basque country clearly demonstrate. By the
end of the Cold War terrorism as a phenomenon had become deeply
embedded all round the world. The Tamil Tigers of Sri Lanka, the
Hutus of Rwanda, the Colombian drug cartels and the Chechnyan
rebels, who even took their fight up to the Kremlin Gates, were all
exploiting one of the oldest forms of warfare in the world in their

various attempts to intimidate the opposition. Terrorism had become a part of most people's lives.

No greater dispute reared its head in the last half of the twentieth century than the Arab-Israeli war. Whatever the rights and wrongs of the case, the fact is that by 1968 the majority of the Palestine people and their Arab friends realised that after the Israeli Defence Force's (IDF) stunning victories on the battlefield in the Six Day War of 1967, there was no possibility of ejecting the Israelis from the land of Israel by main force. Instead the Palestine Liberation Organisation (PLO) opted for terror. In a series of daring coups, televised live around the world, the militants of the PLO hijacked airliners and blew them up on prime-time TV. The world recoiled in horror, but the armed propaganda of the PLO was remarkably successful. Suddenly the world was very inter-ested indeed in the Palestine problem. Within two years, Yassar Arafat, the PLO's leader, was addressing the United Nations General Assembly in New York, pleading his cause at the world's highest political forum. Clearly, terrorism worked.

Where the PLO led, others followed. In 1969 and 1970 Northern Ireland (the six counties of Ulster united with Britain) came under an unremitting terror campaign launched by a new Irish Republican Army. These were the men whose grandfathers had written the first rule book of terrorism back in the 1920s as part of their original war of inde-pendence from the British. The PIRA's attempt to take over Northern Ireland, which started on the back of a civil rights movement in Ulster during 1968–9 was at first remarkably successful as a means of waging a terrorist campaign to 'prosecute a political aim by other means'. By the early 1970s, bombs exploded, policemen and soldiers were gunned down in cold blood and political violence and terrorism had become a way of life. The British desperately tried to buy off the PIRA by giving the terrorists what they wanted. At one stage in 1972 the British gov-ernment was actually considering redrawing Ulster's border with the South in a desperate bid to rid itself of this combative minority of its

OPPOSITE: *Terrorism's impact – British top secret plan to bow to IRA terror, 1972*

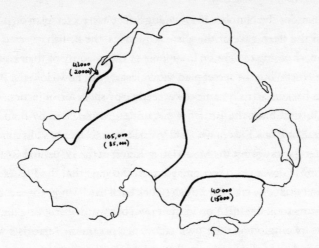

41000
(2000)

105,000
(25,000)

40,000
(15,000)

TOP SECRET

11.   **Conclusion**   It is therefore extremely doubtful
whether a transfer of territory, or population, could be
effectively accomplished, or maintained; ~~and~~ indeed, even
if ~~most improbably~~ it could be achieved, whether it would
produce any worthwhile dividends. Any faint hope of success
must be set against the implications of a course which would
demonstrate to the world that HMG was unable to bring about
the peaceable solution of problems save by expelling large
numbers of its own citizens and doing so on a religious
basis.

12.   The ceding of smaller parts of Northern Ireland
where there is a large Catholic majority (e.g. Newry,
Londonderry) as one element in a settlement raises a
different range of consideration and has not been examined
in this Appendix.

citizens. (See the Number 10 Downing Street 'top secret' plan on p.391) Under the stern gaze of the Ulster Unionists, the British rejected this option, choosing to fight on in support of the majority of their citizens in the North; but the secret plan shows clearly just how close the PIRA and its backers actually came to succeeding by sheer terror tactics.

To fight back the British went underground. Led by men like General Sir Frank Kitson, who had learned his intelligence skills running counter-gangs against the Mau Mau in Kenya in the 1950s, and General Sir James Glover, who recognised from the start that the PIRA's war was an *intelligence* war, the British struck back hard. Undercover special operators took the PIRA on in their own backyard, disrupting the terrorists by employing their own tactics against them. Terrorists were identified and followed by well trained surveillance teams: terrorist arms caches were uncovered and booby trapped; and terrorists carrying out attacks were themselves ambushed and gunned down by undercover troops lying in wait. Above all, the PIRA and its Unionist counterparts were penetrated from top to bottom by government spies and informers. Suddenly terrorists feared betrayal, the midnight raid or a knock on the door just as much as their victims. Thanks to intelligence the hunters became the hunted.

The result of this long running undercover intelligence war was that terrorist leaders like Martin McGuinness and Gerry Adams realised to their surprise (and, it must be said, to many Britons on the mainland too) that successive British governments really did have the stomach for a long, drawn out and bloody campaign. For once, terrorists could not exhaust the British government's will to fight. Eventually in a climate of political failure and mounting losses PIRA's terrorist leaders were forced to seek new, more political tactics to stay in the vanguard of their struggle. The echoes of that decision are still with us today. The combination of the 'bullet and the ballot box' eventually catapulted the PIRA's political front organisation Sinn Fein into power in Northern Ireland, and may have provided a model of terrorism for others to imitate. The price has been high, however. The Northern Irish terrorist campaign lasted over thirty years and claimed over 3,000 lives.

From 1970 onwards, terrorism spread across the globe like a rash. From the Irish to the Basques, from the Baader-Meinhof gangs to the Red Brigades, terrorism became the cutting edge of groups with a grievance. Even criminal gangs and drug barons jumped onto the bandwagon. Technology, publicity, death and terror finally united when a tiny Japanese splinter group, the *Aum Shinru Kyono* (effectively no more than a bunch of fanatical religious crackpots), actually used nerve gas Sarin on the Tokyo subway in 1995 for no clear reason and succeeded in killing twelve innocent people.

In this escalation of horrors one dispute remained as bedrock: the Arab-Israeli war, rumbling along at its various intensities. From a dispute over land in 1948, the Arab-Israeli war escalated into a full-blown clash of cultures, and by the end of the century had become an ideological crusade for Islam. By 1996 the PLO's war of terror against Israel had turned into something even more sinister: it had spread to become an undeclared war against the United States of America, Israel's backer, by Islamic militants from all lands. Islam has a long tradition of political violence and terrorism. The contribution of the modern Islamic terrorists has been to add an explosive fourth factor to terrorism's unholy trinity of success, the oxygen of publicity and lastly, efficient modern technology – now Islamic terrorists could claim that they have Holy Writ as well.

Other factors, too, dawned on Islamic zealots seeking to strike at the West. Terrorism was not only seen to be successful all round the world, it was also able to exploit the very vulnerabilities of Western liberal democracies. Open borders, relaxed and lengthy legal procedures, a culture of free speech, free association and free movement positively greased the slipway for terrorists to move, plan and work. To further the terrorists' cause even more, Western states had for decades avoided getting involved in their neighbours' disputes. Pleas from Britain for American citizens to stop funding Irish terrorism fell on deaf ears. Basque separatists fled over the Pyrenees to sanctuary in France. Nervous governments even sought accommodation with their mortal enemies, and in return for immunity, turned a blind eye to killers seeking sanctuary. Fanatical Islam took note of these feeble Western responses to determined terrorists. Even when governments struck back hard against killers and terrorists (as did the British Special Forces in Northern Ireland, London and Gibraltar), droves of well-paid lawyers and journalists strove to prove that their very own protector, the State, had in fact been acting outside the law. From such pusillanimous responses, Islamic terrorism took much comfort and planned accordingly. For Islam had a serious grievance against the West.

The fundamental roots of Islamic hostility to the West lie deep. A hundred years after the Prophet's death in 632 AD, his Muslim warriors had conquered most of the Middle East, Western Asia, the North African littoral and Spain. Centred on the Caliphate in Baghdad, Islam over the next five hundred years developed an advanced scientific and literary culture previously unknown in history. Mathematics, astronomy, medicine, geography, music, poetry, botany and metallurgy all flourished at a time when most Europeans lived like ignorant swine. Western attempts to set up Christian Crusader kingdoms in Palestine were stopped short by *Salah ad-Din* (Saladin) one of the great heroes of the Moorish world. In 1187 he recaptured Jerusalem and effectively threw the West out.

By the nineteenth century, however, Western commerce and expansionism finally colonised, exploited and took over large swathes of the Islamic Middle East where force of arms had failed nine centuries before. The result was that by the middle of the twentieth century, discontented Islam had a serious grievance against the West. Islamic militancy was reborn.

During the early decades of the century Islamic radicals had focused their thoughts on the idea of a true Islamic state. These activities inevitably brought them into conflict with that other great historic tide, the nationalism of the new Arab leaders now freed from the 'yoke of colonialism'. For men like Nasser of Egypt, Assad of Syria and the reinstalled Shah in Iran, radical Muslim clerics were an unmitigated nuisance and the Mosque a permanent source of discontent. They cracked down hard on their dissident priests. In Shi'ite Iran opponents of the Shah's regime either fled to avoid prison or were exiled. Chief among these Iranian exiles was an obscure Shi'ite Ayatollah, (Leader of the Imams), Khomeini. A clear fault line was emerging between Church and State in the Islamic world.

The new Arab nationalist leaders were openly ignoring the Mosque and centuries of Muslim religious teaching and heritage. For true believers paradise was not a secular Utopia on earth with freedom, liberty, equal economic opportunities for all, votes for women and well-stocked supermarkets. For radical Islam, the true path was instead based on an Islamic ideal and the revealed word of God. In simple, clear modern language the radical Muslim clerics proclaimed a gospel of hope in the 1960s and 1970s to fire up a new generation of post-colonial Muslim youth and imbue them with a single burning slogan: 'The Koran is our constitution.'

Whatever differences divided them, be they of class, nationalism, culture or language, every true believer across the Muslim world was now being offered a simple solution to all their problems on earth – a single Islamic state that would use Shariah law and the sacred texts to bring about God's kingdom on earth with freedom and justice for all. Events on the wider world stage eventually brought the extremists the very opportunity for which they had been waiting and also the God-given enemy against which all Islam could unite – Israel.

In 1973 President Sadat of Egypt's attempt to demonstrate Israel's vulnerability and bolster his own status in the Arab world failed, despite initial success. From the ruins of this defeat, however, emerged a powerful Arab weapon: oil. With the Suez Canal blocked by the fighting and OPEC restrictions on petroleum exports, the price of oil rocketed. At $12 a barrel in 1972, by December 1973 oil had doubled to $25 a barrel. Money poured into the coffers of the oil states. The energy crisis brought Western economies to the brink of disaster. Suddenly the Arab world had discovered real global power. By 1980, Saudi Arabia, the epicentre of both oil power and the Islamic world, became the effective focus for Muslim hopes.

Fuelled by petro-dollars in undreamed of abundance, Saudis

capitalised on their ownership of the sacred places of Islam and established an Islamic society that blended great wealth with a distinctive brand of religious zeal. By 1986, when King Saud formally took the title of Custodian of the Holy Places the Saudis effectively controlled – or at least set the agenda – for Sunni Muslims. With their petro-dollar wealth and newfound friends and allies, Islam was yet again becoming a global force.

Not all Muslims are Sunni, however. The Shi'ites, who make up about 15 per cent of the Islamic world, believe that the true path for Islam lies in the teachings of the Prophet's nephew Ali, martyred in 661 by Islamic rivals during the bitter struggle for the succession to Muhammad and the soul of Islam. Iran's population is predominantly Shi'a and Iran's ruler in the 1970s was facing a wave of discontent. The exiled Ayatollah Khomeini fomented the unrest from abroad. Khomeini's collection of sermons and his 'Islamic Government under the Guidance of the Law' laid the intellectual foundations for an Islamic revolution, advocating a new kind of state ruled by godly men and following strict Shariah law. The combination of angry, young, middle-class students seeking to overthrow the Shah's regime and the dispossessed, plus the revealed Shi'ite word of Allah proved an explosive mixture. By 1977 the Shah's regime was in serious trouble. To cries of 'Allah Akhbar!' the poor, the workers, the middle class, the students and finally, the Armed Services, rose up and overthrew the Shah. The masses of Iran's revolution now pledged allegiance to Allah alone and loyalty to Khomeini. The brooding Ayatollah returned to Tehran in triumph to be enthroned by popular acclaim as the new ruler of Iran. Allah now ruled Iran and the Shi'a world.

With a ruthless single-mindedness at odds with his claims to otherworldly spirituality, Khomeini swiftly set about institutionalising his own version of the rule of Allah. Politics became synonymous with the Mosque. A network of neighbourhood clerical 'komitehs' modelled on the Soviet and French Revolutions monitored and controlled every aspect of Iranian life, from factory floor to government ministries, from peasant farmer to army general. Within the year Iran was officially declared an Islamic republic with Khomeini as Supreme Guide of Allah, and all secular opposition had been crushed or sidelined. Even dissenting clerics were imprisoned or worse. Khomeini's word was law. This new Islamic regime sent shock waves out both to the West and throughout the Muslim world as Iran tried to export its Islamic revolution to the rest of the Islamic world.

Among the teeming millions of this Arab and Islamic world, where 50 per cent of the population is under 30 and dirt poor, the Iranian call to arms struck home. In Lebanon, Palestine, Gaza and the West Bank, disaffected young Arabs rallied to the fundamentalist cause. For the first time the call of Allah became synonymous with opposition to Israel. Hezbollah, the popular movement backed by Iran, invoked the call of martyrdom carrying out a series of spectacular suicide bombings against Western targets. The Islamic revolution inspired passions and united Arabs far beyond Persia's borders. Khomeini, on one level at least, had fired or frightened all Islam.

Nowhere was there a better cause for Iran's fundamentalists than Afghanistan. In 1979 – the same year as Khomeini's revolution and the storming of the US Embassy in Tehran – the Soviet Union had invaded the country of confused, backward and warring tribes that made up one of the world's most primitive states. The Afghans may fight among themselves as a way of life, but against an outside foe they united to fight the invader with a passion rarely seen. Suddenly the Soviets were bogged down in a proxy war with the Afghani Mujahideen. By the mid 1980s Pakistan – and the CIA – was supplying weapons and assistance to the Afghan resistance, in particular a group called Hezb-e-Islam. America, Khomeini's 'great Satan', was actually arming the cause of Islamic fundamentalism in order to fight the Soviet Union.

One of its allies was an obscure resistance organiser, called Osama bin Laden. Bin Laden was born in 1957, the son of a rich Yemeni contractor who had made a fortune from restoring Saudi Arabia's Holy Places. His mother had occupied a lowly place in his father's house, being referred to as the 'slave bride' by the senior wives, and the young boy, his mother's only child, had wandered the family mansion, alone and friendless. From such psychological scars, great consequences can befall.

Bin Laden's early career appears to have followed the standard pattern of rich young Saudis; university in Lebanon, wild drinking sprees with loose women and his friends, and cruising Jeddah in a canary-yellow Mercedes 450SL. The playboy's days of gladness ended abruptly in 1977 when he made his Hajj to Mecca. Suddenly, Osama bin Laden became a born-again Muslim. Like most fanatical converts, his burning zeal to atone for his past now went looking for a cause.

By the time of the Soviet invasion of Afghanistan bin Laden was in his early twenties, devout, clever, ambitious and rich. He had also fallen under the spell of a fiery preacher of Islam called Azzam, who was busy in the 1980s organising Muslim volunteers to fight in Afghanistan. Osama worked in Azzam's Office of Service, recruiting, training and moving the volunteers to a network of camps and bases in Pakistan and Afghanistan. Bin Laden proved to be a good pupil and a skilful organiser, and the Office of Service eventually pumped over 30,000 volunteer Islamic fighters from all over the world into Afghanistan.

When the Soviets finally quit Afghanistan, the battle-hardened veterans of the Office of Service dispersed back to their home countries. These Afghan-Arabs took with them a radicalised, armed view of Islam and a track record of success and victory fighting Islam's foes. From this network of veterans sprang the idea of *al-Qaida*, 'the cell', a loose international grouping of like-minded Islamic warriors and men of action, all bound by a mutual great calling and all determined to carry on their life's work, fighting for the name of Allah. The cautious rulers of the kingdom of Saudi Arabia, however, did not welcome such dangerous ideas. By 1991 a resentful bin Laden found himself effectively driven into exile in the Sudan behind a Khartoum office whose brass plate openly displayed the name of his business: al-Qaida.

Al-Qaida's business remained as it had been when bin Laden worked for Azzam's Office of Service in Afghanistan: raising funds, recruiting and training suitable volunteers, moving men and money round the world and creating an international organisation dedicated to fighting the foes of Islam. But by 1992, the year America invaded Somalia, the foes of Islam were no longer the 'Godless Marxists' of the Soviet Union. They had long gone. The new foe was the United States of America and the 'arch-oppressors' of the Palestinian people – the state of Israel.

Al-Qaida embraced this new struggle with alacrity and openly joined the warlords and clans fighting against American troops in Somalia. At a stroke Israel, the USA, the West and any Muslim who dared to disagree with al-Qaida were brought into their gun sights as legitimate targets. By the time bin Laden was forced to flee once again, this time to Afghanistan, his organisation had grown and had become a clearly identified terrorist threat. The fanatical Taliban regime of young students, fired with missionary zeal in their *Madrasas* or religious schools, provided the perfect haven for bin Laden and his followers. Recruits to the cause began to dribble in from all over the Muslim world to become soldiers of God for al-Qaida. With its global reach, and supporters in every continent, Bin Laden's al-Qaida had become one of the most successful Muslim NGOs ever.

By 2000 Western intelligence services knew all about al-Qaida. On 26 February 1993, a half-ton truck bomb put together by a man called Youssef had detonated underneath the World Trade Centre, killing six and injuring one thousand. Youssef fled. The WTC bombing, timed to correspond with the anniversary of the ejection of Saddam Hussein's armies from Kuwait two years before, had all the hallmarks of a carefully planned terrorist attack. For the next six years al-Qaida grew and prospered, attracting recruits from among the numerous Islamic terrorist groups across the Middle East. One notable addition to its ranks was Mohammed Atef of the Egyptian Islamic Jihad, who was heavily implicated in terrorism, from the murder of the speaker of the Egyptian parliament in 1990 to the attacks on US forces in Somalia in 1993. Al-Qaida grew to become the umbrella organisation under which any Islamic terrorist dedicated to the destruction of Israel, getting America and her allies out of the Middle East and killing Westerners could find a warm welcome and common cause. By June 2000 the organisation even felt bold enough to attack an American destroyer on the high seas off Yemen by bringing a suicide boat alongside. The attack blew the USS *Cole* open and killed seventeen US sailors.

It was clear that the West was now facing a well-organised, clever and fanatical terrorist organisation that was prepared to deliver suicide bombs by unconventional means. They also had incontrovertible evidence that they were up against an enemy that was perfectly capable of planning and executing decisive attacks against well-defended Western targets. Perhaps most alarming of all was the realisation that these new terrorist bombers were prepared to die for their cause in suicide attacks.

Although suicide is strictly forbidden by the Koran the concept of martyrdom is deeply entrenched in Islamic tradition, especially the Shi'ite sect. Hezbollah was the first modern Islamic group to make a policy of suicide bombers, or martyrs. Fanatical young Muslims, many well educated and of whom at least 10 per cent were young women, volunteered to carry the fight to the Israeli camp. It is hard for the Western mind to understand, but an instantaneous death, while smiting down the enemies of God, is for many Muslim extremists a guaranteed passport to heaven – and they believe it. The martyr's last days are carefully controlled by the godfathers of terror, to nurture and reinforce this idea. Fattened up like some human sacrifice, the martyr is fêted before he or she goes off to kill and be killed in the name of Allah. Once trapped in this web of public commitment there is no going back for the suicide bomber. He – or she – is committed, and the waiting audience expectant.

Al-Qaida's suicide bombers had more ambitious targets in mind. The organisation was aiming for bigger targets than Hamas and Hezbollah's attacks against small knots of hapless young IDF conscripts waiting at a bus stop. After the USS *Cole*, Osama bin Laden was after much bigger fish, a wider audience and, thanks to the 1993 attack in New York, he even knew the right target to go for.

The World Trade Center and Madrid beckoned.

The intelligence agencies were well aware of the danger posed by al-Qaida. By 1998 both the CIA and the British JIC had identified the general trend away from the state-sponsored terror of Libya, Iran and Syria and the growth of what were effectively non-government terrorist organisations. The difficulty was knowing what to do about it. The 'more diverse, freewheeling, transnational networks' of groups like al-Qaida were notoriously difficult to track, let alone penetrate. Another problem was that no one knew exactly what al-Qaida would do next. Intelligence analysts in the West, looking at the range of possibilities open to the organisation, concluded that the group would attack high profile targets using sophisticated systems. Part of the problem was that the forward-looking analysts did not consider the lessons of history. The modern terrorists' obsession with *publicity* over the previous three decades had blinded many intelligence experts – and media commentators, too – to the truth about terror. Terrorism is armed propaganda: and the *armed* part is just as important as publicity for the cause.

The West badly underestimated the intentions of these new terrorist groupings to kill and destroy just for the sake of killing. The sheer malevolence and desire to wreak bloody vengeance on their foes seems to have been overlooked. In the words of one al-Qaida leader, after the Madrid bombing of 2004, 'You seek to live – we seek for death'. This perversion of Koranic teachings announced a chilling new element in the conduct of terrorism: terror without a political motive. This reversion to a much older form of Islamic terror, more akin to the Old Man of the Mountain and his Assassins than the PIRA, was not surprisingly, outside the cultural comprehension of most Western analysts. The PIRA and ETA had never gone in for suicide bombings.

There were distinct clues, however, that things were changing. In 1980 there were only two religious terrorist groups recorded by the CIA – by the 1990s this number had mushroomed, and most of them were Islamic fanatics. One estimate of the period showed that Shi'ite terror organisations were accounting for over 25 per cent of all terrorist deaths by the turn of the century. There were other indicators too. Omar Abdul Rahman, a known al-Qaida sympathiser openly announced:

> We have to be terrorists ... the Great God has told us to make yourself
> as strong and powerful as you can, including the seeds of war, in order
> to strike terror into the enemies of God ...

This kind of apocalyptic language, although familiar to many experienced in the hyperbole of Arabic language and culture, nonetheless indicated a clear trend. Al-Qaida was dedicated to an extended fight and would use any means possible to wreak havoc on the West. By 2000 the CIA had recognised the growing threat and was predicting a wave of attacks on Western targets. Unfortunately its assessment was weighted towards 'high end' targets, and alerted its audience that high tech assets such as computers and nuclear weapons were most at risk from terrorist attack. What very few analysts realised was that al-Qaida would go for *any* attack that would allow it to kill Westerners and work off its pathological hatred of the West and all that it stood for. To put it bluntly, slaughtering 'God's enemies' was more important than advertising al-Qaida. Good old-fashioned killing was preferable to knocking out America's national electricity grid. It was the killing that counted. Al-Qaida said so quite openly. In June 2001 Osama bin Laden had threatened in the Arab press: 'Within the next two months, an attack against the great Satan that will shake the world.'

This was a serious miscalculation of Islamic terror's intentions, and led indirectly to the kamikaze flying bomb attacks on the WTC and the Pentagon in 2001. The truth was that a new terrorist phenomenon had appeared on the scene. Al-Qaida's aims of 'exterminating Jews', 'pushing Israel into the sea', 'killing Americans and their allies wherever you find them', and ensuring that, 'the Holy Places of Islam are defended only by the faithful of God' (all verbatim statements of Osama bin Laden and his followers) are incapable of any political redress. This was no ordinary terrorist group and there could be little possibility of negotiation with such an organisation. The only way to deal with 'fanatics armed with power', in Elie Wiesel's vivid phrase, would be to eradicate them completely. No amount of concessions was going to buy off this new wave of terror. The long predicted clash of civilisations and cultures had arrived.

Unfortunately, Western intelligence agencies, particularly US ones, were ill prepared for this new war on terror. For a variety of reasons, the US intelligence community, despite the establishment of a dedicated national Counter-Terrorist Center in 1986 specifically intended to monitor terrorism, failed to piece together the jigsaw so painstakingly collected by its national intelligence agencies. The truth was that the US intelligence community was neither organised nor equipped to meet a terrorist attack on the US before September 2001. Despite the CTC's alleged charter, no single US agency was maintaining an indicator and warning board for the emerging terrorist threat, let alone coordinating the US national effort against terrorism. Part of the problem was that the intelligence agencies had not reorganised to meet the new world order after the fall of the Berlin Wall and the end of the Cold War. It is axiomatic that form and design should mirror function.

In the case of the growing terrorist threat to America that was manifestly not true. There was no counter-terrorist plan, no strategy and no warning system. In the command bunker at Cheyenne Mountain the USAF's impressive automated indicator and warning display could track space junk coming in over the Pole, let alone incoming nuclear missiles. But inside the USA determined terrorists could run around planning an equally deadly strike and there was no comparable system of early warning.

As the images of fully laden airliners plunging into skyscrapers sent shock waves round the world, the initial reaction was that this was a new and totally unexpected development in terrorist tactics. But even this was not true. It transpired that between 1994 and September 2001, US intelligence agencies received no less than twelve specific reports warning that terrorists were scheming to hijack an airliner and fly it into a prestige target. Several of the reports actually named bin Laden and al-Qaida. One of these reports came from a 'walk-in' to the FBI's New Jersey office, where a stunned FBI agent was told that al-Qaida were planning to hijack a plane and fly it into a building. Other reports emerged of a wealth of intelligence indicators which, taken together, should have sparked an immediate terrorist alert. FBI offices in the US had reported unusual activity but had been rebuffed by FBI headquarters' lawyers; the CIA had obviously known some of the hijackers but appeared to have been playing its own game. Despite all this, the intelligence analysts of CTC and the other agencies made no effort to update its collection plan to include indicators that al-Qaida might be planning to use aeroplanes as bombs. No new CIR were issued or called for. The US intelligence community remained fragmented and divided, complacently going about business as usual. The truth was that there was no shortage of intelligence. The real problem was that there was no central control, far too little human intelligence from spies deep in al-Qaida's ranks and the analysis of what intelligence the US possessed was poor.

The seismic shock waves of the attack when it came on 11 September 2001 astounded the whole world. Everyone on board the airliners, including the 19 hijackers, was killed. In the Pentagon 124 people died, and 2,500 workers and visitors from 60 countries died at the World Trade Center, including 418 New York firemen and policemen. It was terrorism's most spectacular and grievous blow against the West.

In Gaza and the West Bank Palestinians danced in the streets, seeing the attack as a mortal blow against *Israel* – for was not the 'great Satan' the backer and supplier of Israeli military might? Had not Israel hijacked America's government by using 'the Jewish vote' to dictate US foreign policy? Some Arab conspiracy theorists even claimed that the whole attack had been planned and orchestrated by the Jews to blacken the name of Islam and the Arabs. Of one thing the world was not in doubt: the slaughter and the publicity of the 9/11 attack were immense and worse than anyone could have expected. There is some evidence that the apocalyptic images of 11 September shocked even bin Laden and his followers. When the Taliban were ejected from Jalalabad as part of the US's retaliation, an al-Qaida videotape was discovered, on which bin Laden admits that even he had been surprised at the effectiveness of the WTC attack.

In the aftermath of 9/11, the American President George W. Bush declared open war on global terrorism. In a series of carefully calculated measures, the US then moved against al-Qaida and its sanctuary base among the Taliban regime in Afghanistan. The American President followed this with a ringing denunciation of an 'axis of evil' naming North Korea, Iraq and Iran. This last was a dangerous choice as yet again it alienated Iran's Shi'ite leadership and moderates. By spring 2003 the United States and its closest allies had moved decisively into the Middle East, invading Iraq, ousting its dictator Saddam Hussein and, coincidentally, providing al-Qaida and its Islamic fanatics with a 'target enriched environment'. US policy had come full circle, confronting the Islamic world and the Middle East head on and providing al-Qaida with US soldiers to kill on their doorstep. With unfeigned delight, the foes of the West fell upon this new opportunity to hit at 'God's enemies' in an indiscriminate terrorist campaign inside 'occupied Iraq', slaughtering Iraqis and soldiers alike. In an ominous portent of new and even more vicious terrorist wars to come, al-Qaida and its suicide bombers went for the Iraqi Shi'a community as well as the occupying Americans. Holy War had spread to Sunni against Sh'ia, Muslim against Muslim. The revolution, yet again, was devouring its children. More ominously still the truth dawned on the West that they were the next targets. The open societies and open cities of Western civilisation offered nothing less than a feast of plump, vulnerable targets to the wolves and jackals of the new terror, as enticing as a herd of complacent grazing sheep.

The US was now involved in a new world war against terrorism. From Bali to Baghdad, from French tankers off Yemen and attacks on Christians at worship in Pakistan, from airliners over the Atlantic to blowing up railway trains in Madrid, the sons of Allah locked into a shadowy struggle with the Western forces of law and order. Centuries of Islamic humiliation at the hands of the West could be avenged. The West itself became the terrorists' target.

In its blind hatred of the US and all that it stands for, al-Qaida transformed itself into a global movement of autonomous local fanatics. Terrorism had effectively been franchised around the world, as surely as any of MacDonalds' hamburger outlets. All good Muslims had to do, according to the fanatics who bought into Osama bin Laden's view of the world, and who rallied to his cause, was to support al-Qaida, kill Americans, Christians, Jews and their allies, no matter where or how, and God's work would be done. It was a lethal combination. No central command and control was needed. Islamic fundamentalism had globalised terrorism.

In doing so it had also transformed the nature of warfare. For, as Michael Collins and the IRA realised in 1918, a war against terrorism swiftly becomes an *intelligence* war. No amount of tanks and guns, no amount of passive defences, police guards and security barriers can stop the terrorist bent on wreaking havoc and even prepared to die for the cause. Like the bomber of the 1930s, the terrorist will always get through. What is required to attack such an enemy is intelligence. Intelligence alone can guarantee success. Intelligence on the terrorists' identities, their plans, their weapons, their training, their targets and their intentions. Only good intelligence can penetrate the terror network to its heart and place the terrorist at risk from the moment he gets up, to the moment he goes to bed. And even then a frightened terrorist must sleep with one eye open, fearful of the heavy knock on the door, or the helicopter overhead, as the Israelis have proved in their own long running undercover intelligence war against Palestinian and Arab extremists. The truth is that the only way to deter the truly committed terrorist is to place that individual at permanent risk of death or capture. To do that requires intelligence from the very heart of the secretive terror groups: and that means spies.

Fundamental Islamic terror also brought a new and troubling factor to the conduct of war: irrationality. In traditional conflict, rational behaviour has been taken for granted: it is assumed that the warring parties wish to survive if possible. Deterrence lies at the heart of much conflict theory. The threat of Mutually Assured Destruction kept the nuclear superpowers' fingers off the trigger for many years during the wary stand off we call the Cold War. No-one really wants to die. The Islamic terrorists have however brought a new and disturbing trend into their new brand of warfare: many of them appear not only to want to die for their cause, but they *seek* to die. They believe that the Koran tells them they are martyrs and will go to heaven. Dying is *good*. As a result, such fanatics are very difficult to deter. They cannot be appeased or bought off with political concessions. Their motivation is little different from that of the psychopath: they want to kill and rend and hurt for the pleasure it will give them and their cause. In fact, only the fear of failure and pre-knowledge – or intelligence – of their plans will ever thwart such suicidal individuals. The only thing that will give them pause for thought is a fear of failing the cause of Islam. Islam and the Koran lie at the heart of everything they stand for and believe.

In its blind hatred of the US and all that it stands for, al-Qaida transformed itself into a global movement of like-minded would be killers. Islamic fundamentalism had globalised terrorism.

The tragedy, and the irony, was that everywhere Islam was failing. Not as one of the great faiths of the world. On the contrary, Islam was growing – as a religion. Islam's failure was, however, manifest as a system of government. The political truth was – and is – that Islam has failed to deliver God's heaven on earth, whatever its fanatical terrorists and adherents claim. The complexities of the modern world demand more practical, secular solutions to the great questions of public policy confronting the Islamic world. Islamic fanatics may bring terror to the West as did their forebear Hassan ben Sabbah, the Old Man of the Mountain, the first leader of the Assassins. But in the great sweep of history, progress and humanity have passed them by.

For the dedicated fundamentalist terrorists such a message does not make things better. On the contrary, it only spurs them to greater violence in an orgy of blood, caring not whom they kill or even if they destroy themselves along with the 'evil world' they so much hate. In their rage all boundaries disappear; no-one, be they western or Muslim, Arab or Christian, is safe from their vengeful determination to strike at their enemies.

All that is left are fanatics armed with power, searching hard for a weapon of mass destruction to slaughter the 'enemies of God'. Only good intelligence can identify them in time.

20

The Newest Profession?

Intelligence is not necessarily the means
to victory...

JOHN KEEGAN

Good, accurate intelligence is the key to
victory...

US FIELD MANUAL

Intelligence exists to serve the national interest and always has. Although it has a lesser purpose in the service of commercial or other minor interests, intelligence's primary role throughout recorded history has invariably been in the service of the State in both war and peace. In that service, be it in a military, diplomatic, domestic, or anti-criminal role, intelligence has invariably exercised a much greater influence than is generally known or admitted.

To describe its practitioners therefore as 'puppet masters' is by no means fanciful: the pullers of invisible strings behind their screens of secrecy and subterfuge are exactly that. They may have reflected their different national cultures over the centuries, and indeed still do, but intelligence officers of all lands and of all times have shared one common desire – to inform those in power and thus to influence great events, preferably in secret. It is a great responsibility and like all responsibilities it can be abused and it often has been. But in its purest form, intelligence is (paradoxically, considering its often low and 'immoral' methods) a very noble calling indeed. In many cases the safety and security of whole nations and their peoples have depended on intelligence and intelligence alone. From the time of the Greeks being alerted to the Persian invasions, down to the interdiction of today's terrorist gangs on their way to plant a bomb, intelligence has proved time and time again that it is both a battle winner and a saver of lives.

Professional soldiers, diplomats and civil servants have long recognised this elemental truth. Novelists and amateurs, seduced by the supposed glamour of this secret world, with all its 'cloak and dagger' paraphernalia popularised in a thousand works of fiction, often forget the purpose of the world of intelligence, which is simply to provide accurate, processed information, in time for policy makers to make the best decisions. All the rest, from clandestine meetings with 'secret agents' at dead of night to satellite images so highly classified and secret that they can only be shown to a head of state, are merely supporting acts. Intelligence exists to inform and warn us – nothing more, and as long as there are enemies harbouring secret plots against us, then we will need intelligence to find out what fresh horrors are being planned.

Part of the problem for intelligence today comes from three revolutionary developments that have altered our whole understanding of intelligence over the last half-century. The first is the information revolution. Computers, the Internet and so-called 'cyber war' have genuinely altered the playing field on which the 'great game' is played. What the information revolution has brought about, more than ever before, is a flood of information. A positive Niagara of material, freely available to all, now roars over the Internet and the world's media and threatens to drown the intelligence analyst and many others beside. Most of this torrent of open source information is unclassified and irrelevant; much of it is either simply drivel or just plain wrong; but some of it is deadly secret or important. For the analyst faced with fishing valuable nuggets from this flood of facts and assertions, the task of sifting the wheat from the chaff is immense, and even computers can offer only so much help in processing information. The information revolution with its supporting banks of computers poses immense challenges to the management of information. Intelligence analysts, diplomats and politicians may well find themselves positively swamped with information in the years ahead.

Computers themselves ironically pose the second great challenge. Computers and their related electronic based toys are *very* tempting targets, and easy targets at that. Cyber war is now a very real possibility. As the whole business of war has shifted towards 'information warfare' – trying to get inside the 'time loop' of an enemy's decision-making systems to paralyse his command and control systems before he can do anything – so information systems and intelligence have actually become strategic *targets*. The very flood of information we rely on to run our lives in both peace and war, from computers controlling bank cash machines to national electricity and military communication systems, is now intensely vulnerable to attack, either physically or electronically. Knock out modern information technology and we are paralysed, both personally and as nations. All the nuclear bombs, rockets, aircraft, guns and ships in the world won't help if they don't work. 'Asymmetric warfare' to get inside an enemy's decision loop is thus a very real possibility and offers as it has over the centuries, a tempting possibility for the terrorist and the weak. Information war is by no means some futuristic pipe dream; as early as 1999 the Indonesian Government attacked the East Timor Liberation Movement's websites with a number of well-coordinated hacking assaults. Since then hacking intelligence ('hackint') has developed into a new discipline as important as any story of Enigma and Bletchley Park in the last century.

Some even believe that 'I-War' is the future of all warfare: this is, however, clearly an overstatement. Even the cleverest computer hacker cannot function effectively if his expensive computer has been demolished by a crude blow from a rifle butt, or some savage decides to knock out his expensively educated brain with a club. (Thus rather neatly proving one fashionable theory that 'the human mind is the true target of the computer age'.) I-War does not replace warfare. Like so many scientific advances over the years, it merely supplements the many unpleasant ways by which humanity can already hurt people and break things.

Software in particular will be especially vulnerable in the future. Strange new weapons like 'stealth viruses' and 'false algorithm bombs' will undoubtedly figure large in the years ahead, both as targets for our own versions of cyber war and, just as important, as deadly threats against which we need sound national defences. No better way can be devised of pulling a nation's strings than to quietly try and take over control of its internal computer mechanisms. Without electricity, fuel and water, modern Western city civilisations would soon grind to a halt and begin a swift slide towards anarchy and chaos. Intelligence had better be on its guard on our behalf.

The third and final development is an apparent drift away from all out war and sheer military power to resolve conflicts. Many will view this as an encouraging development. The idea of some major nuclear war and subsequent nuclear winter forcing the survivors back into a new and chilly Stone Age never really appealed to those of sound mind. However, to paraphrase one ex-CIA director's famous remark at the end of the Cold War that, 'we have slain a large dragon, but we live now in a jungle filled with a bewildering variety of poisonous snakes' may point to an equally dangerous future. The receding threat of nuclear war appears to have been replaced by a new global conflict, which Samuel Huntington characterised as 'the clash of civilisations'. For the truth is that military threats to the West have actually *increased* since the Iron Curtain was dismantled and the Berlin Wall came down.

When the three hijacked airliners smashed as Kamikaze flying bombs into their American targets in September 2001 they signalled the declaration of a war that had been building up for some years. This new war will task intelligence every bit as much as running half-drunk and frightened agents in downtown Moscow, or trying to second guess the Soviet leadership's intentions from a selection of intercepted Kremlin telephone calls plus some fuzzy satellite photographs taken from space. In one single attack the Islamic fanatics killed nearly as many people as thirty years of terrorist war in Northern Ireland and many more than the Cold War ever did. It is no exaggeration to say that al-Qaida's own murderous versions of 'precision guided missiles' were effectively weapons of mass destruction, and without even as much as forty-five minutes warning either. As the threat shifts, so intelligence will have to adapt to meet it.

This will be no easy task. To defend the realm or any other society against fanatics armed with real power is a deadly task. When the fanatics in question are well armed, believe totally in their cause, are suicidal and have no aim but to rend and destroy, mere force against them will be no defence. Where are they? *Who* are they? What capabilities do they possess? What are their intentions? Where do they plan to strike next? It is a chilling prospect and only intelligence can provide the best answers as the future unfolds.

We know what this next enemy wants. It does not make for happy reading. Al-Qaida has made its war aims perfectly clear. In 1998 Osama bin Laden issued a rallying call to the faithful proclaiming his World Islamic Front against Jews and Crusaders (WITJ), whose title appears to be the organisation's mission statement. If there is any doubt, then the words of Hussein Massaur, one of the early leaders of Hezbollah, spell out the intentions of Islamic terrorism clearly enough: 'We are not fighting to win some concession from our enemy: we are fighting to wipe out our enemy.'

The next war will rely on intelligence and its puppet masters as never before.

It has already started.

Notes to the Text

This book was written primarily for the interested general reader and not as an academic textbook. On a subject as vast as a history of intelligence it is only too easy to drown in the flood of learned sources and references from every quarter. However, if more detail or further reading is required, then I have found the following references to be especially useful or interesting. Many of these sources of information can be found nowadays on the numerous Internet websites. Although I have not listed every site's complete www.address in mind-numbing detail, for the dedicated researcher a trawl through any good Internet search engine will reveal many of the references below.

1: On Intelligence

The story of the Magdeburg Field Security Section is recounted by Bob Steer in *FSS: Field Security Section* (Intelligence Corps Association, 1996). The book also contains numerous – and sometimes very moving and funny – accounts of what the reality of intelligence and security is 'on the ground'.

Abram Shulsky, *Silent Warfare: Understanding the World of Intelligence* (Brasseys US, 1991) gives a good overview of a complex and secretive subject.

The Mitrokhin Archive by Professor Christopher Andrew (Penguin, 2000) tells the whole story of Mitrokhin's extraordinary exploit and gives an interesting insight into what it was really like to work for the KGB. Bureaucracies seem to be the same the whole world over.

For a discussion of the whole impact of the controversial question of intelligence and the JIC before the 2003 Iraq War see John Hughes-Wilson, 'Intelligence Blundering or Intelligence Laundering?', *Royal United Services Institute Journal*, February 2004.

2: In the Beginning

For a fuller discussion of the early records of intelligence see Professor Rose Mary Sheldon's numerous articles and writings on intelligence in antiquity. See, for example, 'The Oldest Classified Document?' on the Sumerians in *Espionage in the Ancient World* (McFarland & Co, 2002). Professor Sheldon specialises in Ancient History and Intelligence at the Virginia Military Institute, USA.

'I will lift up mine eyes unto the hills …' comes from Psalm 121: 1.

Moses' spying expedition is described in some detail in Numbers 13.

Moses' intelligence expedition into Canaan makes a little more sense when put into the context of taking his instructions from the wandering Hebrews' god of war. Yahweh or 'Jehovah' has an interesting history, little known to most. He was originally part of a pantheon of gods in the Canaan-Sinai area, sharing the earthly honours with a number of other gods, including Baal, the god of fruit-fulness and nature. '*JeHoVaH*' appears to have been the original Hebrews' god of storm, force, war and might. It is only with the rise of monotheism in the tribes of the region that the Jewish god goes outside the Earth to become an umbrella deity 'above all others'.

Rahab's story can be found in Joshua 2.

Samson and Delilah's story is told in The Book of Judges, 13–16. (The Israeli champion seems to have had little success with women, first marrying a Philistine girl and then, having fallen out with her, taking on delightful Delilah as his second wife. She appears to have been a 'right nag'.) Samson's story will not be unfamiliar to many men!

Histiaeus's story can be found in H. L. Havell, *Stories from Herodotus* (Harrap, 1910), which gives an accessible version of this classical tale and many more besides.

Mithridates, the great king of Pontus, was one of Rome's most formidable enemies and had a victorious track record in the first century BC against Rome's attempts to expand into Turkey and Asia Minor. He was unlucky enough to come up against very good Roman generals at the last (for example, Pompey) and by then he had alienated his Greek allies to such an extent that they gave up the struggle against the might of Rome. A tyrant Mithridates may have been: he was also an extremely good commander.

Macaulay's *Lays of Ancient Rome* gives a wonderful insight into how the Romans might have wished to view the golden age of their supposedly virtuous Republican past.

'Hannibal's Spies' in *International Journal of Intelligence and Counterintelligence* Vol. 1, No.3 by Rose Mary Sheldon tells the full story of Hannibal's intelligence operations. Articles of particular relevance in various other Journals are: 'Slaughter in the Forest, Roman Intelligence Mistakes in Germany';'Taking on Goliath – Jews against Rome'; 'The Ancient Imperative – Clandestine Operations and Covert Action'; 'The Roman Secret Service'; and 'Toga and Dagger'.

See Professor Rose Mary Sheldon's articles and books for a fuller version of the Imperial Roman secret service and its role.

For a more detailed account of the *Peregrini* see Yann le Bohec, *L'Armèe Romaine sous le Haut Empire* (Editions Picard: Paris, 1989).

Greek Fire was developed in about AD 600 and is credited with saving the Byzantines on three key occasions: against Arab fleets attacking Constantinople in AD 673 and 717; and against a Russian invasion from the north in the tenth century. The exact formula still remains a topic of hot debate among scholars of the period: but of its effect, both physical and psychological, there can be no doubt.

The impact of Greek fire against the Crusaders is recorded in *Joinville's Chronicle*. Jean de Joinville was the chronicler of King Louis's Crusade in 1250.

The Mongols' methods of military operations predated Napoleon's and were logistically better organised. Each warrior had a string of six to eight ponies and fought mainly with the bow from horseback as part of his family group or clan. The horde advanced as separate 'corps' along nominated axes of advance that were also tightly controlled as main supply routes. Quartermasters went ahead to set up previously recced campsites, and a fixed system of resupply and depots fed the army as it pushed into enemy territory. Once into the tactical area of operations the individual corps left all their baggage and *impedimenta* behind under guard and advanced as marauding bands living off the land, pausing only for the individual corps to turn in and concentrate against any enemy detected along the main axis. It was a surprisingly modern concept and echoes can be found in both Napoleon's campaigns – which appear *not* to have been as well organised – and in the Wehrmacht's concepts of blitzkreig. See D. Morgan's *The Mongols*.

Few Westerners will have heard of Kautilya – an account of his life and career (around 300 BC) can be found in the *Indian Intelligence Review*, in particular

Brigadier Khan's review of his life and work. Fuller details are also in *The Ancient History Source Book* by Paul Halsall (1968). Kautilya was the first man apart from Sun-T'zu to codify a practice of intelligence as a policy for manipulating great events. In *Arthasastra* he spells out his philosophy and ideas about politics in some detail. They are surprisingly modern. He is often fêted as the greatest early Indian military thinker, and his uncompromising views on spies, dirty tricks, political assassinations and treachery in the pursuit of power have rightly earned Kautilya the title of the Indian Machiavelli.

3: Church and State

Hell exercised a particularly powerful grip on the medieval mind, as the literature and art of the period clearly demonstrates. Coulton's *Five Centuries of Religion* (CUP, 1950) talks about the culturally enduring idea of the fires of hell and its grip on men's – and women's – minds over the Christian period.

The idea of the apostolic succession and the power it conveys is a theological hot potato. See Matthew 16: 18–19 and 28: 19–20 for the concept of apostolic succession and the idea of the 'laying on of hands' as a vehicle by which the Church claimed a direct link back to Jesus and his divine powers. The first record seems to be in AD 95 when Clement, the Bishop of Rome, wrote to the Church in Corinth spelling out the fact that the bishops had been directly linked to Christ through their personal knowledge of the Apostle. 'The 'tradition of the Church' is a hugely significant concept for Christian theology and for the Catholic Church in particular; interestingly, Aquinas makes no such claims.

Lea's *Auricular Confession* gives a comprehensive overview of the whole business of confession and absolution.

Innocent III was arguably the most powerful of all the popes as he was elected to the papacy at a time (1198) when Rome's temporal and spiritual power coincided. He genuinely believed that the papacy was the fount of sovereign authority on earth and that the Holy Roman Emperor was subordinate to him. His attempts to strengthen papal power and influence still further appear to have been based on the fear that papal power might be eroded and the Church weakened. The life and times of the medieval popes at the height of their power is well explored in Clayton's *Pope Innocent III*.

The Inquisition was started in embryo by Innocent's successor Gregory IX in 1231. Innocent IV gave it teeth in 1252. Vacandard's *Inquisition* (Richwood Pub.

Co., 1977) gives a comprehensive overview of just how the Inquisition started, its methods and how it worked.

The sheer in-fighting over Catholic theology in medieval times is astonishing to our modern minds. There really were week long 'theological test matches' as learned academics debated 'How many angels can dance on the head of a pin?' and 'Did Christ possess a purse?' in sometimes very intemperate disputations. The motions for debate were invariably coded statements about contemporary policies. (In the latter case, Rome was understandably hypersensitive to the Franciscans' insistence on 'Holy Poverty' and the fledgling order very nearly went the same way as the heretical Cathars.) Sometimes fiction can give a better understanding and feel for an era than contemporary documents. Umberto Eco's *The Name of the Rose* offers an accurate version of the spirit of the time and the theological disputes that were boiling up inside the Catholic Church. Human nature being what it is, many of these struggles were rooted in a desire by the Church hierarchy to hold on to their power and riches and to snuff out any threats to the established order in Rome.

The Black Friars or Dominicans were the most orthodox of the orders until the Jesuits. For a description of their early role see Henry Kamen, *The Spanish Inquisition* (Weidenfeld & Nicolson, 2000).

Brutal religious executions by burning were often symbolic as the victims had wisely taken themselves off and were *in absentia*. For example, in the *auto da fe* at Barcelona of June 1491, only three converted Jews were actually burnt; another 139 fled but were burnt in effigy.

See Rafael Sabatini, *Torquemada and the Spanish Inquisition* (House of Stratus, 2001) for the best portrait of this fanatical Catholic fundamentalist, whose name has endured as a monument to cruelty and religious persecution.

Lucien Wolf in *The Jews of the Canary Islands* (1925) gives the best, detailed description of the travels of the Jews to escape persecution.

Torquemada's instructions to 'Defending Counsel', can be found in his 'Instructions', Article XVI.

For the unfortunate Alvaro Gonzales' story, see again the *The Jews of the Canary Islands*, cited in www.saudades.org.

4: Money, Money, Money

Lane's *Venice – a Maritime Republic* gives an admirable overview of Venice's rise to power and then her gradual decline. The point about the importance of Venice's geographical position at the confluence of West and East is powerfully reinforced by the timing of her decline. It coincides exactly with the voyages of Vasco da Gama, the Portuguese navigator who rounded the Cape of Good Hope to bring back spices like mace and nutmeg and luxury commodities from the Indies. With this new southerly trade route open to the riches of the East, Venice was increasingly cut out of the European trading loop during the 1500s and 1600s.

Venice's history and influence are well set out in William McNeill, *Venice: the Hinge of Europe* (University of Chicago Press, 1986) and Frederick Lane, *Venice: A Maritime Republic* (The John Hopkins University Press, 1973).

The Role of the Venetian Oligarchy (parts 1, 2 and 3) by Webster Tarpley on the Schiller Institute's website (www.schillerinstitute.org) give a one-sided – if pretty accurate – view of how Venice rose to greatness, and also her methods of staying there.

Ragusa was the historic name of modern Dubrovnik on the Dalmatian coast until 1806. See F. W. Carter, *Dubrovnik (Ragusa): A Classic City State* (Seminar Press, 1972).

For the statement of Ragusa's defence and security policy see the Dubrovnik State Archives, *Reformationes*, 1301.

The ambassadors' written orders were pretty comprehensive. The quotation about passing information on is a modern translation of the original Latin in the instructions to Ragusan ambassadors. It reads in the original: *'Sapientes et inquerandum et inestadum de novis.'*

The story about the Sultan and Lastovorno is to be found in *Narodna Milicijia*, 7/8, 1958. Stevan Dedijer in *Ragusa Intelligence and Security - a model for the 21st Century?* on the Zagreb National Security website examines Ragusa's security policies and their reliance on intelligence in some detail. For more background to Venice and Ragusa's intelligence methods see also S. Dedijer, 'Ragusa "Intelligence and Security"', *National Security and the Future*, Zagreb 1998.

Talleyrand (whom Napoleon once memorably described as 'a piece of shit in a silk stocking') was the archetype of the devious diplomat. Two-faced is an understatement. He survived both the French Revolution and Napoleon. To be admired by Talleyrand would seem to be a very double-edged compliment.

The economics of the 1300s, while not exactly riveting to non-economists, do, however, explain much. For a good description of the great financial market manipulation of the mid 1300s, see Paul Gallagher's 'How Venice rigged the First Global Financial Crash', *The American Almanac*, September 1995 and Lane and Moeller's *Money & Banking in Medieval and Renaissance Venice* (John Hopkins U.P., 1985).

Economic and commercial intelligence are as old as the first market place. For a highly readable and accessible account of how European commercial intelligence worked in Renaissance times, see the excellent monograph by Ian Blanchard of Edinburgh University, 'Foreign Merchants in Early Modern Towns and International Market Intelligence Systems'.

5: States and Churches

Beheading is an especially cruel way to kill, as in some cases the conscious brain lives on until starved of oxygen. Richard Wingfield's *Narration of the Last Days of the Queen of Scots* gives about the best contemporary account of Mary's execution. If the first axe blow had been too high and struck the back of her head, she would have been rendered unconscious by the blow. Logically it must therefore have hit too *low*, i.e. in the upper shoulders, to allow her to speak. The jet of arterial blood from the severed neck was normal, as French guillotining demonstrated until well into the twentieth century. The movement of the eyes, lips and mouth by beheaded victims after the head was struck off was not uncommon. It is well documented that on the occasions when Samson, the French executioner during the Terror, held a head aloft and spat in the victim's face, the eyes in the decapitated aristocrat's head usually blinked.

Luther seems to have been a fairly uncompromising and unlovable character. For a full description of his fierce personality and dogged views, see Beard, *Luther*. He was clearly a very stubborn – even bigoted – individual. To achieve what he did, Luther would have to have been.

There are many – far too many – accounts of Henry VIII's life and doings. See H.M. Smith's *Henry VIII and the Reformation* (Macmillan, 1948) for as good an account as any.

Walsingham's time on the run on the continent is to be found in Dr Karl Stahlin's *Sir Francis Walsingham und Seine Zeit* (Heidelburg, 1908).

The religious fanaticism ('warriors for God engaged in a Holy War') of the first Jesuits seems horribly familiar today. See the fascinating history of the early Jesuits in Jonathan Wright, *The Jesuits: Missions, Myths and Mysteries* (HarperCollins, 2004).

The St Bartholomew's Day Massacre (which began as a limited decapitation exercise by the French Catholic Establishment to get rid of the Protestant nobility at prayer and ended up going horribly wrong with a wholesale massacre of Protestants at the hands of the Paris mob) is well described in many books. For a more detailed examination of the whole background, see Chapter X of the Gunpowder Treason website which looks at the roots of undercover religious plotting in Elizabethan and Edwardian times.

Elizabeth I's life is well documented. Unfashionable as TV sources may or may not be, Dr David Starkey's comprehensive television series *Elizabeth* (BBC, 1999) gives an admirable introduction to the life and times of Elizabeth I.

'The Great Bog' … this splendidly dismissive phrase about the Netherlands comes from a very old book, *A Brief Character of the Low Countries* by one O. Feltham, published in London in 1652. Considering the low-lying nature, swamps, mosquitoes and even malaria of the Netherlands until the middle of the nineteenth century it seems a not unreasonable view. It also explains why the Spanish, the greatest military power of the day, were unable to get to grips with their watery Dutch enemies to crush them in a decisive battle.

Sir Edward Stafford's money worries are discussed in Richard Deacon, *History of the British Secret Service* (Collins, 1987).

Ivan the Terrible's attempts to cosy up to the English queen and recruit her favourite astrologer John Dee were further revealed when the Public Record Office/UK National Archive opened its new files in early 2004 – see the entertaining 'Ivan the Terribly Rude' *Daily Telegraph*, 2 January 2004.

Marlowe appears to have been a model of the volatile, highly strung Elizabethan man, light years removed from the stiff upper-lippery of post-Victorian English males of a certain educated type and class. For a view of Marlowe's complex character see Austin Grey, *Observations on Marlowe*, Modern Language Institute of America, 1928.

Marlowe's murder is a very murky business. All three men involved in Marlowe's death had long records as government agents in the penetration of the Babington plot in 1587 and also in working for Walsingham's intelligence network. The whole affair looks very much like a put up job.

For a comprehensive description of Marlowe's life story, character, exploits and untimely end, see Wraight and Stern, *In Search of Christopher Marlowe* (Adam Hart, 1993).

Marlowe's possible backsliding before the Privy Council is explored in the Gunpowder Treason website along with numerous other examples of Tudor-Stuart double dealing, intrigue and treachery.

The blocking of Spanish Bills of Account in Italy's banks was almost certainly coordinated by an English merchant, Thomas Sutton, working undercover in Northern Italy as one of Walsingham's secret agents.

For a full description of the last days of the galleon *San Juan di Sicilia*, see McLeay, *A Tobermory Treasure*.

The Spanish Armada, and its failure to land Parma's legions ashore, is rightly celebrated as a crucial moment in English history. For a full description of the whole epic tale of Catholic Spain's expedition to invade Protestant England, see Garrett Mattingly, *The Defeat of the Spanish Armada*.

Casualties for the Spanish Armada are notoriously difficult to estimate accurately. The best sources appear to be the Spanish State Archives, Archivo Generale de Simanca, Estado, CMC and GA series, cited in Martin and Parker, *History of the Spanish Armada* (Penguin, 1988). The key judgement, irrespective of precise casualties in men and shipping, must be that the Spanish 'Enterprise of England' failed completely – however much the Spanish may have wished to remount an expedition – and that King Philip II of Spain was deterred from chancing his arm against Protestant England again.

Elizabethan politics were as confused and dangerous to its practitioners as any story of Stalin's Politburo or Hitler's Nazi 'court'. Dictatorships are like that. For an overview of these troubled times between State and Church, and much else besides, see Paul Hammer, *The Polarisation of Elizabethan Politics* (CUP, 1999).

Babington's plot has been described many times and Catholic versions are strongly at variance with the official English accounts and histories. The *Catholic Encyclopedia* takes, not unnaturally, a different view of events. For an excellent account, which also looks at the whole business of the codes and ciphers involved in the devious affair, see Simon Singh, *The Code Book* (Fourth Estate, 2000).

To describe Walsingham and his secret agents as 'puppet masters' is no exaggeration. The machinations of Walsingham, Cecil and Essex and the impact of their secret service on both domestic and international politics are well described in A. Haynes, *Invisible Power: The Elizabethan Secret Service* (London, 1992) which gives a highly detailed account of their operations.

6: Making the Mould

The full story of the life and times of L'Éminence Grise are well described by Arnold Huxley in *Grey Eminence* (Harper Bros: New York, 1942).

Du Tremblay seems to have been a seriously disturbed individual with some kind of pathological mental condition. For an excellent description of his most likely clinical problem see Carl Jung, *Psychology and Alchemy*, vol. 12 (Princeton University Press, 1968). Professor Kaaren Jacobsen of Montana State University has done an original and penetrating critique of du Tremblay's misapplied mysticism from the Christian perspective, 'Is it possible to be a Mystic and Serve the public Good?' (She concludes that it is.)

John Dee appears to have been half astrologer, half scientist. Given the academic and intellectual climate of his day we should not be surprised or dismiss his genius as a result of his reputation as a soothsayer: we are all prisoners of our times and cultures. Even Isaac Newton held some pretty strange beliefs by our modern standards. He was a practising alchemist.

An account of Wallenstein's genius for war and influence can be found in Liddell Hart, *Great Captains Unveiled* (1928). Wallenstein stands as the supreme European example of a warlord.

Du Tremblay's influence and story is told by R. W. Rowan in *The Story of Secret Service* (John Miles, 1938).

For a detailed discussion of Richelieu's career see Orlin Damyanov's article, 'The Political Career and Personal Qualities of Richelieu' (American University of Paris). *L'Histoire du Canada et de l'Acadie* on the Internet has a good review of exactly how Richelieu operated, with a certain emphasis to the New World.

The Diary of Samuel Pepys has references to the importance of and the debate about the secret service vote.

Ambassador Sagedo's quotation is cited in Antonia Fraser, *Cromwell: Our Chief of Men* (Weidenfeld & Nicolson, 2001).

Substitution codes are very simple: e.g. **CAT** can be written XMP if X = **C**, M = **A**, and P = **T**.

D. J. Hill's 'A History of Diplomacy in the International Development of Europe' explores the various devious ways in which the prototypical diplomatic corps of Europe tried to outwit each other. Not much changes.

For a fine description of codes and ciphers and the workings of the *Cabinet Noirs*, see James Bamford, *The Puzzle Palace: Inside the NSA* (Penguin, 1986). Simon Singh's *The Code Book* is invariably fascinating and technically accessible for the lay reader.

Cromwell's story is told in Antonia Fraser's currently fashionable and comprehensive *Cromwell: Our Chief of Men*. For an older and little-read biography, try John Morley, *Oliver Cromwell* (Macmillan, 1901).

D. L. Hobman in *Cromwell's Master Spy: A Study of John Thurloe* (Chapman and Hall, 1961) gives a good account of Secretary Thurloe's accomplishments.

Louis XIV (*'l'Etat – c'est moi!'*) was clearly an extraordinary man and, given the pressures of his father's reign, it is perfectly understandable just why he wished to exercise absolute power and to keep a very close eye indeed on the French nobility. The *Memoirs* of St Simon are a detailed and fascinating insight into what life was like at the French court at the height of the Sun King's power. His successors would suffer for Louis's over-centralisation of political and economic institutions.

The life and times of Charles II are recorded in some detail in Ambassador Colbert's diaries. Occasionally even he sounds shocked by the goings on in the Merry Monarch's court.

For a full description of the Restoration court and the England of the last of the Stuarts, see G. Clark, *The Later Stuarts* (OUP, 1991) and Tony Palmer, *Charles II* (Cassell, 1979).

The early development of Peter the Great's prototypical Russian secret police is laid out in Richard Deacon, *History of the Russian Secret Service* (Muller, 1972).

7: The Age of Battles

For a really good account of the Battle of the Boyne – a small battle that was to have momentous and unforeseen consequences, Richard Holmes' battlefield tour-cum-history in his *War Walks: From the Battle of Hastings to the Blitz* (BBC Books, 1997) cannot be bettered.

Prior's 'confidential report' on the intelligence operator seems remarkably familiar to anyone who has had to deal with spies or journalists in seedy bars at one o'clock in the morning. See 'Matthew Prior, A Study' cited by Richard Deacon in *History of the British Secret Service*.

James Westfall Thompson & Saul K. Padover's *Secret Diplomacy* (Constable, 1937) is a treasure trove of how diplomats used to work.

Security breaches are as old as spies and intelligence. For the laptop losses, see the *Daily Telegraph*, November 2004.

The Treason Act in question was the 'Act the 25th of King Edward III, Stat 5, cap. 2 art. 3'.

Gregg's sorry tale is outlined with some relish in the *Newgate Calendar* (see www.exclassics.com), which contains numerous other accounts of crime and punishment in the eighteenth century.

Defoe led what can only be described as a very unusual life. See Thomas Wright, *Life of Daniel Defoe* (Cassell & Co, 1894) for the full story.

The reference to military finance in the age of Marlborough is taken from Col Clifford Walton, *History of the British Standing Army* (London, 1894). Correlli Barnett's *Britain and Her Army* (Allen Lane, 1970) is a more modern and more perceptive analysis of Marlborough's army.

Eugene of Savoy had fought the Turks and offered his services to Louis XIV of France. Snubbed by the French king, he transferred to the service of the Emperor in Vienna and spent forty years making Louis wish that he had hired him when he had the chance.

For more detail on the second Earl of Stair see the *Columbia Encyclopedia*, www.bartleby.com, 2001.

For the development and 'industrialisation' of cryptography in Vienna and all the capitals of Europe see Simon Singh, *The Code Book*. Derek J. Smith's *Codes and Ciphers in History* on the Internet offers a condensed version.

For the story of the Hannoverians boosting the secret room of the Post Office see Michael Smith, *The Spying Game* (Politico's, 2002), which also gives an excellent overview of the whole background to secret intelligence in Britain by a writer who has made it his career.

D'Éon once heard a noise in his chimney and investigated it with his rapier.

A bleeding French agent fell out, claiming he was 'sweeping the chimney'! D'Éon's extraordinary life fascinated his contemporaries and he was the object – hardly surprisingly, given his history and exploits – of much prurient speculation. However, in view of his well-known skill with the sword, few dared risk his displeasure. There are numerous accounts of his life and the Internet has several readable summaries.

The full story of this unnamed lady's exploit is to be found on the front page of the *Derby Mercury* 18–25 July 1782. Mrs A, we can be sure, was by no means unique.

Frederick's Articles can be read in the original in full in *Oeuvres de Frederic II, Roi de Prusse*, (Voss et Cie, Berlin, 1782) and in modern English in *The King of Prussia's Instructions to his Generals*, ed. Allen (Stanford University Press, 1997).

8: Land of the Free?

The quotation at the head of the chapter is from Washington's own hand, dated July 26 1777. A copy is in the Intelligence Corps Archive (Museum of Defence Intelligence, Defence Intelligence Centre, Chicksands, Bedfordshire).

For the original of Wolfe's secret intelligence on the defences of French Quebec see the beautifully copied copper-plate version of the Stobo report in the Intelligence Corps Archive.

For a good overview of the intelligence operations of the colonial period, see Hamish Eaton, 'British Military Intelligence in North America', Intelligence Corps Journal (*The Rose and the Laurel*).

Washington's early military career – which seems to have taught him a great deal about both what *not* to do on campaign and of the vital importance of intelligence – can be found in Mrs Franklin D. Wildman, *Geo. Washington, The Soldier*, (Valley Forge Historical Society, January 1966). The Historic Valley Forge website is an interesting – if sometimes hagiographic – source of information on the Revolution.

Washington's biography is summarised on the White House's historic website.

For a fuller account of Washington's skill at disinformation see R. F. McIntyre, *George Washington: Master of Misinformation*, Founders and Patriots of America website, 2003. See also Carl Hartman, 'Double Crossing the British', *Philadelphia Inquirer*, 2 July 2003.

Washington was obsessed by the need for intelligence. He wrote extensively –
and often with a very worried air – about the importance of intelligence and his
lack of it. There can be no doubt that he regarded it as crucial to victory: and
indeed the Rebels' very survival. See George Washington's 'writings' and
'George Washington: Manager of Intelligence' (a Smithsonian paper, November
1983) which forms part of Sayle's article 'The Historical Underpinnings of
US Intelligence Community', *International Journal of Intelligence and Counter-
intelligence*, vol. 1, no.1.

Rhodri Jeffrey-Jones' splendidly iconoclastic *Cloak and Dollar* (Yale University
Press, 2002) is an excellent analysis of Washington's strengths and weaknesses as
an intelligence officer and a good, if cynical, analysis of the whole ethos of
American intelligence over the years. The Papers of George Washington, ed.
W. Abbot (University of Virginia Press) are also a valuable source of detail and
well worth a read to get a flavour of Washington's beliefs and character.

As with all myths about the founding of nations, most popular American
accounts of their struggle for independence from Britain are as biased as, for
example, British accounts of the Armada or Australian accounts of Gallipoli.
(There were more *French* casualties at Gallipoli than Australian troops taking
part – but don't try and say that in a Sydney bar at midnight.) The truth is most
of the American colonists were *not* involved in the war and a very large number
of 'Americans' disapproved of it totally, regarding the Founding Fathers as
nothing more than troublemakers and men on the make for their own ends. For
example, by 1781 profiteering and inflation were causing many to question the
war and discontent was widespread among the majority of the settler population. (The French, always happy to twist English tails, were seriously concerned
that the Congress and colonists were about to give up the fight with London.)
For a more objective view of the Revolutionaries' struggle for independence,
see Hugh Bicheno, *Rebels and Redcoats: The American Revolutionary War* (Harper-
Collins, 2003). For a thoughtful exploration of national mythmaking through
war, and its importance, see Professor Michael Howard, 'War and the Making of
Nations', Gallipoli Memorial Lecture, Eltham, 25 April 1997.

Hale's last words are recorded in Nathan Miller, *Spying for America* (Dell-
Doubleday: New York, 1989), which gives an excellent account of the whole
troubled history of American intelligence since pre-Revolutionary times.

British intelligence in the period is given a critical examination by Jeffery Steinberg
in 'The Bestial British Intelligence', Schiller Institute speech, February 1994.

For André's full story see the excellent article 'Hanged as a Spy' in the Intelligence Corps Journal *The Rose and the Laurel,* and the article 'The Long Lost Letters of General Washington', *Life* magazine, 18 March 1968 which carries details of many contemporary accounts.

Franklin was clearly a slippery and rather lascivious old man by this time. Nathan Miller in *Spying for America* and Carl van Doren in *Benjamin Franklin* (Viking: New York, 1938) give an excellent description of the intrigues surrounding Passy, Franklin's entourage and the intrigues at the Paris end of the American rebellion.

9: The Age of Revolution

Catherine's husband, Czar Peter III, was a Caligula-like inadequate, petulant and childish. He is alleged to have giggled at wholly inappropriate moments such as solemn *levées* and council meetings, and even stuck his tongue out at a priest during mass. He was deeply unpopular with the court and nobles. When Catherine learned that the Czar was intending to divorce her, she organised a coup and seized power, with popular support. The unfortunate Czar was confined to a dungeon where he died in mysterious circumstances of intestinal haemorrhage. (History does not relate whether the fatal haemorrhage was encouraged by toxic chemicals, lead or steel.)

The British ambassador's embarrassing gaffe and his fall from grace are cited in Thompson and Padover's, *Secret Diplomacy*.

For a really comprehensive analysis of the Terror, especially in Loire–Rhône, see Colin Lucas, *The Comités de Surveillance and the Structure of the Terror* (OUP, 1973).

Fouché's career and his methods are outlined in a very large number of sources and memoirs. Robert J. Stove in *A Brief History of Secret Police* (Melbourne, 2002) gives a good overview as do the various texts on the Fairfax Archives website. See also Michael Browers, 'The Napoleonic Police and their Legacy', *History Today*, May 1999.

Some idea of Napoleon's intelligence methods can be found in Dave Hollins, 'The Hidden Hand – Espionage and Napoleon', *Osprey Military Journal*, 2/2, 25 March 2000.

The French triumphant Jena campaign is commemorated by the Pont du Jena across the Seine in Paris. After Waterloo Blücher was hell bent on blowing it up as a symbolic gesture, but was dissuaded. Many wags said (privately, for Fouché had many ears) that the bridge should really be named the Pont d'Auerstadt or even the Pont Davout. Given Napoleon's vanity that was always unlikely. See Jay Luvaas's clinical dissection of the 1806 Jena-Auerstadt campaign in *Leaders and Intelligence*, ed. Michael Handel (Frank Cass, 1989).

Napoleon's campaigns, including those in Spain, Germany, Poland and Russia are described in exhaustive detail in numerous books and articles. *The Memoires of Napoleon* (1829) by Louis de Bourrienne describe the man and his methods; the campaigns can be followed in the Napoleon Series by Alexander Mikaberidze on the web. David Chandler's seminal *The Campaigns of Napoleon* (Macmillan, 1973) remains the bible for first reference.

British national intelligence in the time of Nelson, Napoleon and Wellington is well described by Steven Maffeo in *Most Secret and Confidential: Intelligence in the Age of Nelson* (US Naval Institute Press: Virginia, 2000). Although the book concentrates – as its title suggests – on matters maritime, it has an extremely useful chapter on the disbursing of the Treasury's budget on the secret vote, proving, yet again, that even across the years it is the administrative and money chain that gives away supposedly secret activities.

George Scovell is a most underrated figure and deserves more credit for Wellington's victories in the Peninsula than he was given in his lifetime. For a really well-documented account of this remarkable officer and his achievements see Mark Urban's seminal work *The Man Who Broke Napoleon's Codes* (Faber, 2001).

Colquhoun Grant was clearly quite an adventurer and his exploits are well related in Jock Haswell's biography *The First Respectable Spy* (Hamish Hamilton, 1969).

Wellington spent almost as much time wrangling with the Horse Guards back in London as he did fighting the French. For a splendid discussion of Wellington's 'War on Two Fronts' (with the French *and* the Whitehall bureaucrats) see the witty but erudite paper to the Royal United Services Institute, Whitehall, by Captain Josh Moon, US Army, (West Point Historical Staff), *RUSI Journal*, Summer 2002.

10: The Peaceful Century?

Clausewitz and Jomini were the first really deep Western philosophers of war (if indeed philosophy is what they produced). Jomini was Ney's Chief of Staff in the latter stages of the Napoleonic wars and fought on both sides, having left the French service in 1813 'in a huff', feeling snubbed over lack of promotion. In his *Traité des Grandes Operations Militaires* he is the first influential military writer to really distinguish the separate needs of operations, logistics and strategy.

Clausewitz and Jomini's contributions are neatly compared by Col John Osgood in his paper 'Carl von Clausewitz and Antoine-Henri Jomini and Military Strategy' (2000) which can be found on the Internet.

Clausewitz's key thought – or at least the one for which he is most famous – is correctly (but clumsily) translated precisely into English from the German as: 'War is nothing more but a continuation of political intercourse with the admixture of other means'. It remains true, and woe betides the politician or soldier who forgets it.

Clausewitz continues to exert a powerful influence on military and strategic thinking. His work is much deeper than Jomini's, which can be thought of as primarily a technical work. The German's insights and conclusions on the other hand are clearly deeply thought out and yet he is always struggling – as are we all with the realities of human conflict – to reconcile something that is often well nigh impossible to explain away with rational logic. The Hegelian method of the dialectic breaks down sometimes when confronted by the facts and absurdities of insensate battle. Clausewitz himself clearly realised this, emphasising the importance of the *psychology* of war – although he doesn't call it that – and the importance of chance. To such a tidy mind this was obviously an irritation. Like Jomini he identified several important fundamental truths, especially the need to go for the enemy's resource base and 'will to fight' just as much as for his main forces in the field.

A basic overview of Clausewitz's life and work is available on the Houghton Mifflin website, in their *Reader's Companion to Military History*. For a deeper exploration of Clausewitz's work see Michael Handel's fascinating *Sun Tzu and Clausewitz Compared* (US War College, 1991) and Hans Rothfel's 'Clausewitz' in E. M. Earle (ed.), *Makers of Modern Strategy* (Princeton U.P., 1943).

Michael Howard's edited version of Clausewitz's work – Carl von Clausewitz, *On War,* ed. and tr. by Michael Howard and Peter Paret (Princeton University Press, 1976) – remains the bedrock English version.

The extent of Clausewitz's influence can still be found in such recent works as Professor Bruce Fleming, 'Can Reading Clausewitz Save Us From Future Mistakes?', *Parameters* (US Army War College Quarterly), Spring 2004; and John

G. Fox, US National Defense University (National War College), 'Did Clause-witz win the American Revolutionary War?', faculty seminar paper, 2000.

The revolutions of 1848 are described in David W. Koeller, 'Revolutions of National Liberalism', North Park University, Chicago website, 2001; 'War and Social Upheaval – the Revolutions of 1848–49' (unreferenced) on the Historical Boys' Clothing website, 20 December 2002; and also on the Internet 'European Nation States and the New Imperialism', World Civilisations Series, 112.

For a good flavour of the fevered and spy ridden atmosphere surrounding the 1848 revolutions across Europe, see Friedrich Engels' article in the Rheinische Zeitung Archive. See Edition 93 of 3 September 1848.

Metternich's contribution to the nineteenth century is summed up very crisply by Nick Pelling (Charterhouse School) in his article, cleverly masquerading as a 'model answer', 'Metternich: Success or Failure?', *New Perspective*, vol 4/2, December 1998. Professor Gerhard Rempel of Western New England College has published an article on the Internet entitled 'Metternich and the New Social Order: 1815–1848' which also casts light on a complex, vain man who struggled to hold the dam for twenty years and was then swept away when the torrent of social disorder and revolt burst over him.

Günter Grass in *Too Far Afield* (Faber, 2000) draws parallels between the State secret police of the nineteenth century in Middle Europe and the similar work of the DDR's Stasi and its other Eastern Bloc counterparts. For many Europeans the secret police have been a depressing reality for generations.

Britain's lacklustre contribution to the raging heat of social upheaval is described in the work of Professor John Breuilly, especially his website article 'The Revolutions of 1848 and London Compared' and in Emma Macleod, 'Revolutionary Britannia?' *English History Review*, February 2000.

The travails of Lord Raglan in the Crimean War are well described in Cecil Woodham-Smith, *The Reason Why* (Penguin, 1991).

The state of the pre-Crimean army, with its entrenched conservatism, misman-agement and indifference to the new realities of war is well set out in Correlli Barnett's *Britain and Her Army*. Hew Strachan's definitive works 'Soldiers, Strategy and Sebastopol', *Historical Journal*, XXI, 1978 and *Wellington's Legacy: The Reform of the British Army* (Manchester University Press, 1984) are important to understanding just how the army got into such a state.

The intelligence problems of the Crimea are examined in detail in Stephen Harris, *British Military Intelligence in the Crimean War* (Frank Cass, 1999) and Jock Haswell, *British Military Intelligence* (Weidenfeld & Nicolson, 1973).

See Brian Parritt, *The Intelligencers* (Intelligence Corps, 1983) for by far the best, detailed description of Major Best Jervis and all his works. Professor Christopher Andrew in *Secret Service* (Heinemann, 1985) also outlines this redoubtable Victorian's contribution. (*The Intelligencers* was published privately to benefit a charity, and is therefore a much under-read and underrated contribution to the story of British military history.)

11: The American Civil War

For a reminder that the coming war had been long expected see the *Memoirs of General W. T. Sherman* which are published in various editions or can be accessed on the Internet (www.ebooks4all.org).

More has been written on the American Civil War than almost any other. Churchill's *History of the English Speaking Peoples* (Cassell, 1958) gives a typically broad but informative and highly readable account of the history of the war and its outcome. The conflict has been dissected, analysed, brooded on and made the subject of much special pleading by vested interests. (For example, there is a surprisingly large body of literature on the role of Black Americans and women in the conflict, in a way that contrasts with, say, European writings of the Great War.) The actual fighting is well – even exhaustively – documented. The *West Point History* is as always, excellent; J. M. McPherson's *Ordeal by Fire* (Knopf, 1982) and *Battle Cry of Freedom* (OUP, 1988) are both good and detailed accounts of the fighting and campaigns.

The role of intelligence in the Civil War is well documented by Edwin Fishel in *The Secret War for the Union* (Houghton Mifflin, 1995). Arguably there is a great lack of a comprehensive analysis of the Confederates' intelligence system(s).

Alan Pinkerton's self-serving memoir is *The Spy of the Republic* (1883). Rhodri Jeffrey-Jones in *Cloak and Dollar* takes a more sceptical view of what seems to be just another 'snake oil salesman' in a long list of American intelligence con-men. Nathan Miller's *Spying for America* seems to support his thesis.

Belle Boyd in Camp and Prison (New York, 1865) tells Belle's story in her own words. The quotation '[her] trigger finger had ... reached the age of consent' is taken from R.W. Rowan, *The Story of Secret Service*, which goes into considerable detail about the various machinations of North and South to gain intelligence and is especially good on the Webster story.

The Confederate Navy was a major source of concern to both the Union and to relations between London and Washington. The website www.e-spy.org (September 2003) has a nice review of James T. Dekay, *The Rebel Raiders* (Presidio Press, 2003).

The secret trade war in Europe is discussed in more detail in Bulloch's own *The Secret Service of the Confederate States in Europe* (1959). Churchill's *History of the English Speaking Peoples* is a good source for the tensions between the Union and the British.

The dealings with Garibaldi are cited in Nathan Miller, *Spying for America*, which also gives Col Sharpe his due recognition.

For a surprisingly up-to-date pictorial record of the principal players in the intelligence war between the states see *A Photographic History of the Civil War*, ed. Theo F. Rodenbough (The Blue and Gray Press, Secaucus 1987).

Balloons in the Civil War figure prominently on the HistoryNet's *Civil War Times*.

A detailed and critical examination of the use of intelligence in the Civil War is given by Fishel in 'The Mythology of Civil War Intelligence', *Civil War History*, 10/4, December 1964.

Hattaway and Jones in *How the North Won* (University of Illinois Press, 1983) give a good discussion of the Union's road to victory and J. P. Finnegan in *Military Intelligence* (US Army Center for Military History, 1998) gives an honest unvarnished account of just how 'amateurs waged war' in the intelligence sphere.

12: The Great Architect

For a detailed account of the war between Prussia and Austria see Geoffrey Wawro, *The Austro-Prussian War* (CUP, 1996) and Michael Howard, *The Franco Prussian War* (Routledge, 1961).

Jock Haswell in *Spies and Spymasters* (Thames and Hudson, 1977) gives an admirable summary of Stieber's career.

There are numerous references to Stieber's work and legacy on the Internet in both English and German.

Details of Stieber's various machinations are well recounted in R. W. Rowan's *The Story of Secret Service*. Reading his accounts of Stieber's intelligence coups, it is impossible not to feel a sneaking admiration for such a subtle, devious – if thoroughly immoral – intelligence puppet master.

For the details of the 'Green House' in Berlin, see R. W. Rowan's *The Story of Secret Service*.

The use of professional prostitutes as spies is the oldest trick in the book. Men seem to be particularly susceptible to 'honey traps'. Pillow talk is often the loosest talk of all and technology has now made things even easier for the dedicated intelligence officer. Stieber's methods were taken up enthusiastically by others, including the Nazis. Apparently Dr Goebbels kept a similar establishment in the German capital for exactly the same purpose, but was also supported by camera and recording devices to ensure that any juicy compromise was recorded for all to see and listen to. In 1940 the Nazi's chief propagandist was able to use Stieber's methods with great success on the Italian Foreign Minister Count Ciano during a visit to Berlin, much to the later entertainment of Hitler's entourage.

13: Imperial Echoes

The machinations of the Fenians are well recorded. K. Short in *The Dynamite War* (Dublin, 1979) gives a good account of their campaign.

Professor Christopher Andrew in *Secret Service* records the political concerns about Irish terrorists and the formation of the 'Special Irish Branch' to cope with their explosive activities. Tony Bunyan in *History and Practice of the Political Police in Britain* (Quartet, 1977) gives a more critical account of the times and the role of the newly formed Special Branch.

De Blowitz tells the story of his coup for *The Times* at the Berlin Conference in *My Memoirs* (Edward Arnold, 1903).

Brian Parritt's *The Intelligencers* remains the seminal work on the formation and development of the military intelligence system during late Victorian times. See also Thomas Fergusson, *British Military Intelligence, 1870–1914* (University Publications of America, 1984).

For a good account of the reality of intelligence work in Whitehall in late Victorian days see Count Gleichen, *A Guardsman's Memories* (London, 1932).

John Keegan's thoughtful reminiscences in *Warpaths: Travels of a Military Historian in North America* (Pimlico, 1995) give a particularly poignant and well-informed account of George C. Custer, his doomed 7th Cavalry and their slaughter on the Little Big Horn at the hands of Sitting Bull's well led, determined and fighting-mad Lakota-Sioux warriors.

By far the best account of the Zulu Wars is by Ronald Morris, *The Washing of the Spears* (DaCapo Press, 1998).

Fynney's intelligence role against the Zulus is described in some detail in Brian Parritt, *The Intelligencers*.

The colourful encouragement on why it might be unwise to be captured by fanatical Islamic tribesmen and the similarities with the fighting on the North-West Frontier was recounted in an intelligence briefing on operations against insurgents on the Jebel in Dhofar, 1975 (private information).

For a cheery account of British officers' holidays-cum-amateur-spying-missions see Baden Powell's enthusiastic nonsense in his *Boys Own*-type books: for example, *My Adventures as a Spy*, (Pearson, 1915).

The Dreyfus affair is examined in detail in Rupert Hart-Davis, *The Dreyfus Case: A Re-Assessment* (1955).

There are literally hundreds of books about Dreyfus. See Douglas Porch, *French Secret Services* (Macmillan, 1996) for a dispassionate overview of the affair and a long-term appraisal of its impact. Richard Deacon's *History of the French Secret Service* (Grafton, 1990) is also useful and informative on a case that split the French Republic.

Gladstone's sexual targeting by the Czar's agents appears to have failed according to Gladstone's son, Herbert. (Private information, MRD Foor/Cosmo Lang)

The risks of being a Russian minister or chief of police, let alone a member of the Royal Family, in the late nineteenth century are well described in Richard Deacon, *History of the Russian Secret Service*. This was the time that political terrorism really came of age. In their battle against the Czar and the Ochrana, the Russian revolutionaries and anarchists provided the blueprint for most modern terrorist movements.

The deficiencies of intelligence – or to be more accurate the *ignoring* of intelligence – in the run up to the Boer War are well described in Fergusson's *British Military Intelligence*.

For a suitably shocked tabloid newspaper of the day's view of British deficiencies at the start of the Boer War in 1899–1900, see the *Daily Mail* pamphlet *The Ghastly Blunders of the War* (Carmelite Press, 1903).

The full report of the deficiencies of the Boer War is to be found in Lord Elgin's Royal Commission report, 1903.

For the details of the various threats against Black native scouts, see the full letter from the Boer commander (and many others) in the Intelligence Corps Archive.

14: Into the Abyss

See the Eastern District 1909 Intelligence Officers Course Programme and supporting documentation in the Intelligence Corps Archive. It is astonishingly professional and modern, and with technical modification could easily be used today. The programme strongly belies the fashionable notion that Edwardian officers – certainly at this level – were a bunch of socialite layabouts and 'Hooray Henrys': these IOs were clearly worked hard. It also casts a little light on why, five years later, the performance of the BEF so impressed the Germans invading France. This view of the BEF as a very professional organisation indeed is supported by a host of training manuals of the day. See the collection of Army Training and Field Manuals 1909–1914 in the RUSI Library. For further proof, see Brigadier General R. C. B. Haking, *Staff Rides and Regimental Tours* (Hugh Rees, 1912), which discusses the need for intelligence and its importance in some detail. Officers may not have welcomed such demands on their busy social round, but at least it demonstrates the standard required.

Ironside's undercover work in South Africa is described in Professor Christopher Andrew, *Secret Service*, which cites the Macleod Papers in the Liddle Hart Archive.

The late Victorian-Edwardian Revolution in Military Affairs has been well explored by the works of John Keegan, Hew Strachan, Brian Bond and Correlli Barnett. That it was most marked at sea and in the air is obvious: Keegan's *History of Warfare* (Hutchinson, 1993) and Correlli Barnett's 'Sailor with a Flawed Cutlass' in *The Swordbearers* (Indiana University Press, 1975) are well worth a read on this era of dramatic change. Martin van Creveld's *Technology and War* (Free Press, 1989) and J. F. C. Fuller's *The Conduct of War, 1789–1961* (Rutgers University Press, 1961) are invaluable guides.

See Alan Judd, *The Quest for C* for a really detailed account of Commander Smith Cumming's rise to become head of the Secret Intelligence Service. Vernon Kell's steady bureaucratic progress is described in Professor Christopher Andrew's *Secret Service*.

For copies of the correspondence between Bertrand Stewart and his German lawyers see the letters in the Intelligence Corps Archive. Nicolai, in his *History of the German Secret Service*, claims to have seen through the whole thing from the start: however, he calls Bertrand Stewart a lawyer, missing the fact that the latter saw himself as a rather dashing Territorial Forces officer.

Nigel West (Rupert Allason) gives a splendid and detailed account of the impact of wireless communications in the era before the Great War in his *GCHQ* (Coronet, 1986) citing material from the GPO Archive.

For the perceptive comment on the vulnerability of radio transmissions to 'sigint', see the *News Chronicle,* 12 November 1914.

For a good broad-brush account of the huge campaign that began the war in the West in 1914 see Correlli Barnett's *The Swordbearers*.

For details of Tannenburg and the Masurian Lakes see the crisp summary in Richard Holmes (ed.), *Oxford Companion to Military History* (OUP, 2001). A really good short account is included in Montgomery's *A History of Warfare* (Collins, 1968) with clear maps and a passing recognition of the crucial role of intelligence in the stunning German victory. For a fuller account, Ludendorff's *My War Memories, 1914–1918* (1920) are well worth a look. The most balanced, comprehensive account, which gives due weight to the crucial Russian intelligence blunders, is in Barbara Tuchman's admirable *The Guns of August* (Ballantine, 1962.) Her very readable version also explains why the Russian commanders Samsonov and Rennenkamp may not have worked well together: they had a long running detestation of each other going back to the Russo-Japanese war which had once brought them to blows at a railway station.

Douglas Porch in *The French Secret Services* is quite rightly scathing about the intelligence deficiencies of the French High Command in 1914. As early as 1900 the French attaché in Berlin was providing clear and accurate reports on German plans and warning particularly of the threat to the flank. In 1904 Lt Col Gallet based in Brussels outlined the threat from the new German railway construction 'pointing like a dagger' to the Belgian flank of the French defences. Accurate intelligence reports came in steadily thereafter. In 1904, 1908, 1911 and 1912 a string of French intelligence officers warned of the threat posed by von Schlieffen's great plan. See also J. K. Tannenbaum, 'French Estimates of German War Plans' in *Knowing your Enemies*, ed. E. R. May (Princeton University Press).

Part of the intelligence problem in 1914 was the total dominance of policy over intelligence. 'Ops & Plans' generally recruit the brightest officers. Unless they have experienced the upsets of real war, such career-conscious planners tend to disregard the likely activities of the enemy: it only confuses readers of their highly polished schemes.

For the sudden discovery of the value of air reconnaissance and the early need for intelligence on the advancing Germans see Barbara Tuchman, *The Guns of August*; Edward Spears, *Liaison 1914* (Weidenfeld & Nicolson, 2000); Ralph Barker, *The Royal Flying Corps in France* (Constable, 1994) and the *British Official History*. The Intelligence Corps Archive, which shares the Museum of Defence Intelligence at Chicksands with the RAF's Medmenham collection (a history of aerial photography) has a superb collection of aerial photographs taken in 1912 and 1913, clearly demonstrating the value of aerial reconnaissance. See also Dr Anthony Clayton's *Forearmed – a History of the Intelligence Corps* (Brassey's 1993).

By far the best source of information on British Military Intelligence in the Great War in one single book is Michael Occleshaw, *Armour Against Fate* (Columbus, 1989), which gives a complete breakdown on the growth of what was to become a vital part of Britain's war-winning effort.

The importance of a good map cannot be overemphasised. See, for example, Wellington's request before Waterloo, recounted in Max Hastings, *Military Anecdotes* (OUP, 1992).

The reference to good aerial photography comes from The Haig Diaries, 28 August 1917.

The *Official History of the War in the Air*, vol. 1 gives statistics of intelligence work from the air.

Good accounts of the exploits of naval intelligence in the Great War are given in Patrick Beesley's *Very Special Intelligence* (Doubleday, 1978) and *Room 40* (1982). Nigel West's *GCHQ* and Professor Christopher Andrew's *Secret Service* both give good, clear, accessible accounts of the importance of naval 'sigint'. David Kahn's *The Codebreakers* (New York, 1996) remains the bible on the history of 'sigint' in general.

For an account of the intercepted German telegram see Barbara Tuchman, *The Zimmermann Telegram* (Macmillan, 1966) which cannot be bettered.

Silber's 'thank you' letter from the Director of Military Intelligence at the War Office was dated and referenced, D.M.I., 5th July 1919.

15: The Red Peril

See Tony Bunyan's *The Political Police in Britain* for an account of the Sydney Street siege.

The story of the attempt by the king to rescue the czar seems, against all the odds, to have a ring of truth about it. For a full account of this extraordinary exploit, see Michael Occleshaw's *Armour against Fate*, where the gripping story is related in detail, with full references to the primary sources.

New information tends to confirm Meinertzhagen's diary and the circumstantial evidence for the extraordinary story of the attempt to rescue the Czar. Tatiana could well be the mysterious 28-year-old woman buried in Lydd, Kent in 1923, ('Larissa Feodorovna, Wife of Owen Tudor, 3rd Hussars'). 'Feodorovna' was a name particularly associated with the Romanovs and unknown persons cleaned up the grave in 1998 on the day Czar Nikolas's remains were re-interred in Moscow. See also Edwards, Sue, *No Resting Place for a Romanov*, ISBN 095292921.

The whole spirit of the Red Menace is hard for us to understand nowadays. It was, however, very real in the 1920s. The true social history of the time can often be found in popular culture. The reaction of the middle classes of the day to the threat of Bolshevism in Britain is reflected in the 'Just William' books of Richmal Crompton where stories with references to the Reds and the Bolsheviks appear frequently. See Mr Dimtritch's exploits in *William the Conqueror*, which was published in March 1926 (the year of the General Strike) and 'William and the Stolen Whistle' in *William the Outlaw* (1927).

The statistics for the growth of the security service (MI5) are cited in Professor Christopher Andrew's *Secret Service*, as is the splendid story of Thompson's undercover anti-strike men spreading alarm and despondency among the workers.

See Tony Bunyan, *The Political Police in Britain* for an anti-Establishment perspective on the Zinoviev letter. The balance of evidence seems to be that it probably was a forgery, perhaps executed by White Russians in the Baltic States and 'fenced on' to Berlin. The mysterious Mr Thurn turns out to have been an ex-officer of the British Secret Services.

Van Deman's story and the growth of US 'MI' is told in the US *Official History of Military Intelligence*.

The judgement about the French politicians of the 1930s trying to tailor intelligence to suit their domestic policies (with predictably disastrous results) is reflected in Porch, *The French Secret Services*.

The Venlo Incident is well described in brief in Nigel West's *GCHQ* and in more detail in his *MI6* (Weidenfeld & Nicolson, 1983). For the full official version of this extraordinary story, and original texts from the German secret service and Berlin's side, see the evidence submitted at Nuremburg in Appendix A.

16: Total War

For all the facts and figures see *The World at Arms* (Readers Digest Books, 1989) and John Ellis, *World War 2 Data Book* (Aurum Press, 1993).

The secret turning of German agents in the UK is well outlined in Sir John Masterman, *The Double Cross System* (London, 1972).

Popov's story is told in more detail in Nigel West, *Seven Spies who Changed the World* (Mandarin, 1991).

The whole saga of the German radio game against N Section of SOE is well told in Professor M. R. D. Foot's *SOE in the Low Countries* (St Ermin's Press, 2001) and in Herman Giskes, *London Calling North Pole* (London, 1953), which gives the Abwehr's perspective on the operation.

The splendid Major Wintle's court martial is well recounted in R. V. Jones, *Most Secret War* (BCA, 1978).

The saga of the German B-Dienst successes – which unaccountably seems never to have gripped British TV commissioning editors – is well told in *The Battle of the Atlantic and Signals Intelligence*, ed. Syrett (Archgate Books, the Naval Records Society, 1998).Wilhelm Tranow's career is recalled in David Kahn, *Hitler's Spies* (Macmillan: New York, 1978).

For an admission that the USSR knew the plan to attack at Kursk all along see the RUSI article, in particular the evidence of the Russian Army speaker, 'Kursk, 60 Years On', *RUSI Journal*, Summer 2003.

The website 'WW2 Index – Soviet Spy Rings' gives a rather alarming list of all known Soviet espionage activities in the Second World War.

For a full analysis and a controversial view of this startling theory that Martin Bormann was a spy, see Lou Kilzer, *Hitler's Traitor* (Presidio Press: California, 2000). Even if the tale seems too incredible to be true, it still raises important questions that need clear answers, the first of which is, if Werther was not Bormann then who else was it? The idea of a network working in OKW, various ministries and Hitler's headquarters undetected for so long seems incredible. And anyway, how could any physically widespread network react as quickly as it did? Nigel West explores the mystery further in the 'Who was Werther?' chapter in *Unreliable Witness*. General Walter Warlimont, *Inside Hitler's Headquarters* (1964) and F. M. Keitel's Nuremburg confessions both confirm the secure typing procedures used at the *Führerkonferenzen*.

For a detailed examination of the whole Red Orchestra story, based on the Swiss government's own internal investigations as passed to the CIA, see *The Rote Kapelle* (University Publications of America, 1979) and V. E. Tarrant, *The Red Orchestra* (Arms and Armour, 1995).

The story of the operation to ambush and kill Yamamoto is told in Burke Davis, *Get Yamamoto!* (Random House: New York, 1969). There are numerous website versions of the exploit. The aeroplane used was the P–38 Lightning.

For the fullest account of the intelligence effort to track Hitler's V-weapons can be found in David Irving, *The Mare's Nest* (Kimber, 1964) and R. V. Jones, *Most Secret War*.

17: New instruments of War

For the genesis of the idea of the indirect approach to war, see Liddle Hart, *The British Way in Warfare* (Faber, 1932). The lure of cheap and swift victories has, not surprisingly, fascinated British strategists ever since. However, as Professor Christopher Bellamy of Cranfield University has recently pointed out, sometimes the grim reality of war has to be faced and, in order to win, we still sometimes have to bite the hard bullet of attrition. See Professor C. Bellamy, 'Attrition', Inaugural Lecture, Cranfield University, 2000.

Churchill had a lifelong interest in intelligence based on his experiences in peace and war. In his 'wilderness years' in the 1930s he had built up close links with the British intelligence services. (There is some evidence that the government was not unaware that he was getting secret information and indeed may have turned a blind eye to this unofficial 'feed' on some occasions.) Dr David Stafford's excellent study of Churchill's lifelong infatuation with the secret world *Churchill and Secret Service* (John Murray, 1997) is well worth a read.

The bizarre story of Hess's flight to Britain is well told in Martin Allen's *The Hitler–Hess Deception* (HarperCollins, 2004). The secrets of British deception operations, with their close links to intelligence, have been well kept over the years. The Hess story still conceals one final mystery: was it really Hess in the dock at Nuremberg and subsequently at Spandau jail? There are a number of theories that it was a double; for example, the Spandau doctor claimed to be baffled by the absence of bullet scars on prisoner Hess's body – yet the real Hess had been badly wounded in the 1914–18 war.

Lord Haw Haw made a greater impact than many people choose to remember, particularly in the dark days between the Fall of France and the Blitz. Over a million people admitted to listening to his broadcasts and the government was sufficiently alarmed to begin counter-propaganda messages. See Norman Longmate, *How We Lived Then* (Hutchinson, 1971) for an unvarnished view of Britain in wartime. For more detail and a surprisingly sympathetic view of Joyce, see Alex Softly, 'William Joyce – alias Lord Haw Haw' published by the Heretical Press on their website.

Kurzwellensender Atlantik was run by Lt Cdr Donald McLachan RNVR under Naval Intelligence Division cover. According to Professor M. R. D. Foot, on being questioned about what he did during the war, McLachan invariably replied, 'Just some damned dull job in the Admiralty …'.

Stafford Cripps was a curious figure and aroused great emotion. A rich liberal Socialist – in fact he was virtually a Communist – he was a vegetarian, non-smoking teetotaller, and convinced that his way was right for everybody else. Churchill, no admirer, once observed of this particularly self-satisfied, aloof product of the British moneyed classes, 'There but for the grace of God, goes God!'

Cripps was more realistic in his understanding of the difficulties that lay before the advocates of the 'New Jerusalem' in Britain than many of his fellow activists and prophets on the Left. Men like Toynbee, Nicolson, Laski, Archbishop Temple and Kingsley Martin exercised an unshakable stranglehold on liberal progressive thought at the time, firmly rooted in Victorian ideals of 'muscular

Christianity' at best, or open Marxism at worst. Like all those who think that they know best what is right for others, the men and women of Britain's 'Enlightened Establishment' of the day were perfectly prepared to enforce their views on their fellow men as much as necessary. See Correlli Barnett's scathing and clinical dissection of the period and particularly the New Jerusalem in *The Audit of War* (Papermac, 1986). For a political critique of the Left in the 1930s see C. Northcote Parkinson, *Left Luggage* (John Murray, 1967).

See the splendid Milton Keynes website 'WW2 Secret Intelligence Activities around Milton Keynes'. There is a good rundown of the whole subject of radio propaganda in Mark Kenyon, 'Black Propaganda', *After the Battle* series, no. 75, 1992.

Irish views on the integration of North and South are very ambivalent. Public utterances and true policy often seem curiously contradictory. For example, in the Wilson government of the early 1970s when 'the Troubles' were at their height, the British Prime Minister actually opened secret discussions with Dublin to see if the Eire government was interested in a deal to hand over Ulster to the South. The British offered to pull out of the North, leaving Ulster to be absorbed into a united Ireland. Concerned officials in Dublin swiftly rang London to say that this was the last thing they needed. Puzzled British advisers in Number 10 demanded, 'But we thought that was just what you wanted?' The amused aide to the Taisoch, is alleged to have replied airily, 'Oh for sure; but it's a little like Saint Bernadette and her prayer for chastity –"Please Lord, make me chaste – but not just yet!"' This still appears to be the Irish government's official line behind the scenes on Irish Reunification. (Private information.)

J. Edgar Hoover appears to have been a particularly nasty piece of work. His links with the Mafia, sexual preferences and his apparent ability to blackmail elected politicians remain to be investigated and exposed still further. For a description of his true predilections, corruption and lifestyle see Anthony Summers, *Official and Confidential: The Secret Life of J. Edgar Hoover* (1993). See also T. Holt, *The Deceivers* (W&N, 2004).

Operation Pastorius was a very serious attempt to launch a sabotage attack on the USA. For the full story of this extraordinary tale of treachery and corruption, and a fuller account of German activities in the US during the Second World War, see David Alan Johnson, *Germany's Spies and Saboteurs* (MBI Books: Wisconsin, 1998).

For more details of Operation Zeppelin see Andrew J. Swanger, 'Luftwaffe's Secret KG 200', *World War II* magazine, September 1997; cited also on the HistoryNet, 2004.

The source for the 'Prosper' network's possible betrayal comes from Suttill /M. R. D. Foot (private correspondence).

Fletcher's story is well-told in *Sabotage and Subversion*, Ian Dear, (Cassell 1996).

18: Cold War – Intelligence War

The Canadian Broadcasting Corporation Backgrounder Internet Briefs 'Spies' and 'Cold War' plus CNN's 'Cold War Experiences' and 'Spies in the Digital Age' are useful for navigating through thousands of sources.

The stories of the duping of the gullible left-leaning Western intellectuals and apologists for Stalin's savageries are recounted with some humour (and mild contempt) in C. Northcote Parkinson, *Left Luggage*. Lenin's phrase 'useful idiots' seems wholly appropriate.

Sources on the Cambridge spies abound. E. H. Cookridge's book *The Third Man* (1968) is a good start and it is hard to see how Professor Christopher Andrew's books and Andrew Boyle, *Climate of Treason* (Hutchinson, 1972) can be bettered. Philby's own account and *My Five Cambridge Friends* (Headline, 1994) by Yuri Modin (who was for a time the spies' handler) should be treated with caution.

Nigel West in *Venona* (HarperCollins, 1999) gives the best and most detailed account of this extraordinarily long-running exposure of the USSR's Third Front in the Great Patriotic War – spying on her own allies. There is a Venona website, managed by Nova Online, where texts can be viewed.

The role of the KGB in the Cold War is set out in great detail by Andrew and Gordievsky in *KGB: The Inside Story* (Hodder & Stoughton, 1990). Oleg Gordievsky was a Soviet intelligence officer who defected to the UK. His betrayal of the Soviet system contributed to a better understanding between East and West.

The U2 incident and its future policy can be found in 'CIA Future of the Agency's Overflight Capability', 7 July 1960, and supporting documents in the Dwight D. Eisenhower Library, USA. See also the CIA's 'Debriefing of Francis Gary Powers', 1 February 1962 (US National Archives, 1988, now declassified).

The full saga of the Berlin Wall can be found on the AOL Text History site.

For a good Soviet/Russian account of the tense days of the Cuban Missile Crisis, see Alexander Mozgovoi, *The Cuban Samba of the Foxtrot Quartet*, published in Russian (Military Parade Books: Moscow, 2002). Tr. Svetlana Savranskaya (US National Security Archive).

For the details of the underwater standoff that so nearly led to war in 1962 see CINCLANT cables to 'AiG 930', the Joint Chiefs of Staff and CINCCARIB, 'Current Sub-Surface Status', 26-28 October 1962, Top Secret (since declassified).

Details of the underwater intelligence war (that is still going on) are to be found in W. Reed, *Crazy Ivan* (Writers Club Press, 2003).

The Walker story is recounted in some detail on the Crime Library website as 'The John Walker Spy Case'. He and the CIA spy Richard Ames did as much damage as ever the Cambridge spies did – and probably more.

More details of the mystery deaths of trawlermen at sea are to be found on the Manxman Archive website.

The saga of Dutch officers spying for Israel is explored in more detail in the Electronic Intifada website. *Die Telegraaf* newspaper archive records the bare facts of the Smit case. The full story comes from private sources and retired SHAPE officers.

Bernd Schaefer's 'STASI files and GDR espionage information against the West', IFS Info. paper 2/02, gives a dispassionate and rather chilling account of the East German's Stasi penetration of the West and the Federal Republic of Germany in particular.

Markus Wolf's reflections on his extraordinary career as East Germany's puppet master are best summarised in his comprehensive CNN interview, 'The Man Without a Face'. See CNN Interactive, 'The Cold War – Spies in their own Words'. Details of Western spies can be found in the excellent website *Open Source Intelligence Digest* ('OSINT') (Glenmore Trenear-Harvey) including the obituary and celebration of a Polish officer who spied for the CIA 'in the name of peace' for over twenty years. See 'Life in the Shadows', OSINT, 21 February 2004.

19: The Globalisation of Terror

Terrorism has a long and dishonourable history. The World Trade Center attack, better known by its shorthand '9/11', has spawned more books and articles worldwide than one can begin to imagine. At the present rate of progress books on terrorism will soon equal books on Napoleon, who allegedly is only surpassed by the Bible. By far the most thoughtful work on the subject in the long term has come from Richard Clutterbuck at Exeter University and his protégé Paul Wilkinson of St Andrews University, now the doyen of long-term thinking about terror and its impact on politics and populations. In our contemporary concerns about global Islamic terror it is only too easy to forget the horrors that have gone before.

The Russian Anarchists of the nineteenth century are well charted in Richard Deacon, *Russian Secret Service*.

The history of Irish terrorism is explored by Patrick Bishop and Eamonn Mallie in the first three chapters of *The Provisional IRA* (Heinemann, 1987). Tim Pat Coogan's work, *The IRA* (Fontana, 1980) remains the seminal authority.

Jewish terrorism is skipped over lightly by Ian Black and Benny Morris in *Israel's Secret Wars* (Grove Weidenfeld: New York, 1991). A more honest assessment is to be found in Benjamin Beit-Hallahmi, *Original Sins* (Pluto Press, 1992). Martin van Creveld's uncompromising look at the truth in *The Sword and the Olive* (Public Affairs: New York, 1992) remains the most honest account. His research into the background to the struggle by the Zionists to secure a Jewish homeland remains the most dispassionate.

The startling rise in the price of oil after the 1973 war is well charted in the graph of the historic world oil price in *Environmental Conflict*, ed. Paul Diehl and Nils Petter Gleditsch (Westview Press: New York, 2001).

The Fundamentalists' death wish is hard for Westerners to understand. In a shaft of grim humour on a deadly serious subject, during the hunt for Osama bin Laden after the World Trade Center kamikaze air strikes, the US Marines had a bumper sticker which read: 'Osama bin Laden wants to meet his God: the mission of the USMC is to arrange his transportation.'

Democratic governments face a real dilemma in combating determined terrorist attack. They can either try and appease the terrorists by giving in to their demands. Secondly, they can try and deal with terrorism by treating it as a kind of extended serious crime wave. A combination of these two approaches has traditionally been the favoured course for most democracies since 1945. The third course is to attack the terrorists and root them out by a genuine counter terrorist war: this approach requires very good intelligence and has two grave disadvantages: it admits to the world and to the voters that the government is not 100 per cent in charge. More importantly, if there is a genuine grievance and it remains uncorrected, it sows the dragons' teeth of future resistance by creating martyrs and breeding even more resentment. Israel proves the point.

Rohan Gunaratna, *Inside Al Qaeda: The Global Network of Terror* (Hurst and Co, 2002) gives, as its name implies, a detailed insight into just how al-Qaida operates. There have been countless articles on the subject between 2001 and 2004. Significant books on the recent surge of fundamentalist Arab Terrorism are:

Paul Wilkinson, *Political Terrorism* (London, 1974)

Rudolph Peters, *Islam and Colonialism* (Den Haag and New York, 1979)

Sa'd al-din Ibrahim, *The New Arab Social Order* (Boulder: Colorado, 1982)

Oliver Roy, *The Failure of Political Islam* (London, 1994)

The Encyclopedia of World Terrorism (Armonk Pubs: New York, 1997)

John K. Cooley, *Unholy Wars: Afghanistan, America and International Terrorism* (Pluto Press, 2000)

Simon Reeve, *The New Jackals* (André Deutsch, 1999)

B. Hoffman, *The Modern Terrorist Mind* (St Andrew's University, 1997)

Juergensmeyer, *Terror in the Mind of God* (University of California Press, 2000)

US Dept of State, *Patterns of Global Terrorism* (Langley, 2001 and 2002)

Baxter and Downing, eds., *The Day that Shook the World* (BBC Books, 2001)

Why the Twin Towers Collapsed, Channel 4 documentary, November 2001

Peter Bergen, *Holy War Inc.: Inside the Secret World of Osama bin Laden* (Weidenfeld & Nicolson, 2001)

Malise Ruthven, *A Fury for God* (Granta Books, 2002)

Milton Metzer, *The Day the Sky Fell: A History of Terrorism* (Landmark Books, 2002)

Congressional report into the events of 9/11 (US Government Printing Office, 2002)

Yossef Bodansky et al., *Bin Laden: The Man who Declared War on America* (Random House USA Inc., 2001)

Jessica Stern, 'The Protean Enemy: Terror's Future', *Foreign Affairs*, July 2003

'Weapons of Catastrophic Effect', RUSI Seminar, Whitehall, 2003

'Homeland Security and Terrorism', RUSI Seminar, Whitehall, 2003

Andrew Sinclair, *An Anatomy of Terror* (Macmillan, 2003)

The Madrid bombing of Spring 2004 brought two new elements into the war on terror: history and democracy. It was with a sense of surprise that many Westerners realised that to the Muslim world the final expulsion of the Moors from Spain in 1492 – a date better remembered for Ferdinand and Isabella's other decision, to send Columbus to locate the Americas – still rankled as an historic Islamic grievance. The second factor was the shock removal by the Spanish voters of a government that had allied them to US President Bush's war against Iraq in Spring 2003.It was the first time that terrorism and the fear of its consequences had toppled a democratically elected Western government. However, as many observers at the time pointed out, it was impossible to opt out of a terror war waged by an implacable enemy.

20: The Newest Profession?

For the future of intelligence there are numerous speculative articles, some better informed than others. Sun-T'zu's work is widely available on the Internet and on the bookstalls. A good selection of balanced references on the future of intelligence follows.

Michael Herman of St Antony's College, Oxford, in *Intelligence Services in the Information Age* (Frank Cass, 2001) gives a thoughtful review of 'Whither intelligence?' by a long-term practitioner.

John Keegan's *Intelligence in War* (Hutchinson, 2003) aroused considerable discussion among intelligence professionals. His history is, as ever, beyond reproach: his conclusions on intelligence (a subject on which his experience is not regarded as authoritative) are however fiercely debated.

Agents for Change: Intelligence Services in the 21st Century, ed. Harold Shukman (St Ermin's Press, 2000) is an important collection of views from Russian, Israeli, French and British senior intelligence officers.

For a well-reasoned discussion see *The Future of Intelligence*, ABC Australia TV programme, 31 December 2003.

The discussions at the CIA Langley Symposium (see the CIA website) of October 1993 have stayed surprisingly accurate and relevant: cynics might say much more than the CIA's predictions of international events.

The reports (February 2004) of the CIA's chief questioning foreign, especially UK, intelligence before the 2003 Iraqi war has thrown new light on the way intelligence seems to have been used and manipulated for political ends in both the US and UK during the run up to war.

The *Open Source Intelligence Digest* (Glenmore Trenear-Harvey) between October 2003 and January 2004 was crammed with reports and allegations of intelligence being manipulated and spun for political reasons by both the UK and US governments. The subsequent inquiry in the UK by Lord Hutton was generally felt to have been lopsided in its judgements and condemned by most commentators as a government whitewash.

Dan Verton's *Black Ice* (McGraw Hill, 2003) spells out the threat of cyber terrorism in some detail.

For the best crisp and well-informed summary of these new forms of cyber warfare see Professor Christopher Bellamy, 'Tools of Ill Omen', *Cambridge Review of International Affairs*, no. 1 of 2000.

Glossary

20 Committee	UK group for running turned German agents (WW2) (see Double Cross)
Abwehr	Nazi Germany's secret intelligence service
AGER	US Navy Auxiliary intelligence gathering ship
ARCOS	Soviet trading organisation (1920s)
B-Dienst	German 'sigint' and radio intercept service (WW2)
BEF	British Expeditionary Force
BfV	Modern German security service
Black Chamber	Secret codebreaking office of State (Also *Cabinet Noir*)
Bletchley Park	Location of UK 'sigint' service (WW2)
BND	Modern German intelligence service
C3	Command, control and communications
C4I	Command, control, communications, computers and intelligence
Chaff	Anti-radar foil strips (Also 'Window')
CHEKA	Soviet secret service (1917–22)
CIA	US intelligence service
CINCLANT	Commander-in-Chief US–NATO Atlantic Fleet
CIR	Critical Intelligence Requirements
ComSubPac	Commander-in-Chief Submarines, Pacific (US)
Comint	Communications intelligence
CPGB	Communist Party of Great Britain
CPUSA	Communist Party of the USA

CSA	Confederate States of America
Deuxième Bureau	French intelligence staff
DGSE	French secret service
Double Cross	UK committee running turned German agents (WW2)
DST	French security service
Enigma	German encoding machine (WW2)
FAA	Federal Aviation Agency (US)
FBI	Federal Bureau of Investigation (US)
FCO	Foreign and Commonwealth Office (UK)
FISA	Foreign Intelligence and Surveillance Act (US)
Forschungsamt	Research Office (German)
Funkspiel	German radio game (WW2)
G-2	Intelligence and Security General Staff Branch
GC & CS	Government Code And Cipher School
GCHQ	Government Communications Headquarters
GPU	Soviet secret service (1923–34)
GRU	Russian / Soviet military intelligence and security staff
H2S	RAF ground search radar (WW2)
Hackint	Hacking intelligence – protection against computer hackers
Horse Guards	Pre-nineteenth century British Army London Headquarters
Humint	Human intelligence – agents, debriefings, prisoner of war interrogation
I-War	Information war – information technology operations
ICBM	Intercontinental Ballistic Missile
IRA	Irish Republican Army
J2	Joint Military Staff Intelligence and Security Branch
JIC	Joint Intelligence Committee (UK)
JN 25	Japanese naval code (WW2)
KG200	*Kampfgruppe* – Luftwaffe Special Duties Squadron (WW2)
KGB	Soviet secret service (1955–90)
KW-7	US coding machine
Langley	CIA headquarters
LRDG	Long Range Desert Group (Western Desert, WW2)

MAD	German military security service *or* Mutually Assured Destruction
Magic	US codename for breaking Japanese top level code (WW2)
Marechaussee	Netherlands military police and security service
MfS	Ministry for State Security (East German)
MGB	Soviet secret service (1946–53)
MI	Military Intelligence
MI5	British domestic security service
MI6	UK intelligence service (SIS)
MID	Military Intelligence Division or Department (US)
MOD	Ministry Of Defence
Monica	Tail warning radar (RAF, WW2)
Mossad	Israeli secret service
NATO	North Atlantic Treaty Organisation
NGO	Non Governmental Organisation
NKGB	Soviet secret service (1941–43)
NKVD	Soviet secret service (1934–41)
NRO	National Reconnaissance Office (US)
NSA	National Security Agency; US 'sigint' service
Ochrana	Czarist secret police
OGPU	Soviet secret service (1930s)
OKW	Oberkommand Wehrmacht
OSA	Official Secrets Act
OSS	Office Of Special Services (US, WW2)
PI	Photographic Interpretation
PIRA	Provisional Irish Republican Army (1971–)
PLO	Palestine Liberation Organisation
Psyops	Psychological operations
PURPLE	Top secret Japanese diplomatic code (WW2)
PWE	Political Warfare Executive (UK)
RAF	Royal Air Force *or* Red Army Faction (German terrorists)
RB-47	USAF reconnaissance jet (1950s and 60s)
RCMP	Royal Canadian Mounted Police
RMA	Revolution in Military Affairs

Room 40	British Navy codebreaking staff (WW1)
SAM-2	Soviet Surface to Air Missile
SAS	Special Air Service Regiment (British Army)
SBS	Special Boat Squadron (British Marines)
SD	Sicherheits Dienst – German security service (WW2)
SHAPE	Supreme Headquarters Allied Powers Europe
'Sheepdipping'	Falsely 'retiring' intelligence or military officers
Sigint	Signals intelligence – intercept, analysis, codebreaking
SIS	Secret Intelligence Service (UK) *or* Signals Intelligence Service (US, 1930–45)
SOE	Special Operations Executive (UK, WW2)
SR	French intelligence service
Stasi	East German (DDR) State intelligence and security service
SVR/FSB	Modern Russian secret service
T & S Department	Topographical and Statistical Department (UK War Office)
Techint	Technical intelligence – equipment, electronics, weapons
Triad	Three forces of nuclear deterrence: ICBMs, Bombers, Submarines
UNDP	United Nations Development Programme
UNHCR	UN High Commission for Refugees
USAF	United States Air Force
V1 and V2	German rocket bombs (WW2)
Venona	Codename for intercepted Soviet spy communications (WW2)
WO	War Office (UK)
WMD	Weapons of Mass Destruction
WTC	World Trade Center
WTO	World Trade Organisation
Y Service	Radio intercept service (UK)

Bibliography

Allen and Polmar, *Merchants of Treason* (Dell: New York, 1988)

Andrew, Christopher, *Secret Service* (Heinemann, 1985)

– *The Mitrokhin Archive* (Penguin, 2000)

Andrew and Gordievsky, *KGB: The Inside Story* (Hodder & Stoughton, 1990)

Aron, Raymond, *Clausewitz, Philosopher of War* (New York, 1980)

Babington-Smith, Constance, *Evidence in Camera* (London, 1958)

Baden Powell, Robert, *Lessons from the University of Life* (London, 1933)

– *My Adventures as a Spy* (Pearson, 1915)

Bamford, James, *The Puzzle Palace: Inside the NSA* (Penguin, 1986)

Barnett, Correlli, *Britain and Her Army* (Allen Lane, 1970)

– *Marlborough* (Eyre Methuen, 1974)

– *Napoleon* (Penguin, 1970)

Baxter and Downing, eds., *The Day that Shook the World* (BBC Books, 2001)

Beard, Martin, *Luther and the Reformation in Germany* (Keegan Paul, 1889)

Below, N. von, *At Hitler's Side*, tr. (Greenhill Books, 2001)

Bennett, Ralph, *Behind the Battle* (Pimlico, 1999)

– *Ultra and the Mediterranean* (Hamish Hamilton, 1989)

– *Ultra in the West* (Hutchinson, 1979)

Bergen, Peter, *Holy War Inc.: Inside the Secret World of Osama Bin Laden* (Weidenfeld & Nicolson, 2001)

Black and Morris, *Israel's Secret Wars* (Grove Weidenfeld: New York, 1991)

Blake, Robert (ed.), *The Private Papers of Douglas Haig* (Eyre & Spottiswoode, 1952)

Bodansky, Yossef et al., *Bin Laden: The Man who Declared War on America* (Random House USA, 2003)

Bond, Brian, *The Victorian Army and the Staff College* (Eyre Methuen, 1972)

Boyd, Belle, *Belle Boyd in Camp and Prison* (New York, 1865)

Boyle, Andrew, *The Climate of Treason* (Hutchinson, 1972)

Brendon, Piers, *The Dark Valley: A Panorama of the 1930s* (Jonathan Cape, 2000)

– *Winston Churchill: A Brief Life* (Pimlico, 2001)

Brown, Malcolm, *The IWM Book of the Western Front* (Pan Macmillan, 2001)

Bunyan, Tony, *History and Practice of the Political Police in Britain* (Quartet, 1977)

Calvi and Schmidt, *Intelligences Secrètes* (Hachette: Paris, 1988)

Carrell, Paul, *Der Russlandkrieg* (Ullstein: Frankfurt-Main, 1967)

Chandler, David, *The Campaigns of Napoleon* (Weidenfeld & Nicolson, 1967)

– (ed.), *Napoleon's Marshals* (Weidenfeld & Nicolson, 1998)

Chapman, Guy, *The Dreyfus Trials* (New York, 1972)

Churchill, W. S. C., *History of the English Speaking Peoples* (Cassell, 1958)

– *Marlborough* (Scribner, 1968)

CIA Staff, Langley, *The Rote Kapelle* (University Publications of America, 1979)

Clarke, Peter, *The Cripps Version* (Penguin, 2002)

Clausewitz, C. von, *Vom Krieg*, ed. Michael Howard and Peter Paret (Princeton University Press, 1976)

Clayton, Anthony, *Forearmed* (Brassey's, 1993)

Coleman, Janet, *Against the State: Studies in Sedition* (BBC Books, 1990)

Cookridge, E. H., *Inside SOE* (Arthur Barker, 1966)

Cooley, John K., *Unholy Wars* (Pluto Press, 2000)

Corbett, J., *Naval Operations* (HMSO, 1920)

Cowley and Parker, *Osprey Companion to Military History* (Osprey, 1996)

Daily Mail pamphlet, *The Ghastly Blunders of the War* (Carmelite Press, 1903)

Deacon, Richard, *History of the British Secret Service* (Collins, 1987)

– *History of the Chinese Secret Service* (Muller, 1974)

– *History of the French Secret Service* (Grafton, 1990)

– *History of the Russian Secret Service* (Muller, 1972)

Deakin and Storry, *The Case of Richard Sorge* (London, 1966)

Dear, Ian, *Sabotage and Subversion* (Arms & Armour, 1996)

Deighton, Len, *Blood, Tears and Folly* (Jonathan Cape, 1993)

Duffy, C., *Frederick the Great* (London, 1985)

Dulles, Allen, *Great Spy Stories* (BCA, 1984)

Durant, Will and Ariel, *The Lessons of History* (MJF: New York, 1968)

– *The Story of Civilisation,* 10 vols. (MJF: New York, 1975)

Dziak, John, *Chekisty: A History of the KGB* (Ivy Books: New York, 1988)

Ellis, John, *World War 2 Data Book* (Aurum, 1993)

Ellis and Cox, *World War 1 Data Book* (Aurum, 1993)

Encyclopedia of World Terrorism (Armonk Pubs: New York, 1997)

Erickson, John, *The Road to Stalingrad* (Weidenfeld & Nicolson, 1993)

Esposito, John, *The Islamic Threat: Myth or Reality?* (OUP, 1999)

Everitt, Nicholas, *British Secret Service in the Great War* (Hutchinson, no date)

Farrago, Ladislav, *The Game of the Foxes* (Hodder & Stoughton,1972)

Feis, William, *Grant's Secret Service* (University of Nebraska, 2003)

Fishel, Edwin, *The Secret War for the Union* (Houghton Mifflin, 1995)

Foot, M. R. D., *SOE in France* (HMSO, 1966)

– *SOE in the Low Countries* (St Ermin's Press, 2001)

Foote, Alexander, *Handbook for Spies* (Museum, 1949)

Fraser, Antonia, *Cromwell* (Weidenfeld & Nicolson, 2001)

– *Mary Queen of Scots* (Weidenfeld & Nicolson, 2001)

Freedman, Lawrence, *The Revolution in Strategic Affairs,* Adelphi Papers (OUP, 1998)

Garlinski, Jozef, *Intercept* (Dent, 1979)

Gleichen, Edward, *A Guardsman's Memories* (London, 1932)

Graber, G. S., *History of the SS* (Hale, 1978)

Gramont, Sanche de, *The Secret War* (André Deutsch, 1962)

Grey, Austin, *Observations on Marlowe* (Modern Language Institute of America, 1928)

Halsall, Paul, *Ancient History Source Book* (London, 1968)

Handel, Michael, *Masters of War* (Frank Cass, 1992)

– (ed.), *Leaders and Intelligence* (Frank Cass, 1989)

Hastings, Max, *Military Anecdotes* (OUP, 1992)

Haswell, Jock, *British Military Intelligence* (Weidenfeld & Nicolson, 1973)

– *Spies and Spymasters* (Thames and Hudson, 1977)

– *The First Respectable Spy* (Hamish Hamilton, 1969)

Havell, H. L., *Stories from Herodotus* (Harrap, 1910)

Herman, Michael, *Intelligence Services in the Information Age* (Frank Cass, 2001)

Herzog, Chaim, *The War of Atonement* (Greenhill Books, 2003)

Hinsley, Harold, *British Intelligence in the Second World War*, 5 vols. (HMSO, 1979)

Hoffman, B. *The Modern Terrorist Mind* (St Andrew's University, 1997)

Holmes, Richard (ed.), *Oxford Companion to Military History* (OUP, 2001)

– *War Walks 2* (BBC Books, 1997)

Holt, Thaddeus, *The Deceivers* (W&N, 2004)

'Homeland Security and Terrorism', RUSI seminar, Whitehall, 2003

Howard, Michael, *Strategic Deception in WW2* (HMSO & Pimlico, 1990)

– *The Franco Prussian War* (Routledge, 1961)

Huntington, Samuel, *The Soldier and the State* (Harvard University Press, 1957)

Ibrahim, Sa'd al-din, *The New Arab Social Order* (Boulder: Colorado, 1982)

Irving, David, *The Mare's Nest* (Kimber, 1964)

Jeffreys-Jones, Rhodri, *Cloak and Dollar* (Yale University Press, 2002)

Johnson, David, *Germany's Spies and Saboteurs* (MBI: Wisconsin, 1998)

Jomini, *The Art of War*, tr. Mendell and Craighill (Greenwood: USA, 1977)

Jones, R. V., *Most Secret War* (BCA, 1978)

Juergensmeyer, *Terror in the Mind of God* (University of California Press, 2000)

Judd, Alan, *The Quest for C* (HarperCollins, 1999)

Kahn, David, *The Codebreakers* (New York, 1996)

Keegan, John, *A History of Warfare* (Hutchinson, 1993)

– *Intelligence in War* (Hutchinson, 2003)

– *Warpaths* (Hodder & Stoughton, 1981)

Kendall, W., *Revolutionary Movement in England* (London, 1969)

Knightley, Phillip, *The Second Oldest Profession* (André Deutsch, 1986)

Knorr, Klaus, and Morgan, Patrick, *Strategic Military Surprise* (Transaction: Canada, 1984)

Lambert, Andrew, *The Rules of the Game* (John Murray, 1996)

Lane, F., *Venice – a Maritime Republic* (John Hopkins U.P., 1973)

Lea, Henry, *Auricular Confession* (Swann, Sonnerschein, 1896)

Liddell Hart, Basil, *The British Way in Warfare* (Faber, 1932)

Lloyd, Mark, *Guinness Book of Espionage* (Guinness Publishing, 1994)

Maffeo, Steven, *Most Secret and Confidential* (Naval Institute Press: US, 2000)

Margiotta (ed.), *Encyclopedia of Military History* (Brassey's, 2000)

Mason, David, *U Boat: The Secret Menace* (Purnell Weapons, 1968)

Masterman, J. C., *The Double Cross System* (London, 1972)

McLeay, A., *The Tobermory Treasure* (London, 1986)

McNeill, W., *Venice – The Hinge of Europe* (Chicago U.P., 1986)

Metzer, Milton, *The Day the Sky Fell: A History of Terrorism* (Landmark Books, 2002)

Miller, David, *The Cold War* (Pimlico, 2001)

Miller, Nathan, *Spying for America* (Dell: New York, 1989)

Montgomery, Bernard, *A History of Warfare* (Collins, 1968)

Morgan, David, *The Mongols* (Blackwell, 1990)

Morley, John, *Oliver Cromwell* (Macmillan, 1901)

Nicolai, W., *The German Secret Service* (Stanley Paul, 1924)

Occleshaw, M., *Armour Against Fate* (Columbus, 1989)

Parritt, Brian, *The Intelligencers* (Intelligence Corps, 1983)

Payne-Best, Sigismund, *The Venlo Incident* (London, 1950)

Peters, Rudolph, *Islam and Colonialism* (Den Haag and New York, 1979)

Pollard and Allen, *The Spy Book* (Greenhill Books, 1997)

Porch, Douglas, *The French Secret Services* (Macmillan, 1996)

Putkowski, Julian, *British Army Mutineers 1914–1922* (Francis Boutle, 1998)

Queux, William le, *Spies of the Kaiser* (London, 1909)

– *The Invasion of 1910* (London, 1906)

Reeve, Simon, *The New Jackals* (André Deutsch, 1999)

Rowan, R. W., *The Story of Secret Service* (John Miles, 1938)

Roy, Oliver, *The Failure of Political Islam* (London, 1994)

Savant, Jean, *Les Espions de Napoleon* (Hachette: Paris, 1957)

Schama, Simon, *Citizens* (Penguin, 1989)

Shukman, Harold (ed.), *Agents for Change: Intelligence Services in the 21st Century* (St Ermin's, 2000)

Shulsky, Abram, *Silent Warfare: Understanding the World of Intelligence* (Brassey's US, 1991)

Sinclair, Andrew, *An Anatomy of Terror* (Macmillan, 2003)

Singh, Simon, *The Code Book* (Fourth Estate, 2000)

Skillen, Hugh, *Enigma and its Achilles Heel* (Intelligence Corps, 1992)

Smith, H.M., *Henry VIII and the Reformation* (Macmillan, 1945)

Smith, Michael, *The Spying Game* (Politico's, 2002)

Soyinka, Wole, *BBC Reith Lectures 2004*

Stafford, David, *Churchill and Secret Service* (John Murray, 1997)

Stahlin, Karl *Sir Francis Walsingham und Seine Zeit* (Heidelburg, 1908)

Stern, Jessica, 'The Protean Enemy: Terror's Future', *Foreign Affairs*, July 2003

Tarrant, V. E., *The Red Orchestra* (Arms & Armour, 1995)

Thompson, J. and Padover, S., *Secret Diplomacy: Espionage and Cryptography 1500-1815* (Constable, 1937)

Urban, Mark, *UK Eyes Alpha* (Faber, 1996)

– *The Man Who Broke Napoleon's Codes* (Faber, 2001)

US Congress, *Joint Enquiry into Intelligence Community Activities Before and After the Terrorist Attacks of September 11, 2001* (US Govt Printing Office, 2002)

US Department of State, *Patterns of Global Terrorism* (Langley, 2002)

Vaillé, Eugene, *Le Cabinet Noir* (Presse Univ. de France, 1950)

Van Deman, *The Final Memorandum*, ed. Ralph E. Weber (Scholarly Resources, 1988)

– *Memoirs* (unpublished manuscript, US Intelligence Center, Arizona)

Vereton, Dan, *Black Ice: Threat from Cyber Terrorism* (McGraw-Hill, 2003)

'Weapons of Catastrophic Effect', RUSI seminar, Whitehall, 2003

Weigley, Russell, *The Age of Battles* (Pimlico, 1991)

West, Nigel, *GCHQ* (Coronet, 1986)

– *MI6: British Secret Intelligence Service Operations, 1909–1945* (Weidenfeld & Nicolson, 1983)

– *Seven Spies who Changed the World* (Mandarin, 1991)

– *Unreliable Witness* (Weidenfeld & Nicolson, 1984)

– *Venona* (HarperCollins, 1999)

– (ed.), *Faber Book of Espionage* (Faber, 1993)

Why the Twin Towers Collapsed, Channel 4 documentary, November 2001

Wilkinson, Paul, *Political Terrorism* (London, 1974)

Williamson, Murray, *Strategy for Defeat: Luftwaffe 1933–45* (USAF University Press, 1983)

Wolf, Lucien, *Jews of the Canary Islands* (University of Toronto Press, 2001)

Acknowledgements

A book like this does not get written without the help and encouragement of a great many people.

Ian Drury of Cassell Military was the man behind the project; my friends and colleagues in the Study Group on Intelligence all contributed, chief among them Christopher Andrew, Michael Foot, Richard Aldridge and Anthony Clayton. John Montgomery, Librarian of the RUSI was as ever patient and helpful, and without the resources of the Templeman Library at the University of Kent at Canterbury there would be no book at all.

A number of individuals contributed in a variety of ways: Rupert Allason, Bill Barnett, Richard Holmes and Christopher Bellamy remained as always staunch allies, keen to see a serious gap in the armoury of military history filled in. The staff at the Intelligence Corps Archive at Chicksands were not only patient but also extraordinarily helpful and I owe a very special debt indeed to Lt Col John Woolmore, Alan Edwards and Fred Judge at Chicksands. The hard labour of typing the manuscript was done by the ever tolerant Gilly, while the task of turning that text into a real book was thanks to the hard work and patience of Keith Lowe and Jo Murray of Weidenfeld & Nicolson. I thank them all. Their contribution has greatly enriched the book: any errors are mine own.

In addition to these 'open sources' I would like to extend a special thank you to that very small and select group of behind the scenes intelligence helpers who contributed enormously but, for a variety of perfectly understandable reasons, wish to remain strictly anonymous.

Finally, a note on footnotes. A number of keen-eyed academics have observed that there are no footnotes. This is because this is a book for the general reader, which is what the publisher required, not for the ivory tower. However there is a comprehensive and authoritative series of 'notes to the text' which should satisfy most researchers wishing to delve deeper.

Appendix A

Documents referring to the Venlo incident

The 'Venlo incident' (see chapter 15) effectively ruined the British Secret Service's operations against Nazi Germany at the start of the 1939–45 war. The documents produced at the Nuremberg trial show the German and Dutch view of the event:

Memorandum of a Conference of the Führer With the Principal Military Commanders, November 23, 1939[1]

Every hope of compromise is childish. Victory or defeat! The question is not the fate of a National Socialist Germany, but who is to dominate Europe in the future. This question is worthy of the greatest efforts. Certainly England and France have means of pressure to bring Belgium and Holland to request English and French help. In Belgium and Holland the sympathies are all for France and England. Mention of the incident at Venlo. The man who was shot was not an Englishman, but a Dutch general staff officer. This was kept silent in the press. The Netherlands Government asked that the body of the Dutch officer be given up. This is one of their greatest stupidities. The Dutch press does not mention the incident any more. At a suitable time I shall exploit all that and use it to motivate [justify?] my action.

1 This report of Hitler's speech was found in OKW files captured at Flensberg. Its authorship is unknown. Additional information about Hitler's statements during this conference is contained in the testimony of General Halder in the 'High Command Case', *Trials of War Criminals Before the Nuremberg Military Tribunals Under Control Council Law No. 20, October 1946–April 1949*, Vol. X, p.857.

Source: Documents on German Foreign Policy, Series D (1937–1945): Volume III, The War Years, September 4, 1939–March 18, 1940. Document No. 384, page 445.

The strange staccato style of the original (pp.439–446) suggests that verbatim notes were taken by an unknown officer, but never worked up into a polished text. A footnote refers to the document below, written by Otto Christian, Prince von Bismarck.

Memorandum by the Deputy Director of the Political Department

BERLIN, November 10, 1939

The Netherlands Minister called on me at 7:45 this evening and handed me the annexed *note verbale*.

M. de With stated the case as follows:

Yesterday afternoon a Dutch automobile with two Englishmen, who supposedly were to conduct peace negotiations with Germans at the Dutch-German border, accompanied by a Dutch officer in civilian clothes, who had been assigned to them, had come to the border near Venlo, halting at a café there about 40 metres from the border line. As soon as the car had stopped, the occupants were fired upon from ambush; the Dutch officer was seriously, probably fatally, wounded, and one of the Englishmen also was hit. Immediately after the shooting, an automobile crossed the border from Germany and towed the Dutch car with the two wounded men, the second Englishman, and the driver of the car across the German border.

M. de With declared repeatedly that in these troubled times he did not wish in any way to exaggerate the incident. Since the Netherlands Government supported every peace movement, it had given its authority to that trip. To the extent that the incident concerned the two Englishmen, it was no concern of the Netherlands Government. It did request, however, that the wounded or dead Dutch officer and the Dutch chauffeur be returned to Holland. An investigation of the matter was deemed urgent by him because, as he had heard, the incident had already been announced over the Dutch and the foreign radio.

I stated that I knew nothing of the whole matter.

BISMARCK

Bismarck's memorandum contained the following enclosure:

Note Verbale From the Netherlands Legation

BERLIN, November 10, 1939

The Royal Netherlands Legation has the honour to inform the Foreign Ministry of the following:

At 4:30 on November 9 of this year, a Dutch automobile containing four passengers halted at a distance of 40 metres from the border at Venlo; two of them alighted, whereupon two persons emerged from a café at that place and took off their hats. Apparently that was a signal, for immediately six persons dressed in civilian clothes rushed up and opened fire. The two persons who had alighted from the car fell to the ground. Then an automobile approached from Germany and pulled the Dutch car with its remaining occupants and the two persons who had been shot over to the German side. Whether the two persons who had remained in the car were also hit is not known.

Pursuant to instructions the Legation wishes to request the Foreign Ministry to institute an investigation of this matter and inform it of the result.[2]

Source: ibid., pp. 395–6

2 On nine occasions, at frequent intervals, the Netherlands Legation requested a reply to its note of Nov. 10, 1939. On Jan. 25 1940, a new Netherlands note (173 / 84170-72) was presented suggesting that the matter be referred to the German–Netherlands Conciliation Commission or to an international court. To this and several subsequent inquiries no reply was made prior to the German attack on the Netherlands in May 1940.

Additional information and documentation on the Venlo incident were brought out in the course of the so-called 'Ministries Case' at Nuremberg. Some of this material was published in the *Trials of War Criminals Before the Nuremberg Military Tribunals Under Control Council Law No. 10, October 1946–April 1949*, Vol. XII, pp. 1178–1180, 1206–1210, 1214, 1232–1242 and 1248–49.

Appendix B

Britain's plans to crush terrorists, 1972

The following is a facsimile of a top secret government document showing the British plan to swamp the IRA. It shows how a tiny handful of terrorists can wield extraordinary power.

THE MILITARY CONTRIBUTION TO THE PLAN

Concept of Operations

1. The emphasis of military operations will be on vigorous action, Privince wide, to:-

   a. Swamp with troops all extremist strongholds including no go areas or any other area where there is a risk of inter-sectarian strife, to achieve complete domination and demoralisation of extremists of both sides impartially.

   b. Disarm the population.

   c. Prevent anyone taking any offensive action against anyone else.

   d. Maintain essential services.

   e. Be prepared to exercise tighter control of cross-border movement.

   f. In consultation with the civil authorities, restore the normal economic and social life of the Province.

2. Planning to meet this concept will be based on the following criteria:-

   a. <u>Force Levels</u>. Reinforcement above the current force level of 20 battalions will take place in two phases:-

      i. <u>Phase 1</u>. To 40 battalions - for saturation of all the main areas of conflict.

      ii. <u>Phase 2</u>. To 47 battalions - for consolidation in country areas.

      Of the extra 27 units, it is expected that 18 can be provided from Britain and the remaining 9 will be temporarily redeployed from BAOR. (The total number of units from BAOR then serving in Northern Ireland will be 15, which is roughly the equivalent of one of the three divisions' teeth arm units. This would leave only 2 infantry battalions in BAOR.)

   b. <u>Sequence of Action</u>. The day on which HMG declares a State of Emergency will be Proclamation Day (P Day); that on which it is decided to implement the reinforcement plan will be Reinforcement Day (R Day). It is/.....

Index